Africans to Spanish America

THE NEW BLACK STUDIES SERIES

Edited by Darlene Clark Hine
and Dwight A. McBride

A list of books in the series appears at the end of this book.

Africans to Spanish America

Expanding the Diaspora

Edited by
SHERWIN K. BRYANT,
RACHEL SARAH O'TOOLE,
AND BEN VINSON III

UNIVERSITY OF ILLINOIS PRESS
Urbana, Chicago, and Springfield

First Illinois paperback, 2014
© 2012 by the Board of Trustees
of the University of Illinois
All rights reserved

∞ This book is printed on acid-free paper.

The Library of Congress cataloged the cloth edition as follows:
Africans to Spanish America : expanding the diaspora / edited
by Sherwin K. Bryant, Rachel Sarah O'Toole &
Ben Vinson, III.
p. cm.—(New Black studies series)
Includes bibliographical references.
ISBN 978-0-252-03663-7 (hardback)
ISBN 978-0-252-09371-5 (ebook)
1. Blacks—Latin America—History. 2. Blacks—Race identity—Latin America—History. 3. Slavery—Latin America—History. 4. Slavery and the church—Catholic Church. 5. Slavery and the church—Latin America. 6. African diaspora. 7. Latin America—History—To 1830. I. Bryant, Sherwin K. II. O'Toole, Rachel Sarah. III. Vinson, Ben, III
F1419.N4A39 2012
305.80098—dc23 2011047444

PAPERBACK ISBN 978-0-252-08001-2

Contents

Introduction

SHERWIN K. BRYANT, BEN VINSON III,
AND RACHEL SARAH O'TOOLE

On August 1, 1708, the now infamous privateer Woodes Rogers departed Bristol to sail around the world, "first to the South-Sea, thence to the East-Indies, and homewards by the Cape of Good Hope." Sailing down the Atlantic coast of South America, and passing Cape Horn, the Rogers expedition sighted the uninhabited San Fernández Island, located nearly 400 miles off the coast of Chile, on January 31, 1709. After spending nearly two weeks there repairing the *Duke* and the *Dutchess*, the Rogers crew pushed off, prowling the Peruvian coast for several weeks before capturing their first prize—a small, sixteen-ton coastal trading vessel out of Paita. The eight-man crew included one "Negro," a "Spaniard," and six "Indians." The capture of this small bark, which they symbolically renamed the *Beginning*, marked the advent of the seizure of a spate of "prizes"—vessels traveling either between Panama and Lima's port of Callao or within the coastal trading network that joined Chancay and Trujillo to Lima in the south. These cities were also tied to ports such as Paita and Guayaquil and to clandestine trading sites found within the Gobernación of Barbacoas to the north, all of which fell within the kingdom, or *audiencia*, of Quito. Passengers and goods moved constantly within this Pacific trade nexus that fed ultimately into the circum-Caribbean and Atlantic economic system.

Unsurprisingly, people the Europeans categorized as "black," "mulatto," "*bozal*," "free," and "enslaved" were buffeted about within this Pacific trade network. These included the anonymous "negro" who was eventually held captive on the *Beginning*, a man who was representative of the scores of free blacks serving as crew members on other coastal vessels. He was also representative of the countless enslaved Africans shipped to the Pacific from parts of Africa. As evidenced by the English-speaking women taken by Rogers and his crew, some of the slaves who were traded in the Pacific had previously lived in the British Caribbean prior to their forced migration to the Spanish Andes. They, like scores of others, had traveled from west and west-central Africa to the greater circum-Caribbean before being trekked across the Isthmus of Panama for transshipment to the port of Lima's Callao and its outlying entrepôts. By the beginning of the eighteenth century, an increasing number of Africans did not pass through Lima at all, being sold directly in Guayaquil, where ships bound for Lima often stopped to unload passengers headed to the north Andean hinterland. As fortune would have it, being strategically positioned within this regional traffic enabled Rogers and his crew to become rich beneficiaries of movements in the direction of the Pacific. His expedition took six ships within the brief span of a month that yielded no fewer than 125 "negroes and mulattoes."[1]

What we know of this aspect of the Woodes Rogers expedition comes principally from his diary and that of Edward Cooke, a Bristol merchant captain who served as the executive officer of the *Dutchess*.[2] Their account of events enables us to envision some of the violence inflicted upon many of the captives—enslaved, free, black, mulatto, indigenous, and Spanish alike. Yet many questions and issues remain unaddressed. Just who were the men and women they captured and traded? How did their individual sagas unfold, and what were their interrelationships with one another, the broader colonial world, and the merging parts of the Atlantic and Pacific realms? How did their stories fit within a universe of diverse identities? How did their genders shape their enslaved and free experiences? And how did their individual histories contribute to the nascent processes of racial formation and caste signification that were emerging in their worlds?[3]

Despite the silences contained within the pages of the Rogers and Cooke narratives and a panoply of similar texts, such sources still constitute a treasured resource that opens windows onto a range of individuals described as "black" who lived and moved within the territories claimed by Spain. In the Rogers account, for example, we find the case of Michael Kendall, a free black man from Jamaica who, after fighting for the English along the Caribbean coast of New Granada, was forced into slavery by the Spanish in the gold mines of Barbacoas (located along the southwest Pacific littoral of Colombia).[4] Kendall ended up deserting the mines to join the Rogers expedition near the Isla del Gallo in July 1709. Soon afterward, the freedman-turned-slave-fugitive was quickly elevated to a position of leadership within the expedition. It is cases such as these that are illustrative of the black diasporic condition. Kendall's striking example of agony, mobility, achievement, and flight poignantly remind us of the frailty of black social standing in the era of chattel slavery—how crossing colonial boundaries could dramatically impact an individual's fate and how the pursuit of basic liberties was tenuous, framed always in the shadow of slavery and marked by a kind of liminal rootlessness.[5] The extant documentary evidence may not always enable us to completely peer into these worlds, but as with the Rogers narrative, we can catch important glimpses of them.

This volume takes as its cue the need to further expand the framework by which we chart the African Diaspora, based upon a close reading of a variety of texts from the Spanish American colonies. Our setting encompasses some familiar and unfamiliar terrain. The Rogers expedition reminds us that few have considered the expanding importance of slavery in Pacific sites such as Trujillo, Guayaquil, and Barbacoas or the ways that slavery and blackness impacted imperial attempts to restructure governance in the region. But as Charles Beatty-Medina reminds us in this volume, African-descended peoples had long-standing influences upon colonial governance efforts and imperial defense schemes within the Spanish-controlled Pacific/Andean region. Likewise, as Rachel O'Toole's essay shows, the presence of Atlantic Africans and their integration into increasingly Hispanicized Pacific and Andean worlds brought forth complex processes of self-crafting that refracted local sociocultural realities and apparently echoed those found in what might be called "Atlantic Africa." In short, the Rogers story, the case of Esmeraldas (chapter 4), and the lives of individuals such as Ana de la Calle of casta Lucumí (chapter 3) signal the need for explorations of blackness that extend the framework of Diaspora more explicitly to Spanish America. What contemporaries might not have imagined was the emergence of a black Pacific, a zone of contact that ran from Panama southward at least as far as Arequipa, linking feeder communities in the Darien region, Atrato, Chocó, Barbacoas, and Esmeraldas to those in Guayaquil, Paita, Trujillo, Chancay, and Lima-Callao. While these sites were actually old landmarks of the early modern African diasporic experience (keep in mind that Africans accompanied the earliest European expeditions here), today they represent new nodal points that are receiving broader consideration by a current generation of scholars working on the African Diaspora to Spanish America. Work in these areas represents new ways of seeing the African Diaspora and marks evolutionary steps in the growth of the subfield of Afro–Latin American history.

Afro–Latin American History: The Sketch of a Retrospective into the Present

Afro–Latin American history has enjoyed a long tradition since the nineteenth century. Given the ebb and flow of scholarly production and changes in the focal points of academic inquiry, it seems best to categorize the rising tide of Afro–Latin American history as a series of waves. The first wave of scholarship, dominated by scholars writing within Latin America, enjoyed the distinct challenge of trying to situate blackness within nascent nation-states that were trying to articulate their national character for the first time.[6] The challenge was made all the more daunting by the preponderance of positivist and pseudo-scientific theories that marked the black presence as antithetical to the developmentalist aims of these emerging nations.[7] The writings of these historians featured concerns about defining citizenship and assessing the level to which blacks should be included (or excluded) from the body politic and broader civil society. Many of these scholars themselves held ambivalent views regarding black citizenship and equality, but despite their personal biases (which inevitably seeped into their writings), their research and lines of inquiry laid the groundwork for the scholarly questions and agendas that would eventually mold the field. José Antonio Saco provides a great example. His elegant survey of blacks in the Hispanic world was a pioneering accomplishment that helped inspire further work on slavery, emancipation, and free black life. In fact, Saco was influential in launching the career trajectory of the renowned Afro-Cubanist Fernando Ortiz. But at the same time, Saco was undeniably a product of his times. Despite being a forceful advocate of emancipation and the abolition of slavery, he remained unconvinced that blacks and whites should possess full equality in post-emancipation Cuba. Hence, his passion for understanding the historical contours of black life was counterbalanced by his ideas regarding the proper prospects for Cuba's future sociopolitical course. Regardless of these seemingly discordant viewpoints, his work represented a major step forward.

Similar arguments can be made for other trailblazing pioneers. First-wave scholars such as Fernando Ortiz, Raimundo Nina Rodrigues, Gilberto Freyre, and Arturo Ramos concerned themselves with exploring black subjectivity from a range of frames, including slavery, music, folklore, magic, transculturation, and African cultural survivals.[8] By and large, their works are seminal accomplishments of great vision and theoretical foresight. But it must be said that most of these individuals were also perplexed by the questions of the extent to which blacks should be included into the national fabric and how a national identity that absorbed blackness could develop in ways that were not irrevocably marred by what many deemed was a socially harmful African primitivism. Both the best and the worst of their scholarship frequently resurrected pseudo-scientific notions of race and nationalist impositions of *mestizaje*. Sometimes unknowingly, they obliquely endorsed the fear of "the African" and contributed to emergent national narratives that sought to whiten Latin America. Nevertheless, their work introduced some powerful basic tools that steered scholarship into its second wave. Their collective contributions demonstrated the value of studying slavery as a constituent part of national sociocultural development. Equally as important, their work opened debates about how blackness could enhance the profile of Latin America's population, or at a minimum be beneficially blended into *mestizaje*. Finally, these authors showed that blackness and slavery could provide useful and convenient metaphors for persecution and subjugation. In co-opting the black experience in this way, individual Latin American societies could level critiques at their colonial past while also engaging in substantive and meaningful critiques of reputedly "advanced" Western nations such as the United States. Latin America's comparatively successful management of what North Americans called the "race problem" spotlighted the region as progressive and enlightened in ways that showcased failure in the United States. In this way, the nationalist goals of the first-wavers were partly fulfilled. Through blackness, they managed to present their countries as full participants in modernity while also offering tangible recipes for congealing fissures in the larger social fabric: they provided road maps for showing how to reconcile race, blackness, *mestizaje*, and nation.

In some ways, second-wave scholars responded to the clarion calls of first-wave pioneers, and scholars from the U.S. academy entered the fray and reacted (favorably and not) to critiques of the American brand of racial capitalism. Frank Tannenbaum's *Slave and Citizen* (1947) marked a significant move in this direction by exploring the roots that differentiated Latin American and North American race relations. According to *Slave and Citizen*, part of the answer could be found by carefully examining comparative slave systems, legal codes, colonial institutions, and experiences. Although this was not quite a novel idea, his influential work helped launch the comparative slavery school, which took his basic questions and probed even deeper—sometimes with more refined case studies and at other times with larger or different research questions.[9] Eric Williams, for example, used some of the basic paradigms framed by the comparative slavery school to help explore the dynamics of the rise of capitalism itself.[10] In the late 40s, 50s and 60s, new approaches to social science combined with the development of global events made the study of blacks more urgently prescient and helped further propel the comparative slavery school forward. Pan-Africanism, decolonization movements in Africa, and the civil rights struggle in the United States in particular as well as the UN declaration that race was a social construct were among the pivotal contextual events that enhanced the study of Afro–Latin America. Similarly, the emergence of social history as a core disciplinary field and advanced anthropological methods in ethnography (which, when applied to black culture, took seriously the question of African survivals and their expression and transformation in New World cultures) were features of second-wave scholarship. Hence, resistance studies and studies of the nature of creolization, demography, and cultural analysis accompanied the advances made by the comparative slavery school.

How these broad developments worked themselves out in the literature on Afro–Latin America was both diffuse and precise. Within individual Latin American countries, a small foundational literature on the black experience began to emerge between the 50s and the 70s. In Chile, for instance, a trio of core works by Mellafe (1959), Feliú Cruz (1942), and Vial Correa (1957) studied the plight of slaves and traced the saga of their emancipation, while also assessing the place of blacks in Chilean colonial society.[11] Similar works could be found throughout the region—for Venezuela (Acosta Saignes, 1967), Argentina (Scheuss de Studer, 1958), and Panama (Castillero Calvo, 1969), among others.[12]

The 1940s and 50s witnessed a fuller maturation of theoretical and conceptual approaches to the study of the African-descended peoples of Latin America and the Caribbean. Later work by scholars such as Fernando Ortiz helped complete the dismantling of pseudo-scientific racist theories while opening new vistas for theorizing race and nation in Latin America. In particular, first-waver Ortiz's theorization of *transculturation* reimagined blacks and their ability to coexist (and inform) national culture. In a theory that bore faint resemblances to W. E. B. Du Bois's theory of double consciousness, Ortiz acknowledged that blacks held multiple cultural dispositions simultaneously; these were cultural leanings that were rooted in the Americas but were also tied to a primordial African past. While transculturation ultimately imagined an essentialized, though somewhat complex black subject, it offered the possibility of considering identity formation as a fluid and dynamic process, albeit one that moved away from a "traditional" African essence into a more modern, national identity. In addition, transculturation shone a light upon black cultural history, opening the way for ethnohistorical approaches to black Afro–Latin America.[13] These ethnohistorical approaches would be heavily featured in works by scholars such as Miguel Acosta Saignes in Venezuela and Gonzalo Aguirre Beltrán in Mexico.

From the 1970s through the early 1990s a new, third wave of scholars emerged to consider a range of themes and findings advanced by their predecessors. With the continuing advances being made in the techniques of social history, scholars turned increasingly toward context-specific (nation-centered/geographical) analyses of slavery, slave life, law, and caste relations.[14] Indeed, two scholarly strands came to dominate this third wave of scholarship—one dedicated to studying slavery and slave life and the other to exploring the extent to which Latin America was a "caste society." If, during this period, Harry Hoetink's *Slavery and Race Relations in the Americas: Comparative Notes on Their Nature and Nexus* (1973) marked the expansion of the comparative slavery school to include work on slave life, abolition, and the localized economic importance of slavery across Latin America, Magnus Mörner's *Race Mixture in the History of Latin America* (1967) also marked the expansion of a subfield that explored "black" colonial subjects through the prism of the caste system. Insisting that Latin America was a "caste society," Mörner precipitated debates that continue to animate scholarly inquiry even today.[15]

The wide-reaching literature of the third wave has helped us clearly understand the reaches of the plantation complex (with its attendant array of commodities) and other forms of social and economic organization that directly influenced the development of black life and culture. Among these were rural farming, urban labor, and the mining industry.[16] It is during this era as well that the volume and quality of slave resistance literature reached new heights, providing a solid foundation in thinking about how blacks challenged their status in slave regimes and constructed alternative social systems of their own.[17] The implications of this emergent literature were profound in terms of contemplating the degree to which blacks did or did not become Atlantic creoles in the New World. The 1970s through the early 90s also saw major advances in charting the contours of black demography throughout the hemisphere. At the end of the 1960s, Philip D. Curtin's grand synthesis of Atlantic slavery triggered responses by scholars who sought to correct oversights and miscalculations and provide greater empirical depth to areas where Curtin's calculations rested principally upon rough estimates and suppositions.[18] Decades of work along these lines advanced the comparative slavery school considerably, culminating most recently in Voyages: The Trans-Atlantic Slave Trade Database.[19]

The third wave's interest in demography extended to the lives of free blacks, and in concert with scholarship on the caste system and dramatic growth in statistically oriented regional histories, there was a veritable efflorescence in our understanding of the degree to which blacks came to populate individual Latin American cities, towns, and hinterlands. Some of the statistical works published in this vein were not directly focused on interpreting the black experience.[20] Nevertheless, they provided crucial background that informed other studies, and in a few cases, some of these publications emerged into classic works on the black experience.[21] By and large, the 1970s through the early 90s further witnessed the scholarly popularity and gradual adoption of prosopography and nominal record linkages, using the archives of the Inquisition and the techniques of cultural history to examine the lives of Latin America's black populace.[22] These techniques would eventually become standard tools by the middle of the 1990s and have greatly influenced the method of scholarly practice in the early twenty-first century.[23] Finally, primarily within Latin America, third-wave scholarship featured collaborative research projects, specifically Mexico's Third Root project, which was designed to recover the nation's black heritage, but also the international efforts of UNESCO's Slave Route Project, which was launched in 1994 to foster greater understanding of the causes, operation, and consequences of slavery at the global level.[24] In short, the third wave was the most vast and sweeping of any of its predecessors in terms of the volume of knowledge produced, the number of international conversations that emerged from its studies, and the degree of detail to which black life was analyzed.[25] Still, over the stretch of nearly three decades, many of the works were produced episodically at best, resulting in some significant lags in the coherent development of the literature, especially with respect to the experience of free blacks.[26] Similarly, because of the tremendous influence that slavery had upon the trajectory of scholarship as well as the influence of historiographical questions that incorporated but did not center on black life, the corpus of works evolved somewhat unevenly, with an imbalance that partially obscured the black experience as lived beyond the nexus of slavery.

In the past two decades, the emerging prominence of the concept of Diaspora as a way to evaluate the black experience has helped provide new theoretical insight and sophistication into how we should interrogate the black presence.[27] Extensions of older debates regarding the importance of the "African" past on the development of Afro-American culture and American societies have reached new levels of intensity, and new conceptualizations of the very theme "Diaspora" have forced scholars to widen the scope of their lens on the African Diaspora, conceptually, spatially, and temporally.[28] Microstudies of urban Atlantic centers such as Calabar, Cartagena, Charlestown, Havana, Lisbon, Luanda, New York City, Salvador, São Salvador (Kongo), Seville, and Veracruz have recently served to help bring regional and local histories into a more synthetic and networked interregional mainstream.[29] In some senses, the energy and attention expended on documenting the history of the "Black Atlantic," especially the British North Atlantic system, has often substituted for examining the African Diaspora more broadly. However, this research oversight has been duly acknowledged and correctives are under way.[30] Generally speaking, Latin American historians have joined in this productive enterprise. The 1990s and the first decade of the twenty-first century have produced a proliferation of MA theses, dissertations, journal articles, and monographs produced in English, Spanish, and Portuguese that treat Afro–Latin American historical topics.[31] It is now safe to say that a subfield that might be called "Afro–Latin American history" is quickly coming of age.[32] No longer content with merely situating blacks (and people who have been variously defined as blacks) within the histories of Latin American institutions or with viewing these populations primarily through the lenses of slavery, *mestizaje*, and colonial systems of racial dominations (*sistema de casta*), a new fourth wave of scholars (including those in this volume) is raising different research frameworks. Of course, their work stands on the shoulders of those who have come before. Many of these scholars, some of whom are featured here, stress the need to examine questions of identity, connections to blackness, African-derived cultural formations, and ongoing connections to west and west-central African personal aspirations, gender roles, religious relations, and sexuality. Above all, these scholars have articulated one of the field's principal aims as striving to situate African-descended peoples in their own narratives, over and above the more traditional themes that have heretofore dominated the field. This volume represents some of the most explicit attempts at this enterprise.

It is worth pausing here to highlight more precisely what we mean by this fourth-wave turn. Afro–Latin American history as traditionally conceived is being reevaluated as constituting an independent subfield where Africans and their descendants are measured on their own terms, or as "subjects in their [own] plot."[33] The debates surrounding this move are giving life to "Afro–Latin America" as a heuristic category with epistemological value rather than simply a descriptor. While studies concerned broadly with race relations, racial governance, status and honor, or the impact and prevalence of slavery have revealed a great deal about the presence and importance of African-descended subjects, distinctly new research perspectives emerge when the scholarly focus foregrounds black experiences vis-à-vis such themes or when scholarship articulates alternative historiographical research paradigms and subject matter.

As can be appreciated from the discussion in this introduction up to this point, essentially three basic investigative approaches seem to best characterize the traditional themes that have been used to study Afro–Latin America: 1) recovery and insertion (recovering the black past and inserting it into the metanarrative of Latin American history); 2) race relations (emphasizing social mobility, relations with the church and the transition from Baroque forms of piety, the impact of royal authority on black life, and the influence of local politics on black-native-mestizo interactions); and 3) slavery and manumission. One problem with these approaches (as they have been implemented up until this point) is that the primary way to actually *see* blacks in the historiographic record is to look through the lens of the church, slavery, or the colonial bureaucratic order. In other words, it would appear that Africans and their descendants principally enter the narrative of Latin American history when their stories complement the well-framed questions and debates of the larger field or when their stories inform our understanding of elite institutions, aspirations, status claims, or other "elite" preoccupations. Herman Bennett has recently argued this point in *Colonial Blackness* (2009). According to his point of view, Africans are ever the "objects" of historical study, even when they supposedly appear as subjects. Of course, this is not the only way to characterize the state of the field. While we certainly need new ways of "seeing" in order to read through the traditional narrative, much remains to be gained by inserting blacks into the traditional narrative. First, doing so forces scholars to rethink the narrative by considering blackness as essential to it. Second, it explodes the traditional narrative (or at least shows its limitations); in other words, an accommodationist outcome for black life need not always be the end result. Third, we enrich the basic metanarrative by aligning Afro–Latin American history as a coequal component. Essentially, our aim with this volume is to advocate a blending of viewpoints so that a more balanced synthesis can emerge from fourth-wave scholarship.

Since the 1970s, similar moves have been made in the study of women's history and the ethnohistory of Amerindians. Although the advent of social history in the 1960s and 70s promised new approaches that extended beyond the study of bureaucracies and "strong men" to the study of "blacks," "Indians," and "women," arguably the study of Africans and their descendants remains more underdeveloped.[34] Moreover, strikingly, despite the vigor, depth, and energy that has characterized third-wave scholarship, many of the research prerogatives outlined by Frederick Bowser in his 1972 review essay are still of critical importance.[35] Among other suggestions, Bowser argued that scholars should look beyond the Caribbean and Brazil to regions such as coastal Ecuador; that they should explore eighteenth-century Peru; and that they should mine the colonial sources further for what they might say about African ethnicity and the formulation of New World identities. In addition, he called for scholars to investigate the precise methods slave laborers used in gaining their freedom in Spanish America; to examine "the attitudes and actions of the free black population"; to investigate the theme of race mixture; to work to complicate African conversion and blacks' relationship to Catholicism; and to explore the varying roles African-descended people played within colonial society more generally. These concerns remain of critical importance. With respect to the relationship of blacks to colonial institutions, for instance—a prominent feature within some lines of third-wave inquiry—we have yet to achieve a complete understanding of how blacks operated within and used institutions that have been traditionally construed as being the preserve of mestizo, *criollo*, and native populations. For instance, a great deal remains to be done to uncover the relationship between black life and colonial financial structures, such as tribute. Moreover, we know precious little about black land tenure patterns and changes in occupational status over time. We have only begun to ask how gender shaped articulations of diaspora identities within Spanish America. And while scholars have turned increasingly to the law and court cases to study the enslaved, we do not yet know enough about slave legal action or how their engagement with colonial courts (civil and ecclesiastical) developed over time.

As fourth-wave scholarship develops further, it seems inevitable that it will be compelled to wrestle with the ubiquity with which "blackness" prefigures into the conversation of the African Diaspora and the degree to which blackness has ironically operated as both a tangible and phantasmic force in the previous waves of scholarship that have configured the field. In some ways, blackness remains undertheorized, particularly in relation to colonial Spanish America. Part of this is due to a deliberate and conscious ambivalence about the degree to which race and racialization were actually forces that operated in the Spanish colonial regime. Regardless, if the African Diaspora paradigm is to be used for Afro–Latin America, then it is incumbent upon scholars to better define the parameters of one of the integral analytics of the enterprise. This will mean fully addressing 1) the ways that race operated simultaneously in both elite and subaltern circles; 2) the ways that blackness could be constructed, identified with, used, and rejected by a diverse range of social actors; 3) the ways that race was obscured and enabled by other classificatory phenomena of the age; 4) the ways that race both existed and did not exist as a social reality in colonial lives; 5) the ways that race was decidedly gendered; 6) and, finally, the full spectrum of social organization and hierarchical mechanisms produced by Spanish colonialism. Obviously, a great deal of significant work has already been done on many of these topics, but targeted research that keeps all of these aims in mind and incorporates the essential ironies that governed Spanish colonialism may help us to see what we may have been missing up to this point in the recovery of Afro–Latin America.[36]

A few signposts may be useful in further framing the conversation of future fourth-wave scholarship surrounding the issue of blackness. It is important to keep in mind that juridical actors labeled the "subjects of Guinea" and their descendants as "negro" and African (*bozal*) according to a Spanish colonial taxonomy of difference known as the *sistema de castas*. This was done in part to signal these individuals' lack of Spanish/Christian pure blood lineage. In an era when the "Spanish/Christian" heritage had come to be imagined through the metaphor of blood, all who lacked noble, Spanish/Christian lineage were deemed as "others." First applied to Jews and Muslims in Iberia (the quintessential "others"), "Spaniards" (who were actually a newly constructed people themselves, forged from ethnic diversity within Iberia) subsequently construed the inhabitants of Africa as others by virtue of their distinct political, territorial, and religious heritage. Above all, the descendants of the early modern "subjects of Guinea" were conceived of as *negros bozales*, or unacculturated blacks, who were supposedly neither conversant in the Castilian tongue nor attuned to Spanish cultural mores. While Herman Bennett has argued persuasively that Iberians initially viewed the subjects of Guinea as *herrschafts* (sovereign peoples) and *herrschaaftlos* (sovereignless subjects and thus enslaveable pagans and infidels), those forced into the New World as slaves were understood to lack *limpieza de sangre* (Spanish Christian blood purity) even though they were simultaneously envisioned as Old World people with the full capacity for conversion to the faith. Regardless of whether they were newly arrived, *bozales* or New World-born criollos, *negro/as*, *mulato/as*, *pardo/as*, *lobo/as*, *morisco/as*, or *zambo/as* constituted or carried a kind of blackness, despite the fact that many of these labels pointed to varying degrees of proximity to both Africanity and a "*negro*" lineage. In short, these *casta* labels signaled the distinct heritage that Africans had in relationship to Spanish Christian (read: "white") normativity. Thus, while the *sistema de casta* envisioned a range of "coloreds," those of African descent were "blackened," as best seen through the glass ceiling they faced in the caste system—whiteness was never truly attainable despite endless exogamy with *españoles*. Consequently, while few *mulato/as*, *pardo/as*, *zambo/as*, *morisco/as*, or *lobo/as* would have actually identified themselves as "black" (ethnically, racially, or politically), it is possible to understand a kind of *politics of blackening* cross-cut with gender at work in the colonial era that requires excavation and analysis from modern scholars.

The scholars assembled in this volume use a variety of historical questions and approaches, some of which straddle the divide of third-wave and fourth-wave research designs. This underscores the reality that the line demarcating scholarly trends is never neat but continually references, advances, and complements previous publications. What each author shares in common is an unyielding interest in engaging and reconfiguring what Leo Garofalo (chapter 1) calls the "shape of Diaspora," accentuating its early extension into Iberia in the fifteenth century and its reach beyond the Atlantic basin into the Pacific/Andean territories not long thereafter. Thus, while oftentimes scholars speak of the early modern African Diaspora as primarily an eighteenth- and early nineteenth-century Atlantic basin phenomenon, the majority of the essays in this volume study periods before 1700 and strive to stretch the view of Diaspora into lesser known geographic areas (including the Pacific).[37]

Comprised of nine original essays, this volume is organized into three sections. Starting with voluntary and forced migrations across the Atlantic, Part One explores three distinct cases of identity construction that intersect with ongoing debates in African Diaspora scholarship regarding the models of continuity and creolization in the Americas. In chapter 1, Leo Garofalo explores how a diverse group of free and enslaved Africans and Afro-Iberians moved back and forth from the Iberian peninsula to the Americas to suggest a significant impact of the African Diaspora on the sixteenth-century Spanish Atlantic world. Garofalo insists that Afro-Iberians, the descendants of those traded from Africa to Iberia beginning in the 1440s, were conquistadors, passengers, and laborers in the conquest and colonization campaigns. Ultimately, they brought Europeans to the Americas, fought alongside them, carried their goods to colonial sites, and became powerful intermediaries who were as essential to empire as the indigenous intermediaries described by scholars elsewhere. Exploring passenger lists and official licenses to travel to the Americas, Garofalo highlights the movement of Africans and their descendants between Seville and colonial centers such as Santo Domingo, Mexico City, Quito, Lima, and Charcas. In short, not all blacks arriving in the early colonial Americas originated in West Africa and the Atlantic Islands. Moreover, Afro-Iberians were of diverse statuses—free, enslaved, traveling with patrons, or alone. Some were property holders in their own right. While some had been born in the Americas, others were born in Iberia and Africa. Movement within this Diaspora was not unilinear; Afro-Iberians moved back and forth between the peninsula and the Americas and traveled to Africa, and some even made their way to other parts of Europe. Study of the movement of African-descended passengers thus promises many insights into the early colonial Ibero-American world while offering additional texture to theorizations about the African Diaspora, identity formation, and the development of New World systems of labor extraction.

Where Garofalo traces the circular movements of Africans and Afro-Iberian passengers, Frank "Trey" Proctor (chapter 2) explores the development of Diasporan ethnicities. That is, Proctor shows how early waves of ethnic Africans reinvented ethnic and community identities once in Diaspora. Using marriage records from early seventeenth-century Mexico City, Proctor shows that ethnic Africans tended to marry and form communities of association with Africans from the same general catchment areas. In Mexico City prior to 1650, West-Central Africans, for example, tended to marry one another with the support of a host of godparents and witnesses from the same region. This was also the trend among ethnic Africans from other regions, leading Proctor to suggest that Africans formed new ethnic identities based upon Old World backgrounds and commonalities while in Diaspora.

Rachel Sarah O'Toole (chapter 3) seizes on a distinct case of Atlantic Africans who articulated multiple and transforming colonial and transatlantic identities within the Spanish-Peruvian Pacific. She takes the reader into the world of Ana de la Calle, a free *morena* of *casta lucumí* living in the northern Peruvian city of Trujillo circa the year 1719. This unique co-joining of Spanish American "*casta*" nomenclature with that of the transatlantic slave trade by Ana de la Calle herself (a free woman of color from the Yoruba-speaking interior of the Bight of Benin) suggest that men and women constructed identities that grew out of African landscapes and meanings but were shaped in Diasporic contexts. Thus, O'Toole's essay highlights the interstitial nature of African Diasporic identity in colonial Spanish America.

Part Two interrogates how enslaved and free people used their rights as Catholics to present themselves as civilized subjects, loyal Christians, and resisters to slavery. The strategy caught Africans and their descendants in a double bind, however, as inquisitors, royal officials, and neighbors often suspected them of errant behavior or unorthodox beliefs. Charles Beatty-Medina (chapter 4) returns to the early colonial period when African-descended people of various statuses arrived in the colonies under varying conditions. On the northern Pacific coast of modern Ecuador these arrivals occurred by way of a series of shipwrecks beginning in the year 1545. As successive groups of black castaways overthrew their captors and married into local Amerindian chieftaincies, Esmeraldas became a mighty Afro-Amerindian maroon society. Beatty-Medina explores interactions between Esmeraldas and the colonial state. By examining an Afro-Amerindian maroon society on the Pacific coast of the kingdom of Quito, he underscores the little-studied aspects of marronage and maroon societies in Spanish America, showing that missionizing and religious conversion were both part and parcel of the colonial state's efforts at pacification. Here, we see the royal and religious discourse deployed by maroons to gain legitimacy and autonomy and go-betweens within the colonial order. Consequently, his essay shows the central importance of Christianization for Afro-Amerindian rebels seeking political legitimation and continued authority on the Quito frontier. Here, we learn how the Esmeraldas maroons—some of whom were descendants of Garofalo's Afro-Iberians—navigated with great sophistication both clerical intervention and the discourse of Christian conversion in order to situate themselves as the legitimate lords of Esmeraldas.

Joan Bristol (chapter 5) takes us into the alleys of late seventeenth-century Mexico City, where a group of black men and women held clandestine religious ceremonies and claimed to be *religiosos* (clerics) and *religiosas* (nuns) of Saint Iphigenia, in an effort to uncover the possible meanings such gatherings held for the congregants, who were described by observers as "blacks and mulattoes." Bristol shows that while blacks were involved closely in colonial religious life, they might also assert the right to participate in Christianity on their own terms. These second- and third-generation African descendants were seasoned members of colonial society with sophisticated understandings of Christianity, but they often deployed those understandings in ways that flaunted the prescribed tenets of religious orthodoxy. Such individuals were not unique, and Bristol shows that men and women of other *casta* designations were also among the devotees she studies. Thus, her essay has large implications for understanding how colonial subjects related to the racial hierarchy of the society.

Nancy E. van Deusen centers her discussion on the religious lives of second- and third-generation African-descended peoples, in this case free Afro-Peruvian women who served as *donadas* (religious servants) in the female convents of seventeenth-century Lima. By the seventeenth century, convents throughout Spanish America were home to thousands of women of African descent. While very little is known about them, van Deusen takes the reader into the world of seventeenth-century *donadas* in Lima in order to understand how these pious workers maneuvered a hierarchically ordered environment to gain prominence as spiritual beings. The essay offers an original investigation of the actions and motives of sincere devotees, thereby complicating our understanding of "subaltern agency," matronage, and colonial *casta*/gender hierarchies. Ultimately, as van Deusen's essay encapsulates, Part Two explores how official ecclesiastical and secular expectations of Africans and their descendants presupposed a resistance to orthodox Christianity. Collectively, the scholars in this section insist that militant maroons and urban laborers sought Catholic conversion and respected Church practices in a process of ethnogenesis with indigenous communities and colonial *castas* that included other free people of color. They ask that scholars consider the range of ways that African-descended peoples impacted the designs of statecraft, colonial piety, and efforts at gaining access to indigenous labor across time and space.

Part Three shifts our attention from the religious lives of African-descended peoples in Mexico and Peru to the family and professional lives of free blacks in nineteenth-century Cuba. Focusing upon medical workers and the category of "white," this section asks how free people of color claimed categories of inclusion. Linking various strategies, this section reconsiders how communities of Africans and their descendants used professional or familial categories offered by a modern Spanish colonial state.

Examining the strategies of free women of color, Karen Morrison (chapter 7) tackles the question of whitening in nineteenth-century Cuba, arguing that the dichotomous view of "whitening" as either a positive reproductive strategy pursued by blacks and mulattos or a political ideology of the racist Latin American elite to improve the images of their nations is misleading. Morrison insists that people of color did not merely tacitly accept racist, elitist principles, and in so doing she shows that efforts at whitening were not as predictable or linear as previous scholars have suggested. In place of such notions she offers a more detailed and nuanced reading of the principle of whitening, including how it was theorized and the complex and varying ways that Cubans (coloreds and others) engaged with the principle.

Likewise, Michelle Reid-Vazquez (chapter 8) asks how modern impositions of a nineteenth-century colonial state in Cuba eliminated previous inclusions of professional positions and articulations of "whitening." Reid's essay explores race in Cuba through the lens of midwifery—a skilled occupation once dominated by free women of color. As Spain endeavored to modernize its Caribbean territories, colonial authorities in Cuba embraced broader trends in the West aimed at professionalizing medicine. It was under this context, Reid asserts, that midwifery took on new political meaning as Cuban colonists sought to supplant free colored women as midwives. Reid explores the conflicting interpretations of midwifery, revealing a complex dialogue between Cuba's medical establishment and free colored women, who ultimately appropriated elite discourses of honor in an effort to shore up their occupational position.

Completing Part Three, Herbert Klein, one of the leading scholars of colonial Latin America, the transatlantic slave trade, and New World slavery, offers a critical review of some of the "new directions" in Afro–Latin American history. In the concluding essay of the volume, Klein returns us to some of the methods and questions that animated the comparative slavery school. He insists that scholars have jettisoned the comparative model at a real cost. Reminding us of the relationship between slavery and freedom, Klein charts a research agenda for fourth-wavers. In short, questions addressing how the social, economic, and legal positions of slaves impacted manumission and the enjoyment of full social lives remain of critical importance. Klein pushes us to move our examination of Afro–Latin America beyond the frame of slavery to include fuller explications of free black life, an approach that promises a more comprehensive examination of Afro–Latin America that both centers blacks in their own narratives and adds greater complexity to our understanding of the societies of Spanish America and beyond.

Notes

1. Months later, after the siege of Guayaquil, the expedition took another prize off the coast of Barbacoas near Isla del Gallo containing twenty-four "negros," including men, women, and children, bringing the total number of African-descended captives to nearly 150 people. See Rogers, *A Cruising Voyage round the World*.

2. Ibid.; Cooke, *A Voyage to the South Sea*.

3. As Saidiya Hartman points out, we can never know the sentiments or the fate of the woman that Rogers described as "the prettiest young female Negro we had in the Prize," who was given along with "some Bays, Linnen, and other things" to the "young Padre" (a priest of Tacames [Atacames]) for his good services in helping them promote their trade for provisions. According to Rogers, the "young Padre part[ed] with us extremely pleas'd, and leering under his Hood upon his black Female Angel." Like Venus, she has no name, no recording of her sayings, or what she refused to say. See Hartman, "Venus in Two Acts."

4. According to Rogers, Kendall stated that when the last war was declared (most likely the War of the Spanish Succession), he embarked under the command of Edward Roberts, who joined in commission from the governor of Jamaica, along with captains Rash, Golding, and Pilkington. Their company had 106 men, and they were tasked with taking the mines of Taco, situated at the lower Gulf of Darien. The Kendall party, which included twelve other free blacks, was overtaken by an estimated 500 men, reducing the company to sixty, included those wounded in battle. After a skirmish wherein the English lost an additional four men, the Spanish called a truce, fed their captives, took them up river, and killed everyone (except a Scot, a Frenchman, an English boy, and twelve free blacks, including Kendall). At the intercession of a priest, the Spanish decided to keep the free blacks as slaves. Kendall was sold first to the mines of Taco; from there he went to the mines near the Isla del Gallo.

5. Koser, "New African Diasporas: An Introduction"; Carter, "Preface"; and Butler, "Defining Diaspora, Refining a Discourse."

6. Saco and Ortiz, *Historia de la esclavitud de la raza africana en el Nuevo Mundo*; Ortiz, *Hampa afro-cubana*; Nina Rodrigues, *Os Africanos no Brasil*; Freyre, *The Masters and the Slaves*; and Ramos and Patee, *The Negro in Brazil.*

7. Peter Wade's book, *Race and Ethnicity in Latin America*, provides a nice synopsis of these challenges.

8. Ortiz, *Hampa afro-cubana: Los negros esclavos, estudio sociologico y de derecho publico*; Nina Rodrigues, *Os Africanos no Brasil*; Freyre, *The Masters and the Slaves*; Ramos and Patee, *The Negro in Brazil*; and Aguirre Beltrán, *La población negra de México, 1510–1810.*

9. Hoetink, *Slavery and Race Relations in the Americas*; Degler, *Neither Black nor White*; Harris, *Patterns of Race in the Americas*; Mörner, *Race Mixture in the History of Latin America*; and Klein, *Slavery in the Americas*—formerly a master's thesis that addressed questions set forth by Tannenbaum. See also Fernandes, *A Integraço do Negro na Sociedade de Classes.*

10. Williams, *Capitalism and Slavery.*

11. Mellafe, *La introducción de la esclavitud en Chile*; Feliú Cruz, *La abolición de la esclavitud en Chile*; Vial Correa, *El africano en el Reino de Chile.*

12. Acosta Saignes, *Vida de los esclavos negros en Venezuela*; Scheuss de Studer, *La trata de Negros en Rio de la Plata durante el siglo XVIII*; Castillero Calvo, *Los negros y mulatos libres en la historia social panameña.*

13. Barnet, *The Autobiography of a Runaway Slave: Esteban Montejo.*

14. For a comprehensive and still-prescient examination of the study of blacks in Latin America from the 1940s to the early 1970s, see Bowser, "The African Experience in Colonial Spanish America." Examples of studies that emerged in response to Tannenbaum and the comparative slavery school include Bowser, *The African Slave in Colonial Peru*; Blanchard, *Slavery and Abolition in Early Republican Peru*; Brockington, *The Leverage of Labor*; Carroll, *Blacks in Colonial Veracruz*; Chandler, "Slave

over Master in Colonial Colombia and Ecuador"; Chandler, "Health and Slavery in Colonial Colombia"; Crespo, *Esclavos negros en Bolivia*; Hünefeldt, *Paying the Price of Freedom*; Karasch, *Slave Life in Rio de Janeiro, 1808–1850*; Knight, *Slave Society in Cuba during the Nineteenth Century*; Lombardi, *The Decline and Abolition of Negro Slavery in Venezuela, 1820–1854*; Meiklejohn, "The Implementation of Slave Legislation in Eighteenth-Century New Granada"; Souza, *O Diabo e a Terra de Santa Cruz*; Palmer, *Slaves of the White God*; Reis, *Slave Rebellion in Brazil*; Scarano, *Sugar and Slavery in Puerto Rico, 1800–1850*; Schwartz, *Sugar Plantations and the Formation of Brazilian Society*; and Scott, *Slave Emancipation in Cuba*.

15. See for example Chance and Taylor, "Estate and Class in a Colonial City: Oaxaca in 1792"; Chance and Taylor, "The Ecology of Race and Class in Late Colonial Oaxaca"; McAlister, "Social Structure and Social Change in New Spain"; Borah and Cook, "Sobre las posibilidades de hacer el estudio histórico del mestizaje sobre una base demografica"; Arrom, *The Women of Mexico City, 1790–1857*; Seed, "The Social Dimensions of Race: Mexico City 1753"; Anderson, "Race and Social Stratification: A Comparison of Working-Class Spaniards, Indians and Castas in Guadalajara, Mexico in 1821"; Cope, *The Limits of Racial Domination*; Boyer, "Cast and Identity in Colonial Mexico: A Proposal and an Example"; Jackson, *Race, Caste, and Status: Indians in Colonial Spanish America*; McCaa, Schwartz, and Grubessich, "Race and Class in Colonial Latin America: A Critique"; and Chance and Taylor, "Estate and Class: A Reply." More recently, fourth-wave scholars have continued to explore the question of Latin America as a caste society. See for example Lewis, *Hall of Mirrors: Power, Witchcraft, and Caste in Colonial Mexico*; Vinson, *Bearing Arms for His Majesty*; Martínez, *Genealogical Fictions*; Fisher and O'Hara, *Imperial Subjects*; and Greer, Mignolo, and Quilligan, *Rereading the Black Legend*.

16. See Duncan and Meléndez, *El Negro en Costa Rica*; Kristjanson, *Estratificación socio-racial y económica de Costa Rica: 1700–1850*; Guardia, *Los Negros del istmo de Panamá*; Mena García, *La sociedad de Panamá en el siglo XVI*; Leiva Vivas, *Tráfico de esclavos negros a Honduras*; Karasch, *Slave Life in Rio de Janeiro, 1808–1850*.

17. Some great examples include Reis, *Slave Rebellion in Brazil*; Baralt, *Esclavos rebeldes*; and Sydney Mintz's classic work on marronage: *Maroon Societies: Rebel Slave Communities in the Americas*.

18. Curtin, *The Atlantic Slave Trade: A Census*.

19. Available at http://www.slavevoyages.org/tast/index.faces.

20. For example, see Wu, "The Population of the City of Queréetaro in 1791"; and Chance, *Race and Class in Colonial Oaxaca*.

21. Two good examples are Bowser, *The African Slave in Colonial Peru, 1524–1650*; and Lutz, *Santiago de Guatemala, 1541–1773*. Although Lutz's book examines Guatemala City rather broadly, it is nonetheless widely recognized as a foundational text for Afro-Guatemalan studies. For important ground-breaking work on Africans and their descendants in Guatemala, see Lokken, "Marriage as Slave Emancipation in Seventeenth-Century Rural Guatemala."

22. A ground-breaking work in the examination of spiritual lives and the development of folk culture among the enslaved in Mexico is Palmer, *Slaves of the White God*.

23. Superb examples for Mexico include Bennett, *Colonial Blackness*; Bennett, *Africans in Colonial Mexico*; Bristol, *Christians, Blasphemers, and Witches*; Villa-Flores, "To Lose One's Soul: Blasphemy and Slavery in New Spain, 1596–1669"; Proctor, "Slavery, Identity, and Culture: An Afro-Mexican Counterpoint, 1640–1763"; and Restall, *The Black Middle*.

24. The Third Root Project in Mexico has produced a host of Spanish-language publications, including Chávez-Hita, *Pardos, mulatos y libertos*; and Martínez Montiel, *La presencia Africana en México*. The work of the UNESCO Project has resulted in fairly recent publications on Latin America, specifically Cáceres Gómez, *Del olvido a la memoria*; and Cáceres Gómez, *Rutas de la esclavitud en África y América Latina*.

25. Third-wave scholarship also featured pioneering works that addressed African-descended peoples in Ecuador. See Whitten, *Black Frontiersmen*; Slamoral, *Sangre sobre piel negra*; and Savoia, *Actas del primer congreso de historia del negro en el Ecuador y sur de Colombia*. Both Michael Hammerly and María Luisa Laviana Cuetos blazed important trails for scholars interested in the social history of the city and province of Guayaquil, highlighting the presence of African-descended people. See Hammerly, *Historia social y económica de la Antigua provincia de Guayaquil, 1763–1842*; Hammerly, *El comercio de cacao de Guayaquil durante el período colonial*; and Cuetos, *Guayaquil en el siglo XVIII: recursos naturals y desarrollo económico*. More recently, in the wake of greater interest in the history of the North Andes and the African Diaspora to Spanish America, several fourth-wave scholars have begun to explore the history of blacks in the region. Charles Beatty-Medina's work on Esmeraldas promises to deepen our understanding of a familiar yet complex and grossly understudied aspect of colonial history—what he refers to as the colonizing and, at times, anticolonizing efforts of the so-called Afro-Esmeraldeños; see Beatty, "Rebels and Conquerors: African Slaves, Spanish Authority, and the Domination of Esmeraldas, 1563–1621 (Ecuador)." Sherwin Bryant's work promises a comprehensive examination of slavery and slave life in the kingdom of Quito; see Bryant, "Slavery and the Context of Ethnogenesis: Africans, Afro-Creoles and the Realities of Slavery in the Kingdom of Quito, 1600–1800." Still others, such as María Eugenía Chaves and Camilla Townsend, have gone far to enlighten our minds regarding the lives of enslaved black women at the end of the colonial era. See Chavés, *María Chiquinquirá Díaz un esclava del siglo VIII*; Chavés, "Slave Women's Strategies for Freedom and the Late Spanish Colonial State"; and Chavés, *Honor y libertad: Discursos y recursos en la estrategia de libertad de una mujer esclava (Guayaquil a fines del período colonial)*. Sherwin K. Bryant has sought to complement the work of Chavés and Townsend, arguing for the need to examine slave litigation over the *longue durée*; see Bryant, "Enslaved Rebels, Fugitives, and Litigants: The Resistance Continuum in Colonial Quito." See also Lavallé, "Lógica esclavista y resistencia negra en los Andes ecuato-

rianos a finales del siglo XVIII"; and Tardieu, *El negro en la real audiencia de Quito, siglos XVI–XVIII.*

26. Important exceptions to this can be found in the Colombian historiography. For decades now, Colombia has enjoyed a thriving historiographical tradition examining African-descended populations. Critical works include *Instituto Colombiano de Cultura Hispánica, Geografía humana de Colombia: Los Afrocolombianos*; Arrazola, *Palenque: Primer pueblo libre de América*; Colmenares, *Historia económica y social de Colombia*, Tomo 1, *1537–1719*; and Colmenares, *Historia económica y social de Colombia*, Tomo 2, *Popayán: una sociedad esclavista 1680–1800*; de Friedemann, "Estudios de negros en la antropología colombiana"; and de Friedemann, *Presencia Africana en Colombia*; Castillo Mathieu, *Esclavos negros en Cartagena y sus aportes léxicos*; Jaramillo Urbe, *Ensayos de historia social colombiana*; Restrepo, *Brujería y reconstruccción de identidades entre los Africanos y sus descendientes en la Nueva Granada, siglo XVII*; Romero, "Sociedades negras: esclavos y libres en la Costa Pacífica de Colombia"; Sharp, *Slavery on the Spanish Frontier*; Valencia Villa, *Alma en boca y huesos en costal*; and West, *Colonial Placer Mining in Colombia.*

27. Guridy, *Forging Diaspora: Afro-Cubans and African Americans in a World of Empire and Jim Crow*; Dubois and Scott, *Origins of the Black Atlantic*; Manning, *The African Diaspora*; Gilroy, *The Black Atlantic*; Okpewho, "Introduction," xxii; Edwards, "The Uses of Diaspora"; Butler, "Defining Diaspora, Refining a Discourse"; Palmer, "Defining and Studying the Modern African Diaspora"; Manning, "Africa and the African Diaspora: New Directions of Study"; Patterson and Kelley, "Unfinished Migrations: Reflections on the African Diaspora and the Making of the Modern World"; Hine and McLeod, *Crossing Boundaries: Comparative History of Black People in Diaspora*; Zeleza, "Rewriting the African Diaspora: Beyond the Black Atlantic"; and Vinson, "Introduction: African (Black) Diaspora History, Latin American History."

28. For a critically important work that both widens the spatial frame of the African diaspora and theorizes blackness, diaspora, transnationality, and "Black Europe," see Hine, Keaton, and Smallwood, *Black Europe and the African Diaspora.*

29. Byrd, *Captives and Voyagers: Black Migrants across the Eighteenth-Century British Atlantic World*; Cândido, "Merchants and the Business of the Slave Trade in Benguela, c. 1750–1850"; Dantas, *Black Townsmen: Urban Freedom and Slavery in the Eighteenth Century Americas*; de la Fuente, *Havana and the Atlantic in the Sixteenth Century*; Mann, *Slavery and the Birth of an African City: Lagos, 1760–1900*; Young, *Rituals of Resistance: African Atlantic Religion in Kongo and the Lowcountry South in the Era of Slavery*; Law, *Ouidah: Social History of a West African Slaving "Port," 1727–1892*; and Harris, *In the Shadow of Slavery: African Americans in New York City, 1626–1863.*

30. Sweet, *Recreating Africa: Culture, Kinship, and Religion in the African-Portuguese World, 1441–1770*; Sweet, "Mistaken Identities? Olaudah Equiano, Domingos Álvares, and the Methodological Challenges of Studying the African Diaspora."

31. Despite the groundswell of new work on blacks in Latin America, work on blacks in Spanish America continues to lag behind scholarship addressing the Carib-

bean and the United States. The literature produced in the past few years is far too vast to cite in its entirety, but some representative examples (especially in English) include: Helg, *Liberty and Equality in Caribbean Colombia, 1770–1835*; Lasso, *Myths of Harmony: Race and Republicanism during the Age of Revolution, Colombia 1795–1831*; Lane, *Quito 1599*; Walker, "'He outfitted his family in notable decency': Slavery, Honour and Dress in Eighteenth-Century Lima, Peru"; Lohse, "Africans and Their Descendants in Colonial Costa Rica"; Restall, *The Black Middle: Africans, Mayas, and Spaniards in Colonial Yucatan*; Bennett, *Africans in Colonial Mexico*; Bennett, *Colonial Blackness: A History of Afro-Mexico*; Butler, *Freedoms Given, Freedoms Won: Afro-Brazilians in Post-Abolition São Paulo and Salvador*; de la Fuente, *A Nation For All: Race, Inequality, and Politics in Twentieth-Century Cuba*; Restall, *Beyond Black and Red: African-Native Relations in Colonial Latin America;* and *Black Middle*; King, "Introducing the 'New' African Diasporic Military History in Latin America"; Vinson, *Bearing Arms for His Majesty*; Sweet, *Recreating Africa*; Herrera, *Natives, Europeans, and Africans in Sixteenth-Century Santiago de Guatemala*; Ares Queija and Stella, *Negros, mulatos, zambaigos*; Cáceres Gómez, *Negros, mulatos, esclavos y libertos en la Costa Rica del siglo XVII*; Chavés, *María Chiquinquirá Díaz: Una esclava del siglo XVIII: acerca de las identidades de amo y esclavo en el puerto colonial de Guayaquil*; and Aguirre, *Agentes de su propia libertad: Los esclavos de Lima y la desintegración de la esclavitud: 1821–1854*.

32. Synthetic works such as Rout's *The African Experience in Spanish America* and Andrews's *Afro-Latin America: 1800–2000* have helped give some definition and empirical parameters to this subfield. Andrews's book has synthesized much of the existing knowledge on Afro-Latin America while offering some ideas about how to conceptualize the very term "Afro-Latin America" and its populations and geography.

33. See Herman Bennett, "The Subject in the Plot."

34. Lockhart, "The Social History of Colonial Spanish America."

35. Bowser, "The African Experience in Colonial Spanish America."

36. The literature on the caste system is wide and vast, but a few texts seem particularly relevant to the need to think about a genealogy of "blackness" and "race" in the early modern era: Bennett, "'Sons of Adam': Text, Context, and the Early Modern African Subject"; Martínez, *Genealogical Fictions*; Greer, Mignolo, and Quilligan, *Rereading the Black Legend*; and Fisher and O'Hara, *Imperial Subjects: Race and Identity in Colonial Latin America*. See also Silverblatt, *Modern Inquisitions: Peru and the Colonial Origins of the Civilized World*; and Katzew and Deans-Smith, eds., *Race and Classification: The Case of Mexican America*. Barnor Hesse offers a particularly insightful theorization of race and racialization. Hesse insists that race is irreducible to the body and that it is merely one among several elements (e.g. language, culture, religion, geography, climate), albeit a privileged element, that came together in the colonial creations "Europeanness" and "non-Europeaness." Although the body is, as Hesse describes, the "privileged metonym of race rather than its conventional metaphor," it is the colonial governing relationship that race signifies and requires

further consideration alongside attempts to understand how racialized subjects engaged, evaded, and took up the impositions of race in personal and group projects of self-craft. See Hesse, "Racialized Modernity: An Analytics of White Mythologies." For a highly nuanced synthesis of medieval Castillian culture, see Dodds, Menocal, and Balbale, *The Arts of Intimacy: Christians, Jews, and Muslims in the Making of Castilian Culture*.

37. Heywood and Thornton, *Central Africans, Atlantic Creoles, and the Foundation of the Americas, 1585–1660*. The theorization of Atlantic Creoles is for the most part focused on Atlantic Africa, the sugar islands, and cities in Anglo-Dutch North America. Jane G. Landers offers a notable exception in her recent work, *Atlantic Creoles in the Age of Revolutions*. Her work stresses that we simultaneously consider the multiple stations of black journeys as being heavily influential in shaping black identity before (and during) the journey to the Americas. Landers insists that creolization involved give and take, constant reconfiguring, and personal odysseys that crossed vast geographies in which identities were formed and accumulated by accrual and accretion.

PART 1

Complicating Identity in the African Diaspora to Spanish America

1

The Shape of a Diaspora

The Movement of Afro-Iberians to Colonial Spanish America

LEO J. GAROFALO

The presence of Afro-Iberians who helped shape the cultural and physical webs that bound together the African, European, and American continents forces us to broaden our understanding of the history of Iberian empires and the African Diaspora. The creation and activities of populations of African descent in Portugal and Spain, their work in expanding and sustaining the Atlantic system, and their resettlement in the Americas make Afro-Iberian intermediaries as essential to empire as the indigenous go-betweens described by Alida C. Metcalf in the colonization of Brazil.[1] The view of how imperial systems develop and function on display in J. H. Elliot and Henry Kamen's impressive studies and in the work of C. R. Boxer leaves out these key dynamics and actors.[2] An equally important and compelling story of Iberian-style expansion and its intimate link to the movement of millions of African peoples appears when we broaden our view and ask how imperial systems take on a reality and operate and expand through individuals' actions and participation. This fuller picture includes considering the unexpected presence and mobility of Afro-Iberians as they became a part of urban southern Iberian society, moved back and forth to the Americas, and served the Spanish Crown as sailors and soldiers in the Americas and along the coasts of Africa. The African presence in southern Europe fostered an early appearance of intermediate groups and culture mediators, especially in crossroads locations on both sides of the Atlantic. These East Atlantic and Mediterranean dimensions of the Diaspora did not disappear even after the majority of slaves went directly to the Americas. Thus, a history of empire or slavery in the Americas under colonial rule cannot be fully understood without considering the slaves and ex-slaves in Africa and Europe before and during the European invasion and colonization of the Americas.

Significance of Africans in Iberia

By the end of the 1400s, a significant African presence existed in Iberia, and Africans in the south of the Peninsula grew in importance over the next 200 years. Of course, an influential medieval Mediterranean model of slavery in Italy, Barcelona, and elsewhere originally treated slavery as nonracial, as predominantly female, and as a subset of human dependence within the flexibility permitted by legal systems that countenanced buying, selling, renting, and freeing the people captured from societies as diverse as those found in the Black Sea regions, the Mediterranean, Southern Europe, and Africa.[3] Between the eleventh and the thirteenth centuries, Barcelona engaged in small-scale trade in expensive black African slaves with Tunis.[4] Eventually, over the course of the fourteenth century, merchants engaged in the trans-Saharan trade brought slaves from Sub-Saharan Africa to Christian kingdoms in Iberia and to other parts of the Mediterranean. The fifteenth-century expansion of seaborne Iberian raiding and trading expeditions south along the African coast bypassed the Muslim-controlled overland trade routes and significantly increased the number of people brought from sub-Saharan Africa to southern Europe. Following the first sales in Lagos in 1444 of large numbers of West Africans captured by the Portuguese, the presence of enslaved and (eventually) free West and Central Africans in southern Iberian towns and cities of both Portugal and Spain grew steadily during the 1400s and 1500s. In the second half of the fifteenth century, Andalusian nobles, merchants, and ship owners competed with the Portuguese traders by organizing their own raiding missions to bring enslaved West Africans directly to Seville for sale. Although on a smaller scale, direct Spanish participation in the trade continued even after the treaties of Alcaçovas (1479), Tordesillas (1494), and Sintra (1509) recognized a Portuguese monopoly over the trade and defined Spanish and Portuguese spheres of activity in Africa and elsewhere.[5] Seville became Europe's second most important center (after Lisbon) for trading slaves. By 1492, as many as 35,000 people from West Africa—primarily from Senegambia and the Gulf of Guinea—had been sold into slavery on the peninsula.[6] According to Alessandro Stella, between 700,000 and 800,000 people arrived as slaves from the Atlantic trade between 1450 and 1750.[7] The triangle of the Andalusian cities of Ayamonte, Seville, and Cadiz contained the highest concentration of slaves in all of Spain. Perhaps as many as one in four or one in five people in southern Iberian port cities such as Cadiz were of African descent by the end of the 1600s.[8]

An Andalusian market developed for enslaved Africans that preferred them over *morisco/as* for certain jobs. This was the result of a labor shortage, increasingly affordable slaves supplied by the Portuguese, and the erratic nature of the supply of and religious suspicion associated with *morisco/a* and Moorish captives. The new, more direct Portuguese slave trade undercut the competition, lowering the price of slaves and regularizing the flow. Slaves became more common and could be dedicated to a variety of tasks according to sex. Women worked primarily in domestic service and home-based manufacturing. Men labored as domestics; stevedores; assistants to artisans, farmers, miners; and in workshops, construction, and the galleys.[9] As with enslaved *morisco/as*, women may have predominated among Andalusia's enslaved Africans. Much earlier, the caliphates of Muslim-controlled Iberia had imported more female sub-Saharan slaves than males.[10] After the America-bound slave trade grew, slavers shipped men to the Americas and women and children to Iberia. Alessandro Stella argues that the majority of the slaves traded in the Iberian Peninsula were children and adolescents. Although always part of a complex world of slaves and ex-slaves that included Moors and *morisco/a* Bosnians, and even Indians from the subcontinent, Africans from south of the Sahara were perhaps favored in Andalusia because they were considered less likely to harbor an allegiance to Islam and less likely to resort to violent means to escape. Furthermore, the supply of *morisco/as* was limited to those who could be enslaved for rebelling, and capturing North Africans at sea or in raids on shore was no easy task and occurred only sporadically. The population of African slaves and ex-slaves reached some 10 percent of southern Iberia's urban population and contributed substantially to economic and social production in the 1500s.[11]

Enslaved and free people from sub-Saharan Africa became another part of an already heterogeneous urban population in Andalusia. In Seville, all social groups and almost all artisan sectors possessed African slaves.[12] Afro-Iberians became associated with specific southern Iberian neighborhoods such as Seville's San Bernardo and San Ildefonso parishes and formed confraternities (Seville's San Roque confraternity, for example).[13] Sixteenth- and seventeenth-century notary and municipal records and Inquisition cases that refer to Seville indicate that Afro-Iberians influenced daily activities (such as selling in local markets) and beliefs (such as healing and divining).[14] Indeed, Seville was known as a crossroads and a cosmopolitan place: "queen of the world and haven of foreigners," as sixteenth-century picaresque novelist and actor Agustín de Rojas Villandrando characterized it.[15] Perhaps the heterogeneity of local society and the constant movement of people through southern Iberian towns and cities and those of the Algarve and Lisbon allowed space and opportunities for Afro-Iberians to create or claim ways of work, thought, and creativity, maybe even Afro-Iberian ways of doing business and forming trade networks. More certainly, life in southern Iberia offered enslaved and free Afro-Iberians a role as intermediaries at a time when European expansion into the Americas and along Africa's coast demanded many more people with skills as mediators and experience with adaptation and assimilation.

Before he embarked for the Caribbean in 1502, Bartolomé de Las Casas, like so many other Spanish colonizers and missionaries, grew up in Seville with a significant presence of black slaves and free people from sub-Saharan Africa. The practice of bondage as well as Africans and West African ways were well known to the Iberians taking part in the European invasion and colonization of the Americas. In 1565, Seville held 6,327 slaves (including *negro/as*, *moro/as*, *canario/as*, *indio/as*, and *morisco/as*) and perhaps double that number of free people of African or partial African origin in a population of 85,538.[16] Given the historic importance of these West African residents of Seville and the surrounding southern Iberian regions from which most of the Spanish (and Portuguese) emigrants sallied forth to the Americas, it is not surprising that a population and individuals already characterized by multiple uprootings and resettlements might form a key component of the Iberian crews, raiding parties, and trade networks being formed in the fifteenth, sixteenth, and even seventeenth centuries. The nature of that enterprise and its roots in southern Iberia made Afro-Iberians into intermediaries in the transfer of Hispanic society, ideas, and institutions and the creolization of these things in the Atlantic world.

The history of changes and continuities in western and central Africa also shaped the Afro-Iberian experience on the three continents and in that middle space of routes and connections that Afro-Iberians proved so instrumental in forming. Individual Africans arriving in Europe and later in the Americas often suffered multiple forced movements as slaves from one group to another. Sometimes this experience spanned several years before they reached the coast or a slaving network that took them to the coast for embarkation. The Canary Islands became one of Spain's early formative experiments in building an overseas empire through conquest and slavery and through displacing and combining different sorts of people both as colonizers and colonized.[17] The Canaries continued to form an important link in the Spanish and Portuguese slave-trading networks that regularly sent ships to the islands for the final Crown inspections of crews and provisions or to take on additional water and food and occasionally sailors.[18] The Canaries also became home to large numbers of imported African slaves and their descendents (often alongside enslaved islanders and *moro/as*). In the Canaries, the same trends appear of Afro-Iberian integration into local versions of Hispanic society, and the same struggles occurred with the oversight and intervention of Iberian institutions such as the Inquisition.[19]

Other African slave-trading enclaves played similar roles and articulated wider African populations on the continent in the context of this emerging early Iberian Atlantic presence and its extension into the Americas. Networks and routes were established, and Afro-Iberians occupied difficult—but strategic and sometimes shifting—positions within them as intermediaries of many sorts (as traders, translators, missionaries, refugees, sailors, and so forth). Intermediaries appeared in family networks and benefited from a time when identities were often in flux. From the late fifteenth century forward, mixed Euro-African families or even communities appeared in coastal Africa, usually as African women married or formed families with European men.[20] When researchers ask who was actually doing the labor and what was making this trade system work in specific locations, they sometimes come upon these family networks, the children of which were often trained to facilitate contact between different cultures. George E. Brooks credits racially mixed people he labels Eurafricans for making possible much of the commerce between Europe and West Africa.[21] To an extent, the work of these culturally mixed families and individuals helped to create or re-create important parts of what we have come to know as the slave-trade system and to blend Iberian and African economic and cultural practices.[22]

Furthermore, the cultural flexibility evident in Iberia and the Americas among people displaced by the Diaspora also existed in Africa because of conflicts and changes before and during the slave trade. Thus, some scholars argue that creolization happened for many people before they moved to the Americas or Europe.[23] Even as ethnicity broke down, broader categories of shared identity may have arisen or persisted (belief in multiple deities, for example). As people struggled to survive in constantly changing and chaotic situations, perhaps identity could be both fixed (vital elements of identity survived) and changing (perhaps not as essentialized as some survivalists argue). People retained and transformed individual identity. This flexibility continued in the Diaspora. Perhaps the cases of Afro-Iberians help synthesize the survival-versus-creation debate by showing that many elements, practices, and beliefs are created survivals.[24] Catholic religious orders—mainly Jesuits and Capuchin missionaries—also proved active in the African enclaves, African courts, and beyond. The missionaries involved many different sorts of intermediaries including some Afro-Iberians and many of the bicultural or tricultural individuals mentioned above. The missionaries were quite active in the island enclaves and in today's northern Angola and in the kingdom of Kongo, and their work gave rise to important sources on missionary work and African life. In a few cases, African entities with greater military and political parity exerted organized and direct pressure on Iberians in Europe—for example, the Angolan and Ndongo diplomatic delegations that dealt with the Portuguese in Europe and Brazil.[25] The culturally dynamic and complicated arrangements of coercion, negotiation, transformation, and human movement that characterized the African experience on the Iberian Peninsula had their counterparts along the coasts and rivers and in the royal courts of sub-Saharan Africa.

Enslaved West Africans arrived in the Americas as personal servants, artisans, concubines, seamen, and fighters. A few even gained recognition and privileges for their service to the Spanish as "black conquistadores."[26] Some historians have concluded, as did James Lockhart for sixteenth-century Peru, that the African-descent population effectively increased the influence of the Spanish and Hispanic culture in Amerindian societies, thus augmenting the influence and power of Hispanic culture in the Americas.[27] Subsequent historical research has broadened our understanding of the importance of a sizeable—even majority—black and *mulato* population on Peru's coast and this population's presence in the labor systems, religious practices, and daily markets of coastal cities.[28] Recent studies of the intersection of cultural, social, and microeconomic history in the Andean cities question the degree to which people of African descent in the Americas *primarily* promoted Iberian customs and beliefs (in some cases, they adopted, modified, and extended indigenous practices and beliefs, such as brewing and marketing *chicha* corn beer or curing illness with coca leaf, guinea pigs, and invocations of the Inca).[29] Detailed local studies of rural areas show that people of African descent could both bolster and challenge the survival of indigenous communities.[30] Other researchers have revealed the significant presence of the black "anti-conquistador" engaged in marronage.[31] In short, West Africans and Afro-Iberians could both promote and alter Iberian colonization in the Americas, just as they had influenced cultural norms and institutional practices in Iberia and Africa.

Measuring the Afro-Iberian population and its cultural influence on the islands of the Atlantic, in African trading enclaves, and in southern Iberia and the subsequent movement of this population to the Americas offers insights into Iberia's cultural norms and institutions; the organization of colonial life in the Americas, including the Pacific coast of South America; and (especially) the role of intermediaries and the mechanisms of incorporation in the creation of the early modern European empires that embraced various continents. Some Afro-Iberians even left or bridged the economic networks and political spheres associated with Spanish and Portuguese colonialism in the Americas and Africa to enter British, Dutch, and French areas of trade and settlement in the seventeenth century.[32] When historians and demographers examine the scope and nature of the stream of West Africans drawn into and passing through the early Iberian Atlantic world and into the Americas, the Africans who traveled back and forth between Iberia and the Americas (and at times Africa too) stand out. Of the people forced into bondage and taken to the Americas, only a small percentage passed through southern Iberia. However, because of this group's lengthy experience with the Portuguese and Spanish, Afro-Iberians quite possibly became an especially important intermediary group in the Americas and on the Spanish Main. Passenger lists and royal licenses to travel permit a reconstruction of Afro-Iberians' transatlantic movement and their presence and functions both in southern Iberia and the colonial Americas.

Afro-Iberian *Pasajeros a Indias*

Passenger lists and official licenses indicate that both enslaved and free individuals embarked in Seville for various parts of the Americas, often in the company of or with the help of powerful masters or employers. The slave Juan, a typical black *pasajero a Indias* (passenger to the Indies), traveled to Lima with his merchant master and his master's junior business partner, who sold goods from a kiosk (*cajón*).[33] Among the free *pasajeros* was Angelina Díaz. A *negra libre*, Díaz parleyed her status as a free servant of the priest Clemente Pérez de Tudela to obtain an official license to travel alone to Panama.[34] In this segment of transatlantic emigration, wealthy Spaniards and church personnel played a significant part in bringing both free black servants and slaves to the Americas from Spain (particularly to colonial centers such as Santo Domingo, Mexico City, Michoacán, Cartagena, Bogotá, Quito, Lima, and Charcas).[35] In the Iberian cities of origin, ecclesiastical and secular officeholders and merchants were consistently the groups who bought and sold the largest number of slaves.[36] Later in the 1600s, especially from the 1620s on, other black slaves and servants traveled with Jesuits to the missions among the Guaraní in Paraguay, usually via Buenos Aires.[37] In one instance, in 1628, the Jesuits brought eight slave musicians from Angola to bolster their evangelization efforts among the Guaraní. The slaves had been trained to sing and to play *chirimías* (hornpipes), flutes, *bajones* (bassoons), and coronets to accompany the religious services. A royal decree allowed the Jesuits the privilege of transporting these men (after paying the requisite taxes), along with forty Jesuits, from Seville to the missions in South America via Buenos Aires. In fact, the decree gave the Jesuits permission to buy and take on board eight slave musicians in Lisbon, Spain, or Brazil, suggesting the availability of this type of trained slaves in each of these important points in the Iberian Atlantic World.[38] Cases such as this one suggest that a well-established merchant class and a large church presence in the Americas—whether in a historically core zone of major missionary activity or in a peripheral area—drew with it the largest segment of both enslaved and free Afro-Iberians.

In a fashion similar to merchants and clergy, Spaniards and Spanish creoles who were recognized as *vecinos* in the Americas or who were traveling to the Americas to assume non-ecclesiastical posts proved much more likely than most other Spanish travelers to bring black servants or slaves from Iberia with them (or to have come from the Americas with them in the first place).[39] Arrangements of work and social control traveled with these black *pasajeros*. In many of these cases and those of elite Spanish creoles returning to the Americas, the black servants or slaves made up part of a larger household or of an elite Spaniard's retinue en route to the Americas. For example, the *esclavos negros* Andrés and Lucas and the *esclava negra* Gregoria accompanied their owner, their owner's four sons, and her four servants (*criados*) to the Indies.[40] In another case, the Marques de Oropesa traveled to Peru in 1615 with the couple Juan de Ortega and Catalina de Ortega (both *mulatos criados*), part of the retinue of many servants and relatives who also made the journey.[41] At times, these groups also included *mestizo* or indigenous servants from the Americas alongside blacks.[42] These same arrangements also drew *mulatos libres* from the Canaries and from other Atlantic islands to the Americas.[43] Thus, the social status, relative economic power, and institutional association of *pasajeros* helped facilitate the movement of this segment of people of African descent between the Americas and southern Iberia. These same factors helped root people of African descent in an immediate and direct environment of patronage and hierarchy as they moved between the Americas and Iberia. When considering Afro-Iberians' possibilities as intermediaries, links to a patron could mean that the goals and benefits of negotiating a place in a new society could be limited to a patron's objectives. However, if allowed sufficient autonomy and access to resources, an Afro-Iberian could turn these connections into an advantage.

This pattern of merchant, ecclesiastical, and other elite patrons facilitating the movement of Afro-Iberians to the Americas matches more general patterns among all Iberian immigrants.[44] Large numbers of *criados* of all types crossed the Atlantic in both directions as part of the retinue of important individuals, successful relatives, or influential personages from their home regions. In exchange for covering the costs of the voyage and travel over land, men and women committed to serve these patrons during the trip and sometimes beyond. This arrangement—exchanging service for transport across the ocean—in some ways resembled the practice in the British Empire of bringing indentured servants to the Americas. As with indentured servitude, the arrangements were not always fully voluntary or made with full freedom of choice. For instance, agreeing to serve and cross the Atlantic could also form part of an agreement to pay back a loan to buy one's freedom. The *negro* Domingo purchased his freedom in Havana with a loan from Catalina de Angeles, who was en route to Seville from Cartagena de Indias in 1596. He agreed to serve her for eight years, and when she decided to return to Cartagena de Indias a year later with her sister, her daughter, and an adopted boy, Domingo was obliged to accompany the group as a servant.[45] A 1612 lawsuit over back wages for a cook helps expose the workings of the *criado* system as a mechanism of travel to and from Spanish America. Antonio de Ojero, a free *negro* from Peru, sued Seville *vecino* Andrés Ramírez de Molina for 1,000 reales for the time he spent serving him and his traveling companions as a cook and "in everything else." Ramírez de Molina countered that he had agreed to bring de Ojero from Potosí to Spain (at a cost of 200 ducados) in exchange for his service. Ramírez de Molina stated that only out of generosity had he provided 400 reales for de Ojero's clothing and maintained him at his house in Seville without charge for six months (12 reales per month was allegedly the cost of his room). Ramírez de Molina called witnesses who had made this same trip before and could enumerate its expenses. They testified that merchants and other prominent people regularly paid the costs of those people—*españoles* or *negro/as*—who volunteered to serve them during the journey by land and sea. These *criados* even included people who could pay their own way but who preferred to save the money instead. The royal judges agreed that these arrangements were common and fair. However, in this particular case, the court sided with de Ojero's witnesses and his attorney. They had explained that de Ojero was poor and could have sustained himself with less work in the Indies than in Spain and that unlike passengers who might work in exchange for their passage and board because they were returning to home towns or had other opportunities in Spain, de Ojero and his wife, who also helped out in Ramírez de Molina's house in Seville, had nobody to draw them to Spain.[46] Other *criados* crisscrossing the Atlantic were children under the protection and control of influential adults. For their survival, they relied on the patronage and support of those who requested the travel licenses on their behalf, as in the case of fifteen-year-old Melchor de Segovia, a *mulato* from the Yucatan about to return to Mexico in the company of a cleric and the cleric's other *criado*, a *moreno*.[47] In short, the *criado* system promoted the trans-Atlantic movement of many free people of African descent alongside thousands of other Europeans and American-born subjects of the Spanish Empire in ways that ran the spectrum from a simple exchange of labor for a wage of sorts to arrangements wrought with compulsion that allowed the *criado* little (if any) choice.[48] Free labor at this time was simply not as free as the term may imply. And in some cases, slavery in the Iberian world provided more flexibility than might be expected. Perhaps these arrangements can be termed a form of "black indenture" in the Iberian world. Certainly no official indentured servant program existed to force or help artisan and peasant families cross the Atlantic at the state's expense. Instead, the individually arranged *criado* system paid the way for those unable to pay the 20 ducats for the passage and an additional amount of 10–20 ducats for provisions.[49]

Coercion aside, the prominence of *criados* from the Americas making the trans-Atlantic journey is striking and suggests that this was an important mechanism that allowed—or forced—peoples of African heritage to move to southern Iberia for different lengths of time. Service in Spain could take *criados* from city to city, as in the case of Isabel Ortiz, a *negra*, and her *mulato* son, who sailed from their native Mexico in the service of Don Manuel de Ongria and then lived in Madrid and Seville, serving two different patrons. After years in Spain, they had formed connections with Afro-Iberian *vecinos* of Seville, who testified to knowing them well for several years and supported their petition to return to Puebla, Mexico, in 1611.[50] Isabel sailed in 1612. Her successful petition was bolstered by testimony from Seville's sea captains. They explained that she had visited Spain once before, that she had a husband and two children in Puebla, and that her color was "*lora*" (olive), not "negra."[51] Of course, marriage in Iberia could prevent the Crown from authorizing return, and marital status was a common concern in the *informaciones* that accompanied all *pasajeros*' petitions for travel licenses.[52]

The prolonged discussions and voluminous proof offered of black *pasajeros*' free status served two purposes: first, such evidence established their rights and better identified them in the Crown's efforts to control the movement of people; and, second, it guaranteed that import restrictions and taxes levied on the sale of slaves were not being violated. A special tax (*avería*) of 2 to 6 ducats or more was charged on each slave who crossed the Atlantic from Seville unless some special exemption applied (certain numbers of slaves were allowed free of charge to provide personal service for officials, for instance) or a person could be proven to be free and traveling as a *criado*.[53] Two natives of Cuba who were freed after years of service in Cartagena de Indias and Seville, the *negro libre* Pascual de Veas and the *libre* and *de color membrillo* Gracia de la Cruz, presented their *cartas de libertad* as well as their former owners to bolster their 1617 petition to be allowed to return to Cartagena. Pascual de Veas's 1611 *carta de libertad* emphasized his loyal service to a captain employed by the king in the armada and in Lisbon. He allegedly defended his master—and by extension Crown interests—at sea and on land. Gracia de la Cruz's January 24, 1617, *carta de libertad* praised her Christian piety and personal service and expressed the desire that she be allowed to live and travel where she pleased without impediment and be treated as a free person. In February of that same year, the Crown approved Pascual de Veas's petition to return with his former master, who was about to assume the command of a boat in the coastal defense of Cartagena. No mention is made of Gracia de la Cruz's request. Perhaps the granting of freedom was suspiciously close to her date of requested travel (perhaps hiding her sale to a new master headed to the Indies).[54] The Crown also strove to guarantee that free and enslaved Afro-Iberians who traveled to the Americas returned to Europe and that African Americans returned to the Americas.[55] Witnesses were carefully questioned about petitioners' age, their appearance, their dates of travel, and their acquaintances in order to prove that the people who requested licenses were indeed the same ones who had traveled across the Atlantic before.[56] Discrepancies could lead to the denial of licenses and even the seizure and sale of slaves or the arrest of free men or women when they reached the Americas.[57]

Of course, travelers who accompanied secular and ecclesiastic patrons would not have been typical of most enslaved West and Central Africans' experience of crossing the Atlantic bound for the Spanish colonies. In the 328 *informaciones y licencias* and other documents on Afro-Iberians examined for this study, sale in the Americas appeared not to be the primary motive for embarkation in Seville. Possible exceptions to this pattern were the small groups of African-born slaves destined for the notorious smuggling center of Buenos Aires toward the end of the seventeenth century and the small groups of four or five slaves who accompanied men identified as Portuguese and Spanish slave traders passing through Seville.[58] Furthermore, it must be noted that perhaps as many as half of all people passing through southern Iberia, including Africans and Afro-Iberians, neither received official permission to sail nor left a trace of their passage in the official documents. From quite early on, ample evidence exists that unauthorized shipments of slaves and goods arrived regularly in the Caribbean or used the Canaries as cover for the real destination of passengers, merchandise, and slaves.[59] Unfortunately, few of the Contratación records systematically or accurately record the numbers, origins, or destinations of the slaves carried to the Americas by trading operations that originated in southern Iberia. Instead, these records show that the officially authorized black *pasajeros* followed the more general patterns of sixteenth- and seventeenth-century Iberian emigration to the Americas (and to a lesser extent they mirrored the return of American creoles). Clientage and family networks played a principal role in Afro-Iberian and general Andalusian settlement of the Indies. And some 10 percent of all officially licensed *pasajeros* returned to Spain.

Black Sailors and Soldiers on the Spanish Main

The sailors and soldiers of the Spanish Main figure prominently among the poorly documented groups known to have made their way to the Americas and back in a very regular fashion. Pablo E. Pérez-Mallaína shows that by the late 1500s 7,000–9,000 mariners sailed each year on eight- to nine-month voyages aboard Spain's naval and merchant fleet. From the beginning, fully half of the sailors were not Spanish.[60] Enough information exists to demonstrate that black sailors and soldiers also traveled frequently between Iberia, the Americas, and Africa. Black sailors included people born on all three continents, and they included both slaves and freedmen. They usually occupied the lower rank of sailors (*grumetes*) or cabin boys (pages), but the occasional petty officer or even pilot appears. They typically made up a very small number of individual crews and came primarily from the principal seafaring towns and cities of Spain and Portugal. Like all sailors, they were poorly paid, suffered high mortality, and engaged in smuggling or trading on a small scale to supplement their wages. Black sailors and soldiers created yet another set of Afro-Iberian routes crossing the Atlantic and linking families and communities across that divide. They also show that people from Africa and their descendants not only helped make the Americas profitable, they also helped carry hundreds of thousands of people and their goods and wealth back and forth across the Atlantic Ocean.

Sea captains from Andalucia, Portugal, the Canaries, and Galicia collected crews with strong local ties that included free and enslaved Afro-Iberian men, boys, and (very occasionally) women. Typical of captains who owned both slaves and their own ships, Fernán Sánchez Franco filled out his crew with three of his own slaves: a low-ranking *grumete* to assist the other sailors and an *esclava lora* and a *mulato esclavo* to serve him personally during the voyage.[61] Afro-Iberians might also find themselves serving alongside indigenous Brazilians. Both groups sailed armed with their *cartas de libertad*, which they were required to show during the royal inspections.[62] A typical crew for a large boat such as the *San Salvador* bound for New Spain with the fleet from Cadiz included twenty-seven sailors (*marineros*), twenty-nine *grumetes*, and fifteen pages (who were usually adolescent boys). The crew included three black slaves among the *grumetes* and one among the pages. One belonged to the captain, one to each of the chief officers, and the page belonged to a *vecino* of Cadiz who would collect the slave's wages at the end of the voyage. The captain was held legally and financially responsible for returning all of these slaves to Spain and seeing that they were not sold or did not escape in New Spain.[63] Smaller ships licensed by Portuguese monopolists to transport set numbers of slaves sailed for Africa with Afro-Iberians aboard. For example, the *San Bartolomé* left Seville for Angola to buy 130 slaves for sale in Mexico or Cartagena de Indias. The Portuguese captain commanded a crew of twenty-six made up of men and boys from Portugal, Seville, the Canaries, Cadiz, San Lúcar de Barrameda (one of Seville's ports), and Galicia. They included seven Afro-Iberians: the gunner and sailor (*moreno*) from La Palma in the Canaries, a carpenter and sailor (*negro*) from the Azores, the sailor Juan de Salzedo (*moreno*) from San Lúcar, two *grumetes* (*morenos*) from Portugal's Algarve, and the captain's two male slaves (a *grumete* and a ten-year-old page). The five freedmen in the crew had to prove their free status.[64] Afro-Iberian sailors also made their way down along the Pacific Coast of South America.[65] Royal regulations required ships sailing to Africa and the Americas to carry weapons and ammunition and at least two or three trained gunners and soldiers. Other Afro-Iberian soldiers and drummers crossed the Atlantic to work in the forts and garrisons, mainly along the coasts.[66] Sailors and soldiers carried out a small but consistent part of the maritime and soldiering work on ships that sailed into the Atlantic from southern Iberia to carry goods; capture slaves; repel British, Dutch, and French pirates; and transport immigrants to the Americas.

Sailing was not easy work, and jobs—particularly skilled ones—tended to be controlled by particular neighborhoods and families, but a few Afro-Iberians entered this realm, claimed a small place, and advanced their interests and those of their families and neighborhoods. Most African-descended sailors served at the lowest ranks, but enslaved Afro-Iberians who achieved the experience and rank of sailor (*marinero*) enjoyed the slight edge that was normally available to enslaved artisans to negotiate a sale to another owner or buy their freedom.[67] A small number filled the position of quartermaster or first mate (*maestre*)—even as slaves. For example, a sea captain from the Canaries elevated his Puerto Rican–born slave from sailor to first mate because of the experience he had gained sailing to and from the Americas.[68] The *mulato* Gaspar Caraballo from Seville's seafaring neighborhood of Triana occupied the position of quartermaster on a warship in the royal Armada until accusations of sodomy by two subordinates threatened his life while the fleet rested in the Port of Veracruz.[69] Resistance to Afro-Iberian superiors, especially pilots, was not unusual. In 1539, the king and the Council of the Indies intervened to force the *piloto mayor* in Seville to allow Diego Hernández, a free *vecino* of Seville with a wife and children, to be examined for his pilot's license, pointing out his thirteen years of experience and his respectable "life and customs."[70] Thus, Afro-Iberians became a part of the maritime tradition of Portugal's Algarve ports such as Lago and Tavira and of Andalusia's ports of Ayamonte, San Lúcar de Barrameda, Santa Marta, and Cadiz and the Triana neighborhood in Seville. Seafaring and soldiering became two additional paths for Afro-Iberian movement along the routes that connected the Atlantic continents.

Although most sailors and soldiers maintained ties with southern Iberia and returned to families, churches, and friends on the peninsula, they also engaged in smuggling and small-scale commerce in the local economies they encountered in the Americas and in Africa to augment their meager pay. In Cartagena de Indias, and no doubt in many other Atlantic World trade centers, Afro-Iberian sailors, *grumetes*, and pages regularly walked through the streets selling the cloth, trinkets, and other goods they and their relatives had smuggled to the Americas for resale. Ambulatory sales and the knowledge that seamen were a good source of imported items helped make this petty commerce successful. Owners of small dry-goods stores—*pulperos*—also made arrangements with Afro-Iberians to sell merchandise, provide credit and lodgings, and even hide stolen goods for later sale. Even for the few weeks or months they were in port, Afro-Iberians became integrated into local commerce and daily life.[71] Not all Afro-Iberian natives of Ayamonte and the other southern Iberian ports remained close to the sea. Pascual Díaz, a *mulato libre* who established a viable business as a small-scale merchant in Mexico City, left enough property and wealth upon his death to settle his debts, pay his executor, and send some 273 pesos back to his *mulata* wife, a pastry seller living in a house they owned in their Spanish hometown of Ayamonte.[72] Afro-Iberians remaining in the Americas frequently built more extensive networks on the same principle of serving as mediators between suppliers or producers and consumers. In the Andes and Mexico, this often meant developing that role between indigenous farmers and city markets. The *mulato* Juan de Rojas, a native of San Lúcar, amassed 586 pesos and many unsold goods buying, transporting, and selling foodstuffs in Mexico.[73] Families at home in southern Iberia depended on the wages and other earnings from these soldiers and sailors. When the drummer Alonso de Castro, a *negro libre*, died on the voyage, his widow in Seville, a *mulata*, anxiously petitioned for his wages and the money from the auction of his belongings. The widow received 476 reales.[74] Whether or not they were soldiers and sailors, Afro-Iberians who died in the Americas regularly remitted part of their wealth to Spain through bequests to specific religious or charitable institutions, indicating both their roots in southern Spain before travel and how those local connections and influences could be maintained from abroad. Ana Gómez died in Panama, but in her will she founded a chaplaincy in Seville's Magdalena parish where she and her husband had been *vecinos*, donated money to Seville's convents and hospitals, and a paid for a memorial in her hometown of Niebla.[75] At other times, Afro-Iberians' relatives reclaimed all the property of deceased family members in the Americas or claimed other favors due them for service to the Crown.[76] Maritime trade routes and forts distributed Afro-Iberians throughout the Atlantic World, and penury brought these individuals into direct and constant contact with local populations even as they tried to keep the vital links to Iberian hometowns alive.

Conclusions

Tracing Afro-Iberian roots in the Andes and elsewhere in the colonial Americas reveals some important characteristics of the African Diaspora in the Iberian Atlantic World. First, not all the arrivals in the Americas originated in West Africa and the Atlantic Islands. A culturally significant Afro-Iberian population developed in Andalusia and Southern Portugal in the fifteenth and sixteenth centuries and contributed a significant number of *pasajeros* to the Indies and Peru in the 1500s and the 1600s. Soldiering, sailing, and serving as *criados* were three of the principal ways this population moved to and from the Americas. Their proximity to patrons and Crown institutions perhaps gave them unique opportunities to operate as intermediaries and to remain connected to Iberia. Second, these *pasajeros* were a diverse group—free, enslaved, traveling with patrons, on their own, *vecinos* in their own right, and so forth. Some were American born, others were Iberian born, and others originated in Africa. They contributed to a diverse population in southern Iberia and extended that complexity in composition to the Americas and possibly to African trade centers. Third, the movement of African peoples to the Americas was not unilinear; people of African descent moved back and forth between the Iberian Peninsula and the Americas, within the Americas, to Africa, and even occasionally into non-Iberian European areas. These findings, of course, do not deny the overwhelming number of Africans and Europeans who made one-way trips to the Americas. Nor do they challenge the centrality of the slave trade's movement of African people under brutal and horrific conditions from Africa directly to the Americas. Rather, the point is to recognize and begin to explore the possibility that Afro-Iberians carried or changed cultures, institutions, and practices on both sides of the Atlantic and in all parts of the Iberian Atlantic system by focusing on Afro-Iberians' experiences and on the routes and nature of their movement as key to the early Atlantic World. Our understanding of the African Diaspora and the horror of slavery is deepened by adding a new stop in the metropole and by considering the experiences of the Afro-Iberians who helped shape the cultural and physical webs that bound together three continents and many peoples.

The wider implications of this study entail reconsidering where and when we locate some of the central transformations wrought by the African Diaspora. Where and when did Iberian colonizers and Africans work out the mechanisms and practices of slavery implemented in the Americas? Perhaps we must keep the Iberian/Atlantic island dimension within our frame of analysis even after the initial establishment of slavery in an American region and in a particular economic sphere. The experiences and even the individuals who originated in those locations continued to join and participate in the American side of the Diaspora. Excellent recent scholarship draws attention to the "Eurafricans," "Atlantic Creoles," and other such intermediaries, particularly in the British and Brazilian plantation societies and to the "Black Conquistadores" of the early conquest era in Mexico and the Andes. Maybe reconstructing the actions and allegiances of Afro-Iberians in the late sixteenth century and throughout the seventeenth century and outside the major plantation zones and the Caribbean will prove equally illuminating about how imperialism both harnesses its seeming victims to its goals and at times is remade or modified locally to suit their interests. The black sailors and soldiers of the Spanish Main demonstrate another way that men of African origin gained—not fame and sometimes fortune, as the earlier black fighters did during the conquest wars—but survival as plebeian workers and a secure hold on a corner of the seafaring professions. Slavery and the African Diaspora both funded and helped staff the voyages and maritime trade networks that made Spanish and Portuguese power. In addition, this line of work afforded Afro-Iberians a claim to service to the Crown and the concomitant protections of that service, which were denied them in almost every other sphere of Crown activity. In subsequent centuries, this kind of service became more common with the formalization of and black participation within militias. The inclusion of the Afro-Iberian experience thus helps expand Diasporic studies temporally and geographically.

Notes

This research received support from the Program for Cultural Cooperation Between Spain's Ministry of Culture & United States' Universities, Franklin & Marshall College, and Connecticut College's R. F. Johnson and Hodgkins Faculty Development Funds. Ben Vinson III, Jane Landers, and participants in the Annual Workshop on Marking Difference in Colonial Latin America at Connecticut College provided valuable comments on this work.

1. Metcalf, *Go-Betweens and the Colonization of Brazil, 1500–1600.*

2. Elliott, *Empires of the Atlantic World: Britain and Spain in America, 1492–1830*; Kamen, *Empire: How Spain Became a World Power, 1492–1763*; Boxer, *The Golden Age of Brazil, 1695–1750.*

3. Epstein, *Speaking of Slavery: Color, Ethnicity, and Human Bondage in Italy*, 66–102, 114–126, 132–139, 156–191.

4. Rout, *The African Experience in Spanish America*, 15; Hernando i Delgado, *Els esclaus islàmics a Barcelona.*

5. Between 1435 and 1525, smaller numbers of slave traders from Florence, Genoa, England, Flanders, and parts of Spain (above all Vizcaya and Burgos) also participated in Seville's slave trade. Franco Silva, *La esclavitud en Sevilla y su tierra a fines de la Edad Media*, 73–84, 365–387; Cortés López, *La esclavitud negra en la España peninsular del siglo XVI*, 40.

6. Portuguese factories stretched from Sierra Leone to Angola. The most important were Arguim (1448), San Jago on the Cape Verde Islands (1458), San Jorge in Mina

(1481), and São Tomé (1486). See Franco Silva, *La esclavitud en Sevilla y su tierra a fines de la Edad Media*, 68; and Ruth Pike, "Sevillian Society in the Sixteenth Century: Slaves and Freedmen," 346.

7. Stella, "'Mezclandose carnalmente.' Relaciones sociales, relaciones sexuales y mestizaje en Andalucía Occidental," 177.

8. Ares Queija and Stella, "Presentación," 13; González Díaz, *La esclavitud en Ayamonte durante el antiguo régimen (siglos XVI, XVII y XVIII)*, 23.

9. Rout, *The African Experience in Spanish America*, 15–16.

10. Ibid., 14.

11. Stella, *Histoires d'esclaves dans la péninsule ibérique.*

12. Franco Silva, *La esclavitud en Sevilla y su tierra a fines de la Edad Media*, 275–331.

13. Morales Padrón, *Historia de Sevilla: la ciudad del quinientos*, 104.

14. Archivo Histórico Nacional (hereafter AHN), Madrid, Inquisición, Sevilla, leg. 2075, docs. 1, 2, 3, 4, 5, 6, 7, 9, 10, and 11; Kabo, "Les esclaves africains face à l'Inquisition espagnole: les procès de sorcellerie et de magie"; Fournié-Martinez, "Contribution à l'étude de l'esclavage en Espagne au Siècle d'or: les esclaves devant l'Inquisition"; Bernard, "Les esclaves à Séville au XVIIe siècle."

15. De Rojas Villandrando, *El viaje entretenido*, vol. 1.

16. Slaves made up 10 percent of Lisbon's 1552 population of approximately 100,000. Pike, "Sevillian Society in the Sixteenth Century: Slaves and Freedmen," 345, 345n5.

17. Fifteenth-century colonization of the Canaries and Madeira and later São Tomé and Principe also extended plantation sugar production from the Mediterranean into the Atlantic, where Iberians combined enslaved African laborers, plantations, and skilled milling to create a system for sugar production and eventually transplanted it to the Americas in the following century. Kamen, *Empire: How Spain Became a World Power, 1492–1763*.

18. Archivo General de Indias (hereafter AGI), Seville, Contratación 2875, "Registros de esclavos," 1584–1599; AGI, Contratación 2895, "Registros de esclavos," 1638; AGI, Patronato 279, N. 6, R. 65, "Real Provisión requisitoria para las justicias de Lisboa y del Reino de Portugal," 1548; AGI, Patronato 290, R. 183, 1565; AGI, Justicia, N. 4 and N. 5, R. 2, 1569–1572.

19. AHN, Inquisición, Canarias, leg. 1829, doc. 1; AHN, Inquisición, Canarias, leg. 1821, docs. 1, 2, 3, 5, 6, 9, and 14; AHN, Inquisición, Canarias, leg. 1822, nos. 4, 13; AHN, Inquisición, Canarias, leg. 1829, libro 1463; Cabrera, *La esclavitud en las Canarias orientales en el siglo XVI (negros, moros y moriscos)*; Cabrera, *Los libertos en la sociedad canaria del siglo XVI*; Crosby, *Ecological Imperialism: The Biological Expansion of Europe, 900–1900*.

20. Sweet, *Recreating Africa: Culture, Kinship, and Religion in the African-Portuguese World, 1441–1770*; Saunders, *A Social History of Black Slaves and Freedmen in Portugal, 1441–1555*; Thornton, *Africa and Africans in the Making of the Atlantic World, 1400–1800*; Curtin, *Economic Change in Precolonial Africa: Senegambia in the Era of the Slave Trade;* Mark, "Constructing Identity: Sixteenth- and Seventeenth-Century

Architecture in the Gambia-Geba Region and the Articulation of Luso-African Ethnicity," 317.

21. Brooks, *Eurafricans in Western Africa.*

22. Some combined African and European dress, practiced syncretized forms of Christianity, used both European money and African practices of accumulating wealth, or sent sons to Europe and the Americas to master languages and trade techniques.

23. Mann, *Rethinking the African Diaspora.*

24. Miller, *The Way of Death: Merchant Capitalism and the Angolan Slave Trade*; Lovejoy, *Transformations in Slavery: A History of Slavery in Africa*; Thornton, *Africa and Africans in the Making of the Atlantic World.*

25. Heywood, "Queen Njinga Mbandi Ana de Sousa of Ndongo/Matamba"; Northrup, *Africa's Discovery of Europe: 1450–1850*; Hilton, *The Kingdom of Kongo;* Barbot, *Barbot on Guinea: The Writings of Jean Barbot on West Africa, 1678–1712*, vols. 1–2; Cavazzi, "Istorica Descrizione de' Tre Regni Congo, Matamba, et Angola"; Bassani, *Un cappuccino nell'Africa nera del seicento: I disegni dei manoscritti Araldi del Padre Giovanni Antonio Cavazzi da Montecuccolo*; Collo and Benso, *Sogno: Bamba, Pemba, Ovando e altre contrade dei regni di Congo, Angola e adjacenti.*

26. See Gerhard, "A Black Conquistador in Mexico"; and Restall, "Black Conquistadors: Armed Africans in Early Spanish America"; among others.

27. Lockhart, *Spanish Peru, 1532–1560.*

28. Bowser, *The African Slave in Colonial Peru, 1524–1650*; Harth-Terré, *Negros e indios: Un estamento social ignorado en el Perú colonial*; Arrelucea, "Conducta y control social colonial. Estudio de las panaderías limeñas en el siglo XVIII"; Arrelucea, "Slavery, Writing, and Female Resistance: Black Women Litigants in Lima's Late Colonial Tribunals of the 1780s"; Tardieu, *Los negros y la Iglesia en el Perú. Siglos XVI–XVII*; van Deusen, *The Souls of Purgatory: The Spiritual Diary of a Seventeenth-Century Afro-Peruvian Mystic, Ursula de Jesús*; O'Toole, "The Making of a Free *Lucumí* Household: Ana de la Calle's Will and Goods, Northern Peruvian Coast, 1719."

29. For examples see Garofalo, "Conjuring with Coca and the Inca"; Garofalo, "The Ethno-Economy of Food, Drink, and Stimulants: The Making of Race in Colonial Lima and Cuzco"; and Jouve Martín, *Esclavos de la ciudad letrada: Esclavitud, escritura y colonialismo en Lima (1650–1700).*

30. O'Toole, "Castas y representación en Trujillo colonial."

31. AGI, Patronato 234, R. 7, "Cimarones de Limón, Polín y Zanaguare," 1634; Sherwin K. Bryant, "Enslaved Rebels, Fugitives, and Litigants: The Resistance Continuum in Colonial Quito"; Beatty-Medina, "Fray Alonso de Espinosa's Report on Pacifying the Fugitive Slaves of the Pacific Coast."

32. Ira Berlin calls these cultural brokers familiar with the languages, religions, and commercial practices of the European-dominated Atlantic world "Atlantic creoles." See Berlin, *Many Thousands Gone*, 12, 17–31.

33. AGI, Contratación, leg. 5336, N30, 27-II-1614, folios 1–7v.

34. AGI, Contratación, leg. 5251B, N2, R42, 1-II-1596, folios 1–3v. See also AGI, Contratación, leg. 5316, N14, 20-VI-1618, folios 1–4v.

35. AGI, Contratación, leg. 5300, N68, "Relación de pasajeros," 1607. These same groups also carried Afro-Iberians to the Philippines, as in the case of Capitan Mateo de Villerías and his black slave Vicente. See AGI, Contratación, S42,SS1, leg. 5226, N12, 13-I-1617, folios 1–5v; AGI, Contratación, leg. 5354, N12, 13-I-1617, folios 1–5v. The *relaciones de pasajeros* regularly list people headed first to Mexico who then continued on to the Philippines. For example, see AGI, Contratación, leg. 5302, N83, 27-I-1608, folios 1–34v. Afro-Iberians appear in this movement from Mexico to the Philippines and in the return voyages bound for Mexico. See AGI, Contratación, leg. 455, R3, "Bienes de difuntos de 1617."

36. Nobles also held many slaves. See López Molina, *Una década de esclavitud en Jaén: 1675–1685*, 143–145; Martín Casares, *La esclavitud en la Granada del siglo XVI*, 293–297; González Díaz, *La esclavitud en Ayamonte durante el antiguo régimen (siglos XVI, XVII y XVIII)*, 105–109; Franco Silva, *La esclavitud en Sevilla y su tierra a fines de la Edad Media*, 275–337; Cortés Lopéz, *La esclavitud negra en la España peninsular del siglo XVI*, 68–69.

37. AGI, Contratación, leg. 5283, N67, 6-VI-1605, folios 1–2v; AGI, Contratación, leg. 5297, N26, 30-V-1607; AGI, Contratación, leg. 5229, N2, R.10, 26-V-1581, folios 1–2v; AGI, Contratación, leg. 5229, N2, R10, 26-V-1581, folios 2v–13; AGI, Contratación, leg. 5232, N82, 26-V-1590, folios 1–4v; AGI, Contratación, leg. 5261, N18, 7-VI-1600, folios 1–5; AGI, Contratación, leg. 5340, N16, 20-VI-1614, folios 1–2v; AGI, Contratación, leg. 5379, N17, 14-IV-1661, folios 1–5v; AGI, Contratación, leg. 5318, N2, 14-I-1610, folios 1–4v. Clergy also took black slaves and servants with them to the Philippines (e.g., the friar Pedro de Ledesma took Seville-born Luis de Lara as his black servant, leaving Luis's parents behind in Seville); AGI, Contratación, leg. 5250, N1, R30, 23-VI-1595, folios 1–7v. Non-clergy also brought Afro-Iberians to the Philippines, as in the case of Capitan Mateo de Villerías and his black slave Vicente; AGI, Contratación, leg. 5226, N12, 13-I-1617, folios 1–5v; AGI, Contratación, leg. 5354, N12, 13-I-1617, folios 1–5v.

38. Crown inspectors allowed a limited number of ships to sail from Seville to Angola to collect slaves for transport directly to Buenos Aires; AGI, Contratación 2890, "Registros de esclavos," N1, R5; AGI, Contratación 2890, "Registros de esclavos," N1, R11; AGI, Contratación, leg. 5403, N1, 19-I-1628, folios 1–5r.

39. See for example AGI, Contratación, leg. 5275, N48, 7-II-1603, folios 1–2v; AGI, Contratación, leg. 5369, N63, 14-III-1619, folios 1–3v; AGI, Contratación, leg. 5280, N30, 9-IV-1604, folios 1–3v; AGI, Contratación, leg. 5297, N35, 22-XII-1607, folios 1–21v; AGI, Contratación, leg. 5299, N1, R50, 27-II-1607, folios 1–3v. For merchants, see AGI, Contratación, leg. 5237, N1, R35, 10-I-1592, folios 1–4v; AGI, Contratación, leg. 5370, N4, 1-VIII-1620, folios 1–5v.; AGI, Contratación, leg. 5379, N5, 3-IV-1621, folios 1–6v.; AGI, Contratación, leg. 5359, 10-IV-1618, folios 1–2v; and AGI, Contratación, leg. 5275, N49, 7-II-1603, folios 1–2v.

40. AGI, Contratación, leg. 5369, N38, 7-III-1619, folios 1–8v.

41. AGI, Contratación, leg. 5343, N27, 18-III-1615, folios 1–2v. The *corregidor* desig-

nate for the city of Quito, Cristóbal Vela y Acuña, traveled with his slave Francisco Marchena and his servants Pedro de Castro (a *vecino* of Mora) and Luisa Ramírez. See AGI, Contratación, leg. 5360, N21, 3-V-1618, folios 1–12v. Don Juan Cano Moctezuma journeyed from Mexico to Seville and then petitioned to return in 1612 with the same members of his household: his wife, Doña Isabel Mejía y Figueroa; their son; a niece and a nephew; two *criadas*; his slave Baltasar de Los Reyes (*mulato zambaigo*); and his slave Antonia Negra and her four *mulato* children, who ranged in age from twelve to twenty-four. See AGI, Contratación, leg. 5326, N49, 11-VI-1612, folios 1–5v. For additional examples of Afro-Iberians headed for Peru embedded in a larger Spanish contingent, see AGI, Contratación, leg. 5327, N78, 5-IV-1612, folios 1–6v; AGI, Contratación, leg. 5341, N, 15-II-1614, folios 1–8v; AGI, Contratación, leg. 5341, N30, 17-II-1614, folios 1–12v; AGI, Contratación, leg. 5342, N21, 28-II-1614, folios 1–2v; AGI, Contratación, leg. 5353, N18, 28-I-1616, folios 1–10v; AGI, Contratación, leg. 5354, N5, 24-I-1617, folios 1–15v.

42. AGI, Contratación, leg. 5442, N16, 24-III-1678, folios 1–7v; AGI, Contratación, leg. 5270, N2, R57, 11-IV-1602, folios 1–2v; AGI, Contratación, leg. 5352, N18, 24-III-1616, folios 1–3v; AGI, Contratación, leg. 5387, N42, folios 1–2v. Children might also accompany female slaves; see AGI, Contratación, leg. 5431, N5, 10-IV-1658, folios 1–2v.

43. AGI, Contratación, leg. 515, N1, R5, "Autos sobre los bienes de Francisco Carreño," 1614, folios 1–38v.

44. Martínez, *Pasajeros de Indias. Viajes trasatlánticas en el siglo XVI*; Altman, *Emigrants and Society.*

45. AGI, Indiferente, leg. 2103, N92, 10-I-1597, folios 1–12.

46. Both sets of witnesses described a long journey: 400 leagues over land on mules from Potosí to Buenos Aires, then from Buenos Aires by boat to the Brazilian port of Olinda in Pernambuco, and finally from Brazil to Lisbon or Seville, with delays of sometimes months while waiting for ships. See AGI, Contratación, leg. 782, N17, 27-VIII-1612, folios 1–37r.

47. AGI, Contratación, leg. 5348, N67, 16-VI-1615; AGI, Contratación, leg. 5387, N16, 20-VI-1623, folios 1–2v. Some came to help sell shipments of American products and then returned. The *mulato criado* Francisco de Salas helped sell tobacco and hides from Venezuela; see AGI, Contratación, leg. 5350, N44, folios 1–2v.

48. Kris Lane's study of Quito at the end of the sixteenth century provides a useful point of comparison and suggests that slavery heavily influenced all forms of colonial labor in the Andes. See Lane, *Quito 1599.*

49. Elliott, *Empires of the Atlantic World: Britain and Spain in America, 1492–1830*, 51–52, 55.

50. AGI, Contratación, leg. 5324, N30, 17-VI-1612, folios 1–2v; AGI, Contratación, leg. 5356, N40, 17-VI-1617, folios 1–5v.

51. AGI, Indiferente, leg. 2074, N50, 1612, folios 1–9; AGI, Pasajeros, leg. 9, E2882, 17-VII-1612.

52. AGI, Contratación, leg. 5316, N63, 12-VI-1610, folios 1–2v.

53. The *oidor* Don Jeronimo de Herrera traveled with the "captive slave" Juan for whom he paid 6 ducados and the seven-year-old *mulato libre* Damian. AGI, Contratación, leg. 5359, N16, 23-VI-1618, folios 1–11v; AGI, Contratación, leg. 5387, N27, 24-III-1623, folios 1–20v; AGI, Lima, "Licencia," 1628, 9-VII-1548.

54. AGI, Contratación, leg. 5358, N15, 18-II-1617, folios 1–8r. For cases of "*esclavas negras libres*" see AGI, Contratación, S42 S1, leg. 5241, N2, R.63, 5-I-1593, folios 1–3v; and AGI, Contratación, leg. 5252, N1, R11, 30-I-1596, folios 1–6v.

55. AGI, Contratación, leg. 5375, N58, 19-VI-1621, folios 1–4v; AGI, Contratación, leg. 5402, N35, 18-V-1628, folios 1–3v; AGI, Contratación, leg. 5377, N11, 11-VI-1621, folios 1–31r.

56. AGI, Contratación, leg. 5316, N11, 8-VI-1610, folios 1–25v.

57. Royal officials in the Panamanian port of Nombre de Dios confiscated and sold a Christian slave born to *negros esclavos* in Portugal because the registry of passengers listed her as an "*esclava negra*," not as an "*esclava lora*" (olive skinned slave), as they perceived her to be. AGI, Panama, 235, leg. 6, "Devolución de una esclava," 20-IV-1537, folios 106v–107r; AGI, Panama, 235, leg. 7, "Real cédula," 1-VIII-1539, folios 61v–62r; AGI, Contratación, leg. 136, "Autos fiscales," N. 15, 28-III-1566, folios 1–10v.

58. AGI, Contratación, leg. 5270, N2, R47, 23-IV-1602, folios 1–7v; AGI, Contratación, leg. 5452, N148, 27-X-1690, folios 1–13v; AGI, Contratación, leg. 5453, N31, 12-XII-1690, folios 1–2v; AGI, Contratación, leg. 5453, N32, 23-IX-1690, folios 1–5v; AGI, Contratación, leg. 5453, N33, 22-XII-1690, folios 1–2v; AGI, Contratación, leg. 5453, N34, folios 1–2v; AGI, Contratación, leg. 5453, N30, 28-XI-1690, folios 1–2v.

59. AGI, Indiferente, 426, leg. 25, "Real cédula," 14-VI-1569, folios 4v–5, 63r–63v; AGI, Santo Domingo, 899, leg. 1, "Real cédula," 10-VIII-1562, folio 265v; AGI, Justicia, 870, N1, "Pleito fiscal," 27-X-1569, folios 1–77r; AGI, Patronato, 175, R. 9, "Relación de los esclavos descargados," 1519–1520.

60. Pérez-Mallaína, *Spain's Men of the Sea: Daily Life on the Indies Fleets in the Sixteenth Century.*

61. AGI, Contratación, leg. 5412, N48, 7-V-1631, folios 1–5v; AGI, Indiferente, 2048, N62, "Relación de pasajeros," 17-V-1596, folios 1–1v; AGI, Contratación, leg. 5307, N2, R32, 6-VI-1608, folios 1–2v.

62. AGI, Lima, "Registro de nao," 1625, 27-X-1573, folios 1–18; AGI, Contratación, leg. 1151B, "Registro," N5, 18-XII-1607, folios 1–390v; AGI, Contratación, 2890, "registros," R2, 7-X-1633.

63. AGI, Contratación, leg. 1151B, "Registro," N7, 19-XII-1607, folios 1–390v.

64. AGI, Contratación, 2890, "Registros," N2, 5-XII-1632, folios 45r–48r; AGI, Contratación, 2875, "Registros," 1584–1599, folios 1–698r.

65. AGI, Contratación, leg. 473, N5, R1, "Autos sobre los bienes," 31-VII-1572, folios 1–23r.

66. AGI, Contratación, 296A, N2, R4, 1610, folios 1–26v, 1–4v; AGI, Contratación, 296A, N2, R3, 1610, folios 1–20v.

67. AGI, Panama, 235, leg. 8, 18-VI-1546, folios 1–3r.

68. AGI, Indiferente, 2054, N127, 1572, folios 3r–10r.

69. AGI, Contratación, 5730, N8, R4, 6-III-1591, folios 1–29v.

70. AGI, Indiferente, 2054, N127, 8-XI-1539, folios 34v–35r. The document can be read in English in Garofalo, "Afro-Iberian Sailors, Soldiers, Traders, and Thieves on the Spanish Main."

71. AGI, Contratación, 772, N13, "Autos del capitán Pedro de Murguía," 20-II-1609, folios 1–110r. Portuguese Afro-Iberians also became enmeshed in local affairs; see AGI, Contratación, leg. 488, N3, R 2, "Bienes de difuntos," 1594, folios 1–10v.

72. AGI, Contratación, leg. 413A, N1, R5, "Autos sobre bienes de difuntos," folios 1–94v.

73. AGI, Contratación, leg. 293A, N1, R6, "Bienes de difuntos," 10-XII-1610, folios 1–91. For an Andean example, see AGI, Contratación, 439B, N3, "Bienes de difuntos," 20-V-1658, folios 1–40v.

74. AGI, Contratación, 526, "Bienes de difuntos," N1, R1, 19-XII-1626, folios 1–6r. When enslaved sailors died, their owners claimed their wages and belongings. AGI, Contratación, 533B, N2, R77, "Auto sobre el sueldo," 11-XI-1632, folios 1–2v; AGI, Contratación, 574, N2, R5, "Autos de bienes de difuntos," 14-II-1633, folios 1–1v; AGI, Contratación, 963, N2, R11, "Autos de bienes de difuntos," 5-III-1673, folios 1–10r.

75. AGI, Contratación, leg. 257A, "Bienes de difuntos," R12, 1600; AGI, Contratación, leg. 526, R1, N8, 1626, folios 1v and 2r.

76. AGI, Contratación, leg. 938A, N10, "Autos sobre bienes de Bartolomé Martín," folios 1–163v; AGI, Contratación, leg. 303, N2, "Autos bienes de difuntos," 7-IV-1612, folios 1–37v. Soldiers' Afro-Iberian spouses and children could secure Crown permission to move to the Americas as did the *negra atezada* Felipa de Santiago of Seville and her three *mulato* sons. In 1594, she requested permission to join her husband, a gunner identified as an *español blanco*, who had been sent to a fort to defend Veracruz in Mexico three years before. Her petition and her witnesses emphasized her free status—that her mistress had freed Felipa de Santiago with a *carta de libertad* when she married in Seville's San Vincente church in 1583—and her children's legitimacy and their baptisms in the church with godparents. AGI, Contratación, leg. 5248, N1, R1, 22-VI-1594, folios 1–6r. When accused in court, *marineros* from the fleets claimed their rights to admiralty jurisdiction and a trial. AGI, Contratación, 805, N14 "Autos de Sebastián de Vargas," 8-III-1617, folios 1–10v.

2

African Diasporic Ethnicity in Mexico City to 1650

FRANK "TREY" PROCTOR III

On January 21, 1640, Pedro Sánchez and Mariana filed a petition for the right to marry at the Catedral Metropolitano, which served the main parish of Mexico City. The prospective bride and groom were both slaves, owned by Diego de Barrientos and Antonio de Almaras, respectively, and, as required in all such applications, both listed their *calidad* (personal quality, which was generally expressed in racial or ethnic terms),[1] as "Angola." In addition, Juan de la Cruz and Ana María, also identified as Angola slaves, served as *testigos* (wedding witnesses) for Pedro and Mariana, testifying that the bride and groom were not already married, had not taken some form of religious vows that would prevent them from marrying, and were unrelated to each other and were therefore free to marry. Juan stated that he and Pedro had been friends for over twelve years and that he had known Mariana for over six. Ana María said that she had known the prospective groom for over twenty-five years and the bride for twelve.[2]

In a similar case, on September 20, 1645, Lorenzo de la Cruz, an Angola slave owned by Isidro de Caja, and Maria de la Cruz, an Indian woman, petitioned in the same parish for the right to marry. As her *testigos*, Maria presented Bartolomé Fortuna, a Spaniard, and Dominga de la Cruz, a free creole black woman, both of whom testified that they had known the prospective bride for ten years. Juan Francisco, a creole black slave owned by Don Bernabé de la Vega y Amarilla, served as Lorenzo's witness, claiming that they had been friends for nearly fourteen years.[3]

Each petition provides tantalizing evidence about the social worlds inhabited by slaves in colonial Mexico in the 1640s. One of the first steps in constructing new communities was the formation of real and fictive kinship ties, both of which are evident in colonial marriage records. In Spanish America, when a couple wished to marry they were required by the Church to first apply for a marriage license. Those licenses include information about the free or enslaved status and the race or ethnicity of brides, grooms, and their *testigos*. Scholars concur that *testigos* were most often close personal friends or community leaders, and thus they can be used to chart at least three and as many as seven important social relationships that slaves formed. Therefore, marriage registers and marriage applications from Catholic colonies such as New Spain provide a special opportunity to explore the creation and evolution of slave communities in the New World.

Colonial Mexico provides an important arena for the consideration of slavery and slave ethnicity. The height of the slave trade to New Spain was 1580–1640. After 1640, the slave trade to the colony slowed to a trickle because Spain redirected its slave imports to South America. At that point, New Spain was home to the second largest slave population and the largest free population of African descent in the Americas. Demand for slaves in Mexico began in earnest in the last decades of the sixteenth century in response to the demographic decline of the indigenous population. Initially, demand was strongest in urban centers such as Mexico City and the burgeoning mining and sugar industries. After the "regular" slave trade to the colony ended in 1640, however, demand shifted away from sugar production in Veracruz and mining more generally to sugar and woolen textile production in central New Spain, and it remained constant through the middle of the eighteenth century.[4] The focus here on the pre-1650 era allows for an examination of slave community formation within one of the first significant African populations in the New World.

Moreover, the methods and sources used by scholars interested in racial hierarchies and identities in colonial Spanish America, particularly the ability to track self-proclaimed racial and ethnic identities in parish and court records, allow for new considerations of ethnicity and community formation within the African Diaspora. Doing so requires the integration of the heretofore largely distinct historiographies of the African Diaspora and precolonial Africa and of race in colonial Spanish America. That transnational and transregional focus promises to challenge previous conclusions about slavery in New Spain and throughout the Atlantic World by tracing how individual Africans and groups of Africans reinvented ethnic and community identities once they were in the Diaspora. The result will be significant revisions of considerations of race, ethnicity, and slavery in Spanish America and the African Diaspora.

While few recent historians of slavery would assert that slaves did not play a central role in determining their own communities and identities in the Diaspora, there are serious disagreements about what the foundations of those communities were. Scholars of British North America and the British Caribbean such as Sidney Mintz, Richard Price, and Philip Morgan, who represent the "creolization school," have offered a series of arguments about Afro-American cultural construction that focus on the transition of disparate groups of African slaves into African Americans.[5] For example, Morgan contends that the slave trade (specifically delivery of slaves to the Americas) and, perhaps more important, the recruitment of slaves within a single African region was too random for African ethnicities to provide the basis of emerging and evolving slave cultures throughout the Americas. They propose that we explore the creation of slave cultures in the New World as "ethno-genesis," implicitly urging historians to focus their attention on the transition from "African" to "African American," a shift in identity best described as a move from a collection of peoples hailing from numerous and distinct cultural traditions in Africa to a cultural identity based largely upon race that grew out of the syncretism of African beliefs/practices.[6]

On the other hand, a growing number of Africanists such as John Thornton, Joseph Miller, and Paul Lovejoy, who represent the "diasporic" position, argue that the slave trade was neither as destructive nor as random as once asserted and that enslaved Africans successfully formed identities and communities based on their shared ethnic pasts. John Thornton asserts that the trend of treating African cultures as innumerable and mutually exclusive is dangerous. Rather, he contends that Africans should be treated as originating from three slaving regions along the West African Coast, which can be further divided into seven subregions or general cultural zones based upon linguistic similarities (see Map 2.1).[7] The nature of the slave trade, he argues, tended to result in the delivery of significant numbers of slaves from one of those subregions to particular slave societies in the Americas. Slaves originating from within any one of those subregions had enough in common linguistically and culturally with others from the same subregion to be recognizable to them, and those commonalities, he argues, provided the foundation for cultural communities based on ethnic identity in the Americas.

These divergent hypotheses provide important methodological signposts that should inform the study of African ethnic identities in the Americas even as they both fall short in their common attempt to define a universal model grounded in patterns within the slave trade to describe all historical contexts. They encourage a closer look at the specific ethnicities *bozal*

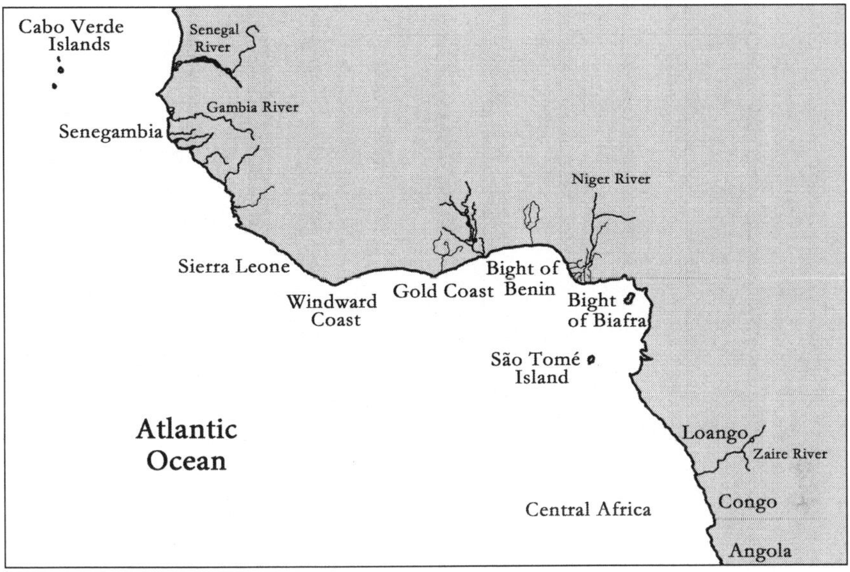

Map 2.1. Primary Slaving Region on Atlantic Coast of Africa

(African-born) slaves claimed in particular colonial contexts to chart whether the articulation of communities in the New World occurred along the lines of preexisting African, pan-African, racial, or new ethnic identities. Marriages from Mexico City allow us to do just that by focusing on how slaves actually comported themselves in the colony. We can explore how slaves named their own ethnicity and chart the race or ethnicity of their spouses and *testigos*, who also named their own ethnicities in these documents, to highlight the creation of distinct cultural communities. This study relies on 106 marriage applications from Mexico City for the period 1640–1649 that are housed in the Ramo de Matrimonios at the Archivo General de la Nación.[8] I will compare this data with similar data collected by Herman Bennett and Colin Palmer for the pre-1650 period in New Spain. This study joins a growing trend among Latin American historians (such as Garofalo and O'Toole in this volume) of investigating sources in which Africans named their own identities to explore how they constructed cultural communities in specific chronological and geographic contexts, thereby moving beyond a reliance on general patterns in the slave trade.[9]

Key to this growing scholarship is the awareness that common origins in one of the African subregions Thornton identified did not necessarily translate into a shared sense of identity and/or community with others from that subregion in the New World. In his study of slavery in sixteenth- and seventeenth-century Peru, Frederick Bowser found that Africans "showed some preference for marriage with their African ethnic group."[10] But, reflecting the era in which he wrote, Bowser did not delve into the potential meanings of the specific ethnicities those slaves claimed. Using evidence in criminal records, Rachel Sarah O'Toole takes up that challenge by arguing for the creation of African diasporic ethnicities in seventeenth-century Peru through the articulation of Bran identities. Her work explores conflict between bondspeople who defined themselves using the same ethnonym and offers an important corrective to the assumption that common origins automatically created alliances among slaves.[11] In another example, Nagôs (Yoruba speakers) and Jejes (Fon speakers), both groups that originated from the Bight of Benin, did not identify with each other as members of a common ethnic group in nineteenth-century Brazil. However, in nineteenth-century Cuba, the links between these two groups were significant enough that they constituted a common community.[12] The different articulations of community in these contexts call for regionally specific studies of community formation using sources in which slaves proclaimed their own ethnicities.

The question remains, however: Which of the two marriages that opened this study—the one that brought together four Angola slaves or the one that included Africans, free and enslaved Mexican-born blacks, Indians, and Spaniards—was the norm in Mexico City prior to 1650? Echoing the "creolization" argument, early scholarship on *novohispano* (New Spanish) slavery asserts that despite the fact that slaves had the right to marry in the church and to select their potential spouses free from interference by owners, the overwhelming physical and psychological effects of enslavement in Africa, of the Middle Passage, and of colonial slavery isolated slaves from each other, preventing the formation of lasting family relationships among both Africans and Afro-Mexicans.[13] In addition, because slaves and their progeny were always a marked minority in colonial society, numerous scholars, such as the eminent Gonzalo Aguirre Beltrán, contend that slaves were forced to turn to the indigenous majority and the growing mestizo population for marriage partners or to engage in concubinage with Spanish men.[14] Such an understanding subsumes Afro-Mexicans into a dominant trope of colonial Mexican cultural history, *mestizaje*, understood as the racial and cultural mixing between Indians and Spaniards.[15]

A more recent consensus, influenced by the "diasporic" position, is emerging that during the period before 1650, Afro-Mexicans defined their group identities by referring to common African origins. Colin Palmer and Herman Bennett have found significant levels of marital endogamy among slaves in Mexico before 1650, evidenced by high marriage rates between slaves who shared a common ethnic moniker (e.g., Angola).[16] Although they are not explicitly interested in marriage, Joan Bristol and Nicole von Germeten agree with that assertion for the pre-1650 period, but they suggest that as the colonial period progressed and the population transitioned from African-born to Mexican-born, blacks and mulattoes tried to assimilate to a general *casta* (mixed race) or to Spanish culture.[17] A key assumption that appears to underlie these discussions is that Afro-Mexicans internalized the negative judgments of their Africanity and blackness that emanated from official Spanish discourses.[18] R. Douglas Cope, however, found strong patterns of Afro-Mexican marital endogamy as late as the 1690s, a finding corroborated by Ben Vinson's exploration of free colored militias in eighteenth-century New Spain.[19]

This chapter proposes to go beyond those studies in three important ways in order to illuminate how Africans constructed multiple new ethnic and community identities in Spanish America. First, selection patterns of *testigos* (wedding witnesses) are considered alongside marriage choice to chart the webs of social relations slaves formed. Second, instead of assuming that the ethnic monikers found in marriage registers referred to a common identity derived from a shared African past, this study explores the potential meanings slaves themselves associated with the terms in question. I argue that the foundations of the ethnic communities under formation were not intact African ethnicities (articulated at the village or lineage level in Africa), pan-African identities (i.e., shared by all Africans), or race-based identities (i.e., shared by all colonial Mexicans of African descent). Rather, slave marriages in Mexico City highlight the creation of African diasporic ethnicities that were spontaneously articulated in the Diaspora and were based on the redefinition of the common linguistic and cultural traits shared by slaves who originated from within common regions in Africa. Third, selection patterns for Mexico City suggest that slave understandings of African diasporic ethnicities were not necessarily confined to nor fully represented by monikers Europeans imposed such as "Angola" and "Congo."

That African slaves were marrying in New Spain at all suggests that they had begun to be integrated into Catholic society. One of the first known sets of royal ordinances on Spanish American slavery clearly associated Christianization with benign treatment because it ordered masters to baptize and indoctrinate their slaves in Catholicism.[20] Joan Bristol suggests that the reiteration of these expectations by Spanish authorities throughout the colonial period might suggest that masters largely ignored their Christianizing duties.[21] Still, despite expectations that all slaves be Catholic and that all Catholics should marry, few slaves actually did so in New Spain. Illegitimacy rates of slave children were as high as 80–90 percent; the overwhelming majority of slaves did not marry.[22] Those who did had all been baptized, had taken Hispanicized names, and had learned at least rudimentary Spanish (there is no evidence that priests employed interpreters) and the basic elements of the Catholic faith necessary to petition to marry, all of which highlights their integration into *novohispano* society. Whether that knowledge of Catholicism began in Africa (some scholars argue that Central Africans in and around the kingdom of Kongo were incorporating Catholicism into their cosmological visions by the early fifteenth century), in the Americas, or, as Garofalo suggests in this volume, in Iberia, is not readily evident in marriage applications.[23] Yet despite the powerful acculturative force of Catholicism, Africans in New Spain proved more than able to manipulate Catholic institutions such as marriage and confraternities to define and maintain distinctive identities.[24]

Analysis of patterns of slave marriage for Mexico City in the years 1640–1649 reveals three general trends representative of the pre-1650 period. First, the majority of slaves who married in that decade were *bozales*. Among the 185 slaves who petitioned for a marriage license in those years, approximately 72 percent were African born and just over one in four were creole or Mexican-born blacks and mulattos. Second, only eleven slaves selected a spouse who was not also of African descent. These numbers undermine the argument that Africans were forced to marry Indians and mestizos due to the nature of colonial slavery and the slave trade. And third, *bozales* and creoles exhibited very different marriage patterns. As shown in Table 2.1, African-born slaves overwhelmingly married other *bozales*. Creole slaves, as will be discussed below, very rarely married Africans.

Once we acknowledge the patterns manifested in Table 2.1, we must reconsider the racial and ethnic foundations of the Mexican slave community. The exploration of the specific ethnonyms of African-born slaves in marriage applications reveals two important points: the overwhelming majority of Africans in Mexico City hailed from Bantu-speaking West Central Africa, and they exhibited high rates of marriage with other slaves from that region. The ethnicity of over nine in ten slaves in marriage applications from the 1640s was listed as Angola, Congo, Banguela, Anchico, and Malemba, all of which refer to West Central African origin (see Table 2.2). Official importation records

Table 2.1. Slave Marriage Patterns, El Sagrario Metropolitano Parish, Mexico City, 1640–1649

	Grooms			Brides		
	Bozal	*Negro*	*Mulato*	*Bozal*	*Negra*	*Mulata*
Spouses						
Slaves						
Bozal	58	6	—	58	4	2
Negro/a[1]	4	3	4	6	3	2
Mulato/a	2	2	2	—	4	2
Free						
Bozal	1	—	—	—	—	—
Negro/a	—	1	—	1	—	—
Mulato/a	2	4	2	—	2	1
Indio/a	1	2	—	—	—	—
Mestizo/a	—	—	7	—	—	—
Español/a	—	—	—	—	—	1
Total	68	18	14	65	12	8

Note: 1. Creoles or Mexican-born blacks.
Source: AGN, Ramo de Matrimonios, 1640–1649.

Table 2.2. Ethnicity of African-Born Slaves (Brides, Grooms, and *Testigos*) Listed in Marriage Applications of Slaves, Mexico City, 1640–1649

Nomenclature in the Ramo de Matrimonios	Number of Slaves		Percent	Shipping Region (See Map 2.1)
West Africa		13	4.7	
Caboverde	1			Senegambia
Mandinga	1			Senegambia
Nalu	2			Senegambia
Bran (Bram)	7			Senegambia
Arara	1			Bight of Benin
Carballi	1			Bight of Biafra
Central Africa (Map 2)		258	92.4	
Angola	218			Luanda and its hinterland
Congo	26			Between the Zaire and Kwanza rivers
Malemba	9			East of colony of Angola
Anchico	4			Interior, Zaire estuary
Banguela	1			Banguela and its hinterland
Southeastern Africa		8	2.9	
Mozambique	3			Southeastern Africa
Xhosa	5			South Africa
Total		279		

Source: AGN, Ramo de Matrimonios, 1640–1649.

reveal that before 1640, over 84 percent of the 150,000–175,000 slaves legally imported into Veracruz (the principal slave port in New Spain) originated from West Central Africa.[25] An obvious question is What do the ethnic monikers listed in Table 2.2 actually refer to? In the context of slavery, did they mean anything other than point of origin? Are they African ethnicities? Do they represent new ethnicities forged during the slave trade and under slavery that drew upon African elements even as they were distinct from African ethnicities? Are the answers to these questions necessarily mutually exclusive? Answering those questions will serve to revise and refine arguments about ethnic identities within the Diaspora.

To begin to answer these questions, we must shift our attention to pre-colonial West Central Africa. In doing so, we find that the terms listed in Table 2.2 did not refer to pre-colonial African ethnicities.[26] From the perspective of slave traders and masters, each term appears to designate the general region of Africa from which slaves were recruited. Among Central Africans, "Angolas" originated from what became the Portuguese colony of the same name in the region surrounding the port of Luanda, including territories once controlled by the Mbundu peoples (Kimbundu speakers) around the Kwanza River. The majority of slaves exported from Luanda, the primary slave port in Central Africa, were called "Angolas" by Portuguese slave traders even if they were originally Mbundu, Ovimbundu, Imbangala, or Congo (subdivisions within the family of Western Bantu languages). In non-Spanish and Portuguese colonies, however, the term "Angola" referred to slaves taken from bays to the north of the Zaire River, underscoring a potential lack of geographic specificity in such ethnonyms.[27] "Congo" slaves were recruited in or near the areas controlled by the kingdom of Kongo between the Kwanza River to the south and the Zaire River to the north. But the moniker "Congo" should not be equated with either a former subject of the kingdom of Kongo or a speaker of the Kikongo language because not all slaves exported from the region would have recognized such an identity.[28] "Banguela" referred to slaves recruited around the southernmost Portuguese slave port of the same name and its hinterland. "Anchico" designated a group of peoples who inhabited the interior along the Zaire River and would eventually establish the Tio kingdom. "Matamba" and "Malemba" referred to principalities formed along the eastern edge of the Portuguese colony of Angola in the interior (see Map 2.2).

Thus, these terms did not refer to specific ethnicities in Central Africa but rather to fairly specific areas in that region from the perspective of the slave trader and master. From the perspective of slaves, however, Paul Lovejoy

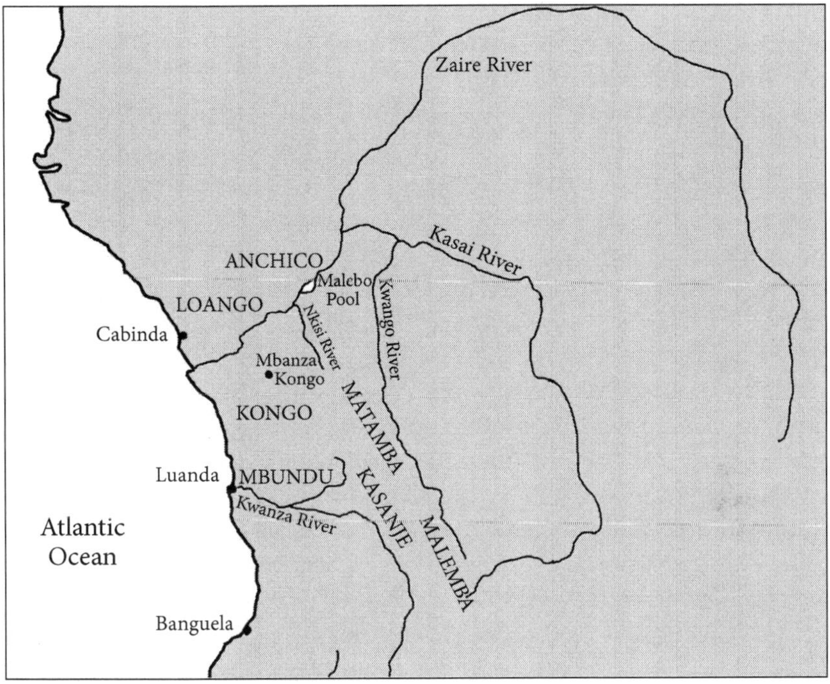

Map 2.2. Major Ethnic Groups of Coastal Central Africa

suggests that scholars treat these ethnic monikers as representing cultural creations within slavery and aboard slave ships. He wrote:

> Ethnic identification implies a mechanism for preserving and highlighting culture and hence is a key concept in examining the constructions of diasporas. Applying the concept of ethnicity to slave societies, one would expect to find a series of autonomous or semi-autonomous groups that traced their roots to Africa, often with continuing linkages or later connections that were intended to recreate associations that had been "lost." These connections have sometimes been recognized as "shipboard" bonding, but in most of these cases, these linkages or bonds were consolidated along *spontaneously generated* ethnic lines and communicated through a common language, whatever the dialectal difference that had to be overcome.[29]

Furthermore, concerns that the random nature of slave recruitment made such self-fashioning impossible are undercut by the nature of the slave trade in Central Africa before 1650. Up to that point, the slaving frontier extended at most 200 kilometers inland and was limited largely to the kingdom of Kongo and the region that would become the Portuguese colony of Angola. The great majority of slaves were recruited from the region south of the Kwanza River because of the Angola wars and Portugal's military encroachment into the region. Raids on the Kongo border by Portuguese and African slave-trading groups and the release of a limited number of slaves recruited in the interior regions supplemented those slaves.[30] Moreover, these two regions of Central Africa had a long history of interaction before the arrival of the Portuguese and the initiation of the slave trade.[31] Thus, the great majority of slaves drawn from Central Africa shared common cultural and linguistic heritages that might have facilitated the generation of new ethnicities within the Diaspora.

Turning our attention back to Spanish America, parish records should not be seen as an objective tool for understanding race and ethnicity in colonies and the African Diaspora; rather, they should be seen as potential sites of contestation. As discussed in O'Toole's chapter in this volume in reference to notary records, these sources were mediated and questions about who actually defined a person's race or ethnicity in these documents leave doubts, for some, about whether they reflect social reality. As what follows will demonstrate, the evidence suggests that self-definition outweighed priestly opinion a great majority of the time. If that is the case, the ethnicity and race of persons found in parish records indicate personal declarations of ethnic or racial identities.[32]

Still, one might wonder why Africans in New Spain did not use ethnic monikers that better reflected their various localized ethnicities in Africa. Herman Bennett argues that the nature of colonialism forced Africans to use terms stipulated by their Spanish enslavers, which, in turn, set "discursive limits" on their ability to fashion cultural communities of their own. Such categories could be infused with meaning by Africans, but, he would argue, the power of Spaniards to "name" shaped the ways Africans self-identified in the end.[33]

Yet upon further inspection, Spanish authorities do not appear to have been as concerned about the distinctions within the African population as they were between Indians and mestizos (mixed Spanish-Indian) or Indians and mulattos, distinctions that marked significantly different rights and responsibilities based upon race within the colonial system. They showed a similar disinterest in the ethnic distinctions within the indigenous population, listing indigenous individuals only as *indios* (Indians) in such sources. Differences among African ethnicities had no official implications, which suggests, perhaps, that Spanish authorities were not as responsible for (nor as interested in) policing the distinctions between the ethnic communities ethnonyms represented as we might have assumed.[34] For example, the marriage register for the Sagrario parish in Mexico City indicates that ecclesiastical authorities were not overly concerned with recording the ethnic differences among "black" (African and Creole) slaves who married. The marriage register from the Sagrario parish for 1647–1648 includes 177 "black" slaves who married. Among this group, only twenty-eight (15.8 percent) of the related entries included data on the ethnicity of the slave in question. The rest were simply listed as "*negro*" slaves. In contrast, of the 163 "black" slaves in extant marriage applications from the Ramo de Matrimonios for Mexico City during the 1640s, 133 (81.6 percent) listed an African ethnicity. In fact, I was able to cross-reference thirteen marriages involving at least one *bozal* in extant marriage applications to actual marriages in the registry. Among the twenty-five slaves who claimed an African ethnicity in those applications, only six (24 percent) also saw it listed in the registry. One might argue, then, that the enslaved status and the race of slaves mattered more to colonial authorities than did their ethnicity. Terms such as Angola, Congo, and Arara may have simply meant "*bozal*" or "*negro*" to priests. They certainly translated them as such when recording the race or ethnicity of slaves in Mexico City's marriage registers. The impetus for ethnic naming came not from Spaniards but from Africans themselves. Thus, we should treat such ethnonyms in marriage registers as proclamations of self-identity and not as distinctions imposed by the recording cleric.

Yet the possibility that the use of ethnic monikers reflected issues within the African (rather than the Spanish) community does not adequately address why slaves used ethnonyms created by slave traders rather than those that reflected local African ethnicities. In fact, despite the "bewildering variety" of ethnonyms in Africa (and even in the Americas), the great majority of "named Africans" from a common slaving region in Africa tended to group themselves into two or three major ethnicities in the Americas, and once established, the names of those groups remained quite stable.[35] For example, the ethnic monikers slaves in New Spain used were almost exactly the same as the various ethnicities the Jesuit Alonso de Sandoval identified in his ministrations to recent slave imports in Cartagena de Indias in the first decades of the seventeenth century. Alejandro de la Fuente found a similar consistency of ethnic monikers from seventeenth-century Havana, Cuba.[36] Therefore, we should not expect that slaves claimed localized African ethnicities, and this strongly underscores the need to understand the meaning of these ethnonyms specifically within the context of the Diaspora.[37]

With that knowledge of diasporic ethnonyms and Central Africa in mind, Catholic marriage applications from New Spain provide an important opportunity to explore the potential for the creation of slave communities based in new diasporic ethnicities. In such sources, slaves identified their ethnic and community identities using the monikers initially used by Europeans, but these terms were quickly appropriated by slaves in the Diaspora to name the distinct but (as we will see) not necessarily mutually exclusive ethnic communities.

It is possible that newly arrived Africans began to experience a new sense of self upon their arrival in Mexico City. Most historians highlight the importance of newly arrived Africans for maintaining ethnic divisions within slave populations through their continuous importation of African cultural elements. From another perspective, however, those new slaves, who spoke little or no Spanish, were drawn to other slaves with whom they could communicate who had been pulled from similar regions in Africa. That gravitation likely resulted in their continued integration into a larger community of slaves whose cultural and linguistic heritages from Africa were similar enough to their own to be mutually intelligible. We know from *testigo* testimonies, for example, that Africans often spent considerable time in the colony before marrying. Only fourteen of 133 African brides and grooms presented a *testigo* who had known them in the colony for less than five years. That time in the colony allowed new slaves to familiarize themselves with other Africans and to better grasp the distinctions within the enslaved population. Through those interactions slaves learned of and continuously redefined new diasporic ethnic identities that were distinct from those they would have claimed in Africa. Those identities became identified by terms such as "Angola" or "Congo" because such terms marked distinctions between "us" and "them" that had resonance for slaves in this particular historical and geographic context.

Thus, based on the cultural similarities of slaves drawn from a common region in Central Africa, marriages between two people using the same ethnonyms will be treated as endogamous and as part of an attempt to construct a new community based on shared cultural traits. In Mexico City during the period 1640–1649, slaves originating from West Central Africa almost always married other Africans who hailed from the same region. Among the fifty-eight marriages uniting two Africans, forty-two were clearly endogamous: forty-one Angola-Angola unions and one Malemba-Malemba couple (see Table 2.3). Among Angolas, nearly 80 percent married endogamously (82 of 104). This pattern appears to describe the marriage market for slaves in

Table 2.3. Marriage Patterns of *Bozal* Slaves, El Sagrario Metropolitano Parish, Mexico City, 1640–1649

African Grooms		African Brides	
Groom's Ethnicity/Bride's Ethnicity	Number	Bride's Ethnicity/Groom's Ethnicity	Number
Central Africa		Central Africa	
Angola/Angola	41	Angola/Angola	41
Angola/Banguela	1	Angola/Congo	6
Angola/Congo	1	Angola/Malemba	2
Congo/Angola	6	Banguela/Angola	1
Malemba/Angola	2	Congo/Angola	1
Malemba/Malemba	1	Malemba/Malemba	1
Subtotal	52	Subtotal	52
Angola/Negra	4	Angola/Arara	1
Angola//Mulata	4	Angola/Caboverde	1
Angola/India	1	Angola/Negro	5
Angola/China	1	Congo/Negro	1
Subtotal	10	Subtotal	8
South African Grooms		South African Brides	
Mozambique/Mozambique	1	Mozambique/Mozambique	1
Xhosa[1]/Xhosa	1	Xhosa/Xhosa	1
Congo/Xhosa	1	Xhosa/Congo	1
Subtotal	3	Subtotal	3
Other *Bozal* Grooms		Other *Bozal* Brides	
Arara/Angola	1	Nalu/Bran	1
Bran/Nalu	1	Subtotal	1
Caboverde/Angola	1		
Nalu/Angola Libre	1		
Subtotal	4		
Total	69	Total	64

Note: 1. Aguirre Beltrán places Xhosa within the Bantu language group originating in West Central Africa, while Colin Palmer asserts that this ethnic group originated from Southeastern Africa. See Aguirre Beltrán, *La población negra*, 241; and Palmer, *Slaves of the White God*, 23.

Source: AGN, Ramo de Matrimonios.

Mexico City; both Bennett and Palmer report that over 83 percent of Angola slaves married other Angolas in the period before 1650.[38]

However, my data from Mexico City for the years 1640–1649 indicates that an important minority of Angolas married Central Africans who were not Angolas, a finding supported by Herman Bennett's data. He found that Angolas were quite important as spouses for Congo slaves. Of the sixty-seven Congo slaves who married from 1584 to 1640, twenty-eight married

Congos and another twenty-eight married Angolas.[39] Were those unions also endogamous?

A possible answer to that question lies in treatments of the cultural history of pre-colonial Central Africa. According to specialists, Central Africa was the most culturally and linguistically homogenous of the slave-exporting regions of Atlantic Africa. Jan Vansina, in his seminal *Paths in the Rainforests*, charts how the region came to be populated by a single linguistic family—the Western Bantu—over the last two millennia BC.[40] Subsequently, these peoples with a common ancestry developed distinct traditions and dialects over time that reflected local conditions. Accordingly, people throughout the Western Bantu speaking region of Central Africa would *not* have identified themselves as sharing the same ethnic identity.

Yet within the regions most involved in the slave trade, West Central Africans spoke two languages, Kikongo and Kimbundu, that were as linguistically similar as Spanish and Portuguese.[41] The region was homogenous linguistically as well as culturally. Pre-colonial West Central Africans, historians of the region contend, shared a single overarching cultural and political tradition *before* they arrived in the Americas. In other words, the cultures and societies of the area constituted a single unit when compared to the outside even if Western Bantu speakers failed to recognize it as such while in Africa.[42] In trying to explain how West Central Africans may have transitioned from African to "diasporic" ethnicities, Joseph C. Miller wrote,

> The distinguishable aspects of the lives of the Central Africans ensnared in slaving on which they might have drawn as they *redefined* themselves [in the slave trade and] in the New World centered on shared understandings of community—generally in the arenas of human experience characterized as "religious," the security of family, symbols of power and authority, wariness toward strangers, and particularly the broad linguistic similarities through which people who talked with one another on a day-to-day basis expressed the easy familiarity of spontaneous commonality.[43]

Such descriptions of the cultural unity of Central Africa suggest that any unions between slaves originating from that region, regardless of ethnic appellation, could be treated as endogamous. Returning to our discussion of Congo slaves in Mexico City, that twenty-eight of sixty-seven Congo slaves who married prior to 1650 selected Congo spouses highlights high levels of ethnic endogamy among a small population dominated by the Angola majority. At the same time, however, the other twenty-eight Congos who married Angola slaves were also exhibiting cultural endogamy because the communities represented by those ethnonyms were not necessarily mutually exclusive. Thus, approximately 85 percent of West Central Africans who married in Mexico City prior to 1650 did so endogamously.[44] Even more telling, in the 1640s, only three of 107 Central African slaves married other Africans who were not also from that region (see Table 2.3).[45]

Marriage patterns among the minority West African slaves also highlight their desire to search out spouses and friends among slaves with similar origins, even when their small presence in the colony would seem to complicate that task. Although my sample is too small, Bennett's study includes valuable information on the marriage patterns of slaves from West Africa. For example, he found that among forty-six slaves identified as Terra Nova (hailing from the Bight of Benin), twenty-six found spouses who self-identified with the same ethnonym. Similarly, among the thirty-four Bran slaves (from Senegambia) included in his study, sixteen married another Bran. Recall that in the 1640s less than 10 percent of the slave population was West African. Incredibly, therefore, even when particular diasporic ethnic groups represented clear minorities within the overall slave population, they still tended toward ethnically endogamous marriages. At the same time, however, the West Central African majority interacted with these other ethnic groups with West African origins, which were simply too small to remain completely separate. For example, the second largest number of spouses for both the Terra Nova (15) and Bran (7) ethnic groups hailed from Central Africa.[46] The patterns highlight that various "diasporic ethnicities" were under construction in Mexico City as slaves sought out other Africans who defined themselves with similar ethnic monikers, marking their sense of belonging to common cultural communities.

In contrast, creole slaves rarely married Africans (Table 2.1). This group—particularly men—looked to the free population and even to non-Afro-Mexicans for spouses. Interestingly, the rate of racial endogamy among creole slaves increased and the relative number of creole slaves who married Indians and mestizos decreased over time as creoles became the majority of the slave population. That trend highlights an important transition—similar to the transition Michael Gomez proposes for British North America—in the basis of the cultural identity of slaves in Mexico from diasporic ethnicity to race, an issue that is beyond the scope of this study.[47]

The marriage patterns discussed above suggest both a strong sense of community among the Central African majority before 1650 and that minority West African groups saw themselves as distinct from that majority. But the small number of non–Central African slaves and the increasing population of creoles appear to have operated on the fringes of that community, suggesting that there was some social distance among Africans based in ethnicity and between Africans and creoles in the colony. This evidence suggests that neither pan-Africanity nor race formed the basis of slave cultural identity in New Spain prior to 1650, a finding that undermines the applicability of the ethnogenesis/creolization thesis to Mexico.

Marriage applications for slaves in Mexico City provide a second way to measure the importance of West Central Africans to each other. The preference of this group for endogamous marriage also manifested itself in *testigo* selection patterns in the 1640s. For West Central African brides and grooms, 203 of 252 *testigos* (81 percent) were also *bozales* from that region of Africa.[48] In addition, the Ramo de Matrimonios contains seventy-three marriages in which the bride or the groom or both were West Central Africans during the 1640s. In sixty-three of those marriages (86 percent), at least one *testigo* was also of West Central African origin. Conversely, there were only four instances among fifty-two marriages when two West Central Africans married each other without at least one West Central African *testigo*. Mirroring trends from spousal choice, *testigo* selection clearly indicates that non-localized African ethnic identities—diasporic ethnicities—provided the foundation of the Afro-Mexican community.

If we consider spousal and *testigo* choices simultaneously, the overlap between the Angola and other West Central African diasporic ethnicities becomes even more evident. For example, in the fifty-two marriages that united two Central Africans, nineteen included persons of at least two different West Central African ethnicities. Ten couples married despite the fact that the bride and groom claimed different ethnicities (the most common example being an Angola groom with a Congo bride). Those couples showed the greatest variability in terms of the ethnicities their *testigos* listed. For example, when Manuel, a Malemba slave, and Juana, an Angola slave, petitioned to marry on August 3, 1648, their *testigos* included Manuel de Santiago and Domingo, both of whom self-identified as Congo.[49] That three different ethnonyms marking distinctions within Central African slaves appear in a single record suggests that it was slaves and not clerics (who likely were ignorant of the real distinctions among Africans) who assigned them. Additionally, another nine "ethnically endogamous" unions included at least one *testigo* who claimed a West Central African ethnicity different from that shared by the bride and groom. For example, when Francisco and Margarita, both Angola slaves, petitioned for the right to marry on April 2, 1744, Bartolomé, an Angola slave, and Juan Francisco, a Congo slave, were among their *testigos*. Both claimed to have been friends with the bride and groom for over twelve years.[50]

If, as argued above, the primary impetus for maintaining the different Central African "diasporic ethnonyms" came from within the African community in New Spain, then we must assume that Africans used them to demarcate what they perceived to be important divisions within their larger community, even if those divisions did not translate into mutually exclusive ethnic communities. The sources considered here do not provide clear causes of those differences. They might be geographic (marking slaves from different regions within Central Africa) or linguistic (in that Congos more than likely spoke Kikongo while Angolas predominantly spoke Kimbundu) or they might recognize the longer historical association with Christianity in the regions dominated by the kingdom of Kongo as opposed to the region that became the Portuguese colony of Angola. Whatever the cause, it emanated out of African and African diasporic concerns rather than Spanish imperial concerns.

Equally important, African slaves were able to construct these overlapping ethnic communities across the urban landscape of Mexico City. In only nine of the eighty-two marriages joining two slaves were the bride and groom owned by the same person. In another eleven cases, the bride or groom and at least one *testigo* were owned by a common master. But there was only one case in which the bride, groom, and all the *testigos* were owned by one person. Thus, three in four marriages brought together a bride, a groom, and *testigos* owned by different masters spaced throughout the viceregal capital.

While examples are quite rare, largely due to the limited number of extant marriage petitions, it is possible to find particular slaves who appear in more than one marriage party. Two Angola slaves, Francisco and Marcos, served as *testigos* for Mateo, an Angola slave owned by Joseph de Arauz, and Isabel, an Angola slave owned by Mathias del Castillo, when they petitioned to marry on January 4, 1640, testifying that they had known Mateo for ten and eight years, respectively. On the next day, Mateo again appeared before the ecclesiastical authorities, this time as a *testigo* for Francisco and Christina, two more Angola slaves. Mateo testified that he had been friends with Francisco (who was not the same person as Mateo's *testigo* with the same name) for eight years and that he had known the bride for over twenty years. Francisco, the second groom, and Mateo's fiancée, Isabel, were owned by the same person, Miguel del Castillo. Combining these two marriages we can chart five different long-term friendships Mateo established with Angola slaves owned by four different masters, suggesting that Africans sought out social relations with people of common ethnic backgrounds throughout the city.[51]

In addition, in many cases, the process of community formation based on diasporic ethnic identity began before slaves actually reached the Americas.

In some cases it is clear that the origin of the relationship among slaves who wished to marry and their *testigos* began in Africa or during the Middle Passage. When Pedro, an Angola slave owned by Francisca Navarro, and Christina de la Cruz, an Angola slave of Antonio Langes, petitioned for the right to marry on December 15, 1646, Francisco, an Angola slave belonging to Luís de Vergaza, testified that he had known both the bride and groom since the three of them had left Angola aboard a slave ship. The language of his testimony suggests that they became acquainted after their capture, either while waiting to be placed on board ship or once they were aboard. Despite the fact that they all had different masters in Mexico City, they maintained the bonds they had forged during the Middle Passage.[52] Similarly, when Antonio de la Cruz, the Congo slave of Domingo Caritebraña, and María de la Cruz, the Congo slave of Juana Basan, petitioned to marry in 1680 they presented two other Congo slaves—Francisco de San Pedro and Antonio de San Miguel—who testified that the couple had met in Africa and that the four of them made the Middle Passage together.[53]

The importance of shipmates as the pillars of nascent Afro-American slave communities cannot be overstated.[54] Ties that slaves from a common cultural region of Africa forged on board slave ships despite differences in local identity provided the initial relationships upon which African diasporic communities were built throughout the Americas. But those bonds were based upon common cultural backgrounds, not just common experiences as chattel on a slave ship.

The ability of shipmates to maintain ties across the urban landscape of Mexico City represents no small feat. It is nearly impossible to provide an accurate demographic picture of Mexico City's population and the importance of slaves within the city for the colonial period. However, Colin Palmer estimates that for the period under consideration, the total slave population of Mexico City was 10,000–20,000 and that approximately half that number were Africans.[55] The importance of the ability and desire of slaves to maintain such connections in a city whose total population was nearly 50,000–100,000 should not be underestimated.

In conclusion, African ethnicities rarely survived the slave trade intact. Although the slave trade destroyed the family and kinship ties that were central to identity in pre-colonial African societies, it did not destroy memory, belief, experience, and expertise.[56] The survival of those cultural elements made it entirely possible that a slave originating from any of the Central African subregions listed in Map 2.2 could have recognized common cultural traits with another slave from the same region even though that they might have come from different ethnicities in Central Africa. Such individuals likely claimed different diasporic ethnicities in the Americas and would then have been able to build new communities upon those ethnicities. The first step in articulating those new ethnicities would have been through establishing new kinship ties, which makes marriages a key element in community formation within the Diaspora. Thus, as old identities—articulated at the level of lineage or village—were destroyed, new ones—diasporic ethnicities—were being constructed.

Central Africans, the great majority of slaves in Mexico City in the 1640s, did not turn to creole slaves, Indians, or any other ethnic or racial group in significant numbers when selecting a spouse or wedding witness. Rather, their endogamous marriage and *testigo* selection patterns provide important evidence that new ethnic identities were being formed within the Diaspora—aboard slave ships and within the colonies—that before 1650 cannot be adequately described as African ethnicities, pan-African identities, or racial identities. The ability of scholars interested in race and ethnicity in colonial Spanish America to explore the self-definition of Africans in specific regional and chronological contexts revises and refocuses theorizations about ethnic formation in the Diaspora. The selection of a spouse and/or *testigo* who proclaimed a similar ethnicity was a tangible expression of the intricate, enduring, and complex set of relationships that bound together slaves with similar origins and backgrounds in New Spain.[57] In that sense, terms such as Angola, Congo and the like were more than shorthand for geographic origin. They also had meaning in the lives of slaves and served as cultural markers. Africans appropriated ethnonyms imposed by slavers and masters to describe the new identities they were constructing in the Atlantic World—identities that moved beyond localized African ethnicity as they built upon the cultural and ideological commonalities shared by societies within Africa.

Notes

1. McCaa, "*Calidad, Clase*, and Marriage," 477–478. McCaa reminds us that "in many instances [calidad] was an inclusive impression reflecting one's reputation as a whole. Color, occupation, and wealth might influence one's calidad, as did purity of blood, honor, integrity, and even place of origin."

2. Archivo General de la Nación de México (hereafter AGN), Ramo de Matrimonios, vol. 126, exp. 28, folios 81–88.

3. AGN, Matrimonios, vol. 19, exp. 22, folios 118–119.

4. Proctor, "Afro-Mexican Slave Labor," 33–58.

5. Berlin, "From Creole to African," 251–288; and Mintz, *An Anthropological Approach to the Afro-American Past*, 5–8; and Stuckey, *Slave Culture*, esp. Ch. 1.

6. Morgan, "The Cultural Implications of the Atlantic Slave Trade," 122–145.

7. Thornton, *Africa and Africans*, 186–192. Thornton divides Upper Guinea into three linguistic groups, 1) the North Western Atlantic cultures; 2) the South Western cultures; and 3) the Mande. Lower Guinea contained two subgroups: 1) the Western Kwa including the Akan, Ewe-Aja, and Ga speakers from the Gold Coast and the Western part of the Bight of Benin; and 2) the Eastern Kwa language group, including the Yoruba-Oyo-Edo ethnic groups from the Eastern Bight of Benin and the Igbo speakers who originated from the Bight of Biafra. Last, he divides West Central Africa into two Bantu language groups, Kikongo in the north and Kimbundu in the south.

8. These marriage applications represent approximately 10–15 percent of all slave marriages in Mexico City in the years 1640–1649. For the years 1647–1648, I found 155 slave marriages in the two most important parishes in Mexico City, Sagrario Metropolitano (123) and Salto de Agua (22). AGN, Matrimonios.

9. Lohse, "Slave-Trade Nomenclature," 73–92; O'Toole, "Inventing Difference"; and Sweet, *Recreating Africa*.

10. Bowser, *The African Slave*, 261.

11. O'Toole, "From the Rivers of Guinea," 32.

12. Morgan, "The Cultural Implications of the Atlantic Slave Trade," 140–141; and Reis, *Slave Rebellion in Brazil*, 146–159.

13. Alberro, *Inquisición y sociedad en México*, 456–462; Cortés Jácome, "La memoria familiar de los negros y mulatos," 128; Martínez Montiel, *Negros en América*, 167.

14. Aguirre Beltrán, *La población negra de México*, 255; Cortés Jácome, "Negros amancebados con indias," 285–293.

15. Aguirre Beltrán, *Medicina y magia*, 109; and Behar, "Sex and Sin," 48. Some scholars argue that Afro-Mexicans served as an important bridge between the Spanish and indigenous worlds, thereby playing a fundamental role in *mestizaje*. See Carroll, "Los Mexicanos negros," 403–438; Lewis, *Hall of Mirrors*.

16. Bennett, *Africans in Colonial Mexico*, 64–95; Bennett, "Lovers, Family and Friends," 91–104; Palmer, "From Africa to the Americas," 223–235.

17. Bristol, *Christians, Blasphemers, and Witches*; von Germeten, *Black Blood Brothers*, 11–40.

18. Bennett, "Lovers, Family and Friends," 114; Lewis, *Hall of Mirrors*, 31–32.

19. Cope, *The Limits of Racial Domination*, 81–83; Vinson, *Bearing Arms for His Majesty*, 4. For an argument that Cope may have underestimated the racial endogamy of Afro-Mexicans, see Proctor, *"Damned Notions of Liberty,"* esp. chapter 2.

20. "Ordenanzas acerca de la orden que se ha de tener en el tratamiento con los negros," 237–240.

21. Bristol, *Christians, Blasphemers, and Witches*, 78.

22. Proctor, "Slavery, Identity, and Culture," 148. For similar findings, see Calvo, *Guadalajara y su región en el siglo XVII*, 91. Legally, only children whose parents were married were defined as legitimate. See Borah and Cook, "Marriage and Legitimacy in Mexican Culture," 947.

23. Thornton, "Religious and Ceremonial Life in Kongo and Mbundu Areas," 71–90.

24. For a discussion of Afro-Mexican confraternities, see von Germeten, *Black Blood Brothers.*

25. Carroll, *Blacks in Colonial Veracruz*, 32–33 and 160; and Ngou-Mve, *El África Bantú en México*, 97–147. These figures may underestimate the importance of West Central Africans to the slave population of New Spain; Joseph Miller calculated that 91 percent of slaves exported from Africa prior to 1650 originated from West Central Africa. See Miller, "Central Africa during the Era of the Slave Trade," 67.

26. For similar findings on other ethnic monikers employed in the diaspora, see Byrd, "The Slave Trade"; Chambers, "'My own nation,'" 72–97; and Hall, "African Ethnicities," 43–65; and Law, "Ethnicity and the Slave Trade," 205–219.

27. See Miller, "Central Africa during the Era of the Slave Trade," 29.

28. Ibid., 40; and Thornton, *The Kingdom of Kongo*, xv.

29. Lovejoy, "Identifying Enslaved Africans," 9, my italics.

30. Miller, "Central Africa during the Era of the Slave Trade," 23–27.

31. Vansina, "The Kongo Kingdom," 546–587.

32. Cope, *The Limits of Racial Domination*, 54–55 and 69. The growing consensus that parish records generally reflect self-proclaimed ethnic or racial status contrasts greatly with the oft-cited inability of witnesses to agree on the racial classification of defendants in criminal and inquisition records. For a discussion of that variability, see Boyer, "Cast and Identity in Colonial Mexico," 1–17.

33. Bennett, *Africans in Colonial Mexico*, 91.

34. O'Toole, "Inventing Difference," 307.

35. Chambers, "Ethnicity in the Diaspora," 26. Also see Lovejoy, "Ethnic Designations," 9–42.

36. See Sandoval, *De instauranda aethiopum salute*, 90–97; and de la Fuente, "Esclavos africanos en La Habana," 135–160.

37. Byrd, "Eboe, Country, and Nation," 126.

38. Bennett, "Lovers, Family and Friends," 69 and 88; and Palmer, "From Africa to the Americas," 233–234. This represents a recalculation of Bennett's data, as he counted only marriage applications (p. 65), a strategy that underrepresents endogamy because it does not count both slaves in endogamous marriages.

39. Bennett, "Lovers, Family and Friends," 66. Importantly, these patterns reflect the general size of the Angola and Congo presence in New Spain; ten times as many Angolas as Congos married in Mexico City prior to 1650.

40. Vansina, "Equatorial Africa and Angola," 551–577; and Vansina, *Paths in the Rainforests.*

41. Thornton, *Africa and Africans*, 191; and Vansina, "Western Bantu Expansion," 129–145.

42. Craemer, Vansina, and Fox, "Religious Movements in Central West Africa," 458–475; Vansina, "Foreword," xii; and Vansina, *Paths in the Rainforests*, 5 and 249.

43. Miller, "Central Africa during the Era of the Slave Trade," 35–36, my italics.

44. See Table 3. Similarly, Bennett's research found that 88 percent of Angolas and

85 percent of Congos married endogamously in Mexico City prior to 1650. Bennett, "Lovers, Family and Friends," 66, 69.

45. Studies of Brazil have found a similar tendency. See Schwartz, *Sugar Plantations in the Formation of Brazilian Society*, 392; and Sweet, *Recreating Africa*, 45–48.

46. Bennett, "Lovers, Family and Friends," 66–69.

47. Gomez, *Exchanging Our Country Marks*; Proctor, "*Damned Notions of Liberty*," 54–55, 60–64.

48. It is possible to tell from the sources if a particular *testigo* was testifying on behalf the bride or groom. Therefore, these figures include only *testigos* who testified on behalf of a slave. I excluded *testigos* for the free spouse because they do not necessarily speak to the intimate relations of the slave in question.

49. AGN, Matrimonios, vol. 172, exp. 170.

50. AGN, Matrimonios, vol. 172, exp. 4.

51. AGN, Matrimonios, vol. 126, exp. 126 and 127.

52. AGN, Matrimonios, vol. 172, exp. 84.

53. AGN, Matrimonios, vol. 67, exp. 59, folios 291–292.

54. Mullin, *Africa in America*, 161; and Slenes, "'*Malungu, ngoma vem*,'" 48–67.

55. Palmer, "From Africa to the Americas," 229.

56. Frey and Wood, *Come Shouting to Zion*, 36.

57. Palmer, "From Africa to the Americas," 234.

3

To Be Free and *Lucumí*

Ana de la Calle and Making African Diaspora Identities in Colonial Peru

RACHEL SARAH O'TOOLE

In 1719, Ana de la Calle paid a notary in the northern Peruvian city of Trujillo to compose her will. She identified herself as a free *morena* of *casta lucumí* or, as I will argue, a free woman of color from the Yoruba-speaking interior of the Bight of Benin.[1] In doing so, Ana de la Calle asserted her identity using terms, *morena* and *lucumí*, that were familiar to the notary and to slaveholders (such as herself) in coastal Peru. Yet unlike her Spanish and creole counterparts, she used the term "*lucumí*" to name not only her slave but also her own status.[2] Furthermore, by claiming to be a *morena* she included herself among other free people of color who used the colonial term to set themselves apart from enslaved men and women. Why did Ana de la Calle use these appellations together? Her assertion was unusual, since free people did not publicly identify themselves using terms such as *lucumí*, a word that was normally used to describe enslaved men and women in official documents. These terms were useful to Ana de la Calle even if their meaning is puzzling today. By exploring how the terms served her purposes, this chapter suggests that men and women constructed identities that were rooted in African meanings but were shaped in diasporic contexts.

Ana de la Calle's example highlights the interstitial nature of African diasporic identities in colonial Spanish America. Ira Berlin, Philip Morgan, and other historians have argued that Africans rapidly became acculturated creoles to create an Atlantic or African American culture within and in resistance to slavery.[3] John Thornton, James Sweet, and others have explored how Africans, in Sweet's terms, re-created communities, practices, and identities that were distinctly African in the Americas.[4] Yet the compelling invitation remains to explore African adaptations of individual identity in a specific historical diasporic context. As Kristin Mann has urged, historians need to understand "how, when, and why slaves were able to draw on material, social, ideological, and other resources" from traditions in both Africa and the Americas "to fashion communities for themselves and cope with the demands of bondage."[5] By presenting and interrogating testimonials of Africans who experienced the Middle Passage and then freed themselves from slavery, such as Olaudah Equiano and Mahommah Gardo Baquaqua, historians have drawn closer to understanding both individual choices and the variety of experiences among enslaved Africans.[6] In the Spanish Americas, documents of individual experiences are rare and historians are only beginning to explore (as does Frank "Trey" Proctor III in this volume) collective expressions of identities that would provide evidence of how or why men and women of the African Diaspora chose certain identities or joined particular communities.

Historians increasingly have turned to the inscribed "nations," or the ways that enslaved and free people articulated their origins, to uncover individual affiliations and community identities within the African Diaspora. For example, Douglas Chambers argues that captives sold from the Bight of Biafra constituted many geographic, social, and religious collectivities but formed a "diasporic African nation" of Igbo in the context of New World slavery. Thus, the slave-trading term "Calabar" named a "meta-ethnicity" in the Americas.[7] Likewise, Michael Gomez ascribes ethnic solidarity (or at least recognition) to Africans from similar cultural zones of the transatlantic slave trade such as Senegambia or the Gold Coast. For Gomez, communities of diasporic populations first articulated common origins or a unique set of beliefs and then established "polycultural life-styles" before identifying as a race in the southern United States.[8] Other scholars caution against assuming that Africans shared affinities based on their sale from slave-trading ports affiliated with regional cultural zones.[9] For example, Peter Caron argues that labels of "nation" such as Bambara (from Senegal) did not always describe ethnicity. As a result, a demographic concentration of enslaved Africans from a common origin did not necessarily translate into "the foundation of an ethnic, linguistic, or other community" in the Americas.[10] Questions remain regarding which terms men and women of the African Diaspora employed and why. Sandra Greene urges more historical specificity rooted in African history when ascribing religious, linguistic, or social characteristics to cultural zones such as the one labeled *lucumí*. For one thing, not all communities along the Slave Coast shared the same exposure to Yoruba polities.[11] Nevertheless, enslaved and free people in the Americas used terms that denoted "nations," cultural zones, slave trade ports, or what is now known as ethnicity to name themselves. These terms were called *casta* in colonial Spanish America, and they remain useful to historians interested in African diasporic identities. Building on this scholarship, this chapter focuses on how people of the African Diaspora activated *casta* terms in the Americas to counteract assumptions that particular terms signified a shared identity. The challenge is to understand what people meant when they used certain words to describe themselves (and others) at particular historical junctures.

This chapter deconstructs the terms Ana de la Calle used in order to suggest how enslaved and free people of the African Diaspora used *casta* terms. Complementing Proctor's exploration of terms employed in marriage applications (chapter 2 in this volume), I ask what these words would have meant to a woman of the African Diaspora. Instead of assuming what the significance was of a *casta* term, I approach these words as composites of meanings that were historically specific. Kirsten Fischer provides a model for this method in her book on colonial North Carolina, where she explicates how official racial categories hardened with the increasing sexual violence that accompanied slavery. By emphasizing the severe impact of racial violence, Fischer cautions that race was rarely fixed and suggests that historians explore its multiple constructions.[12] Likewise, Kathleen Brown urges historians to see race as an "ongoing historical and cultural construction." She argues that in colonial Virginia, although lawmakers attempted to impose a "template of binary difference" to naturalize slavery as connected to blackness, in practice race was continually created.[13] With a keen eye to both the impositions of slaveholders and the agency of Africans with their descendants, this chapter also explores *casta* as a construction. In doing so, I respond to Paul Lovejoy's call for historians to approach what he calls ethnic identification as a process of "reinterpretation and re-invention of the present and the past."[14] In this spirit, I assign agency to an African woman and her descendants who infused terms such as *lucumí* with historical meaning. Rather than assume an understanding of Ana de la Calle's choices, I will instead engage in an interrogation of why such terms may have been useful to a free woman of color in northern coastal Peru.

Slavery and Freedom in Colonial Peru

Free and enslaved Africans and their descendants joined Spaniards during the conquest wars of Peru and would come to serve as domestic servants, overseers on estates, and as artisans throughout the new viceroyalty. As landholders demanded more enslaved laborers, men and women of the African

Diaspora quickly grew in number and by the 1640s constituted roughly 40 percent of the total population in coastal cities such as Lima and Trujillo.[15] Along the coast and outside highland cities such as Cuzco and Cajamarca, enslaved men (primarily) labored on sugar estates, cattle ranches, and wheat farms.[16] Enslaved women sold cooked food, bread, and other products in city markets and streets.[17] Whether urban or rural, Africans and their descendants also joined Catholic confraternities with others of the same origins, such as those from Guinea-Bissau who were active in Trujillo's San Nicolas de Tolentino.[18] Concentrated in the neighborhoods of San Lazaro and Malembo in Lima, Afro-Peruvians also adapted Andean religious beliefs just as indigenous Andeans sought out African Diaspora ritual specialists.[19] Thus, though separated by law from inhabiting indigenous villages and not incorporated as "citizens" within the republic of the Spaniards, Africans and their descendants were integral to colonial Peruvian society.

Individual negotiation of legal freedom or manumission was possible in colonial Peru, but this was largely limited to people of color who had been born in the Americas. Enslaved Africans usually lacked the networks necessary to secure loans to pay for their freedom. In addition, women of color were more likely than men to successfully purchase themselves or their family members because of their ability to sell goods and labor in the cities.[20] Free men of African descent also worked as muleteers, sailors, and even commercial agents in the Pacific routes between Lima and Panama and served as militiamen.[21] Free people became slaveholders, shopkeepers, and (in rare cases) wealthy merchants who sold textiles, tobacco, and alcohol in regional markets. By the eighteenth century, Afro-Peruvians were prominent architects and musicians. For example, seventeenth-century Dominican *donado* Martín de Porres gained considerable fame as a protector and a healer in spite of the Vatican's reluctance to canonize a man of African descent.[22] Excluded from universities, the medical profession, political office, and the clergy, Afro-Peruvian men nevertheless created public positions of prestige within and outside communities comprised of people of African descent.

Lucumí as an Elite Status

Ana de la Calle's claim to free status represented a significant achievement for a woman of color in colonial Trujillo. Assuming that she had been born in West Africa and sold into the transatlantic slave trade, it was unusual for a woman in her circumstances to gain her freedom. African-born enslaved women were less likely to purchase their freedom than those born in the Americas. In a sample of 140 notarized freedom agreements recorded between 1640 and 1730 in colonial Trujillo, twenty (four men and sixteen women) were registered for Africans. The rate of manumission in colonial Trujillo reflected social realities for Africans in the Americas. Africans' claims to freedom were thwarted by their status as recent arrivals. They were unable to prove their descent from free people using baptismal records or other Spanish legal documents. In addition, Africans were separated from kin and family and needed to develop new networks and build local patronage connections to secure the funds required for manumission. Thus, Ana de la Calle was unusual among free women (who most often identified themselves as *mulata* or *criolla*). If she had been enslaved (as I suspect she had been, given the manumission rates of Africans), she had also done much more than secure her freedom. She purchased a house and a slave, arranged legitimate marriages for herself and her offspring, and paid for a full Catholic funeral and additional masses that were sung for her soul. What strategies did she use to achieve these things?

Her 1719 will indicates that Ana de la Calle developed personal networks and patron-client relations that secured and even advanced her family's status. Her first marriage, with Pasqual de Segama, a freed *moreno*, played a role in establishing her among Trujillo's free colored community, members of which used the terms *moreno* and *morena* to separate themselves from enslaved *negros* and *negras*.[23] In this way, Ana de la Calle participated in strategies similar to those used by *criolla* women of color such as María Margarita Alvarado, who declared herself a free *morena* to distinguish herself from the charge of being a recently freed *negra*.[24] Ana de la Calle worked to maintain her *morena* status. After burying her first husband in the Franciscan monastery (at significant expense), she brokered a second marriage with a free *moreno*, Agustín de Saabedra. Saabedra had familial connections with the enslaved and free Cavero family, members of which served wealthy Spanish sugar estate owners, worked as rural overseers and urban *chicha* (indigenous corn beer) makers, and engaged in local commerce and the highland transportation of lucrative tobacco to coastal markets.[25] As scholarship about free women of color in other parts of Spanish America suggests, Ana de la Calle could have expanded her networks through this marital connection and expanded her property holdings.[26] In any event, her status as a *morena* was strengthened through her marriages.

Ana de la Calle and her family continued to develop their status in colonial Trujillo. Indicating the importance of the Caveros, Ana de la Calle's only daughter from her first marriage called herself María de la Cruz Cavero. While "de la Cruz" suggested a humble status, taking the name Cavero can be understood as a tribute to patrons as Ana de la Calle (and her daughter) cemented their alliances. What is certain is that Ana de la Calle successfully inserted herself into an extensive personal and commercial network of her peers, petty traders, and urban vendors whose networks included free and enslaved people. Whether she was born in West Africa or in the Americas, she was connected to free people as kin or patrons in colonial Trujillo.

As a free, married property-holder, Ana de la Calle continued to advance the public prominence of her family through marriage. Her only daughter married *alférez* (second lieutenant) Baltasar de los Reyes, who did not appear to bring substantial wealth to the marriage (as indicated by his destitute status when a widower) but supplied a public title of "lieutenant" to the household. His title matched that of his wife—Ana's daughter—whom the civil notaries recorded as "*doña*" in the subsequent judicial investigations. In addition to a public reputation as free people of color, Ana de la Calle's family claimed titles of respect. More, Ana de la Calle used colonial categories that reflected the changing status of her family. In her will, she (or the notary she hired) identified her daughter as a *parda* while labeling herself and her husbands as *morena* and *morenos*. While slaveholders used the terms of *morena* and *negra* interchangeably, free women of color in colonial Trujillo clearly preferred the term *parda*. For example, in 1692, the women of color who argued that a young girl named Ana was free clearly used *parda* when describing a free woman and used the term *mulata* to identify an enslaved woman.[27] Likewise, in 1718, Valentina de San Joseph called herself a "free *parda*" while her patrons labeled her a *mulata*.[28] In the context of the preferences of other women of African descent in colonial Trujillo, it is clear that Ana de la Calle used terms that she intended to distinguish between the generations of her family. She appears to have advanced the status of her family through marriage and to have claimed colonial terms that signified a free and respectable status.

Ana de la Calle also called herself a *lucumí*, an unusual claim for free people of color in colonial Trujillo. Free African descendants born in the Americas usually did not reproduce the terms that slaveholders used to categorize the

Ana de la Calle's family

Ana de la Calle—Pasqual de Segama (1st husband)—Agustín de Saabedra (2nd husband)

↓

doña María de la Cruz Cavero—*alferez* Baltasar de los Reyes

↓

Juana de Dios y Silva—*alferez* don Faustino de Vidaurre

perceived regional distinctions among enslaved Africans. However, as in other parts of the Americas, it is plausible that Africans and their descendants, both free and enslaved, named themselves and others as Lucumí, Arara, or Angola but did not do so when they interacted with the court scribes and urban notaries who produced official documents. So why did Ana de la Calle certify herself in writing as a *lucumí*? As Kathryn Burns explains, colonial inhabitants used notaries to create a legal document or a "legally valid cover—a paper trail to which they might have recourse should the occasion arise." A notarized account, such as a will, was not so much about recording the actual truth (though it included this aspect) as it was about ensuring a legal record for "an imagined litigious future."[29] Moreover, a notary was paid to compose and archive important documents, and, as Burns argues, people "bothered to have their business recorded so that they could adduce the relevant documents to enforce and defend their interests at a later date."[30] Thus, Ana de la Calle's claim to be of *casta lucumí* was a purposeful act of documentation. She created a legal paper trail that, among other things, provided a record of her status as a *morena* and her family ties and certified her commercial successes. Her claim to be "of *casta lucumí*" must have also fit into these strategies, but how?

Ana de la Calle may have included the term in her notarized will to signal a status that was publicly known but required legal registration. By calling herself a *lucumí*, Ana de la Calle claimed an affinity with the Yoruba-speaking polities located inland from the Slave Coast on the Bight of Benin in West Africa. Along this coast, "*lucumí*" indicated a quality or a status that people could purchase or adapt in the seventeenth century. Historian Robin Law asserts that coastal inhabitants of the Bight of Benin used "Lukumi" (Yoruba) as a lingua franca. By the mid-seventeenth century, even wealthy people from the coastal kingdoms of Allada and Whydah preferred Yoruba as a noble language instead of their own.[31] John Thornton explains that as the Oyo kingdom expanded to the south, coastal peoples not only preferred to speak Yoruba but also adapted Yoruba deities and divination practices.[32] Also, for coastal traders who relied on interior merchants, in the mid-seventeenth century the name Lucumí signified the hinterland source of Yoruba-speaking slaves as well as other valuable commodities such as salt, corn, and cloth.[33] Historian Sandra Greene cautions against Thornton's and Law's assertions to argue that it was not until the early to mid-eighteenth century that the Anlo (in southern Ghana and Togo) adopted Yoruba divination. Furthermore, Greene asserts that "the use of the Yoruba language cannot be used as an indicator of cultural homogeneity" along the multiethnic, multipolity, and multilingual western Slave Coast.[34] Indeed, without further information about Ana de la Calle's origins, her exact intentions remain elusive. Perhaps she was from the eastern Slave Coast and not the western region of the Anlo. More important, I would suggest that she was not claiming a homogenous collectivity in West Africa or the Americas. Furthermore, she was not necessarily concerned with establishing her West African origins. Instead, Ana de la Calle constructed an individual identity to be recorded by an attending notary in the Americas. By calling herself a *lucumí*, Ana de la Calle associated herself with the multiple meanings of a superior status that were familiar to particular communities along the Bight of Benin (and in the African Diaspora) and not necessarily a fixed identity.

Enslaved Africans and their descendants in colonial Trujillo may have recognized the term *lucumí*, which would have made the term useful to Ana de la Calle. Captives from southern Benin and Nigeria (east of the Anlo) were increasingly sold into the transatlantic slave trade in the late seventeenth and early eighteenth centuries.[35] Merchants who sold slaves into the Spanish empire called men and women from the eastern Slave Coast either Arara (sold from the kingdom of Allada) or Popo (sold from both ports called Popo). In Trujillo those called Arara, Popo, and Lucumí appeared on a significant percentage of the purchase agreements recorded by city notaries between 1670 and 1720.[36] Furthermore, Popos, Araras, and Lucumís were also prominent among adult slaves that clerics baptized in Trujillo between 1695 and 1730.[37] Would these enslaved men and women have understood Ana de la Calle's claim to be "of *casta lucumí*"? The number of men and women sold from the eastern Slave Coast would suggest that other inhabitants of colonial Trujillo understood a greater significance than one of origin behind the rare identification of *lucumí*. If *lucumí* was a signifier of superior status, as Law and Thornton argue, then Ana de la Calle registered an identity that was known among a significant audience whose perspectives were not recorded in colonial documents.

Indeed, there is evidence to suggest that men and women from the eastern Slave Coast understood the word *lucumí* as a marker of an elite person. During the late seventeenth and early eighteenth centuries, the expansionist wars of the Yoruba-speaking kingdom of Oyo and other polities generated captives for the coastal slave markets.[38] The Oyo also obtained slaves as tribute payments from subject states such as Dahomey or from trade with northern peoples and polities.[39] As an intermediary between the north and the coast, the Oyo traded people who may not have spoken Yoruba, worshipped its deities, or shared other cultural attributes.[40] Yet traders and merchants may have called these captives Lucumí once they reached the coast as a way of signifying their origin or point of sale from the Yoruba-speaking kingdoms of the interior. European merchants were only superficially aware of the significance of the term *lucumí*. French trader Jean Barbot described those from the kingdom of Oyo as enemies of the Arara, while earlier in the seventeenth century Jesuit informants characterized the Lucumí as loyal in warfare and loyal to their owners.[41] Sandra Greene's careful historical analysis cautions about assuming that Lucumí was a widely recognized status among the coastal inhabitants of the Bight of Benin. Yet as the English dominated the eighteenth-century transatlantic slave trade and sales into the Spanish Americas, the Yoruba language and religion were becoming more widespread. In 1719, the year that Ana de la Calle composed her will, *lucumí* was a rare term among slaveholders and enslaved Africans. Its unusual nature is suggestive, however, of its authoritative use by knowledgeable individuals.

The evidence of her will suggests that Ana de la Calle created and communicated her status as *lucumí* within her household. Indeed, as Proctor points out in this volume, intimate, inner-household relations were critical to strategies of Africans and those of African descent. In 1719, Ana de la Calle declared she owned two slaves, Isabel Lucumí and her "*negrita criolla*" daughter, who had been "born in her house."[42] Because very few people were categorized as Lucumí in colonial Trujillo, Ana de la Calle would have had to specifically seek out Isabel Lucumí or "made" Isabel into a Lucumí as a dependent member of her household. Together, the two women may have been witnesses to each other's status as Lucumí or developed its meaning in exile on the northern Peruvian coast.

Regardless of her motivation, in the context of colonial Trujillo, Ana de la Calle's claim that she was *lucumí* complemented her status as a propertied free woman of color. Her marriage to first a freed man and then a free man as well as her children's titles matched the status of Yoruba speakers on the eastern coast of the Bight of Benin. Together, *morena* and *lucumí* amplified an elite position—even if only one can be documented within Ana de la Calle's household. By legally declaring herself to be a member of these categories, she attempted to fix her status for the benefit of her family and household. In fact, Ana de la Calle's kin used her will (and by extension her status) to defend their inheritance after she died. In the 1720s, her descendants had to fight a cleric's attempt to repossess the house she had willed to them. The fragility of their claim on her property underlines the astuteness of Ana de la Calle's strategy of buttressing her superior status with as many markers or terms as possible. Her assertion to multiple identities of elite status was, then, necessary among free people of color in colonial Trujillo.

The Isolation of *Lucumí*

Ana de la Calle's claim to be free and Lucumí made her unique and perhaps isolated her from other free women of color in colonial Trujillo. As mentioned above, in a sample of notarized manumission agreements from 1640 to 1730, only twenty, or 14 percent of the few enslaved people who gained their legalized freedom, were registered for Africans. In addition, of the African manumissions between 1700 and 1730, only four were people categorized as Araras.[43] One was for a Popo woman (in 1710) and another was for Juan Bautista, who was identified in a notarized sale as a black man of *casta lucumí* and was manumitted in 1730 because of his good service.[44] Even if the Slave Coast polities shared linguistic and cultural connections (as Thornton suggests) there were few freed people from the Bight of Benin to form a cohort for Ana de la Calle suggesting the special status of Lucumí. Why did it matter that Ana de la Calle articulated a rather unique identity in colonial Trujillo?

Ana de la Calle did not document a network with other free women of color; instead, she articulated a patronage relationship that resembled connections between freed women and their former owners. Apart from her husbands (one deceased and one living) and her children, she named only one other person in her will. She requested that a prominent cleric, don Ambrosio Girón de Estrada, serve as executor of her estate. According to subsequent civil cases, Girón de Estrada, who was the local bishop's assistant, owned the mortgage on Ana de la Calle's house and had been the primary customer of her bread-making business. Ana de la Calle did not name Girón de Estrada as her former owner; she indicated that he was her patron—for better or worse. She may have acted like other freed women who also named patrons who had been former owners. In her 1675 will, Ana Juana Pardo, a *mulata* from the Alto Peruvian (Bolivian) city of Cochabamba living in Trujillo, declared that her "industry and personal work" and the charity of her owner, the current bishop of Panama, were what had enabled her to free herself.[45] By firmly declaring that her husband had "never had the capacity or intelligence or know how to look for ordinary sustenance," Ana Juana Pardo asserted that she had paid for her manumission with the assistance of her owner, whose patronage she had cultivated. She recognized that her relationship with her owner, not her husband (who had abandoned her), had contributed to her free status. Freed women of color sometimes publicly recognized the past or continuing patronage of their former owner. For example, María de Alvarado took (or was given) the name of her former owner when she paid for her manumission.[46] Regardless of the arrangements that did or did not include manumission, freed people of color continued to mark their patronage relationships in colonial Trujillo in public and personal ways. Their example suggests that Ana de la Calle may have named the bishop's assistant as a patron who continued as a significant figure in her life even after she had achieved freed status.

Unlike her connections with white men, Ana de la Calle did not document close relationships with other free women of color even though she, her daughter, and her granddaughter married free men of color. In contrast, other free women of color named networks with other people of African descent in order to secure and to maintain the freedom of their families. For example, Ana de Montoya, a fugitive slave woman, accessed a network of urban free people in 1681, when she left her infant daughter on the doorstep of Beatriz de Valverde, a free *parda*. For eleven years, Beatriz de Valverde and her free daughters hid the young *mulata* by first having an indigenous neighbor baptize the infant in the Indian urban parish and then claiming that the child was a relative.[47] The women of Beatriz de Valverde's family relied on arguments regarding the child's parentage to deceive Ana de Montoya's owner. Yet the real strength was their extensive connections, which included ties with a female neighbor and the other enslaved and free women of color who testified in the resulting trial that the child belonged to the Valverde family. Their explanations reveal two distinct yet overlapping networks: one of free urban women of color who raised the young *mulata* (and even sheltered her in the convent) and one of enslaved rural women who relayed information between the adopted family and the fugitive enslaved woman. While we lack additional information regarding Ana de la Calle's associations, her will and her descendants' subsequent civil cases do not provide evidence of similar ties to free or enslaved women outside her household.

Most interestingly, Ana de la Calle was not a member of Trujillo's religious confraternities and thus was not included in any of the most prominent public institutions open to people of color of the colonial city. For example, she was not a member of the religious brotherhood of Nuestra Señora del Rosario, a popular choice for wealthy and honorable men and women of color in Guayaquil, Mexico City, Goiás (Brazil), and other colonial urban centers.[48] A religious brotherhood would pay for a public burial for its members complete with a Mass and a public procession. In Trujillo, Ana Juana Pardo, the freed *mulata* from Cochabamba, was an active member of Nuestra Señora del Rosario and even kept articles (such as a small table) used for the festival of the revered saint in her home.[49] She was considered wealthy enough to belong to Nuestra Señora del Rosario partly because she supported herself from the daily wages of her enslaved *conga* woman. It is thus likely that she had the funds to pay membership dues and could claim that she did not work outside her home, a signifier of honor among colonial women. Her active participation in the pious organization helped reproduce her status as a *recogida*, or honorable, publicly withdrawn woman.

Claiming a similarly prestigious status, Francisca de Esparca, a free *parda*, was a member of two religious brotherhoods, including Nuestra Señora del Rosario. Francisca de Esparca's list of small debts and her collection of tables and chairs suggests that she ran a tavern or an eatery on her piece of property in Trujillo. Francisca de Esparca was not as wealthy as Ana Juana Pardo. A patron had donated a house to Esparca, and she owned no other property besides her clothing and modest household goods. Still, unlike Ana Juana Pardo, who had to free herself (and thus could identify herself as a freed *mulata*), Francisca de Esparca was a free *parda* and the daughter of a free *morena*. Though Francisca de Esparca could not name her father (and therefore would have been considered an illegitimate daughter), free people of color considered her honorable enough to be accepted into their religious brotherhood. Her membership and her publicly recognized descent from free parents (even if one was not publically acknowledged) mutually reinforced her claim to an elite status within a free colored community.

While confraternities were prestigious, they did not exclude Africans. In Trujillo, Beatriz de Siles, a free *morena* of *casta congo* was a member of a religious brotherhood. Siles may have been a practicing Catholic and a member of Nuestra Señora del Rosario in West Central Africa before her enslavement in the Americas.[50] She expressed both her Catholicism and her free status through her membership in and generous donations to the confraternity.[51] Other confraternities included Africans, including the impoverished San Nicolas de Tolentino. Unlike the prestigious Nuestra Señora del Rosario, the membership of the more humble brotherhood included enslaved Senegambians and indigenous urban laborers. Nonetheless, Ana de la Calle was not a member. It is plausible that if Ana de la Calle was sold from the Bight of Benin, she probably was not exposed to Catholicism until a perfunctory baptism in São Tomé or in Cartagena.[52] Yet she paid for a funeral for herself and for her first husband in the Franciscan church, suggesting that she was a publicly practicing Catholic but was not a member of the religious institutions of her supposed peers. Why?

For free women of color, public religious institutions provided a way to achieve honorable status as well as a mechanism of marking their public prestige. Ana Juana Pardo and Francisca de Esparca, free women and members of the Nuestra Señora del Rosario confraternity, maintained religious shrines in their households and left legal documents indicating their disavowal of intimate relationships with men. In particular, Ana Juana Pardo declared that her husband "was of no use" and that he had abandoned her fifteen years before she composed her will.[53] Francisca de Esparca did not marry. In contrast, Ana de la Calle spared no expense when she buried her first husband. She also left special provisions in her will that stipulated that her second husband be provided with a stipend and a room until his death. Ana Juana Pardo and Francisca de Esparca created connotations of religious removal from worldly and secular affairs. Combined with their Catholic religiosity, they presented themselves as lay holy women. In both cases, the women maintained households and property to earn a modest living and to maintain a version of honorary seclusion.[54] In contrast, Ana de la Calle did not mimic these claims and perhaps did not replicate the claims to gendered honorable status of her peers.

Even women of color involved in judicial cases to prove their free status would have attempted to maintain some level of honorable removal from public labor. Manuela de Punine, the daughter of a Quito indigenous noble and an African-descent woman, maintained honorable, withdrawn residence in the house of a militia lieutenant while her case was being litigated. Petronila de Avila managed to find refuge for her niece in a convent while she argued for the minor's freedom.[55] In both cases, free women of color sought to protect their honor (or those of others) by removing themselves (or those in question) from public view. Honorable status was coupled with an honorable livelihood. Most wealthy women of color owned property that enabled them to earn enough income to support their households. María de Herrera (a free *parda*) and Elena de Serrobeno (also a free *parda*) owned houses in the city that they rented or sold. Josefa de Escobar (another free *parda*) owned an enslaved man who earned wages to support her.[56] In these cases, free women of color managed significant investments that meant that they did not have to perform manual labor or work outside their homes.

Ana de la Calle may not have had the ability (or the inclination) to claim these types of honorable removed status. In her will she called herself Ana de la Calle or "of the Street," indicating that she allowed or proudly declared her work in her own name. She sold bread, probably along the alleys and thoroughfares of Trujillo.[57] There, she likely joined free and enslaved women of color who sold prepared food and produce. By the time of her death, perhaps the enslaved woman Isabel Lucumí assisted in the baking and selling. When understood in the context of her life achievements, Ana de la Calle may have claimed her past through her name, suggesting that she did not or could not choose the withdrawn status that propertied free women of Trujillo claimed.

While she did not participate in the Catholic institutions for free women of color, Ana de la Calle was not alone in her public livelihood. Other free women in Trujillo made their living in very visible positions. Elena de Paz tended the store of a Chicama landholder, watched his home when he was away, and cooked for all the members of his large household. When her status as a free woman was publicly contested, she maintained that her family was free and that she, a free woman, earned her living by serving within and outside the slaveholder's house.[58] Similarly, Antonia Giron ran a store with her husband and asserted that she was a married woman who was living honestly and decently, much like Ana de la Calle.[59]

Other free women of color claimed a public religious piety to accompany their free status. María de Segura, a free *mulata* whose father recognized her but did not marry her mother, was also not a member of the Nuestra Señora del Rosario confraternity. Like other women of color, María de Segura entered her marriage with a modest dowry and worked with her husband to purchase two enslaved African women. The urban free woman had a number of small debts and loans when she composed her will, indicating that she had active trade networks. Moreover, she (not her husband) owned warehouses in Trujillo's port, suggesting that she participated in the lucrative coastal trade in liquor, lumber, and tools. María de Segura claimed her imperfections. Though she had children who were born legitimately, she confessed to having a number of illegitimate children who carried her surname.[60] As petty merchants, María de Segura and her *pardo* husband were among the wealthiest free people of color in colonial Trujillo, yet she did not own religious imagery or claim membership in the local religious institutions. Instead, María de Segura, like Ana de la Calle, advanced her family through economic stability, not the standards of Catholic piety. Whether or not they were integrated into the honorable and religious networks of free people of color, María de Segura and Ana de la Calle achieved a financial success that they communicated in their wills with tangible pride.

With or without the acceptance of a particular sector of free people of color, Ana de la Calle claimed powerful terms when she named herself as *morena*, Lucumí, and "of the street." Perhaps the combination of these terms added extra insurance to her status, especially if she or the notary did not include doña in her list of titles or claim a particular confraternity membership. Ana de la Calle created her will as legal proof of her free status so that her family could call on this notarized document during any litigation that might (and did) arise later. Using all the tools at her disposal, including the unlikely term of Lucumí, she claimed free and respectable status in the multiple terms of identity available to members of Trujillo's African Diaspora.

Conclusions

Heterogeneous and somewhat smaller communities of Africans and their descendants were more likely in the Andean nations of the Pacific Rim than among their Caribbean or Brazilian counterparts. Sold as domestic servants to urban households or laborers on rural estates, enslaved and free Africans drew on their cultural interpretations and societal affinities to articulate diasporic identities. Among those from the Bight of Benin polities, shared languages and cultural forms may have provided a basis for the expression of affinities that hint at religious communities or public ranks that are not visible in the secular archives of a provincial city. Identities were collective affairs, and other enslaved and free people provided a discerning audience for Ana de la Calle's claims. Even though captives from the Bight of Benin were a significant majority in urban and rural Trujillo by the early eighteenth century, they had not yet achieved free status and thus were not peers (by colonial standards) for propertied women of color. Although she is unusual in the archival records, Ana de la Calle was not alone in her claims to an elite status if that status is understood within the larger context of the colonial northern coast. Even if local slaveholders confused Arara with Lucumí, women and men such as Ana de la Calle left evidence of how they chose to be identified. For Ana de la Calle, multiple indications of her elite or at least superior status were required given her multiple audiences.

Categories such as Lucumí were both a tool for members of the African Diaspora and a clue about their identities for historians. As evidenced by Ana de la Calle's claim to be a free *morena* of *casta lucumí*, her identity served to advance and to mark her status simultaneously. She, like other urban enslaved and free people, had access to ecclesiastical institutions or could have seized on her right as a baptized or married Catholic to express public identities that had significant meaning in the Diaspora. Yet her claim to Lucumí identity hints at submerged strategies of African communities on the Pacific coast that were not understood by Spanish slaveholders. Besides the vigilant Jesuits who tried in vain to write an "Angolan grammar" in Peru and the observations of fathers Pedro Claver and Alonso de Sandoval in Cartagena, local colonizers and royal officials seemed ignorant or confused by the critical cultural distinctions among enslaved and free people.[61] Perhaps the notaries and their scribes, especially those frequented by Trujillo's free people of color, were not so mystified. They were happy to be paid or knew, as did Ana de la Calle, that there were many terms that enslaved and free people used to describe their identities. Royal mandates were repetitive, and slaveholders used a limited vocabulary that named the status of Africans and their descendants (as slaves or free) and some variables that identified descent (such as *mulato* or *zambo*). Yet free and enslaved people re-articulated how status was marked in multicultural polities, vast commercial networks, and intricate hierarchies of home communities in West and West Central Africa. Transatlantic categories such as Lucumí interacted with gender positions in rural and urban arenas in the Americas to further complicate the meanings of *morena* or *negra*. Through these categories, northern coastal Africans and their descendants claimed multiple identities by imagining communities and kin within—and beyond—the hegemonic boundaries of colonial terminology.

Appendix A. African Slaves Sold in Trujillo, 1670–1720

Castas	1670	1680	1690	1700	1710	1720
Biojo	0	1	0	0	0	0
Folupe	0	1	1	1	0	0
Baños/Bañol	1	0	0	0	0	0
Capo Verde/Guinea	0	1	3	1	0	1
Mandinga	1	0	0	4	0	1
Sape/Zage	1	1	0	0	0	0
Mina	8	0	7	3	16	23
Lucumí	3	0	2	7	11	7
Arara	37	2	8	35	21	18
Popo	3	0	0	22	4	1
Carabalí	3	0	0	9	0	2
Congo	13	8	12	39	4	14
Angola	4	0	0	6	0	0
Malemba	1	0	0	0	0	0
Other	1	0	0	4	1	2
Totals	237	29	54	211	137	132

Source: These numbers are based on a sample of surviving slave sales in the notary records of the ADL. For the full sample, see O'Toole, "Inventing Difference," Appendix C.

Appendix B. Adult Baptisms by Casta, Sagrario Parish, Trujillo, 1690–1730

	Arara	Lucumí	Popo	Mina	Chala	Carabalí	Congo/ Angola	Cancan	Mandinga	Yolofa/ Bran
1690	0	0	2	0	0	0	1	0	0	0
1695	3	0	1	0	0	0	3	0	0	0
1700	1	0	2	1	0	1	1	0	0	0
1705	1	3	0	0	0	0	3	0	1	0
1710	5	4	3	3	4	3	5	0	0	2
1715	7	3	2	0	3	0	1	0	2	0
1720	13	1	2	3	8	3	12	0	0	0
1725	6	0	1	5	9	5	10	7	1	0
1730	7	0	0	1	2	1	1	3	0	0

Source: Archivo Parroquia El Sagrario, Iglesia San Francisco, Trujillo, Libro de bautismos de mistis, 1717–1729.

Notes

I thank Joan Bristol, Sherwin Bryant, Leo Garofalo, Karen Graubart, Ann Kakaliouras, Silvia Lara, Charles Beatty-Medina, Jeremy Mumford, and Ben Vinson III for their suggestions on multiple versions of this essay as well as participants at the Tepoztlán Institute for Transnational History of the Americas (2005) and audience members at the Conference on Latin American History, American Historical Association Conference (Philadelphia, January 2006). Research funding for this chapter was provided by the American Historical Association's Albert J. Beveridge Grant for Research in the History of the Western Hemisphere (2003), a Faculty Research Support Grant from Villanova University (2004), a John Carter Brown Library Post-Doctoral Research Fellowship funded by the National Endowment for the Humanities (2004), and a HASTAC Residential Research Fellowship of the Law in Slavery and Freedom Project (coordinated by Rebecca Scott and Martha Jones) at the Institute for the Humanities, University of Michigan (2006–2007).

1. Archivo Departamental de La Libertad (hereafter ADL), Trujillo, Peru, Cabildo Ordinarias (hereafter Ca. Ord.), leg. 41, exp. 753, "Expediente seguido por don Ambrosio Giron de Estrada promotor fiscal del obispado de Trujillo albacea de Ana de la Calle, morena libre difunta contra don Faustino de Vidaurre albacea y tenedor de bienes de doña María de la Cruz Cavero difunta sobre pago de los carridos que estubiere debiendo del censo impuesto acerca de la casa que hubo y heredo de la dha," 1727, folio 8.

2. Like other *castas* in colonial Latin America (including *español*), notaries did not capitalize the term. In modern usage, this identity would be capitalized.

3. Berlin, *Many Thousands Gone*, 39–45; Morgan, "The Cultural Implications of the Atlantic Slave Trade."

4. Thornton, *Africa and Africans in the Making of the Atlantic World*; Sweet, *Recreating Africa*.

5. Mann, "Shifting," 6. This direction James Sweet has further developed in his second book, *Domingos Álvares.*

6. Equiano, *The Interesting Narrative of the Life of Olaudah Equiano*; Baquaqua, *The Biography of Mahommah Gardo Baquaqua.*

7. Chambers, "Tracing Igbo into the African Diaspora," 57, 60.

8. Gomez, *Exchanging Our Country Marks*, 4, 6, 13.

9. For an example of regional cultural zones affiliated with specific terms, see Thornton, *Africa and Africans.*

10. Caron, "'Of a nation which others do not Understand,'" 101, 113.

11. Greene, "Cultural Zones in the Era of the Slave Trade," 88, 98.

12. Fischer, *Suspect Relations*, 9, 10.

13. Brown, *Good Wives*, 109, 212.

14. Lovejoy, "Identifying Enslaved Africans in the African Diaspora," 10, 11; Lovejoy and Trotman, "Introduction," 2.

15. Bowser, *The African Slave in Colonial Peru*, 341; O'Toole, "Inventing Difference," 8.

16. Tardieu, *El Negro en el Cuzco*, 127, 130.

17. Hünefeldt, *Paying the Price of Freedom*, 117, 177.

18. ADL, Protocolos Paz, leg. 202, numero 84, 1637, folio 177v.

19. Garofalo, "Conjuring with Coca," 69.

20. Hünefeldt, *Paying the Price of Freedom*, 109, 117.

21. Bowser, *The African Slave in Colonial Peru*, 317–319.

22. Morales, "Arquitectura virreynal," 79; Cussen, "Fray Martín de Porres," 177, 218.

23. O'Toole, "Castas y representación en Trujillo colonial," 52–54.

24. Archivo Arzobispal de Lima (hereafter AAL), Apelaciones de Trujillo, leg. 23, exp. 9, "Trujillo. Martín Alonso Romero, en nombre de Margarita de Alvarado, morena libre, vecina de la ciudad de Trujillo, como madre de Antonia Simona, Tomasa y Francisco, mulatos, apela de la sentencia pronunciada por el juez que los declaró esclavos," 1697, folios 3, 7v.

25. ADL, Corregimiento Criminales (hereafter Co. Cr.), leg. 247, exp. 2616, "Mandamiento de don Francisco Pitta Catrillón, corregidor de Trujillo para que se haga cabeza de proceso contra un negro de casta arara Sebastian esclavo del maestro de campo don Albaro Cabero Tinoco, por haber dado de puñaladas a Alonso Rodriguez, su mayordomo," 1677, folios 2v and 6v; ADL, Ca. Ord., leg. 203, exp. 1446, "Auto del Capitán don Juan Ruíz de Lallana Alvarado, Theniente General de Corregidor y Justicia Mayor de Trujillo, para que el presente escribano ponga fe de muerte de doña María de Acosta, viuda de Gabriel Solano y se haga inventario de sus bienes que hubiere dejado," 1681, folios 47 and 50; ADL, Ca. Ord., leg. 25, exp. 533, "Provisión Real receptoria para hacer provanza en las ciudades de Chachapoyas y Trujillo ante las justicias de ellas por parte de Andrés Saenz de Salas en la causa executiva que contra él sigue don Pedro Jaramillo de Córdova sobre pago de 2350 pesos de a 8 reales procedidos del tabaco que le vendió," 1681, folios 11 and 15.

26. Hanger, "Patronage, Property and Persistence," 56.

27. ADL, Ca. Ord., leg. 209, exp. 1556, "Autos seguidos por el Cap. don Joseph Zenteno Machado de Chávez, alcalde ordinario de Trujillo; albacea y tenedor de bienes del Cap. don Manuel Zenteno Machado de Chávez, su hermano; sobre entrega de una mulatilla Ana," 1692, folios 4, 5v, and 7.

28. ADL, Ca. Ord., leg. 37, exp. 714, "Autos que sigue el Defensor de Menores de este Corregimiento don Ignacio de Salinas por lo que toca a Valentina de San Joseph, parda libre, menor de 25 años sobre que seponga por causa de estos autos testimonio del testamento de Joseph Ortiz de Morales que en su nombre otorgó y en virtud de su poder el Capitán don Francisco Risco," 1718, folios 1 and 10v.

29. Burns, "Notaries, Truth, and Consequences," para. 38; Burns, *Into the Archive*, 102.

30. Burns, "Notaries, Truth, and Consequences," para. 48.

31. Law, *The Kingdom of Allada*, 43.

32. Thornton, *Africa and Africans in the Making of the Atlantic World*, 33, 190; Law, *The Kingdom of Allada*, 43.

33. Law, *The Slave Coast of West Africa*, 188; Law, "Ethnicity and the Slave Trade," 209–210.

34. Greene, "Cultural Zones in the Era of the Slave Trade," 98.

35. Eltis, Lovejoy, and Richardson, "Slave-Trading Ports," 20.

36. See Appendix A.

37. See Appendix B.

38. Law, *The Kingdom of Allada*, 101, 102.

39. Law, *The Oyo Empire*, 226.

40. Ibid., 228.

41. Barbot, *Barbot on Guinea*, 2:639; Sandoval, *Un Tratado sobre la esclavitud*, 123–124.

42. ADL, Ca. Ord., leg. 41, exp. 753, 1727, folio 1.

43. Francisco Arara in ADL, Protocolos Cortijo, leg. 110, 1700, folio 577; María Arara in ADL, Protocolos Espino y Alvarado, leg. 161, numero 238, 1705, folios 326v–327v; Isabel, *casta arara*, in ADL, Protocolos Espino, leg. 329, 1720, folio 227v; María, *casta arara*, in ADL, Protocolos Espino, leg. 338, 1730, folio 433.

44. María Popo in ADL, Protocolos Cortijo, leg. 120, 1710, folio 388v; Juan Bautista in ADL, Protocolos Espino, leg. 338, 1730, folio 102v.

45. ADL, Protocolos Alvarez, leg. 90, numero 178, 1675, folio 366.

46. AAL, Apelaciones de Trujillo, leg. 23, exp. 9, 1697, folios 9, 17v, and 23v.

47. ADL, Ca. Ord., leg. 209, exp. 1556, 1692, folio 2.

48. Garay Arellano, "La Elite económica de los negros en Guayaquil de 1742 a 1765," 115; von Germeten, *Black Blood Brothers*, 104–105, 124; Karasch, "Free Women of Color in Central Brazil," 259.

49. ADL, Protocolos Alvarez, leg. 90, numero 178, 1675, folios 363v and 365.

50. Sweet, *Recreating Africa*, 191–197.

51. ADL, Protocolos García Sancho, leg. 166, numero 31, 1660.

52. Sandoval, *Un Tratado sobre la esclavitud*, 413; Valtierra, "El Padre Alonso de Sandoval," xiv.

53. ADL, Protocolos Alvarez, leg. 90, numero 178, 1675, folio 366.

54. Van Deusen, *Between the Sacred and the Worldly*.

55. ADL, Ca. Ord., leg. 199, exp. 1364, "Autos de demanda que Manuela de Punine, samba sigue contra Onofre de Montoya, su amo; sobre que se le declare libre y no sujeta a servidumbre," 1670, folios 2–2v; Archivo Arzobispal de Trujillo, Trujillo, Peru, Testamentos, leg. 3, 1672, folio 1.

56. ADL, Protocolos Espino y Alvarado, leg. 161, numero 21, 1704, folio 28; ADL, Protocolos Espino y Alvarado, leg. 161, numero 326, 1706, folio 469v; ADL, Protocolos Espino y Alvarado, leg. 161, numero 513, 1707, folio 672; ADL, Protocolos Espino y Alvarado, leg. 161, numero 189, 1705, folio 253.

57. ADL, Ca. Ord., leg. 41, exp. 752, "Expediente seguido por el alferez don Faustino Vidaurre como marido lex. de Juana de Silva, albacea, heredero, y tenedor de bienes de María de la Cruz Cavero su suegra difunta contra el alferez Baltasar de los Reyes, pardo libre, vecino de Trujillo sobre que desocupe el cuarto de la casa situada en la calle del Postigo del dean," 1727, folio 1.

58. ADL, Ca. Ord., leg. 196, exp. 1319, "Expediente seguido por Elena de Paz y Vela, mulata en la causa de demanda contra el maestro de campo don Juan de Herrera Salazar, alferez real y regidor perpetuo de Trujillo; sobre su libertad, de sus hijos y nietos con lo demás deducido," 1663.

59. ADL, Ca. Ord., leg. 204, exp. 1455, "Expediente seguido por fray Pedro Galindo, presidente del convento Nuestra Señora de la Merced, contra Antonia Giron, negra libre, sobre pago al dicho convento de 87 pesos y 3 reales del alquiler de una tienda en que vive," 1682, folios 1 and 4.

60. ADL, Protocolos Espino y Alvarado, leg. 149, numeros 75, 1684, folios 122–124v.

61. Tardieu, "Jesuitas y la 'lengua de Angola' en Peru (siglo XVII)"; Sandoval, *Un Tratado sobre la esclavitud*, 370, 373–374; Fernández, *Apostólica y Penitente*, 107.

PART 2

Royal Subjects, Loyal Christians, and Saints in the Alley

4

Between the Cross and the Sword

Religious Conquest and Maroon Legitimacy in Colonial Esmeraldas

CHARLES BEATTY-MEDINA

It has repeatedly been remarked that the beginning of African slavery in Spanish America brought with it the earliest rejection of slave life. Revolt, rebellion, and escape, along with myriad other forms of resistance, emerged in Spain's colonies in the 1500s. Among these, perhaps the most successful (and longest lasting) was escape followed by the formation of maroon societies. Colonies across Spanish America—in Panama, Santo Domingo, Mexico, Colombia, and Peru—witnessed the formation of communities (and sometimes roaming bands) of escaped slaves. In many cases they were short lived, but others, such as the maroons of Esmeraldas, managed to maintain their independence for longer periods of time. Unlike other maroon societies, the Esmeraldas maroons began independent life as runaways and as castaways. Their escape resulted from shipwrecks on the coast of Ecuador in a region where ships frequently ran aground. From the sixteenth through the eighteenth centuries, Esmeraldas contained few (and often sporadic) Spanish settlements. As a result, the maroons enjoyed extensive interactions with the region's native population.

A combination of conflict and cooperation at the initial meeting between the maroons and local native communities in the mid-sixteenth century evolved into political and social alliances as well as territorial competition in the region. The charter group of Africans that landed in 1550 numbered approximately twenty-five. They intermarried with native people, produced a mixed-race progeny, and began participating in regional warfare. By the second generation, the maroons were fully fluent in local languages and customs; so much so that in 1600, the Spanish referred to them as *caciques*, or local lords, and colonial administrators legitimized their rule. The union of Africans and natives thus gave birth to a new ethnic entity called *mulatos*. Later they would be known by one of the *casta* labels for the offspring of African and Indian unions: *zambos*.

Although it might not seem to be the case, understanding how missionizing and religious conversion was viewed among maroon societies in early colonial Spanish America is critical for understanding the politics of African resistance in the Iberian Atlantic world. While missionizing among native peoples provided the moral underpinnings of conquest in the sixteenth century, it also proved to be an important tool of pacification among Africans who escaped slavery and made their home on the demographically devastated landscape of the post-conquest period.[1] As Joan Bristol's chapter in this volume makes clear, perceptions of Christian practice among communities of African descent acquired importance in the colonial context. In Ecuador, Santo Domingo, Mexico, and Panama, legitimizing and non-violently "pacifying" maroon societies depended largely on their acceptance of Spanish Catholicism. Moreover, Christianization often turned on the relationships that maroons formed with Catholic clerics—and at times with secular authorities as well. While Spanish cultural hegemony worked to inculcate religious submission, some individuals of African descent transformed Christianization into a political tool of subaltern agency.[2] Maroons, like other Africans throughout Spanish America, quickly learned that Catholicism was the essential condition of political legitimation. Yet the adoption of Christianity did not preclude maroon agency or interrupt the development and evolution of local practices that observed religious traditions of both African and indigenous American origin. This chapter examines Afro-Amerindian maroon communities on the coast of early colonial Ecuador to understand how Christianization became an indispensable tool for Afro-Amerindian rebels seeking legitimation and continued autonomy on the frontiers of Spain's empire and within an African diasporic world. While an Afro-Christian diasporic identity may have been in its formative stage during the sixteenth century, transfers of knowledge between the old world and the new were readily apparent in European interactions with maroons on the Esmeraldas coast. This case study of the maroons of colonial Ecuador will allow us to see in three acts, or phases, how clerical intervention and the discourse of

Christian conversion shaped colonization over time: ultimately yielding a modus vivendi between rebel African slaves and Spanish colonial authorities. My analysis begins with a vignette from the end of the period I examine—the four decades from 1577 to 1617.

On December 18, 1605, in the coastal town of San Mateo in colonial Quito, Fray Hernando de Hincapie, a Mercedarian missionary, provided sworn testimony against his congregation, the *mulatos* of Esmeraldas—descendants of African fugitives and unconquered coastal Amerindians who had resided on the coast of colonial Quito for over fifty years.[3] Despite their long tenure on the Quito coast, the Esmeraldeños had sworn their loyalty to the Crown only five years earlier. In 1605 they stood accused of carrying out devastating raids on two native communities under Spanish protection. While Fray Hincapie's devotion to his flock might have moved him to exonerate or apologize for their actions, instead he roundly condemned them. Hincapie all but accused the maroons of participating in the raids and then began to inveigh against their many bad habits. According to the catechist, in the five years he had spent proselytizing, they had not learned to lead Christian lives. Each maroon leader had five or six wives, and none would take confession. Hincapie saw the maroon leaders as little more than drunkards and laggards who had learned little of the obedience due to Christ and his servants.[4]

Fray Hincapie and others advocated a military incursion and swift punishment for the maroons, but another set of testimonies soon cast doubt on the notion that the Afro-Amerindians were no longer serving the Crown and Cross—that is, the king of Spain, to whom they had pledged their loyalty, and the Spanish Catholic Church, to which they had bound their souls through baptism. Barely a month after Hincapie made his sworn statement, a ship bound for Lima from Panama foundered on the Esmeraldas coast. The trading vessel, *Nuestra Señora de la Concepción*, lost its goods and left its passengers clinging to life as it sank into oblivion.[5] Vaguely aware of the interminable march to the nearest Spanish settlement, the survivors had few provisions and were hopelessly stranded. With hundreds of miles before them of rough coastland broken by numerous river estuaries, abrupt cliffs, and expansive bays, they would have had to hike for weeks (and maybe months) in order to reach the nearest Spanish settlement. If the marching and lack of food did not exhaust and deplete them, then bellicose Amerindians might have finished them off instead.

The passengers were spared such misfortune, however, when some days after landing, the Afro-Amerindians discovered the twenty-five passengers.

They offered them food, clothing, and shelter, and over the next weeks led them upland toward the highland city of Quito. Upon arrival, royal authorities, eager to hear of their rescue, also made inquiries to help them determine the maroons' involvement in the raids on the indigenous villages. They pointedly asked the passengers about the character of the Esmeraldeños and their "spiritual" state, apparently to determine if the maroons indeed deserved the punitive retribution suggested by Fray Hincapie.

Passengers Hernan López and Pedro de la Santa Cruz, along with others, insisted that the maroons were pious and devout Christians. The Spaniards admired the loyalty the Esmeraldeños gave their catechist and commended their selflessness in rescuing and feeding the lost and weary passengers. They made note of the new church built by the maroons and the beauty of the holy images within. For the passengers of *La Concepción*, the Afro-Amerindians were true models of Christian devotion and charity. In sum, they rejected Fray Hincapie's conclusions, casting doubt on his depiction of life in Esmeraldas.[6]

Nonetheless, the Afro-Amerindian attacks required continued investigation, and royal authorities requested numerous testimonies in their efforts to untangle the events of 1605–1606. These statements reveal that Spanish perceptions of piety and norms of Christian behavior played a meaningful role in the way authorities and colonial elites viewed and interacted with the maroon of Esmeraldas. As John Leddy Phelan has observed: "The religiosity of the seventeenth-century Spanish world stressed the pathos rather than the ethos of religion. Outward display rather than inner piety seemed to predominate."[7]

Of course, other factors colored colonizers' perspectives. Quito's principle interest in helping to establish these Afro-Amerindian settlements was the development of a shipping port in Esmeraldas. Peaceful maroons were an added benefit. Indeed, the entire structure of these communities—autonomous Afro-Amerindian villages with missionaries paid by the Crown—was a response to the repeated failure of the Spaniards to achieve direct military conquest. Thus, even as some authorities inveighed against the Esmeraldeños, Quito's royal judges were unsure if they could mount an effective retribution for the attacks. Christianization, however imperfect and unfinished, was the authorities' only viable course of intervention. Moreover, while the maroons could be seen in an illuminating and favorable light because of their conversion and piety, their independence derived from their unflagging resistance to Spanish incursions and careful diplomacy with colonial authorities.

Conversion in Three Acts: The Drama of Religious Interventions in Esmeraldas

As the preceding vignette indicates, the events in Esmeraldas reported on by Spanish administrators in the sixteenth and seventeenth centuries had little to do with the day-to-day business of survival and resistance. How the Africans who landed in Esmeraldas formed such societies with local indigenous communities and how they evolved over time can only be guessed at through reports and letters addressing issues of the moment. Testimonies of the period sprang forth during times of maroon engagement or conflict with Spanish authorities. Even clerical interventions were largely episodic and discontinuous as missionaries cycled through these communities on their rounds through the lowland region. The available documentation, therefore, denotes not process but "project." Each batch of documentation is detached in time from another and yet all are intimately tied to the successive attempts to pacify and subject the maroon communities. Furthermore, these colonial "performances" were fragmented and interrupted by lengthy intermissions of five years or more. It is their very lack of uniformity and continuity that makes the sources pertaining to sixteenth- and early seventeenth-century Esmeraldas so interesting to historians of the Atlantic diaspora, for such performative interactions allow us to see the role of religion in subduing African rebels as a complex function of colonization that came in numerous forms that were all geared toward distinct yet related ends. For maroons, these moments comprised the turning points in their struggle to successfully legitimize themselves and their communities.

From the African perspective, each intervention brought distinct challenges and opportunities. Spanish clerics of the early modern Atlantic world were not always willing partners to military conquest. Their defense of Native American rights at certain times and places questioned the prerogatives of Spanish rule. The evidence I present here demonstrates that fugitive Africans and their progeny used clerical interventions and perceptions of their adherence to Catholicism to maintain their autonomy and safety.

The three episodes I have chosen stretch from 1577, when the *audiencia* (the colonial court and ruling body in Quito) responded to the first African overtures for peace, to 1617, when Mercedarian missionaries embarked on the first joint commercial ventures with Quiteño merchants and the maroons. These events bookend the course of events on the Esmeraldas coast and shed light onto the obscure workings of early modern diasporic marronage.[8] Three distinct phases, or acts, occurred over these four decades: religious intervention as a diplomatic arm of secular authority, religious intervention as a form of advocacy and resistance, and missionizing as a path to pacification and commercial development. Each of these phases, while chronologically isolated, was interconnected. Unlike a stage show, these segments were not uniform in length, but they were intended to build up to a predicted denouement: the colonization of Esmeraldas and its people. Each act was more than a set of events. They provided experience and perspective: another lesson for Esmeraldeños and Spaniards in their attempts to find common ground. Every failure gave collective pause to the maroons and Spanish authorities, although none provided clear indications for future action. However, religious authorities found renewed inspiration in their desire to extract the wealth of potential riches and prospective souls in Esmeraldas.[9] The motivating force of material opportunity was too great to be ignored.

What follows is not an examination of maroon religion and the spiritual practices of the Esmeraldeños.[10] Rather, it is an examination of the role of Christianization in establishing a discourse of legitimation between rebel Africans and Spanish authorities. While religion formed a principle foundation of culture in Afro-Atlantic communities, it also became a meaningful part of political dialogue.[11] The Esmeraldeños were not only subjected to Christian conversion, they used agents of the church and religious rhetoric and symbols in their efforts to consolidate their position and power on the coast of colonial Ecuador. In so doing, they subverted religious indoctrination in their efforts to form independent communities based on African leadership and rule.

FIRST AND LASTING ENCOUNTERS

The first meetings between Spanish clerics and the Esmeraldeños were not missions sent with the express purpose of conversion. While some encounters had official approval, others occurred incidentally. The earliest, in 1568, took place when a priest known only as Escobar helped a maroon leader escape imprisonment. Most similar activities before 1598 cannot be considered missions, though sometimes they were missionary in character. Indeed, they might be thought of simply as "clerical interventions" because they were neither sustained by nor affiliated with a religious order. However, they served the Africans and Amerindians of Esmeraldas by revealing the role that religious authorities could play in their relations with Crown authorities. Thus, the Esmeraldeños came to realize that religion meant much more than faith in a specific set of beliefs. It occupied a central place in Spanish political thought and ritual life. The maroons also learned that clerics had significant (if somewhat narrowly defined) powers, and they did not always agree with the aims and purposes of *audiencia* judges or the local elite. This knowledge would be instrumental in the Afro-Amerindians' attempts to use the agents of religion—priests, friars, and mendicants—as a wedge between local and transatlantic colonial authorities.

In the following section, I examine first the 1577 intervention of Padre Miguel Cabello de Balboa, a case of clerical involvement as an integral part of secular colonization, and second, the case of Fray Alonso de Espinosa, who provides a less typical example of clergymen who acted to defend the interests of maroons and their followers. Each intervention adds to our understanding of the maroons' response and provides clues about how they learned to navigate the difficult waters that would lead them from a state of rebellion to the status of freedmen. With great acumen, the Esmeraldeños proved their capacity to read into the politics of these intrusions and make choices that served their interests and needs. This chapter does not take on the question of maroons' religious beliefs per se. However, it is my view that even if the Esmeraldeños had been completely cynical about Christianity and its central tenets, they knew enough to believe in the church as an institution of formidable power in colonial Spanish America.

The first example, Miguel Cabello de Balboa, provides a view of the cleric as *oficial*, a Spanish governmental official. He was first and foremost a representative of the *audiencia*. Cabello was also, however, chosen by the bishop of Quito, perhaps because he had experience as a soldier in Philip II's armies. His mission began as an attempt to make the maroons allies of the Crown by offering their leader, Alonso de Illescas, the governorship of Esmeraldas. Illescas began the dialogue that led to Cabello's mission as the result of yet another shipwreck in 1576, from which the maroons again rescued survivors. To occupy the position of *gobernador* (or officially appointed leader) Illescas would have to relocate his people from their inland *palenque*, their well-hidden hamlet, to the coast, where the *audiencia* wished him to formally establish the town of San Mateo de las Esmeraldas. While the aims of Cabello's mission were secular, his method of securing an alliance with the rebel leaders was largely based on his religious authority and his ability to demonstrate to the maroons the error of living outside the jurisdiction of the Catholic Church.

Cabello de Balboa penned a lengthy report of that visit called the *Verdadera descripción de la provincia de Esmeraldas*. As one of the earliest first-hand narratives of a maroon community in Spanish America, it is both fascinating and disappointing. It provides a vivid portrayal of Cabello's journey with detailed scenes of maroon life that would captivate almost any reader. Yet Cabello's eagerness to display and flaunt the superiority of all things Spanish leaves one wondering about its many omissions and Cabello's penchant for writing dramatic prose. Overall, there is little mention of maroon life and much on his interactions with Illescas. Without recounting the entire story, we can focus on how Cabello turned a secular mission into a religious crusade. This shift was as much a function of the literary structure of the *Verdadera descripción* as it was of actual events on the coast.[12]

Cabello casts himself throughout the work as equally representing the Church and Crown. Quito's bishop had proposed he lead the venture, and the audiencia judges agreed. He viewed his "descent" into the wilds of Esmeraldas as achieving its full value in the redemption of souls. When his peaceful mission failed, Cabello was sure that a military incursion to punish the "blacks" would open the way to salvation.

He arrived with three companions at a well-known landing point called Tacames (today known as Atacames). Cabello was authorized to offer Illescas two important rewards, or *mercedes*: the title of *gobernador* and an official pardon for his followers' misdeeds. Upon reaching the Esmeraldas shore, Cabello and his companions built a small chapel with an altar. It was then consecrated and blessed with the cross and holy images brought from Quito. Days passed before they were detected by the Esmeraldeños, and when Illescas learned of their arrival, the maroons went to visit Cabello. The Spaniards greeted him and took him immediately arm in arm to their grass-hut chapel. Cabello described how Illescas wept tears of joy and sorrow. He showed such great emotion that he moved the Spaniards to tears as well. To Cabello, the encounter seemed "blessed by God himself."[13]

A few days later, Illescas brought with him two more maroon chiefs. They were younger than Illescas and spoke only a little Spanish. The young men arrived with offerings of gold for Cabello's chapel.[14] Illescas, led them by the hand to the chapel, tutoring them to understand the symbolic importance of the little grass hut on the shore and the cross and other holy images within. The younger chiefs placed bits of gold on the altar. They swathed them in cotton, leaving the bundle as a payment for their sins. The small flecks of metal, the maroons hoped, would help them achieve legitimation and permanent release from captivity—that is, the chains that still bound them legally if not physically. Among them, only the maroon leader Alonso de Illescas, who had spent seventeen years of his life in Seville, and a Portuguese soldier who lived with the maroons easily understood the significance of the chapel and the offerings made to Cabello.[15]

Notwithstanding these gifts, Cabello became the firebrand. He reminded the maroon leader and his followers that they had fallen into great sin and that living away from a Spanish settlement, away from the Holy Church, made their offense even greater. They had placed themselves outside the physical space of redemption and salvation. Their rebellion had left them to languish in an "untamed" land that of itself was a cause of evil: a quagmire for God's workers and a factory for the devil. These many pronouncements, which Cabello made to Illescas and his people both publicly and privately were but the strong stick to match the carrot of new titles and legitimation sent by the *audiencia*. But the rebels rejected the offer in the end. At the moment when the maroons were to resettle, war erupted among the chieftaincies. Something—Cabello was unsure what—created such furor among the maroons and their allies that even he could not imagine the cause. In all likelihood the conflict resulted from fear over the specter of Spanish colonization and Alonso de Illescas' attempt to heighten his own power. Cabello and his men could only flee. Miguel Cabello de Balboa never returned to Esmeraldas.

THE APOSTOLIC MISSIONARY

Between 1578 and 1583, Spanish plans to subjugate Esmeraldas veered toward military conquest and clerical interventions of the period took a new direction. Fray Alonso de Espinosa , a member of the Trinitarian order, emerged as a passionate advocate for maroon autonomy. His influence in Esmeraldas empowered the Afro-Amerindian rebels and infuriated authorities and elites in Quito. Like Cabello, Espinosa was not a long-term resident of Quito. He arrived from Spain by way of Lima as a novice of an order founded in 1198 to free crusaders from captivity in the Holy Land. As with members of the major orders, such as Dominicans and Franciscans, Trinitarians were mendicants, dedicated to preaching the gospel and serving the poor. Unlike the major orders, Trinitarians had no mandate to travel and serve in the Americas. As a rule, all members of religious orders had to receive permission to travel and minister in Spain's colonies. Most likely Espinosa traveled to Peru without declaring his affiliation. Upon arriving in Quito, however, he attached himself to the Mercedarians.

Quiteños had little reason to scrutinize the young friar who offered to serve the soldiers sent to conquer Esmeraldas in 1583. Only five years after Cabello's failed mission, Quito's authorities placed their hope in Diego López de Zúñiga, newly named *gobernador* of the region. López de Zúñiga gathered nearly a hundred Spanish soldiers for an expedition to conquer the maroons and find the region's legendary gold and emeralds. The incursion had been under way for a few months when López de Zúñiga's wife, Doña Mayor de

Bastides, received word that the men were struggling with disease and dying. She sent Espinosa with two soldiers to find and help them. By that time, most of the expeditionaries were returning to Quito decimated and dejected. They had seen no more than a few Afro-Amerindians, and they had lost at least seven men to disease.[16] Fray Espinosa, who was sent to minister to the sick and dying, instead encountered the "*mulatos y negros*." He found them distraught over the recent Spanish incursion. Espinosa immediately befriended them and persuaded the maroons to submit to Gobernador López de Zúñiga. But the *gobernador*'s desire for gold was greater than his will to establish a settlement or pacify the maroons. López de Zúñiga coerced a number of the Esmeraldeños to guide his men to the source of the region's mineral riches, but they found nothing. After two unsuccessful journeys, López de Zúñiga retired, but Fray Espinosa stayed on, transformed by the experience.

Over the next few years Espinosa became the maroons' loyal advocate. From his letters we can identify many of the maroons' desires and goals. And from the maroons' correspondence and actions we can detect Espinosa's ideas and support. However, they were not coequal. Espinosa endeavored to shape maroon aims under a benign colonial authority. The maroons hoped to retain their independence and autonomy within a Christian missionary context. The conflict between these goals was not immediately visible, perhaps even to the players involved, but as they surfaced, both the maroon leaders and Spanish authorities increasingly expected Espinosa to act solely as their advocate.

Espinosa began by writing numerous times to the Crown and the *audiencia* about Esmeraldas and the maroons in attempts to resolve the conflicts between two hopeful colonizers: López de Zúñiga and Rodrigo de Ribadenyra, a wealthy Quiteño merchant with commercial interests in the region. Ultimately Espinosa denounced López de Zúñiga to the Crown, stating: "When the governor reached the Bay of San Mateo he sent a captain with soldiers to capture the blacks and mulattoes at night. His intent was to torment them due to his greed and desire for gold. The soldiers were detected and your vassals escaped and they knew that your governor had no good intentions."[17]

In Espinosa's letter the maroons were not criminals subjugating the indigenous people but *desventurados*, unfortunates. They were not heathens in the lap of sin but wretches living barbarously with an "extremely intense desire to be instructed in the laws of god so that they may save themselves."[18] For Espinosa, the maroon chief Illescas was not an element to be stamped out and brought to justice (as Cabello and others had advocated), he was "the key to the land because it is under his hand and dominion."[19]

Finally, Espinosa had some things to say about the *audiencia*. During his first stay in Esmeraldas, Espinosa convinced the maroons to send representatives directly to Quito to speak with Oidor (Judge) Pedro Venegas de Cañaveral. The two "Indian chiefs" who went to Quito and stood before the judges, were, in Espinosa's words, "poorly treated, they [the judges] sent them back to their land alone or to where God may help them."[20] From the *audiencia*'s perspective, the meeting was quite different. Oidor Cañaveral simply wrote that four "*indios*" arrived in Quito, where they were well treated.[21]

In time, the Crown granted Ribadenyra license to conquer the region, but all parties realized that military conquest would be costly and ineffective. Thus, following López de Zúñiga's failure, Espinosa appeared to be the *audiencia*'s only hope. Even though the young friar had been critical of Oidor Cañaveral, they expected that he would successfully pacify the maroons. In 1586, Espinosa was sent into the province once more. This time he was well supplied with cheeses, hams, sugar, and biscuits, along with gifts for the maroons: machetes, combs, butchers' knives, and hats.[22]

At the same time, Rodrigo de Ribadenyra also started to make serious overtures toward the Esmeraldeños, showering them with additional gifts and expecting that Fray Espinosa would convince them to submit. Each time Espinosa encouraged them to do so, the maroons refused. Nonetheless, they strongly defended their relationship with Espinosa and sought to maintain it for the "good of their souls" and as a buffer with Spanish authorities.

A letter to the *audiencia* and the Crown from maroon chief Alonso de Illescas in 1586 made his position clear on both matters. The maroons would submit, but they would not aid Ribadenyra. They wished to serve the Crown, but they did not trust the captains and soldiers who had entered the province. They desired a priest to instruct them in Christianity, but they only trusted "the devoted father who we trust because we understand from his heart the great kindness that he has to pacify us."[23] This did not seem to be Espinosa's goal, and yet the letters make clear that the young priest came to see the maroon leader as the true chief and lord of the region.

In his article on Esmeraldas, historian Adam Szaszdi referred to Alonso de Espinosa's stay among the maroons as his "*apostolado*," or his apostleship, perhaps because in Szazdi's view, Espinosa was a true missionary.[24] He seemed to humbly reflect the ideals of his order: to redeem those made captive.[25] Interestingly, at first the African maroons were not the captives that Espinosa liberated; rather, it was Amerindians that the Africans had captured years earlier! Another view of this apostleship might be Espinosa's willingness to dedicate himself to his new flock. One thing is certain, however; even with lofty aims it appeared that Espinosa could not extricate himself from the fierce competitive atmosphere among Quito's religious orders. In his first letter, he made clear that he would protect his right to remain among the Esmeraldeños, "because after I have pacified the land no other clerics should enter and take possession of her and throw me out as so often happens."[26]

Additionally, Illescas's letter declared that he wished himself to be named *gobernador*—the position presented to him years earlier by Miguel Cabello de Balboa on the orders of the *audiencia*. Espinosa underwrote Illescas' declaration in one of his own letters to the Crown and supported the move when he delivered that letter to the *audiencia* in Quito accompanied by another maroon leader named Juan Mangache. It proved to be a turning point. After receiving Mangache and Espinosa and realizing that Illescas would not yield, the authorities turned against young Fray Espinosa, deciding that he was no longer suited to the task. They charged Espinosa and Mangache soon after with the death of a soldier named Diego Felipe and then began to heap further accusations upon them: from collaboration with enemies of Spain to the sin of *nefando*, or sodomy.[27] In 1587 the *audiencia* even wrote to the Crown accusing Espinosa of making himself into a native leader: "the *fraile* emerged [from the land] naked with a long beard and mustache carrying a spear and with a small Indian page." They stated that Espinosa had not only taken advantage of the Amerindians but that he damaged them with his bad customs and habits.[28] Espinosa was accused of treachery against the state and the corruption of souls. The Crown and the Council of the Indies did not seem to mind the accusations. They sent an immediate order for Alonso de Espinosa's arrest and for his return to Spain to face charges. And in 1589 they restricted the entry of all Trinitarians to any part of the Americas.[29]

Between 1577 and 1587, the maroons had lived through at least two very different types of Christian intervention. Cabello de Balboa's expedition showed them that state and religious authorities worked in tandem, while Espinosa demonstrated that clerics could act as important advocates for their interests. The lessons of experience also indicated that advocacy was contingent on their own demonstrations of faith and their sincere desire to live by the guiding hand of Christian missionary authority. In addition, they realized that royal government could also curb priestly authority. But it must have seemed by 1587 that clerical intervention provided the best means toward their ultimate goal of continued autonomy and legitimation.

DIPLOMATIC PEACE IN ESMERALDAS

The narrative journey that ultimately brought more dedicated missions to the Esmeraldas region required a break from the former methods of intervention on the coast. After Espinosa's failure, some of the maroon rebels sought religious intervention from Mercedarians, who began to enter the Esmeraldas lowlands. For the *audiencia*, however, further oversight was needed to be sure that colonial goals would be met. In the meantime, authorities could see that plans for immediate Spanish settlement of the area would not work. Feeling their hands tied, the *audiencia* discouraged all missionary work in the early 1590s.[30] However, as Quito's religious orders competed to enlarge their missions, the Mercedarians began to heed requests from the Esmeraldeños to missionize among them.

According to the official historian of the Mercedarian order in Ecuador, Joel Monroy, it was around 1590, when father Juan de Salas was missionizing in the Yumbos region near Quito, that true missionizing began among the maroons of Esmeraldas.[31] This is misleading; Salas, of course, was not the first to missionize among the maroons. More important, in a letter Juan de Salas wrote to the Crown, he admits it was Amerindians who brought him from his *doctrinas* among the Yumbos to the maroons' village. They took him to where there was a "*población de negros y mulatos*" (a population of people of African descent) to whom a large number of Amerindians were subject. He went on to say that they desired Christian indoctrination and wished to pledge their obedience to the Crown. Incredibly, they also asked for a Spanish *gobernador* and Spanish settlers.[32] One must wonder whether Salas accurately portrayed maroon desires. Could the maroons have changed their minds about a Spanish settlement so quickly? It may be that Salas, at least in part, either reported what he wanted to hear or had convinced the maroons to conform to his expectations. Salas also claimed that the maroons denounced Fray Espinosa for his "bad living." In all, what Fray Juan de Salas effectively proposed was the creation of a joint venture with Spanish settlers: an arrangement like the *doctrina/encomienda* system by which military and religious conquest operated hand in hand, as did the establishment of a parish and a labor force.[33] Indeed it was Salas's inroads that gave the Mercedarians an advantage that would lead to their establishment of missions across the lowlands of Esmeraldas.[34] Unlike previous interventions, their project was exclusive to the maroon territory; it involved missionizing among thousands of lowland indigenous people (including the Cayapa and Malaba groups north of the maroon homelands) and connecting them to previously established Mercedarian missions further south in Puerto Viejo. Indeed, it was partly as a result of the maroons' invitation that the Mercedarians helped Crown authorities conclude a permanent peace between the royal court and the *mulatos* by the end of the 1590s.[35]

However, the *audiencia* recognized that a missionary presence was all it should hope for in Esmeraldas.[36] Juan Barrio de Sepúlveda, the Crown judge who negotiated the final settlement, noted that the maroon had to be treated with care and respect: that meant a moratorium on further expeditions to the area.[37] In addition, they compromised with the Afro-Amerindians on numerous points, not only accepting their legitimate rights to freedom and to rule Esmeraldas but adding an exemption from tribute obligations to the Crown. Finally, the Crown would underwrite all costs associated with the missions. In exchange, the *audiencia* expected the maroons to resettle at the Bay of San Mateo, a first step in reestablishing their project to open a transit port.

The establishment of missions was a gradual process involving indigenous communities throughout the region. Between 1595 and 1600, missionaries cast their nets through various parts of Esmeraldas, converting many Amerindians and establishing strong ties with the maroons. After 1598, enough trust was built that the maroons traveled to Quito to stand before the *audiencia* and swear their loyalty to the Crown. The judges and the bishop of Quito conveniently saw an opportunity to use the outward appearance of religious ceremony to solidify their position on the coast when two of the maroon leaders, Sebastián and Antonio de Illescas, requested the sacrament of confirmation.

While confirmation did not require the instruction and preparation in sixteenth-century Quito often associated with the sacrament today, it still symbolized a passage to a higher level of spiritual responsibility and knowledge. In Quito, it became even more important as the *audiencia* proposed to celebrate the event with a large public ceremony, thus authenticating the pacification in the collective memory of Quiteños. However, for the maroons, confirmation was of equal importance with their new appointed positions. Receiving the sacrament in Quito from the city's bishop and before the leading political authorities furthered their legitimate status. The rites required that Sebastián de Illescas and his brother Antonio receive brief religious instruction. They were taken to Quito's Jesuit school for lessons and were interviewed by the bishop. Days later they received the sacrament before a large crowd that included members of all the religious orders, the leading residents of Quito, and the judges of the *audiencia*.[38] They had just received the minor titles of nobility, their "Don," from the *audiencia*, which helped establish them as legal lords of the land, and now through the sacrament of confirmation they were raised from adolescence to adulthood in the eyes of the church. Sebastián took his father's name, Alonso, during the ceremony. His brother Antonio took the name attributed to the black king of the magi, Balthasar. For both of the maroons these were conscious choices to identify themselves with powerful leaders both within their family dynasty and the

Christian cosmology. The court judge chiefly responsible for effecting the peace, Juan Barrio de Sepúlveda, and the attorney of the court, Blas de Torres Altamirano, served as godfathers to the sons of Alonso Sebastián's brothers, creating fictive family ties of *compadrazgo* (godparentage) that further cemented their new relationships. Thus, Christian ritual served not only to tie the Spanish Crown to the rebel communities as a mediating agent but also to create formal bonds of godparentage between members of the royal court government and the maroon leaders.

Between 1599 and 1601 clergymen of the Mercedarian order continued to build their missionary settlements. A report from Padre Juan Baptista de Burgos in 1601 commended the two maroon communities for building churches, one at the newly named San Martín de los Campazes and the other at the mouth of the Esmeraldas River at a site named San Mateo. The maroons were thus keen to demonstrate their piety within their homelands. The Crown assisted with the cost of these missions and appeared satisfied with the maroons' desire to receive the missionaries into their communities.

The raids of 1605–1606 reminded Spaniards that colonial encroachments could still lead to dramatic aftershocks and that Spanish authorities were still largely impotent in the region of Esmeraldas. Notwithstanding Father Hincapie's condemnation of the maroons and the *audiencia*'s conclusion that both the San Mateo and San Martin communities were involved in the raids, the plan to send punitive expeditions against the *mulatos* never materialized. Ironically, instead, the destruction of the port settlement at the terminus of the Ibarra overland route by other groups of lowland Indians in 1607 pushed Quiteños to once more consider a port settlement in maroon territory.

The maroon raids did, however, expose certain aspects of life among the Afro-Amerindians that were related to issues of conversion and religious adherence. They also opened a window unto the views of the Mercedarian missionaries charged with catechizing the maroons. Their testimony included, among other things, Father Hincapie's observation that the *mulatos* would not practice any of the important Christian rites: they would neither marry nor confess themselves, nor would they observe the feast days.[39] These outward acts thus constituted Christian life for Hincapie and Spanish Catholic society. In all likelihood, maroons had to strike a delicate balance to convince the missionaries of their adherence to Christianity while practicing local customs and Christian religion in parallel.[40] Christian observance for maroons and for Spaniards (as Phelan remarked) may have remained largely in the realm of outward appearance and ritual, while everyday life was conditioned by the norms of African and Amerindian lifeways.

The Mercedarians continued in their missionary work among the maroons after 1605. As Quito's merchant elite looked for alternative routes to the coast, the Mercedarians began to collaborate in their efforts to establish a port settlement. By 1615, a new project was under way under the direction of a Quiteño merchant named Martín de Fuica. Assisting Fuica in moving one of the maroon communities was Fray Diego de Velasco. From 1617 to 1620, Velasco was instrumental in relocating the Illescas community to the Bahía de Caráquez, situated at the southern extremity of Esmeraldas. Velasco's project reveals the type of colonization that some Mercedarians had hoped to achieve in Esmeraldas all along, a mercantile *doctrina*. Rather than a closed missionary system to protect and oversee the spiritual wellbeing of the Afro-Amerindians, they moved to tie their new parishes to commercial ventures in the region.

Conclusion: Religious Intervention and Marronage in Esmeraldas

In an article examining the record of conquest attempts in colonial Esmeraldas, José Alcina Franch proposed that the aims of the expeditions changed over time from military to religious to commercial.[41] However, the record of religious interventions in the region demonstrates that the African and Afro-Amerindian maroons of the area actively engaged clerics and expanded upon early religious inroads during the entire period of their contact with Spanish authorities. Through their experiences prior to arriving in Esmeraldas and the knowledge they gained from Spanish clerics, they utilized religion for their own ends: the maintenance of their autonomy and authority in the region.

While studies of Africans' religious conversion in colonial Spanish America tend to center on the plantation, Christianization in the context of marronage alters our notions of religion's role in a diasporic context. Among maroons, religion could not be used as a promise of salvation in the midst of captivity, deprivation, and physical violence. Rather it furthered legitimation for them and assisted administrators in their efforts to pacify a rebellious frontier region. Religion became a double-edged sword, usable by both colonizer and rebel to manifest claims of legitimacy before the Crown.

This chapter demonstrates how religion defined the terms of engagement between African rebels and Spanish authorities. Importantly, the rules were taught by religious authorities—the clerics, who visited and proselytized among the maroons of Esmeraldas. They provided the Esmeraldeños with the tools they would ultimately use to maintain their autonomy. While these clerics played different roles as either defenders of or detractors of these African-based communities, it was the maroons who successfully incorporated the symbols of religious conquest and helped maintain religious discourse at the center of their interactions with colonial agents.

Notes

1. In the case of Panama, for example, Mena García states: "*Dada la rápida y total desaparición de la población aborigen de Tierra Firme, el esclavo africano desempeñó desde muy pronto un papel de indudable importancia en la sociedad panameña por cuanto* vino a sustituir al indígena en la totalidad de las actividades laborales del istmo, sobre todo en las dos capitales más importantes, constituyendo la plataforma básica sobre la que reposaba la actividad económica de los principales centros urbanos." (Given the rapid and total disappearance of the aboriginal population of Tierra Firme, African slaves came to have a role of undeniable importance in Panamanian society *as they substituted the indigenous in all areas of labor. This was most important in the two key cities where Africans were they formed the foundation of all economic activity.*) Mena García, *La sociedad de Panamá*, 391, my emphasis.

2. *Cofradías* were among the first church-related institutions seen as providing positive space for empowerment and self-help among enslaved and free Africans. See Karasch, *Slave Life in Rio de Janeiro, 1808–1850*. A more recent example that examines these institutions in the Mexican context can be found in von Germeten, *Black Blood Brothers*. For works with a more syncretic cast, see Thornton, *Africa and Africans in the Making of the Atlantic World*. An even more recent study that examines the multiple manners of religious-based interaction can be found in Mills and Grafton, *Conversion: Old Worlds and New*.

3. While a number of terms were current in the sixteenth century to label the progeny of the escaped African slaves and native people, including "*zambos*," "*mulatos*," and "*negros*," I have chosen to follow Kris Lane's usage of the terms Afro-Amerindians and Afro-indigenous as well as the term *mulatos* when referring to contemporary Spanish sources. See Lane, *Quito 1599*, Chapter 1.

4. De Goyler Library, Southern Methodist University, Jowdy-Duque del Infantado Microfilm Collection, Conde de Montesclaros Papers, Roll 2, libro 15, expedientes 6–7, Esmeraldas, 1605–1607, testimony of Fray Hernando de Hincapie, folio 4r. Many thanks to William Taylor for providing the microfilm copy used for this article.

5. *La Concepción* was merely one of many ships that ran aground along pieces of the Esmeraldas shore. Indeed, a shipwreck was said to be responsible for Africans' arrival in 1553. See Szaszdi, "El transfondo de un cuadro," for an excellent narrative of events from 1553 to around 1601. Kris Lane provides an excellent recounting of the 1599 wrecks of the *San Felipe* and *Santiago* (along with a full narrative of the maroons' exploits on the coast) in *Quito 1599*; the account can also be found in Rueda Novoa, *Zambaje y autonomía*.

6. De Goyler Library, Conde de Montesclaros Papers, testimony of Hernan López and Pedro de la Santa Cruz, Duque del Infantado, folios 18r–18v.

7. Phelan, *The Kingdom of Quito in the Seventeenth Century*, 177.

8. As Sherwin Bryant points out, while many areas such as Esmeraldas and the audiencia of Quito are considered outside the mainstream of African slavery in Spanish America, they are, in fact, more typical of Spanish slave societies for the period. Bryant, "Finding Gold, Forming Slavery."

9. Kris Lane touches on these two compelling colonial forces in "Captivity and Redemption."

10. Maroon religion is of course part of a hotly debated field of study that examines the questions of syncretism and cultural survival among Africans in the Americas. See Mintz and Price, *The Birth of African-American Culture*; Herskovits, *The Myth of the Negro Past*; Bastide, *African Civilisations in the New World*; and Thornton, *Africa and Africans in the Making of the New World*. Another important recent contribution to the field is Sweet, *Recreating Africa*. Among the few specific examinations of maroon religion are Kopytoff, "Religious Change among Jamaican Maroons"; and Bastide, *African Civilisations in the New World*.

11. See Viotti da Costa, *Crowns of Glory, Tears of Blood*, for an excellent example of political upheaval inspired by Protestant missionizing.

12. For instance, in the opening dedication of the "Verdadera descripción," Cabello laments that the region has become "a Babylon of abominations, what should have been the home of baptized and Christians"; Cabello Balboa, "Verdadera descripción," 3.

13. Ibid., 36.

14. Ibid., 42. It is difficult to assess from the passage whether it was the Arobe's idea to bring the gold offering or if they were influenced to do so by Illescas: "When we finished, Alonso de Illescas said this to us while still in the chapel, 'the vicar and his companions do not want or seek gold: these brothers offer this small amount in order to decorate this altar.'"

15. At one point, Cabello recounts, Illescas even offered him 1,000 gold pesos to purchase a "pair of blacks"; "Verdadera descripción," 38.

16. López de Zúñiga's expedition generated enough litigation and testimony to trace fifty-seven of its members. They belonged to some of the most prominent families of Quito. However, many of the soldiers came from the frontier region of Baeza on the eastern side of the Andes. See Beatty, "Rebels and Conquerors," chapter 3.

17. Alonso de Espinosa to the Crown in Rumazo, May 22, 1585, in Rumazo, *Documentos para la historia*, 4:7–13. *Audiencia* judge Venegas de Cañaveral noted Espinosa's work among the Esmeraldeños in his 1584 report to the Crown, Archivo General de Indias, Seville (hereafter AGI), Quito 8, Ramo 19, numero 50, digital image 7.

18. Alonso de Espinosa to the Crown in Rumazo, May 22, 1585, 4:8.

19. Ibid., 4:10.

20. Ibid., 4:11.

21. Pedro Venegas de Cañaveral, report to the Crown, 1585, AGI, Quito 8, Ramo 19, numero 50, image 7.

22. *Audiencia* to the Crown, April 19, 1586, AGI, Escribania 922b.2, f. 203r–203v.

23. Alonso de Illescas to the Crown, February 24, 1586, AGI, Escribania 922b, folio 11.

24. Szaszdi, "El transfondo de un cuadro," 111.

25. Ibid., 115.

26. Alonso de Espinosa to the Crown, May 22, 1585, in Rumazo, *Documentos para la historia*, 4:11.

27. Report from the *audiencia* to the Crown, AGI, Quito 8, Ramo 21, numero 54; and royal orders contained in AGI, Quito 209, L1.73v–75v.

28. *Audiencia* to the Crown, AGI, Quito 8, Ramo 21, numero 54, image 9; and AGI, Quito 8, Ramo 21, numero 59.

29. Royal order contained in the Archivo Nacional Historico, Quito, Cedulas, Caja 1.

30. Fray Juan de Salas to the Crown, February 24, 1590, AGI, Quito 83.

31. Monroy, *Los Religiosos*, chapter 2.

32. See Alcina Franch, "Textos para la etnohistoria de Esmeraldas," 1–4.

33. For more on the differences between these forms of Christianization and the transitions between them in the sixteenth century, see Tibesar, "The Franciscan Doctrinero."

34. Monroy, *Los Religiosos*, passim.

35. Juan de Salas in Burgos Guevara, *Primeras doctrinas en la real audiencia de Quito*, Document 24.

36. As Kris Lane points out in his introduction to *Quito 1599*, it was around this date that Quiteños came to realize both the possibilities and limitations of their region in the larger Ibero-Atlantic economy.

37. Barrio noted that the settlers should "know how to treat and care for them [the maroons] with love and Christian charity and that they abhor all avarice and disordered greed and in everything procure their good and that of your majesty and his vassals." AGI, Quito 9, Ramo 3, numero 21, p. 004.

38. Report of Capitán Pedro de Arévalo to the *audiencia*, December 2, 1600, in Rumazo, *Documentos para la historia*, 4: 25.

39. Conde de Montesclaros Papers, Roll 2, libro 15, expedientes 6–7, Esmeraldas, 1605–1607, testimony of Fray Hernando de Hincapie, Duque del Infantado, folio 4r.

40. This phenomenon is explored by James Sweet in *Recreating Africa*.

41. Alcina Franch, "Penetración Española en Esmeraldas."

5

Afro-Mexican Saintly Devotion in a Mexico City Alley

JOAN C. BRISTOL

In October 1699, María Lópes de Avilés informed Mexico City inquisitors about a rumor that Isidro the sweet seller, along with others, had "made in his house a certain feast, or celebration to which a variety of men of all species gathered."[1] She claimed they "had founded there in their fashion a *religión* of Saint Augustine," saying Mass and other prayers in Spanish and Latin.[2] According to her, they wore "habit[s]" of brown scapulars with red hearts and "suits of seculars" (referring to secular clergy, those unconnected to an order).[3] She reported they had other "religions," including one for women called the "Iphigenias," and "they name their Priors, Provincials, Masters of novices . . . and Isidro of Sweets is the abbot."[4]

María's informant was Lucas Mercado, identified as Spanish. Under the questioning of inquisitors, Lucas claimed that the previous year he had witnessed a meeting on the Calle de Escalerillas that was held in a room with a pulpit and an image of Saint Augustine. Among the attendees "most [were] blacks and mulattoes."[5] Lucas had attended similar meetings elsewhere. He claimed that "the congregants, blacks and mulattoes, and the rest . . . name themselves as if they were *religiosos* [clerics]."[6] He also had heard of Afro-Mexican women called *religiosas* (nuns) of Saint Iphigenia.[7] On the feast day of Saint Francisco, he had seen another group processing with an image, probably the saint himself, from the convent church to their meeting place. Members had then marched around a room carrying crosses, placed a man in the middle as if he were dead, and sung a response. He identified these as "exercises like those the Third Order of Saint Francisco practice."[8]

This chapter explores the possible meanings this gathering and others like it may have had for these "congregants, blacks and mulattoes, and the rest," as Lucas identified them.[9] The case reflects Afro-Mexicans' level of involvement in colonial society and religious life and their desires to gain social power as defined by colonial authorities. Yet at the same time it shows us Afro-Mexicans asserting the right to worship as Christians on their own terms. Both of these positions, which really are two sides of the same coin, reflect their roles as Christians and colonial subjects. These attitudes and actions are understandable when we consider the context in which the case against Isidro and the other worshippers occurred. By the turn of the eighteenth century, half a century after the peak of the Mexican slave trade, the "blacks and mulattoes" Lucas identified would have been American-born creoles rather than Africans. It is likely that mulattoes (commonly defined as the mixed descendants of Europeans, in this case Spaniards, and Africans) predominated, since they formed the majority of the Afro-Mexican population in this period. Unlike their African-born ancestors of the previous centuries, who had to quickly learn about Christianity in order to escape suspicions of blasphemy and heresy, Afro-Mexicans of the early eighteenth century acted as seasoned members of colonial society who were familiar and comfortable with Catholic practice. Free Afro-Mexicans were also present in significant numbers among the larger population by this period and were no doubt represented among this group. María's description of "men of all species" reminds us that most early eighteenth-century Afro-Mexicans were fully part of colonial society; many had lived alongside Spaniards and others for at least a few generations and had some Spanish or indigenous ancestry. This integration was also reflected in the descriptions of the gathering, which involved members of different social groups.

Yet in his emphasis on the black and mulatto composition of the meeting, Lucas's testimony indicates that Afro-Mexicans formed a discrete group that was distinguished by the particular challenges its members faced and by shared values and cultural practices. Like Africans and their descendants all over Latin America, Afro-Mexicans had to negotiate the limitations and opportunities that were provided to them by colonial rulers who were committed to limiting their freedom. Even legally free Afro-Mexicans were not allowed to go to the university or profess as clerics, for example. This inquisition case against Isidro and his fellow congregants shows that Catholic practice was central to the negotiation of the space between restriction and opportunity. Many of the identities and opportunities available to Africans and their descendants all over Spanish America were shaped by imperial and church policies.[10] In addition, Catholic practice brought Afro–Latin

Americans material and spiritual opportunities, as the chapters by Charles Beatty-Medina and Nancy van Deusen in this volume show.

An important form of Christian practice for Africans in the Diaspora came through membership in Catholic confraternities. These lay groups were organized around venerating saints and often served as mutual aid societies for their members. In Mexico, as in Peru, Brazil, Argentina, Cuba, and elsewhere, black and mulatto confraternities gave their members a place to gather and a sense of corporate identity based in ideas about shared African origin. Africans and their descendants maintained and developed African-based practices through confraternities, particularly in Brazil and the Caribbean.[11] Yet these groups also gave their members knowledge about Catholic practice and Ibero-American social practices and a way to integrate into these societies.[12] This was especially true in places such as Mexico and Peru, where Africans and their descendants formed a smaller part of the overall population than in Brazil and the Caribbean. While Africans and their descendants formed a larger group than Spaniards in Mexico, they were a distant second to the demographically dominant indigenous population. This facilitated Afro-Mexicans' cultural integration into the colonial population, since members of different groups necessarily lived and worked alongside each other, especially in urban areas. Afro-Mexicans possessed an African consciousness and practiced African-influenced rituals, and their confraternities were frequently organized along the lines of African ethnicities, especially in the sixteenth and seventeenth centuries.[13] Yet overall it seems that their confraternities did not function as sites of African-based practices in the way that confraternities in Brazil and the Caribbean did.

The group described above was not a legally recognized confraternity, yet in its communal Catholic practice it seems to have shared some characteristics with confraternities. As we will see below, the members clearly expressed their identities as Christians and as colonial residents through their communal practices. The Mexico City case described here thus reflects larger processes by which members of the African Diaspora negotiated their responsibilities and rights as Christian and imperial subjects, yet it also gives us a specifically Mexican perspective on this process. As in other parts of the Diaspora, these descendants of Africans formed a community based on Christian practices. Yet in the Mexican case these blacks, mulattoes, and others seem to have been participating fully in mainstream Christianity rather than separating themselves through unsanctioned practices (although, paradoxically, they did so through an unlicensed group).

The group differs from many African-descended groups in its composition as well. In this case Afro-Mexicans joined with members of other social groups. Lucas Mercado, the Spaniard who first told María Lópes de Avilés about the group, emphasized the role of mulattoes, yet his description reveals that the group included others. At least one Spanish student and several Spanish clerics attended the meetings on Escalerillas and elsewhere and served as officials in the purported "religion." Lucas claimed that they were mostly young friars and priests with low positions in the ecclesiastical hierarchy.[14] Several were "ordained as *epístola*," referring to individuals who were permitted to chant the epistles and prepare the Eucharist but not to say Mass or perform the sacraments.[15] Clerics did not organize the meeting, however; Lucas explained that two men, Isidro de Peralta and another named Juan, rented the house. He identified both as mulattoes.[16] After interviewing three other witnesses who corroborated Lucas's story, inquisitors put the case aside.

Three years passed. Then, in September 1702, a Spanish weaver named Francisco Xavier told a priest, Bachiller Simon de Dera y Ulloa, that a group of mulattoes had erected an altar in a house next to his in the Callejón [Alley] de Lainez in the San Juan de la Penitencia neighborhood. Francisco claimed that they had held a "celebration for Saint Nicholas" with a procession that brought the saint's image from the convent church of San Juan de la Penitencia to their altar. They then "celebrated or said mass in the house." He did not mention any clerical supervision.[17] Bachiller Simon immediately went to the house and, peering in from the alley, saw the altar. Two men whom he identified as black and mulatto left the house. Eavesdropping, Bachiller Simon heard them discuss firecrackers, presumably for use in a celebration, and a Mass to be held the following morning.[18] Fearful of unlicensed religious activities, he sent word to don Andres Moreno Bala, the ecclesiastical court's *promotor fiscal* (public prosecutor). The next morning Bachiller Simon; Moreno Bala, a notary; and several officials dispatched a boy to the alley see if "in the house of the mulattoes they sang."[19] He reported that he heard singing, it seemed to him in Latin, coming from the house. With this, the investigators headed to the alley.

In his inquisition testimony the *promotor fiscal* claimed that Bachiller Simon had told him about "a gathering of blacks, mulattoes and other people with the title of confraternity, or religion of Saint Augustine" who had "celebrated a procession without license." The *promotor fiscal* explained that the participants were heard singing "as if they celebrated mass" and possibly preaching.[20]

The scene in the house seemed to confirm these reports. According to the notary, the room was arranged like a chapel, with benches and an altar at the front supporting several saints' images. A pulpit stood against a wall.[21] The *pro-*

motor fiscal testified that nineteen men and two women were present, most of them mulattoes. He also mentioned three students, who were therefore Spanish.[22] He described another man, the sexton of the Monserrate convent, as a native of Spain, although other witnesses identified him as a creole Spaniard. One woman, later identified as the wife of Juan Baptista, the mulatto man who rented the house, was described as *mestizo* (of mixed Spanish and indigenous descent), and the other as mulatto.[23] The *promotor fiscal* apprehended twenty people (one man was too ill for detention). Most would spend two months in prison while inquisition censors assessed the books and other objects found in the house. Isidro de Peralta and Juan Baptista, who were identified as the ringleaders, were held for three months. Isidro de Peralta, also known as Isidro de Loya, was mentioned in the 1699 accusation.

For accusers and investigators, whether or not wrongdoing had taken place rested on whether the participants had "usurped the ecclesiastical jurisdiction," as a notary accompanying the *promotor fiscal* stated.[24] Had the Lainez participants worn ecclesiastical vestments and said Mass? Such honors and functions were reserved for those who had taken holy orders. Several neighbors implied that they had. Francisco Xavier, who raised the alarm, claimed that "it is public and notorious in this neighborhood that the mulattoes say mass and preach."[25] The notary reported that three neighbors had heard singing, "like in the churches when they sing mass in Latin," as well as preaching and violin music, and on the day of Saint Nicholas they heard the litany and smelled incense.[26] They had not seen anything, however, because "the mulattoes shut themselves in and with draperies covered up the doors."[27] To be fair, the neighbors were not all suspicious. Some claimed that they had heard that the members had a license for a confraternity. Either they had not worried that something was amiss or they wanted inquisitors to believe that they were unaware of suspicious activity.[28] There was no license, however. Like the more damning testimonies, these reports reflected and added to the confusion about the meetings.

Taken as a whole, testimonies of investigators and neighborhood residents offer a vivid image of a renegade mulatto congregation whose members wore clerical garb and celebrated Mass illicitly. If these rumors proved true, the group posed a direct challenge to the colonial social order, in which high religious office was reserved for Spaniards. Afro-Mexicans, on the other hand, were to be closely monitored.

This picture of a maverick group changed, however, when three clerics testified. One, a priest and chaplain connected to the cathedral, had been to services on Escalerillas and Lainez. A Dominican friar attended the Saint

Nicholas celebration on Lainez, while an Augustinian had attended a meeting over a decade earlier, as a boy. They reported never having seen the participants wearing vestments or saying Mass. Even when the vespers, litanies, and other prayers that did not need to be said by priests had been chanted, clerics and students had been present.

This testimony did not completely dispel the confusion, however, since it suggested that the congregants had pretensions about forming a religious order. One friar testified that although he "never saw a mass, or other ecclesiastical ceremonies that the church uses . . . it is also called a *religión*." He claimed the group elected "officers of the *religión*" from among the students and said that Isidro de Peralta was named sexton.[29] Ultimately, however, investigators found no clerical clothing in the house and inquisitors did not judge the recovered materials to be heretical. The lack of evidence proved decisive. At the end of December, inquisitors declared that they found "no result of heresy nor flavor of it and that it only seems to have been an indiscreet devotion to . . . Saint Augustine and Saint Nicholas." They affirmed that "celebrating private fires in their houses in the eight-day period of their feasts [is] a common and customary thing in this city not only to the said saints but to others as it is well known."[30] The alleged ringleaders were not let off the hook entirely. Isidro de Peralta, Juan Baptista, and Miguel Ramirez, the sexton of the Monserrate convent, were ordered to report to the Inquisition weekly and were threatened with excommunication and exile to the Philippines if they made a misstep.[31] Yet the judgment transformed the congregants' activities, which investigators and some neighbors had depicted as dangerously subversive, into behavior that was mundane, if imprudent.

Such competing interpretations of the events in the alley raise questions. Were the group's activities evidence of Afro-Mexican defiance of religious norms and policies, as alarmed accusers suggested? Or was this an ordinary series of events with no larger significance in terms of church practice, as inquisitors decided?

On the surface, the group's activities seem to represent a challenge to state and ecclesiastical authorities. Although licensed Afro-Mexican confraternities had met under clerical supervision since the mid-sixteenth century, this was an unlicensed group that did not have the official oversight that came with being certified by the church hierarchy. Moreover, even if the Lainez congregants were practicing Christianity in officially accepted ways—by organizing services and venerating saints—their identities as Afro-Mexicans would render these activities suspicious, since Afro-Mexicans and other non-Spaniards were prohibited from occupying important positions within the ecclesiastical hierarchy.

Furthermore, it is possible that the congregants were performing unorthodox rituals alongside Christianity, a common yet officially prohibited practice all over New Spain and throughout the Diaspora. Lucas Mercado's description of a ritual in which a person was placed on the floor and members sang a response may call to mind West Central African forms of healing and divination in which practitioners were possessed by spirits who acted through them. Although it might be tempting to see the ceremony as having non-Christian origins, we have no further information to support such an interpretation. Moreover, we must remember that Lucas identified this as a practice of the lay brothers of the Franciscan order, perhaps one with which he was familiar. While chanted responses were often associated with African and African Diaspora ritual practice, they were a common part of the Catholic liturgy as well. However, whether the congregants were practicing unorthodox rituals or orthodox rituals in an unorthodox context, the services deviated from prescribed behavior, and some witnesses read such deviation as subversive.

Then again, perhaps inquisitors were right and this was an example of conventional communal worship. With its public processions and clerical involvement, the group was hardly clandestine. The materials that investigators found make sense within the context of colonial ritual practice. Wealthy people owned saints' images and chapels for private devotions.[32] Moderately prosperous residents owned canvases painted with religious images and small statues of saints.[33] Instead of representing subversion, these services might be read as evidence of the degree to which Afro-Mexicans were integrated into colonial religious life. The possibility that congregants were self-consciously participating in Christian society through their services is borne out by the neighborhood witnesses who found the congregation unremarkable, or at least not worth reporting to inquisitors. With the exception of the weaver who alerted Bachiller Simon, neighbors did not come forward but were called by inquisitors for questioning.

The interpretation that the congregation was part of mainstream religious life is not completely satisfying, however. If the meeting was largely accepted by neighbors, what troubled María Lópes de Avilés, the original 1699 informant, and Francisco Xavier, the original 1702 informant, so much that they reported it to authorities? What led investigators to suspect the participants of overstepping social boundaries?

Accusations and Social Change

One of the oft-repeated "facts" in the testimonies was that congregants were black and mulatto. Even witnesses who mentioned that the group was composed of "men of all species" emphasized its Afro-Mexican composition.[34] Indeed, Afro-Mexicans were prominent among those apprehended. According to witnesses, the leaders Isidro de Peralta and Juan Baptista were mulattoes. The rumored "women's *religión*" was dedicated to Saint Iphigenia, a first-century saint associated with Africans and with confraternities with members of African descent in Mexico and Brazil because of her Ethiopian origins.[35] The Spanish detainees were mostly clerics or clerical students who seem to have been supporters rather than central members of the group. Yet it is also true that only 50 percent of those apprehended were Afro-Mexican—seven were Spaniards and three were mestizos (the Afro-Mexicans included nine mulattoes and one creole black).[36] The contrast between the list of detainees and the descriptions of the "mulatto and black" congregants is telling. Perhaps suspicions about illegal activity led neighbors to perceive congregants as Afro-Mexican.

If Afro-Mexican congregants had called themselves "religiosos" and performed Mass they would have been committing a serious infraction, violating not only the law but also the hierarchical assumptions that underlay the law. This is not to say that non-Spaniards were completely prohibited from holding religious office; *castas* (colonial residents of mixed descent) and indigenous men took minor orders, were tonsured, became lay brothers, and occasionally professed as friars.[37] Isidro de Peralta was identified as a lay brother of San Juan de Dios, although one witness claimed that he had not worn the habit for a long time.[38] As van Deusen shows in this volume, Afro–Latin American women lived in convents as servants and devoted themselves to spiritual practice. They could not become nuns, however.[39] And Afro–Latin American men could not take major orders, which were required for saying Mass. Thus, if the Afro-Mexican congregants had held masses, they would have been flouting the ideology that underlay the legal and social systems and rejecting the colonial hierarchy. This would have been a grave affront to Spanish officials, whose prestige and authority derived from that system.

The claims that congregants were assuming unsanctioned roles may have reflected witnesses' fears that they were actually transforming themselves into something they were not, a sort of occupational "passing," or mimesis. Michael Taussig explains that "the wonder of mimesis lies in the copy drawing on the character and power of the original, to the point whereby the representation may even assume that character and that power."[40] Mimesis can support colonial rule; Homi Bhabha shows that colonizers encourage mimicry, hoping that in striving to emulate colonizers' cultural practices and appearance, the colonized will accept their supposed superiority as natural. Yet for mimicry to work in favor of the colonizers, difference, expressed through constructions of race and culture, must always exist. Thus, any blurring of categories of difference threatens imperial power.[41] The Lainez meeting may have seemed to threaten Spanish categories of difference. The rumors that congregants were impersonating clerics by wearing ecclesiastical clothing and calling themselves a religious order would have seemed to officials and witnesses like a claim to the category of Spanishness itself.

Spanish officials were interested in preserving social divisions based on status throughout the colonial period. The bread riot that erupted in Mexico City in 1692, less than a decade before the case examined here began, had only added to this desire. It exposed class tensions as rioters shouted anti-Spanish and anti-government slogans. The rioters were not the poorest members of society; in fact, artisans predominated among those convicted of participating.[42] In the wake of the riot, elites tried to reinforce the system that legally divided different castes (social groups defined by both color and class)[43] and legislated their privileges.[44]

Distrust of non-Spaniards, especially Afro-Mexicans, was not new in the 1690s. Spaniards often identified blacks and mulattoes as violent, unreliable, and culturally deficient and had long doubted their loyalty to their masters and the Crown.[45] This attitude was widespread in Spanish America; Beatty-Medina's chapter in this volume documents negative attitudes about Afro-Ecuadorian piety from the early seventeenth century and before. Spanish fears had been stoked by indigenous uprisings, slave revolts, and urban disturbances that involved multiple castes across Spanish America in the sixteenth and seventeenth centuries. Legislation reflected such fears. The section broadly labeled "Mulattoes, Blacks, Berbers, and the Children of Jews" in the 1681 *Recopilación de leyes de los Reinos de las Indias* was almost exclusively concerned with controlling Afro-Mexicans.[46] A 1645 decree urged colonial officials to monitor "slaves, blacks, and any other people, who can provoke caution, and suspicion" with their disruptive activities.[47] The assumption was that Africans and their descendants were a major subset of suspicious people. Other decrees issued throughout the sixteenth and seventeenth centuries prohibited blacks and mulattoes from carrying arms or limited their right to do so; such laws sometimes mentioned mestizos as well.[48]

The fear that Christianity could be practiced in subversive ways was also not new in the 1690s. Rumors in Mexico City in 1612 about an alleged slave conspiracy planned in Afro-Mexican confraternities show that Spaniards had long been uneasy about the nature of these religious institutions.[49] A 1659 accusation against a Jesuit for preaching a sermon critical of the colonial government to a "church full of mulatto men, mulatto women, black men, and black women, and very few Spaniards" reflects anxiety that religious institutions could nurture insurgent tendencies.[50] The accuser, a Spanish official, warned about rebellion, arguing that "the word of God in the pulpit is meant to restrain them."[51] Fears of active uprising could have been behind the worry that the Lainez activities generated in witnesses.

Disturbances such as the 1692 riot do not, however, fully explain the negative reactions of some neighbors to the services held in their midst. While many were Spaniards, they were not elites. Despite their non-elite status, these Spanish neighbors occupied a higher social status than the non-Spaniards involved in the case, who were largely part of the underclass, a marginalized group.[52] Among the non-Spanish detainees whose occupations were listed, one mestizo worked in a textile mill doing unskilled labor. Three mulattoes were servants and two were slaves, both of which were positions at the bottom of the social hierarchy. Isidro de Peralta sold sweets and food in the marketplace, a financially insecure occupation. The congregants were not all on the lowest rungs of the social structure, however. For example, in the 1699 accusation an associate of Isidro de Peralta's named Juan Baptista, the other mulatto leader, as a cobbler, a skilled occupation.[53]

In general, the Spaniards involved in the case, whether as participants or witnesses, could be defined as lower middle class or middle class, unlike their non-Spanish neighbors.[54] Among the detainees, four Spaniards were clerics or students, one was a sexton, one was an artisan, and another was a *peninsular*, the majordomo of a bakery. Of the five Spanish neighborhood witnesses, one was a clerical student and four were artisans or were connected to artisans. Francisco Xavier, who first sounded the alarm about the processions, was a weaver. Another witness was a master potter. One woman was married to a tailor, albeit one identified as a *morisco* (a light-skinned Afro-Mexican). One man was an unemployed journeyman who had worked in the playing-card factory and another currently worked there. Although the range of occupations among neighborhood witnesses was broad—students and artisans occupied different social positions, a master artisan had much higher status than a journeyman, and the occupation of tailor did not rank high within the artisan class—their status was much higher than that of the Afro-Mexican slaves and servants who attended the meeting.[55]

Yet similarities also existed between Spanish and non-Spanish workers, especially when compared to elites. Lower-class Spaniards faced significant limitations on social mobility. Journeymen did not have many prospects of becoming master artisans, and lower-class Spaniards did not attend university. The fact that a Spanish witness was married to a *morisco* shows that the interests of some lower-class Spaniards and non-Spaniards were intimately linked. Perhaps it was the very thinness of the boundary that existed between Spanish and non-Spanish workers that led Spanish neighbors to emphasize the mulatto nature of the Lainez group when they made their allegations about illicit activities. They may have wanted to maintain social divisions, just as Spanish officials and clerics did.

Their reasons for wanting to emphasize social differences would have differed from those of higher-status Spaniards, however. Lower- and lower-middle-class Spanish neighbors may have been less concerned about overt signs of social disruption such as riots and more concerned with subtle social distinctions. The class positions of Spaniards were being challenged by the late seventeenth century. Lower- and lower-middle-class Spaniards, who were already in a socially intermediate position between lower-class *castas* and prosperous elite Spaniards, were particularly vulnerable. Although in the eighteenth century a color-based division of labor existed, it was less easy to differentiate Spaniards from non-Spaniards: parents of different caste categories had children who could not be immediately classified, lower-caste people acted in ways that were associated with those of higher status, and some *castas* had wealth or power that rivaled that of wealthy Spaniards. Such blurring of social boundaries, which began in the sixteenth century, accelerated in the seventeenth and eighteenth centuries as the ratio of free to enslaved Afro-Mexicans increased and the mulatto population outstripped the black population. Spaniards worried that free mulattoes could pass as mestizo or even Spanish. This possibility increased in the eighteenth century as it became possible to buy certificates of whiteness, although this did not happen often in practice. Intermarriage was more frequent in the eighteenth century as well.[56]

Middle-class Spaniards felt the effects of social change, perhaps even more keenly than elites. Spanish artisans lost status in the eighteenth century. They were less likely to have the honorific "don" used before their names, and non-Spanish artisans became more common in all but the highest-status crafts.[57] Seen in this context, perhaps the rumors of mulattoes wearing ecclesiastical clothing and saying Mass reflected anxieties that mulattoes were assuming elite identities to which neighborhood witnesses could not aspire.[58] Unlike the 1659 witness who accused a Jesuit of inciting rebellion, the 1702 witnesses did not use the language of insurrection. They may have been afraid of a more insidious kind of subversion of the social order.

Objects and Authority

Witness testimony, much of which was based on rumors and hearsay, raised questions about what went on behind the closed doors of the house on the alley and what those inside hoped to accomplish. Eyewitness sources are limited. We have testimony from three clerical attendees and two congregants—one from the Spanish-born baker Juan de Paiba and another from Miguel Ramírez, the Spanish creole sexton of the Monserrate convent. The court received their testimony, accompanied by pleas for freedom, after they had spent two months in jail. Paiba claimed that he had gone to the services for Saint Nicholas to deliver bread and that he had not previously attended the meetings.[59] The prosecutor claimed that Ramírez was in charge of the services along with Isidro de Peralta and Juan Baptista. These three were held longest, although Ramírez was freed one month before the others.[60]

Paiba and Ramírez gave ambiguous information. Paiba had seen students singing prayers before the altar but "did not hear them sing the epistles nor gospel nor . . . use other ceremonies of the church nor sacred vestments."[61] (Epistles from various texts and the gospel are chanted during Mass.) Paiba said that he believed that the congregation was "governed," or supervised, by Augustinians.[62] He claimed that he had heard a clerical student pray and recite the Creed (the profession of faith that is part of a Mass) and had heard that the Kyrie and Gloria (hymns sung during Mass) had been chanted the day before he attended.[63] Ramírez also claimed that he had heard young clerics sing the Kyrie and the Gloria at services, suggesting that masses were performed. He did not know, however, whether the Eucharist had been blessed or the congregants had been granted permission for their activities.[64] These firsthand accounts suggest that clerics or clerical students at the services may have recited some of the prayers associated with Mass, even if a full Mass with the Eucharist was not held. Perhaps the Eucharist was celebrated and witnesses did not admit it: Paiba's bread may have been intended for the ceremony of communion.

This testimony is not the only source of information about congregants' activities and motivations, however. The investigators' descriptions and inventory of the contents of the house provide a material record. The meeting was held in a room in a small adobe house that seems to have been located either in the alley itself or in the patio of a *vecindad*, a building composed of small apartments.[65] The room's organization supports allegations of group worship; as mentioned earlier, it was arranged like a church, furnished with benches and an altar. The altar was lit with forty tallow candles in candlesticks, some of silver-plated wood and others of clay.[66] Two or three silver- and tin-plated wooden *ciriales* (tall candlesticks carried in religious processions) also held tallow candles. The illumination suggests that investigators interrupted a worship service. A statue described as Saint Nicholas the Penitent, or Saint Nicholas of Tolentino, about a foot and a half tall, sat on a throne made of Chinese gilded paper. Two smaller wooden statues, a little over half a foot tall, sat on small wooden thrones flanking Saint Nicholas. One depicted Saint Peter Apostle dressed as a pontiff with a cushion at his feet, and the other depicted Saint Augustine dressed as an archbishop. The altar's *frontal* (front covering) was fashioned from a Chinese silk tablecloth. Other altar cloths were made of Rouen cloth, a French cotton fabric with stamped decoration. A piece of white wool decorated with black silk and amber beads, which investigators identified as a *palia* used in the Eucharist to cover the wine, lay on the altar. The altar also held engravings of Saint Joseph, Saint Rose, Saint Gertrude, and Our Lady of Guadalupe, as well as clay jugs, some of which were painted, and bouquets of flowers. To the side of the altar was a small clay jar containing ashes, which investigators identified as a censer. They also found books containing psalms and hymns, "badly written" in Latin.

A painted cloth stretched horizontally across the room to section off a choir space.[67] Nearby stood a bench and a stand investigators described as a *facistol* (a lectern used in churches). It supported a damask-covered handwritten book that contained Latin psalms, the Creed, and printed masses. A pointer with a tin-plated tip rested on the bench, along with an old breviary (which priests used to say the daily office) and a handwritten book of logic. A wooden structure, described variously as a *puntal* (prop or brace) or *poste* (post), stood in the center of the room, and stuck to it were two papers listing names of clerics, perhaps those who preached at the meetings. A pulpit covered in yellow silk was located on the right side of the room.

If the rumors of masses had not already aroused suspicions in investigators, the scene before them surely would have. Their use of specialized terms for certain objects ("*palia*" for wool cloth, "*facistol*" for lectern, and "*incensorio*" [censer] for jar) reflects their belief that Mass was being said. The *promotor fiscal* also specifically noted that the Creed, one of the written prayers they found, was said during Mass. Although the issue of whether Mass was being performed remains unclear (investigators found no bread or wine), the inventory certainly suggests that the room was being used as a chapel. What, then, did this chapel mean to the congregants?

It is obvious that congregants placed great importance on creating the chapel. They were not wealthy, as the size and construction of the house indicates. Adobe huts that were squeezed into alleys and the patios of larger buildings were poorly constructed and uncomfortable.[68] The house was probably not used solely for worship; it seems to have served as living quarters for Juan Baptista and perhaps others, since behind the cloth that formed the choir investigators found a wooden cot with tattered bedclothes. One investigator claimed that a man was in the bed when the officials arrived, although the *promotor fiscal* did not.[69] Many of the objects were in poor condition. The *promotor fiscal* claimed the pulpit was "formed of sticks,"[70] and the notary described it as made of "mistreated wood."[71]

Yet the apparent quality of some of the objects indicates the importance congregants placed on Christian worship. It was unusual for slaves and servants to own such objects. Although they did not have the silver candlesticks found in the chapels of wealthy patrons or churches, the congregants had silver-plated candlesticks along with others of clay and tin plate. They used tallow candles rather than expensive wax candles, but the fact that they burned over forty candles at once indicates that they devoted significant funds to their activities. The Chinese and French textiles used to cover the pulpit and the silks and taffetas listed in the inventory were not cheap. While imported cloth was widely available in Mexico City and sold in neighborhood stores,[72] it was not routinely accessible to the poorest of the poor. When these goods are juxtaposed with the modest occupations of those apprehended, it appears that the congregants used whatever extra money they could scrape together to buy these objects and dedicate them for collective worship.

Congregants did not buy everything new, however. The origins and condition of some of the objects points to their creativity and determination. They did not need to have the exact materials found in churches or chapels to pursue their spiritual practice. First, many objects were used in ways not originally intended. The censer was described as a "small plate of clay"[73] and a "little clay jar."[74] Investigators identified the altar *frontal* as a tablecloth, and the many bedspreads noted in the inventory may have been used as decoration or room dividers. Second, participants did not own all the objects. A man petitioned inquisitors to return a bedspread that his wife, a mulatto slave, had taken from her master to lend to Juan Baptista. The petitioner explained that she would be in trouble when its owner missed it.[75] This practice of jury-rigging and borrowing gives us a sense of the lengths members went to so they could have what they considered necessary for their services. It also shows us how acts of mimesis can acquire new meanings. The objects in the house in the Lainez alley and the devotions practiced there had such meaning for participants that they created new objects to use in conventional devotion. In so doing they were assuming the authority to define their own devotional environment.

The participants also went to significant lengths, literally, to attend services.[76] The original meeting was on the Calle de Escalerillas, the street that formed the northern boundary of the cathedral; it was located in the heart of the *traza*, the non-indigenous city center. In spring 1702, it moved to the Lainez alley, in the San Juan de la Penitencia neighborhood, southwest of the cathedral. Many detainees were not from either area. The mulatto Francisco de Salazar lived in the Calle de Tacuba, the street that the Calle de Escalerillas became to the west of the cathedral. San Juan de la Penitencia was about five blocks west and five blocks south of this area. The Spaniard Nicolas de la Cruz also lived near the cathedral on the Calle del Arzobispado. Juan de Paiba worked at a bakery on the Alameda, about four blocks north of San Juan. Although these distances might not seem far to a modern sensibility, these congregants left their residential zones. Juan de Paiba mentioned a sermon in which a clerical student described Saint Nicholas's rural upbringing, claiming that the celebration on Lainez was appropriate because it was "outside this city."[77] This reflects congregants' sense that Lainez was some distance from the urban center. Yet they traveled there to worship.

If the descriptions of the house and objects indicate that it was used as a chapel and if its location vis-à-vis congregants' homes suggests that the chapel was important to them, what do the objects and the house itself reveal about how the congregants conceptualized power and authority, a central concern of investigators? Was this an attempt to subvert a system that denied lower-class people, especially Afro-Mexicans, access to religious office? Were the participants attempting to gain glory by borrowing from the Church's symbolic repertoire?

Rather than appropriating authority, congregants might have been asserting their identities as part of New Spain's mainstream Christian culture. Although the censer, the *palia*, and the books suggest that congregants might have held masses, inquisitors did not find the presence of these items objectionable, perhaps because they accepted that these objects were used by clerics who came in to recite prayers and not by members to say Mass. Clerical witnesses did not find the meetings offensive. Presumably they participated to encourage the congregants in their religious practice and possibly because they were paid, as chaplains were. The fact that the congregants participated in the rituals of orthodox Christianity under the tutelage of Spanish clerics indicates that they respected clerical authority. Perhaps secret meetings were held when clerics were absent, although it is hard to imagine how this would have been possible given the crowded conditions of the alley.

The saints' images that investigators found on the altar, including engravings of Saints Joseph, Rose, and Gertrude and Our Lady of Guadalupe, and the small statues of Saints Nicholas, Peter, and Augustine also suggest that participants saw themselves as part of mainstream spiritual life. Many of these had New World connections and well-developed cults. Saint Joseph was made patron of Mexico in 1555 and of Spain in 1679, and Saint Gertrude became patroness of the West Indies in the late seventeenth century.[78] Two had American origins: Saint Rosa, the first American saint, was a Peruvian creole. Our Lady of Guadalupe first appeared to a Nahua witness near Mexico City in 1531. Saint Nicholas was named patron of Mexico City after the 1611 earthquake.[79] In venerating these saints with American (and some specifically Mexican) connections, congregants identified themselves as Christians, colonial subjects, and Spanish Americans.

Yet these symbols could also have been a way for congregants to identify themselves as a discrete group within colonial society. The congregants' veneration of saints calls to mind the cult around the Virgin of Charity developed by royal slaves in El Cobre, Cuba. They emphasized their role in finding her image and maintaining her shrine and made this the basis for the creation of a corporate identity and requests for land and economic benefits based on their corporate status.[80] In other areas of Latin America, particularly Brazil and the Caribbean, Africans and their descendants transformed the meaning of Catholic saints, remaking them to match their specific needs and developing confraternities around them.[81] In the Lainez case, the saints in the alley had special connections to the poor and downtrodden. Saint Joseph's cult developed in Spain and Spanish America at a time of concern about poverty and social disorder. He became an important symbol of hope for the poor, the homeless, and the orphaned.[82] Guadalupe was the champion of Mexico's native population, another impoverished and exploited group. As we have seen, the Lainez congregants were probably on the low end of the lower class. If not poor themselves, they were probably from poor backgrounds, and these saints may have seemed especially suited to help them in their daily negotiation of colonial society.

Another clue about how congregants identified themselves lies in the fact that these saints' cults were new in the early modern period. The cults of Saint Joseph and Guadalupe formed in the sixteenth century but became popular in the seventeenth.[83] Saint Rose was canonized in 1671 and Gertrude made a saint in 1677. The mulatto leaders' interest in newly recognized saints may have reflected their sense of themselves as relative newcomers to Mexico. While mulattoes living in New Spain in the late seventeenth century were creoles, they were only a few generations removed from Africa and probably fewer generations removed from slavery. Some of those apprehended were enslaved or were married to slaves. Perhaps for the Afro-Mexican members of the gathering as well as the other non-Spaniards, veneration of these saints reflected their interest in establishing themselves as colonial subjects of the Crown and the Church.

Finally, the statues on the altar reflect the mulatto leadership and the heavily mulatto membership of the meeting and indicate that the leaders, at least, identified as Afro-Mexicans as well as colonial residents. Many Afro-Mexican confraternities were dedicated to Saint Nicholas of Tolentino, an Italian saint canonized in 1446, perhaps because of his focus on evangelizing the poor.[84] If it was true that a women's group named the Iphigenias was connected to the group, as some witnesses claimed, this demonstrated an Afro-Mexican, and even Diasporic, identity as well. This African saint was often associated with black and mulatto confraternities in both Mexico and Brazil, particularly with groups of women within these organizations.[85] Saint Augustine may have had significance for Afro-Mexicans because Saint Nicholas was an Augustinian saint. Yet Saint Augustine was born in North Africa, and it is possible that this enhanced his meaning for Afro-Mexicans. Although African-based ritual practices such as those found in Brazil and the Caribbean did not thrive in Mexico, blacks and mulattoes were aware of themselves as a discrete group and may have been aware on some level of their location within the African Diaspora.

Overall, these objects and images reveal a group that was navigating colonial society with care. The congregants' desire to practice orthodox religiosity by holding worship services and venerating important saints reflects their sense of themselves as Christian members of colonial society and shows their respect for official forms of authority. Yet we may also read the use of the objects as bespeaking a desire to gain or approximate such authority. This is what their accusers feared. Even if they did not say Mass themselves, the congregants borrowed from the church's symbolic repertoire by using objects such as a censer, a *palia*, a pulpit, and a lectern. These symbols reflected the status of those who used them but also imparted authority to them.

What was the meaning of this approximation of the symbols of authority? Did the meetings on Lainez constitute usurpation, respect, or something else? In Bhabha's formulation, colonial institutions and attitudes are fundamentally ambivalent and hybrid, and respect and usurpation are not mutually exclusive.[86] Even if the use of ecclesiastical symbols was more a matter of imitation than overt usurpation or subversion, imitation is rarely benign; Bhabha and Taussig remind us that mimesis is related to power. Imitation may go beyond mimicry to embodiment so that imitators begin to take on the power inherent in the activities they are imitating.[87] The non-ecclesiastical objects such as textiles that worshippers possessed may point in this direction as well; consumption could be a way to not just reflect but also to change one's social status.[88] Rather than merely trying to express their Christian identities through their collective worship, the members of the Lainez gathering may have been trying on some level to become Spanish through emulation, hoping that by behaving as Spaniards they would acquire the power that came with Spanishness. The goals of trying to integrate into mainstream society and trying to move up in that society are not distinct.[89]

On the other hand, the Christian objects congregants used may have held a different significance for them. Scholars of native Mesoamerican culture have shown that the meaning of Christian symbols can be transformed. For example, in Chiapas in 1712 indigenous rebels fought Spanish authorities in the name of the Virgin Mary. They were struggling to preserve their autonomous practices and institutions, including a cult based around an apparition of the Virgin that Spanish authorities tried to eradicate.[90] In such cases, practicing Christianity was tied to fighting Spanish authority. Bhabha discusses this aspect of mimicry as resistance, claiming that through mimicry colonized subjects reveal the weaknesses and ambivalence in the colonial enterprise.[91] In using ecclesiastical tools the Lainez congregants embodied the ambivalence at the heart of the Christian imperial order. Their actions and the accusations against them made manifest the paradox of colonial rule—that Afro-Mexicans and other non-Spaniards were expected to emulate Spaniards and act as Christian subjects yet were denied opportunities to do so fully. In their accusations, fearful witnesses and investigators may have been responding to the sense that at its heart colonial authority was malleable and subject to change.

Whatever the congregants' goals, however, the attention of the inquisitors must have hurt them materially and symbolically. Servants and marketplace vendors experienced economic uncertainty under any circumstances, and the loss of work while imprisoned for weeks or months may have destroyed them. The loss of honor would also have hurt them.[92] Although the investigations of the inquisitors were theoretically secret, witnesses called to testify knew that the congregants were under suspicion, and the news must have traveled quickly in the close quarters of the alley. Their absences from their neighborhoods while imprisoned must have been noticed as well. This would have made it difficult for them to maintain their reputations as workers and reliable members of society. It must have stunted the development of the meeting as well, if it did not end it completely.

Whether the congregants hoped to express their Spanish American or African-descent identities, challenge the boundaries of the social order, or perform some more complicated combination of these goals, their mimicking of ecclesiastical forms may have served to distance them from their goal. The reactions of witnesses and investigators indicate that this mimicry challenged Spanish ideas about status and the meaning of membership in colonial Christian society in significant ways. Although this case demonstrates the limitations Afro-Mexicans faced in creating places for themselves in colonial society, it also shows how urban Afro-Mexicans at the turn of the eighteenth century participated in colonial institutions as Christians and as colonial subjects. They practiced Christianity, formed relationships with clerics, and understood the language of hierarchy and power embodied in religious objects and rituals. They understood *novohispano* society so well that they were able to use its symbols to imitate—and in the process create alternate meanings of—authority. Africans in the Diaspora played central roles in the societies they entered, even when their numbers were not as large a part of the population as they were in places such as Brazil and the Caribbean. Africans and their descendants in Mexico learned quickly about the imperial and religious order and how to navigate it. They did so in ways that expressed their specific identities as Mexicans while also participating in patterns of cultural creation and community building that characterized Africans in other parts of Latin America and across the Diaspora.

Notes

I would like to thank the University of New Mexico Press for permission to publish this work and the Huntington Library for the research fellowship that supported it. I am very grateful to Rachel Sarah O'Toole, Sherwin Bryant, and Ben Vinson III for their help and comments, and I also thank the anonymous reader for the press.

1. For more discussion of this topic within the larger context of Afro-Mexican ritual practice see Bristol, *Christians, Blasphemers, and Witches*, 191–222.

2. Huntington Library, Huntington Manuscript Collection 35168 (hereafter HM 35168), El Señor Fiscal de este Sancto Oficio contra Isidro de Peralta, mulato, [por fundar a su modo una religion de San Agustin], 1699, Mexico City, folios 2–2v.

3. Ibid.
4. Ibid., folio 2v.
5. Ibid., folio 4v.
6. Ibid., folio 4v.
7. Ibid., folio 5v.
8. Third orders are lay groups connected to religious orders. Ibid., folio 6v.
9. Ibid., folio 4v.
10. Bennett, *Africans in Colonial Mexico*, 5 and passim; Bennett, *Colonial Blackness*, 1 and passim.
11. See Karasch, *Slave Life in Rio de Janeiro*, 82–88, 280–284; Sweet, *Recreating Africa*, 205–210.
12. Von Germeten, *Black Blood Brothers*, passim; Bowser, *The African Slave in Colonial Peru*, 247–251.
13. For a discussion of African-influenced religious practices see Bristol, *Christians, Blasphemers, and Witches*, 99, 149–189.
14. For a discussion of similar gatherings, see O'Hara, *A Flock Divided*, 123–127. The group that O'Hara discusses had no clerical supervision.
15. Huntington Library, HM 35168, folio 4v.
16. Ibid., folios 5–6.
17. Huntington Library, Huntington Manuscript Collection 35169 (hereafter HM 35169), Autos contra diferentes personas que formaban nueba religion de San Augustin . . . el principal, Isidro de Peralta, 1702, Mexico City, folios 18–18v.
18. Ibid., folios 19–19v.
19. Ibid., folio 20.
20. Ibid., folio 7v.
21. Ibid., folio 14.
22. According to later testimonies, these were seminary students.
23. Ibid., folios 9v–12.
24. Ibid., folio 28v.
25. Ibid., folio 25.
26. Ibid., folio 15v.
27. Ibid., folios 15–15v.
28. Ibid., folios 31v and 40.
29. Huntington Library, HM 35169, 46, folios 51–51v.
30. Ibid., folio 89.
31. Ibid., folios 89v–90.
32. Loreto López, "Familial Religiosity and Images in the Home," 26–49.
33. Cope, *The Limits of Racial Domination*, 110.
34. Huntington Library: HM 35168, folio 2; HM 35169, folios 7v, 11v, 15v, 18v, 19v, 20v, 22v, 25, 25v, 26v, 31v, 32, and 33v.
35. Von Germeten, *Black Blood Brothers*, 20.
36. Huntington Library: HM 35169, folio 11; HM 35169, folio 3.
37. Ganster, "Churchmen," 151.

38. Huntington Library: HM 35169, folios 39–39v; HM 35168, folio 2.

39. For an exception see Bristol, *Christians, Blasphemers, and Witches*, 23–62; Bristol, "'Although I am black, I am beautiful,'" passim.

40. Taussig, *Mimesis and Alterity*, xiii.

41. Bhabha, *The Location of Culture*, 86.

42. Cope, *The Limits of Racial Domination*, 158.

43. Cope describes the caste system as composed of "dual ladders, one for race and one for class, that parallel and reinforce each other, so that a specific racial label becomes naturally associated with a specific economic status." Cope, *The Limits of Racial Domination*, 162.

44. Viquiera Albán, *Propriety and Permissiveness in Bourbon Mexico*, 9.

45. Martínez, "The Black Blood of New Spain," 487–490.

46. Manzano, *Recopilación de leyes de los Reinos de las Indias*, 2, folios 285–290v.

47. Ibid., folio 287.

48. Ibid., folios 287–287v; Konetzke, *Colección de documentos para la historia de la formación social de Hispanoamérica*, vol. 1, part 1, folios 239, 290, 299, 420, 427, 433, 436; vol. 2, part 1, folios 479, 182, 262, 317, 417, 427; vol. 2, part 2, folio 513.

49. Martínez, "The Black Blood of New Spain," passim; von Germeten, *Black Blood Brothers*, 77–82; Bristol, *Christians, Blasphemers, and Witches*, 93–102.

50. Archivo General de la Nación de México, Inquisición, 458.21, 1659, folio 236.

51. Ibid., folio 237.

52. Kinsbruner, *Not of Pure Blood*, 108–109.

53. Huntington Library, HM 35168, folio 6.

54. Kinsbruner, *Not of Pure Blood*, 83–84, 103–107, 108–109.

55. Kicza, *Colonial Entrepreneurs*, 208.

56. Katzew, *Casta Painting*, 12.

57. Kicza, *Colonial Entrepreneurs*, 207.

58. The caste system (really an ambiguous set of attitudes and policies more than a set system) began as a way to differentiate Spaniards from non-Spaniards in a context in which race did not correlate directly to class. Cope, *The Limits of Racial Domination*, 24–25.

59. Huntington Library, HM 35169, folio 66v.

60. Ibid., folios 75–76.

61. Ibid., folio 69.

62. Ibid., folio 70.

63. Ibid., folio 68.

64. Ibid., folios 81–83v.

65. Cane-roofed wood or adobe huts were often located on the bottom floors of *casas de vecindad*. Muriel, "La habitación plurifamiliar en la ciudad de México," 275.

66. Huntington Library, HM 35169, folios 14 and 28v.

67. Ibid., folios 9v, 11v, and 21.

68. Gonzalbo Aizpuru, "Familias y viviendas en la capital del virreinato," 82, 92.

69. Huntington Library, HM 35169, folio 15.

70. Ibid., folio 11v.

71. Ibid., folio 15.

72. Kicza, *Colonial Entrepreneurs*, 110.

73. Huntington Library, HM 35169, folio 16v.

74. Ibid., folio 22.

75. Ibid., folio 85.

76. The following discussion relies on maps reproduced in Lombardo de Ruiz and Terán Trillo, *Atlas histórico de la Ciudad de México*, vol. 1. These include the 1772 map of José Antonio Alzate y Ramírez, Lamina 4 (pp. 56–57); the 1628 map of Juan Gómez de Trasmonte, Lamina 119 (pp. 290–291); the 1671 map of John Ogilby, Lamina 125 (pp. 302–303); the ca. 1690 map attributed to Diego Correa, Lamina 126 (pp. 304–305); the anonymous map of ca. 1690, Lamina 127 (pp. 306–307); the 1760 map of drawn by Carlos López and engraved by Diego Troncoso, Lamina 135 (pp. 322–323); and the ca. 1760 anonymous map, Lamina 136 (pp. 324–325).

77. Huntington Library, HM 35169, folio 68v.

78. "St. Gertrude the Great," *Catholic Encyclopedia*, available at http://www.newadvent.org/cathen/06534a.htm.

79. Chimalpahín, *Diario*, 251.

80. Díaz, *The Virgin, the King, and the Royal Slaves of El Cobre*, passim.

81. Sweet, *Recreating Africa*, 205–210; Karasch, *Slave Life in Rio de Janeiro*, 82–88, 280–284.

82. Villaseñor Black, "Saints and Social Welfare in Golden Age Spain," 22–23, 200–218.

83. Ibid., ix–xii; Taylor, "Mexico's Virgin of Guadalupe in the Seventeenth Century," 277–298.

84. Von Germeten, *Black Blood Brothers*, 18, 97. Von Germeten suggests that either Afro-Mexicans developed their devotion to Nicholas independently or that Augustinians encouraged it, perhaps seeing themselves in Saint Nicholas's place because of their work among the New Spain's humble classes.

85. Ibid., 20, 62.

86. Bhabha, *The Location of Culture*, 86–92.

87. Taussig, *Mimesis and Alterity*, xiii.

88. Jamieson, "Bolts of Cloth and Sherds of Pottery," 445–446.

89. For further discussions of Afro-Mexicans' desires for mobility in the seventeenth and eighteenth centuries, see Vinson, *Bearing Arms for His Majesty*; and von Germeten, *Black Blood Brothers*. Both show that the institutions they look at (*pardo* militias for Vinson and Afro-Mexican confraternities for von Germeten) were used by Afro-Mexicans to try to improve their social positions.

90. Gosner, *Soldiers of the Virgin*, 106–121.

91. Bhabha, *The Location of Culture*, 86–92.

92. In the case of non-Spaniards this was honor-virtue, based on personal qualities, rather than the honor-status accorded Spaniards. See Johnson and Lipsett-Rivera, "Introduction," 3–4, 10–11.

6

"The Lord walks among the pots and pans"
Religious Servants of Colonial Lima

NANCY E. VAN DEUSEN

In his sermon given in 1681 at the profession of a *donada*, José de Aguilar emphasized that each nun was the señora of her own cross but that each servant, whether a *criada* (servant) or a *donada* (religious servant who took informal vows), carried the cross of the señora "upon which they could not recline":

> To profess as a Nun and remain a Nun among the Señoras . . . is to carry the Cross of Christ, each with the honor of being the Señora of her Cross. But to profess as a Nun and not remain among the Señoras, but rather among the Servants of this Monastery [as a *donada*] is to carry the Cross of the Servants of this Monastery and to carry the Cross of Christ without it being her own. Those who profess as Servants carry everyone's Crosses because they have to serve them all, and help carry those who are not as able. . . . The Nuns carry the Cross hoping to be chosen to do the honorable tasks of the Convent. The Servants [*donadas*] carry the cross without such expectations. Those are the Wives who hold the title of Señoras. These are the Wives who hold the title of Servants.[1]

By virtue of having taken informal religious vows, *donadas* were more distinguished than the *criadas*; still, they could not rest, because the cross they carried was not their own. For free Afro-Peruvians and *parda*, *mulata*, and *morena* women of African descent, becoming a *donada* was their best option, because all religious orders prohibited them from professing as nuns of either the highest-ranked black veil or the lower-status white veil.[2]

The term "*donada*" literally meant that the candidate had been donated by someone to a monastery or that she had donated herself perpetually to "engage in service to God and the community."[3] Generally, when adolescent girls entered the novitiate with the ultimate goal of becoming a *donada*, they agreed to perform certain tasks in exchange for a home (the convent), living quarters, and food. During the seventeenth century, some 500 free or freed women of African or Indian descent chose to spend their lives in a cloistered setting. Most of these women were less than twenty years old when they made their choice.

In an attempt to explain the discriminatory barriers these aspirants faced and the differences between them and the nuns and the *criadas*, historians have often viewed the vocation of the *donada* as an "attractive alternative" to an insecure life in secular society.[4] Both skilled and unskilled Afro-Peruvian women, they argue, could find gainful employment, food, and shelter as religious domestics. Some, perhaps, might avoid rape or sexual torment by lascivious masters. Yet because conventual life was difficult and racial and occupational hierarchies were more rigidly enforced in the convent than in the secular world, nuns and ecclesiastical authorities considered *donadas* to be only one notch above *criadas* and slaves.[5] While they were meant to serve the community first and then the individual nuns, in fact, according to historian Luis Martín, *donadas* were viewed as nothing more than "exalted maids."[6] We only have to think of the words the black *donada* Ursula de Jesús (1604–1666) wrote in her diary—"They say the profession of the *donada* has no value"—to understand that some nuns did not even see them as "exalted."[7]

Studies based upon sources generated by nuns and ecclesiastical authorities iterate the position that *donadas* were laborers first and spiritual beings second. The documents imply that young women voluntarily submitted themselves to the conditions and *calidad* (prestige, ranking) associated with this position because of inequality and poverty. In fact, a review of the extant 237 rather formulaic *autos de ingreso* (entrance petitions) and *expedientes de profesión* (profession documents) for the largest convents of La Encarnación, La Concepción, and Santa Clara, all located in Lima, Peru, do not always reveal the motivations of the aspirants. Indeed, most of what we know about *donadas* comes from sources generated by individuals talking about them, not to or with them. When *donadas* do appear in the documents, they often speak as litigants in the ecclesiastical court to complain about the physical and emotional abuse of previous owners or nuns, to assert their hope that a testamentary legacy would be honored, or to settle a property dispute.[8] Given these constraints and given that *donadas* are often depicted as shaping the lives of the elite women they served, how can we access their other, "unstoried" lives?[9] Perhaps by repeating what the dominant discourse tells us we are only reaffirming their subordination as the "tethered shadow" to those who portrayed them in that light.[10]

Other methodological brambles tend to ensnare us. Scholars tend to focus on how the dominant legal and religious discourse about people of African descent marked and racialized them by excluding them from certain positions and spaces and by including them in other inferior ones.[11] Indeed, the historiography tends to cast men and women of color as being apart from rather than a part of monastic life in particular and colonial society in general. This tendency is further reinforced when scholars pigeonhole and classify servants as "marginal peoples" and see servitude as an institution just one notch above slavery.[12]

More recent diaspora studies that focus on the intercultural religious exchanges and lived experiences of Africans in the Americas often use Inquisition records to discern how diverse African notions of the beyond were transculturated in daily life practices. However, when discussions of Christian practices arise, scholars tend to juxtapose African religious "traditions" with the compliance with, strategic use of, or resistance to dominant Christian theological discourses.[13] But as recent scholarship on the diaspora has shown, Christianity was not always a "superficial veil," especially among the descendants of Central Africans long familiar with the basic tenets of Christianity.[14] Studies of confraternities as centers of Catholic spirituality and kinship and as communal religious gatherings, as evinced in Joan Bristol's fascinating work, and examinations of wills detailing the acquisition of relics and images and bequests to Catholic charitable organizations all demonstrate that Catholicism was a centripetal and not a marginal force in peoples' lives.[15] Conversion, itself, as Charles Beatty-Medina argues in his chapter, could serve as a means of empowerment—in this case, for the mulattos living in the Esmeraldas maroon society. In this sense, a consideration of the mutable and diasporic nature of spiritual beliefs throughout the Atlantic World can only be strengthened by transcending bifurcated Christian (read: European)/African (read: non-Christian) epistemological paradigms. Furthermore, it is important to differentiate among Africans already influenced by Catholic tenets—that is, *bozales* (recently arrived Africans) who were willing to adapt Christian tenets that resonated with their own spiritual practices—and creole Africans or Afro-Peruvian family members whose prime focus from birth was Catholicism. By seeing African peoples in America as complex colonial subjects with different understandings and proximities to African culture and religious beliefs we can rethink diasporic experiences as ever-evolving, interpenetrating, and culturally layered rather than as unidimensional. On a larger level, understanding the multigenerational experiences of people of diasporic heritage helps deflate the tensions that exist in defining diaspora: as Thomas Holt has pointed out, "one must see a sameness of experience in order to think about 'diaspora' but must conceive of a difference of experience in order to analyze and understand the experiences in meaningful ways."[16]

This chapter contends that for many people of African descent, Christianity was a deeply lived experience, both in the world and in the cloister. By the seventeenth century, monasteries and convents throughout Latin America were home to thousands of free and enslaved men and women of African descent, although we know little about their experiences as slaves, servants, and spiritual beings. Some of us are familiar with Martín de Porras—statues of this humble seventeenth-century *mulato* saint grace restaurants and sacred spaces throughout the Spanish-speaking world. Although less renowned, black visionaries such as Juana Esperanza de San Alberto in Puebla, Mexico, and Ursula de Jesús (1604–1666) in Lima, Peru, have been acknowledged in a spate of recently published encyclopedia entries, books and articles.[17] Hundreds of girls and women of African descent lived in *beaterios* or *recogimientos* (lay religious houses) in the urban areas of Brazil, Peru, and Mexico.[18] The most famous *beata*, or woman affiliated with a third order of the regular clergy, was the African Rosa de Egipcíaca (Courana) (1701–?), an enslaved prostitute turned holy woman who lived in Minas Gerais and Rio de Janeiro. She helped found the Recogimiento of Our Lady of the Good Birth (Bom Parto) (1754) for Portuguese, Brazilian, and Afro-Brazilian women before finally disappearing from the historical record in 1765 after being tried by the Lisbon Inquisition as a false visionary (*embusteira*).[19] These exemplary figures are representative of the thousands of obscure pious men and women serving as *donado/as*, *lego/as*, or *freilas* (synonyms for religious servants) who walked the dimly lit corridors of convents scattered throughout Spanish and Portuguese America.

Fortunately, the assemblage of testimonies from and about *donadas* enables the historian to reveal their discrete motivations and ways of dealing with the exigencies of life in the seventeenth century. While it is nearly impossible to get into the heads of these women and "make the subaltern speak," it is possible to speak about the dimensionality of *donadas*—especially, the external and internal pressures they faced, the matriarchal intimacies they formed with their owners and patrons, and the broader economic and religious climate in Lima that influenced their decisions. Clearly *donadas* were not a homogenous group, and their motivations for taking the veil varied. Most important, they made choices that did not always mimic those of the nuns. However, when considering *donadas*—whether as individuals or as a collectivity—we should be careful not to deemphasize the considerable constraints they faced. As José de Aguilar noted in his sermon, *donadas* occupied themselves in the "humble ministries of the house," and, on a daily basis, they had to strike a balance between communal tasks and the incessant requests of the pampered nuns they also served. No doubt the demands placed upon their time and their bodies caused resentment and enmity.

The vast majority of *donadas* were labeled as free *pardas, sambas, mulatas, negras,* or *quarteronas de mulata.*[20] Certainly these essentializing labels, defined in the masters' terms, reinforced the "myth of [an] essential core" based upon skin color or physical appearance.[21] Yet, in convents and in secular society, these de jure "fixed orderings" were less important than the de facto positionality and valuations relative to economic and social status and the occupations women held in the convent.[22] In determining the relationship of a *donada* "self" to others, these labels identified not an ethnoracial *parda* essence but rather one of many figurative lines in the sand that were eventually consumed by time and the prevailing winds of power. Nor did *donadas* have a fixed "*donada*" identity, because the relationships they established with "others," including nuns, servants, and God, occurred positionally, in a manner related to status, which was internally; the distinctions that were drawn between white-veil nuns, *donadas, criadas,* and slaves; the development of kinship networks; and spirituality. There is no question that the title "*donada*" symbolized the hierarchical, unequal nature of social relations based on the extraction of their labor for the benefit of others, but it also represented an opportunity to serve God and Christ honorably. This tension makes their positionality somewhat paradoxical.

To Better Serve Our Lord

Procedurally, an aspirant had to follow several time-consuming steps before becoming a *donada*. First, the candidate herself (if she was over the age of twenty-five), a nun, or a family member requested formal admittance (*auto de ingreso*) into the religious community as a novice. A nun promoting a *donada*'s candidacy to the community generally emphasized her occupational skills and any distinguishing virtues of spirituality. The candidate (occasionally several applied at once) typically specified her occupational talents, her spiritual motives, how much of her life she had spent in the convent, and her fear of living in the *siglo* (the secular domain) as some of her motivations.

The candidate or the person nominating her also had to specify who would pay the required dowry of 500 pesos.

According to canon law, the candidate had to be free from bondage and over sixteen years of age. If the community of nuns voted to approve the candidate's entry, the abbess would then request that the archbishop sign the *auto de ingreso*.[23] At that point, the novice entered the novitiate, technically for one year, during which she was trained by teachers and kept under strict vigilance.[24] In the novitiate she learned how to be obedient, charitable, and humble and how to make postures and gestures of humility; she studied the attributes of oral and mental prayer and the lives of the saints; and she memorized the rules and constitutions of the order.[25] The most privileged learned to read designated spiritual texts. Once the candidate had completed her studies and training, a delegate of the bishop oversaw the novice's required examination (*examen de profesión*). Following the mandates established by the Council of Trent for all female religious, the candidate answered several questions, after which the novice took simple vows (*votos simples*) of poverty, obedience, chastity, and enclosure. They were not formal vows (*votos solemnes*) in the juridical or canonical sense, but most convents and *donadas* took them very seriously and the penalties for breaking them could be severe.[26] For example, the *morena* María de San Francisco made the following vow before the nuns and the most important celestial beings:

> I, María de San Francisco, out of love and service for Our Lord and Savior, Jesus Christ, and for the Blessed Virgin Mary, His mother, and for the devotion I have for the Immaculate Conception, without original sin, hereby vow and promise God and Mary and all the glorious apostles, Saints Peter and Paul, and the columns of the Church, and the Most Excellent and Reverend Archbishop don Bartolomé Lobo Guerrero and, thee, Abbess doña Aldonsa de Viveros, and all the female prelates who are and were of this convent, to live my entire life, in obedience and poverty, in chastity and perpetual enclosure under the Bull given by Pope Julius II (in living memory) and to our order, granted and confirmed. This I promise to uphold until I die.[27]

After reciting her vows, the *donada* was then given a white shoulder-length *velo simple* to distinguish her from the nuns, and her life as a religious servant began.[28]

Establishing Parameters

Before the 1630s, entry procedures and the careful application of the order's constitutions may have been more the exception than the rule. Records for the first third of the seventeenth century show nuns openly petitioning for a *donada* to enter first and foremost as a personal servant and then to serve the community.[29] In fact, many young girls of African descent entered convents as "*donadas*" to replace ill, deceased, or fugitive slaves or, conversely, slaves replaced *donadas* when their numbers decreased.[30] Several convents distinguished *donadas* who entered the novitiate from those who were formally admitted as servants or slaves who never took their vows and served individual nuns.[31] While these categorical distinctions provide clear evidence of the "exalted maids" to whom historian Luis Martín referred, these inconsistencies and discrepancies changed somewhat after 1631, when Archbishop Fernando Arias de Ugarte (archbishop 1618–38) issued a mandate declaring that service to an individual nun should not in any way interfere with the "obligations to perform designated tasks."[32] The mandate also formalized the *autos de ingreso* to ensure that *donadas* would remain in the cloister, and the required ratio of one *donada* for every ten nuns was then more strictly enforced.

At any given time, the population might range from between thirty and fifty *donadas*, which for a smaller convent such as Las Descalças de San José, which had seventy nuns, could be significant.[33] Candidates were nearly always free from bondage, unmarried, and of African or native Andean descent. The age of *donadas* at the time of entry and profession varied between sixteen (when the novice could legally profess) and twenty. However, occasionally a married woman gained permission from her husband to take vows of celibacy to enter a convent.[34]

If, as I have already argued, positionality involved establishing divisions between one category and another, were *donadas* really treated differently from or considered superior to the *criadas*? In some ways, the answer is yes. For one, *donadas* had "tenure," and the fact that they could not be expelled from convents became more significant after mid-century, when probing archbishops sought to curtail the excessive number of *criadas*, slaves, lay women, and children. Additionally, as permanent members of the religious community, their premium positions were coveted, especially when a vigilant archbishop determined in an ecclesiastical visit that some *criadas* should be expelled because their numbers surpassed the acceptable limit.[35] On such exigent occasions, nuns threatened with the loss of prized servants would scurry to promote the candidacy of specific *criadas* to the rank of *donada*. But even then, the acceptance of servants into the novitiate was not always guaranteed because the allotted slots for *donadas* were so limited.[36]

Ascending to the rank of *donada* certainly did not mean working less than servants or slaves, and those privileged enough to make the transition from *criadas* to *donadas* knew that their lives would be labor intensive. To reinforce the subordination of their position, *donadas* taking their vows would be pointedly asked if they knew that their profession was not meant to be a form of "escape" from a heavy workload.[37] However, to obscure this fact, ecclesiastical authorities tried to glorify the sacrifices involved in their labor-intensive position. As José de Aguilar proclaimed in a 1678 sermon presented at the Monasterio de La Encarnación's celebration of *donadas*, "the *pardas donadas*" could follow the example of the hard-working Marcela, the *criada* of Martha, in whose "castle and home" Christ resided.[38] The notion of sacrifice, so imbued in Christian thought, also permeated the words of young aspirants such as the orphaned *mulata* Josefa de la Concepción y Meneses, who stated in her entrance petition that "it is my deepest desire to be the *criada* of the *criadas* in [the convent] and to do whatever is ordered in the infirmary and other offices.[39]

Unlike *criadas*, *donadas* were listed on the annually designated task lists (*tablas de oficios*) along with the black- and white-veiled nuns. In this sense, the positions they held served as differentiating occupational "buffers" between them and the nuns of the white veil, on the one hand, and between them and the servants and slaves, on the other.[40] For instance, the *tablas de oficios* frequently listed *donadas* as the assistants to their supervisors, the nuns of the white veil, who oversaw the more mundane tasks of the convent. Yet as they performed an array of duties, they worked alongside their subordinates, the servants and slaves.[41] As assistants to the *silleras* (women in charge of the pantry), they assured that the flour, wheat, barley, wine, oil, and legumes were properly protected against humidity. The *fuelleras* stoked and fanned the fires that heated the organ with bellows, and the *entonadoras* made sure the organ was properly tuned and ready to play. *Donadas* also aided the *donadas*' and *criadas*' teachers, the laborers (*obreras*), and bakers (*panaderas*).[42] They fetched the nuns who received visitors, while the more senior *donadas* stood guard (as *celadoras*) at the laundry and other public spaces.[43] In an environment where surveillance and being attentive to the actions of others was paramount, only the most responsible and trustworthy *donadas* were appointed as guardians of the *donadas*' dormitory.[44]

Teresa de Ávila's proclamation that "God lives among the pots and pans"[45] probably resonated deeply with the convents' servants, but still, they could not negate the fact that more than anything, it was the combination of communal duties (*la obediencia*) and service to individual nuns that caused exhaustion and incited anger and frustration.[46] Although *la obediencia* meant following orders, being slotted into inferior positions and occupations produced infighting and rancor because both the nuns and the servants determined the value and prestige of specific tasks according to their own criteria.[47] Evidence suggests that for these reasons, the *donadas* (and nuns) jealously guarded their "rights" to maintain the same post year after year and might take "extraordinary measures" to prevent the abbess from properly executing her duties to assign these coveted or but onerous positions.[48]

Of course, finding a slave to take on the more onerous tasks was an option only a few privileged *donadas* had. Documents reveal the occasional *donada* who owned a slave whom she had inherited as part of a testamentary legacy or who had been donated or loaned by a family member or a pious individual.[49] Not only did slaves relieve the labor burden in the convent, they also allowed those particular *donadas* to garner additional income from the slave's work outside the convent.[50] Ownership of a slave also helped *donadas* gain additional status relative to the other *donadas* (some *donadas* were referred to as "*doñas*" by the nuns) and to the nuns of the white veil who did not own slaves. It also lessened their dependency upon their black-veil-nun patrons because they could live more comfortably, either in their own cell or with a companion or relative.[51]

The internal rankings of specific tasks and spaces in the convent were most apparent in the designation of occupations related to assistance in the divine office.[52] Although supervised by nuns of the white veil (who were called *sacristanas mayores*), some *donadas* worked as sextons who cleaned religious objects and washed the linen for the altar in the sacristy.[53] *Donadas* such as Juana de Sejas (who held the position for consecutive years at La Concepción) rang the bell to specify the liturgical hours and to indicate when "sermons, processions, anniversaries and religious commemorations" were about to occur.[54] An aptitude for a particular vocation also helped a candidate gain a slot in the novitiate. The 26-year-old Lorenza de Mesa entered La Encarnación because she had been carrying the cross in processions for over ten years and considered that task to be her vocation.[55]

"Matriarchal Intimacies"

The prestige associated with particular tasks allowed *donadas* to position themselves favorably relative to other members of the religious community. But on many different levels, matronage, or the association with a powerful female figure in the convent, played an even more crucial role in determining which young women would become *donadas*, when they would do so, and what their status would be afterward. Nearly 85 percent of the postulants examined in all the extant documents had lived for years (if not decades) in a convent serving a nun as a *criada*.[56] Some were even the daughters of slaves who had been freed by their owners. This suggests an internal ranking among servants who were privileged enough to advance to the next level—from slave to *criada* to *donada* or from *criada* to *donada*—and also suggests that candidates whose patron was a well-known and powerful nun (or *donada*) stood a better chance of entering the novitiate.[57] Although the statistics reported in conventual chronicles are not always reliable, we might assume that in a given year (before 1689, when the numbers of servants increased significantly) less than one-quarter of the total number of servants would be fortunate enough to ascend to the rank of *donada* or even enter the novitiate.[58] (Some *donadas* even remained in the novitiate as a type of "holding area" for years.)[59] In fact, the percentage of *donadas* relative to the overall free servant population in the convents of La Encarnación, Santa Clara, La Concepción, and Las Descalças de San José (a smaller convent) rarely exceeded one-third of the total population of free women of color in convents.[60] The selective privileging of particular *criadas* who became *donadas* can be explained in several ways. As elite Spanish women entered the novitiate to become nuns of the black veil, they brought with them young slaves and servants, some of whom would eventually become *donadas*. The connection established between a future *donada* (who often did not know whether she would ever become one) and a powerful female family "cluster" base created distinct positionalities vis-à-vis other nuns and "their" servant girls.

However, non-consanguineous and power-based matriarchal networks were not exclusive to the elite *mestiza* and Spanish nuns. One can also trace intragenerational linkages among the slaves and servants who entered with Spanish novices and daughters, nieces, and granddaughters who continued to serve the next generation of nuns.[61] But not all servant and slave girls had relatives in the convent to rely upon for support and matronage. At a tender age, young girls arrived in Lima from various parts of the viceroyalty to serve a particular nun, often for life. Lacking contact with family members who were far away, they were likely to develop crucial ties within the cloister—particularly with a nun who would offer financial support.[62] Institutional "exchanges" also occurred when orphans from another convent or the Hospital de la Caridad transferred to a new monastic setting.[63] But, again, this matronage was not the exclusive domain of the powerful and the elite. Just as nuns raised young servant girls to become *donadas* (and remain their servants), *donadas* also raised young girls and provided for them financially as best they could.[64] Wealthier *donadas* such as María de San Joseph might leave a *celdita* (little cell) to a girl she had raised, hoping that she, too, would eventually take her vows.[65]

The formation of alternate kinship linkages and matriarchal intimacies was further reinforced by servants and even *donadas* who lived in the cells of their patrons along with slaves and servants.[66] In this intimate, familial context, nuns, servants, and slaves shared material objects such as linens, candles, and furniture; they listened to the same scriptural passages being read; and from youth to old age, they witnessed each others' lamentations and small victories. In some cases, the relationship between owner or matriarch and servant or slave was considered so "intimate" (*estrecha*) that the girls assumed the surnames of the matriarchs. For the *donada*, this deepened ties of identity with her female patron. Such was the case with the young *mulatilla* María Marchan, the legitimate daughter of the *pardo* sexton of La Concepción, Jerónimo Carrión, who took the name of her patron, doña María Marchan, a nun of the black veil who supported her candidacy to become a *donada* in 1681.[67] Others passed down their patrons' surnames to their daughters.[68] Although the practice was more common before the 1630s, some *morenas conventuales* such as Isabel Casanga, Ana Casanga (her sister?), Cecilia Bran, and Maria Fulupa maintained the "African" surnames of their mothers.[69]

Some nuns of the black veil had the ability to support a controversial candidate.[70] This was significant in cases when an enslaved novice was declared "free" at the stroke of a pen, usually after behind-the-scenes negotiation.[71] *Donadas* without a patron were financially and politically dependent upon the good graces of the abbess.[72] In these instances, *donadas* often expressed a willingness to take on the least desirable occupations, to carry the cross of Christ and donate their personal service to the convent for life.[73] Such was the case of Ventura de la Fuente, a free *criada* who dictated her own petition in 1687: "I was born a slave, and my master gave me a letter of freedom when I was still young. I am a mulatta and *mosa*, and in order to serve in religion with the merit of being a nun I desire to take the habit of *donada*. I have no money to give [as a dowry] because I am poor, but I am obligated to serve the community." Below Ventura's petition, the abbess scribbled one line: "She is useful to the community."[74]

Freedom from Bondage?

To carry the cross of Christ, one had to be free from legal bondage. The destinies of girls who were slaves were often linked to the will of their owners. "Because I raised her from infancy in my home" seemed to motivate a charitable owner to leave a bequest to or grant freedom to a young girl who had worked as a household servant (sometimes alongside her mother).[75] Others cited affection, piety, or Christian charity as their main motives. When Ana de Alvarado wanted to have some*thing* (my emphasis) from her home "to offer to the Mother of God," she offered her slave's daughter, Andrea, to two nuns in La Concepción.[76] Some owners agreed to pay a dowry or support a candidacy because the girl's mother had served them well or because they expressed a strong attachment to the infants.[77] But such bequests were sometimes "deathbed gestures," decisions that were made when the girl was extremely young.[78] Such a charitable act might have positive consequences for a young woman freed from bondage before she entered a convent, but the situation was far more complex if the *carta de libertad* (declaration of freedom) contained labyrinthine clauses that specified that the potential *donada* would receive her freedom only if she became a *donada*.[79]

Although some slave mothers were happy knowing that the future of their daughters would be different from their own, not all girls viewed the position of *donada* as a salutary alternative to slavery, nor did all of them appreciate that their owners had made the decision for them, in some cases before they had the use of reason. In one instance, Isabel María, the daughter of the slave Constanza Terranova, was donated by her owner, Catalina Velásquez, at age four to the Convent of Santa Clara and entrusted to a black-veil nun. In her will made in 1641, Velásquez inserted a clause stipulating that Isabel María would be free from bondage as long as she would serve in Santa Clara her entire life. It specified that if she left the convent, she would remain a slave, but the convent would not be able to sell her. Once she reached the required age of sixteen, she would be "free" to become a *donada* and 200 pesos from the estate would pay her dowry.[80] When Isabel María finally came of age, she stated to the ecclesiastical court that she had never wanted to become a *donada*, and knowing that she had to spend her life in the convent, she fled, became pregnant, and, contrary to the legacy, was then sold to an owner outside the convent.[81] Becoming a *donada* under such conditions did not appeal to her, even though not doing so meant continued bondage.[82] In the end, Isabel María stated that she was willing to pay the 200 pesos she owed the convent on the condition that the archbishop dispatch a license that would free her from "whatever rights the nuns claim to have against me."[83]

Just as Spanish families pressured girls to become nuns of the black or the white veil, *donadas* also occasionally took the veil "against their will." Although she was not successful, María de San Francisco's petition to annul her vows provides an example a *donada* who felt constrained. She had entered the convent as a servant of María de Retes, but then, as María de San Francisco's lawyer explained, her uncle, Friar Manuel Franco, a lay brother (*lego*) in the Convent of San Agustín forced her to profess. She did so, she claimed, "out of respect and the reverential fear I had for him." Because he had threatened to cut her off economically, she had acquiesced. Her other arguments were equally compelling: she lacked the strength to do the tasks required of the *donadas*, the convent did not provide her with proper clothing and other items, her health was declining, she felt that she was being held against her will, and she claimed that she had taken her vows before the legal age of sixteen. The nuns mistreated her because she was poor and miserable. In spite of such forceful arguments, the judge denied her appeal to nullify her vows.[84]

The Prospects of a Good Future

As the cases of Isabel María, María de San Francisco and others attest, some *donadas* resented the onerous tasks they had to perform and being treated (or labeled) as slaves. No doubt their understanding that "the obligations of religion are greater than those of the world" resonated differently with them than it did for the nuns they served.[85] However, such responses contrast sharply with the sentiments of other young women who cherished the thought of carrying the cross of Christ (and others) and who would entreat the abbess in tears to let them profess.[86] The transition from *criada* to *donada* was a logical one given the fact that most *donadas* had spent most of their lives serving a nun. But some 15 percent of *donadas* who entered the convent had never lived there or had entered only briefly. They came from all walks of life. Some *donadas* were legitimate daughters whose families who could afford to pay the 500-peso dowry.[87] Other applicants came from humble economic backgrounds and family members, including single mothers who labored as domestics or food sellers, struggled earnestly to gather the capital to secure their daughters' futures.[88] The adopted families of orphans also offered to pay their dowries.[89] Finally, sisters and nieces from more well-to-do families entered the novitiate together, sometimes with their own servants.[90]

What might motivate a parent to place his or her child in a convent under the care of a nun as a *criada*? No doubt a better future for their daughters entailed escape from poverty, protection from a ruthless master, and a rudimentary education in a convent.[91] For that, they were willing to part with their children.[92] Yet spiritual reasons also motivated them. In the seventeenth century, God opened his doors to everyone, including (and especially) people of African descent. As hundreds of colonial documents attest, Spaniards were not the only ones to fully embrace the multitudinous expressions of Catholicism that occurred on a daily if not hourly basis. Many Afro-Peruvian *limeños* knew someone who served as a *mayorala*, *hermana*, or *cofrada* in any one of the dozens of confraternities designated for *moreno/as*, *pardo/as*, and *mulato/as* in a city overflowing with monasteries. Not only did these lay religious brotherhoods finance the ceremonious displays of religious devotion, they also helped the sick, paid burial fees, and oversaw the establishment of chaplaincies for souls in purgatory.[93] They also fostered new networks of kinship relations based upon a common organizational thread. Although men generally held the most prestigious offices, grandmothers, mothers, and aunts sewed the banners that represented their particular confraternities, they maintained the cult of the Virgin by helping dress her image for a particular procession, they traveled from house to house begging for alms to buy candles, and they cleaned and arranged sacred objects in the chapel of their confraternities.[94]

It is also misguided to think that if a girl had spent most of her young life working in the service of a nun, she would sever or relinquish family ties outside the convent. Although girls were separated from their families for lengthy periods of time, evidence shows that family members set aside the money to pay for a young woman's dowry to enter the novitiate.[95] Parents' voices also appear in *autos de ingreso* soliciting the acceptance of their daughters as novices.[96] For instance, Pablo de los Rios, a lieutenant, described his legitimate daughter, Agustina, as being "[endowed] with such virtue, that she never left the cloister, not even when the earthquakes occurred." He requested that she be given the opportunity to pursue her noble goal of taking the veil and serving Christ.[97]

It is important to remember that the convent was a sacred space, where the possibility of a spiritual life was strong. God's presence could be perceived in every room, in every icon, and in every deferential gesture. Indeed, years and even decades of enclosure facilitated the development of characteristics and virtues that might lead to acceptance into the novitiate.[98] Many also believed that a life of enclosure was their destiny.[99] Indeed, because the convent was the only world many had ever known, some girls raised "in the Blessed Virgin's house" felt incapable of returning to *el siglo* (the world) because it had always been portrayed as a dangerous place where they might roam aimlessly.[100] As girls made the transition from novice to professed *donada*, each vow of obedience, chastity, enclosure, and poverty taken was a step down the path of religious perfection.[101] Here their positionality of self to other related most profoundly to the most powerful force of life: God.

Donadas sometimes referred to their profession as a vocation and claimed to have received God's calling to the state of religious perfection. Following the example of the servant Marcela, "they pursued their devotion with ardor, until assured they were in a state of grace, a sure sign they would reach Glory."[102] Day after day, the rigorous conventual routines, which were divided methodically into component parts related to prayer, silence, and work formed steps on the path toward perfection, a path for everyone—nuns and *donadas* alike. Those with more capital invested in the religious culture of the convent. Melchora de los Reyes borrowed 800 pesos to build an altar screen for Our Lady of the Incarnation.[103] Other *donadas* left bequests in their wills to maintain the cult of a particular saint or to ensure a steady supply of wax for the candles placed at the foot of the statue of the Virgin.[104] In La Encarnación, the *parda* servants even established their own confraternity.[105]

In the seventeenth century, prospective *donadas* had many models of sanctity to draw upon for inspiration and support. As officials sought to bring all members of the republics of Indians and Spaniards into the fold of a Christian commonwealth, sermons and chronicles began to emphasize the spirituality of particularly devout men and women of color graced by Mary or Jesus. From priests and nuns, women heard about the genealogy of venerable blacks and exemplary saints such as Benito Palermo, whose cult in Lima flourished after 1620.[106] But *limeños* had no shortage of their own local heroes. Many whispered tales of the miracles of Martín de Porras, who never closed his heart to anyone. Stories of lesser-known exemplary *criadas* and *donadas*, who, according to one chronicler, did not merit a lesser place than the nuns, also circulated widely.[107] Eventually the miniature *vidas* of these blessed servants of God were immortalized in the conventual chronicles of Diego Córdova y Salinas (1651), Juan Meléndez (1681), and Francisco de Echave y Assu (1688), in the hope of inspiring young souls.[108]

Of course extolling the virtues of servants and *donadas* also served the didactic purpose of *exemplum*, and each religious order and convent competed to have the most illustrious, most saintly nuns and servants. Although to a certain degree the women of color in Lima internalized the vision of the exceptionally humble and penitent servant Marcela, this model did more than encourage mimesis and accentuate the unequal distinctions between them and their Spanish superiors.[109] For *donadas*, the parameters of difference were clear in the tasks they were assigned and in the need to accrue capital or find a powerful matron. But their deeply felt experiences of Catholicism were not always shaped by church authorities, nor were they devout Catholics only because mimesis gave them power or prestige vis-à-vis the nuns. For receptive and observant girls who worked alongside pious women of color day after day, their elders served as models of sanctity in the flesh. For them, these "saints" did not need to become "white" to be venerable. For instance, in 1673, María de Escobar, a 50-year-old *quarterona de mestiza* who had been the *compañera* of the blessed *mulata* María de Rojas for over twenty years, petitioned to receive the habit of *donada* because it was the wish of María de Rojas, whom María de Escobar referred to as this "*donada*, a great servant of God."[110] Occasionally the entrance petitions mention particularly devout *donadas*, such as the "virtuous" Inés de la Concepción, who served in the sacristy of Las Descalças for over twenty years.[111] Shortly after the venerable Ursula de Jesús (or de Christo) died, an aspirant named Francisca de la Cruz petitioned to enter the novitiate. The abbess claimed that "for over twenty years Francisca has served the convent with great virtue and perseverance. Following the example of the Mother, Ursula de Christo [,] she has determined to take the habit of *donada*."[112]

Even if *donadas* were unable to share the full status as brides of Christ, their testimonies display a fervent desire to serve God and the Blessed Virgin. In many cases, this motivation took precedence over other, more "material" concerns.[113] The black mystic Ursula de Jesús argued that *donadas* sought to define themselves primarily as spiritual beings in spite of how others perceived them.[114] Although priests often expressed the sentiment that God did not distinguish between servant and señora and that all the bones of the dead were equal, the question is how women of color internalized or appropriated this discourse. When Ursula de Jesús lamented as she talked with God that "they say the profession of the *donadas* has no value," she received the following reply: "There is a difference because the nuns are white and of the Spanish nation, but with respect to the soul, all is one: Whoever does more is worth more."[115] Clearly, Ursula de Jesús believed that all were equal before God. In their hearts, *donadas* carried the cross of Christ, even if they could never hope to rest upon a satin pillow to relieve their weariness.

Conclusions

As a close reading of the documents shows, a variety of issues motivated women of African heritage to become *donadas*—some material, others psychological or spiritual. Some chose this path to ensure their freedom. The matriarchal intimacies of convent life and the positionality of *donadas* relative to others within the convents as well as their ability to effectuate a spiritual life influenced the opportunities presented to them and their decisions about those opportunities. Relations between *donadas* and other members of the religious community depended less upon essentialized "racial" taxonomies, as Jean-Pierre Tardieu has argued, than upon their status as a free or enslaved person, whether they had entered the convent as a donation or had they been raised there from early childhood, whether they had been pressured by family members or nuns to take their vows, and how much power the "patron" supporting their candidacy wielded in the convent.[116] The power *donadas* wielded within the convent also depended upon the economic capital they could garner during their lifetime. Equally important, their positionality relative to others also depended upon how devoutly they ministered to God.

Clearly these "subjugated" women did not just accept the world imposed upon them, but neither did they always resist, negotiate their "identities," or mimic Spanish superiors. Nor were *donadas* marginalized, repressed servants, "placated with unfulfilled promises."[117] If, as historian Luis Martín has argued, *donadas* served as a "buffer between nuns and the hundreds of servants and slaves who inhabited the cloisters," what can the intimate politics of power relations tell us about the interstices of difference in colonial non-elite society? What do they tell us about the ever-changing complexities of the diasporic experiences of bondage and spirituality for people of African heritage?[118] Unveiling the matriarchal and restrictive relations between nuns and *donadas* also raises questions about the positionalities of self in relation to other and the "theatrics of dominance" that took place in other domestic spaces of colonial Lima.[119] The routes taken and the roots sown by generations of diasporic subjects involved different positionalities in relation to the rich variability of baroque Catholic expression.

Given the constraints *donadas* faced and knowing that Spaniards considered them to be inferior did not mean that for those reasons they believed that they had to suffer like Christ in order to enjoy eternal glory. The fact is that many Catholics from America, Europe, and Africa believed that "only he who perseveres until the end will be saved."[120] Knowing they would work diligently until death, men and women of African heritage might say to themselves: "We should not cease to carry our Cross in pursuit of Christ, because what other way is there? What good does it do us to have navigated our way favorably over a very long distance only to lose our way at the door?"[121] Ultimately, everyone carried the cross of Christ, in their hearts, on their shoulders, and in their obligations to others in their world.

Notes

I would like to thank the anonymous readers, Ilana Aragón Noriega, Sherwin Bryant, Patricia Díaz, Rachel Sarah O'Toole, Megan Riddle, Preston Schiller, Susanne Seales, Serena Sprungl, and Ben Vinson III for research assistance and comments that aided in the completion of this chapter.

1. Aguilar, *Sermones varios*, 48v.

2. The first and second Lima councils prohibited blacks and Indians (and implicitly, the *castas*) from becoming nuns; see Tardieu, *Los negros y la Iglesia en el Perú*, 1:385. The term *freila* was synonymous with *donada* or *hermana*; see Covarrubias, *Tesoro de la lengua castellana o española*, 557; Real Academia Española, *Diccionario de autoridades*, 3:794.

3. Real Academia Española, *Diccionario de autoridades*, 3:334–335; Real Academia Española, *Diccionario de la lengua española*, 493.

4. In particular see Martín, *Daughters of the Conquistadores*; and Tardieu, *Los negros y la Iglesia en el Perú*.

5. Martín, *Daughters of the Conquistadores*, 188. Tardieu, *Los negros y la Iglesia en el Perú*, 1:393, 397. Although they ranked higher than the *donadas*, the nuns of the white veil were sometimes viewed as servants. For examples see Archivo Arzobispal de Lima (hereafter AAL), Monasterio de Santa Clara (hereafter SC), *legajo* (hereafter leg.) IV, *expediente* (hereafter exp.) 25, "Autos . . . María Nuñez y Francisca de Guevara para monjas de velo blanco." See also AAL, SC, leg. IV, exp. 32, "Autos . . . Francisca de la Cruz."

6. Martín, *Daughters of the Conquistadores*, 185.

7. Ursula de Jesús, *The Souls of Purgatory*, 121 [32r].

8. Banerjee, "Down Memory Lane: Representations of Domestic Workers in Middle Class Personal Narratives of Colonial Bengal," 682.

9. Burton, *Dwelling in the Archive*, 17.

10. Bhabha, *The Location of Culture*, 88. See also Steedman, "Servants and Their Relationship to the Unconscious," 328.

11. Fra Molinero, "Ser mulato en España y América," 123.

12. Bennett, "The Subject in the Plot," 122–124; Fernández Álvarez, *Casadas, monjas, rameras y brujas*, chapter 5; Fairchilds, *Domestic Enemies*, 102.

13. Davis, "Introduction," xiii, xvi; Bennett, *Africans in Colonial Mexico*, chapter 6.

14. Thornton, "The Development of an African Catholic Church in the Kingdom of the Kongo," 147–148; Vanhee, "Central African Popular Christianity and the Making of Haitian Vodou Religion," 245, 257; Rey, "Kongolese Catholic Influences on Haitian Popular Catholicism," 266; Bowser, *The African Slave in Colonial Peru*, 40–41.

15. Bristol, "Negotiating Authority in New Spain," 82–124; von Germeten, *Black Blood Brothers*; Gómez Acuña, "Las cofradías de negros en Lima (siglo XVII)"; Bowser, *The African Slave in Colonial Peru*, 247–251.

16. Holt, "Slavery and Freedom in the Atlantic World," 33; Palmer, "The African Diaspora."

17. Bristol, "'Although I am black, I am beautiful'"; Cussen, "Fray Martín de Porres and the Religious Imagination of Creole Lima"; Martínez i Alvarez, *La libertad femenina de dar lugar a Dios*; Ursula de Jesús, *The Souls of Purgatory*; van Deusen, "Úrsula de Jesús"; van Deusen "Ursula de Jesús, a Seventeenth-Century Afro-Peruvian Mystic"; Wood, "Religious Women of Color in Seventeenth-Century Lima."

18. Mott, *Rosa Egipcíaca*, 202–226; Algranti, *Honradas e devotas*, 175–178; van Deusen, *Between the Sacred and the Worldly*, chapter 6; van Deusen, "Circuits of Knowledge among Women in Early Seventeenth-Century Lima," 142–143.

19. Mott, *Rosa Egipcíaca*, 157, 202–203, 226, 300–301.

20. This total is based upon all the extant *autos de ingreso* and *autos de profesión* documents for La Concepcion (83); Santa Clara (86); and La Encarnación (68). See also Tardieu, *Los negros y la Iglesia en el Perú*, 1:394. The Council of Trent stipulated that the applicant had to be free from bondage. See Tardieu, *Los negros y la Iglesia en el Perú*, 1:394; AAL, SC, leg. VI, exp. 35, "Autos de profesión . . . Pascuala del Pulgar, negra donada"; AAL, SC, leg. VI, exp. 37, "Autos de profesion . . . Maria Rodriguez, cuarterona donada"; AAL, SC, leg. XII, exp. 27, "Autos de profesion . . . Gracia Maria de Jesus, negra."

21. Minh-ha, "Not You/Like You," 1.

22. Boyer, "Respect and Identity," 492. Fifty-five of the 237 cases reported no data on physical characteristics.

23. Fernández, *La mujer en la conquista y la evangelización en el Perú*, 190.

24. AAL, Monasterio de La Concepción (hereafter LC), leg. XXV, exp. 17, "Profesion de Beatriz del Arco."

25. AAL, LC, leg. XXII, exp. 8, "Solicitud . . . Maria de la Concepción." See also AAL, LC, leg. XXVII, exp. 38, "Paula Maria de Albur."

26. AAL, Monasterio de La Encarnación (hereafter LE), leg. XI, exp. 86, "Autos . . . Antonio de Cordova y Juana Maria Hurtado"; AAL, Monasterio de La Trinidad (hereafter LT), leg. I, exp. 37, "Autos criminales . . . contra Jerónimo Alvaro."

27. The name of the newly professed *donada* was recorded in a *libro de profesiónes*. For an example, see AAL, LC, leg. V, exp. 44, "Autos . . . doña Jeronima de Sejas." I have not been fortunate enough to find one of these *libros de profesiónes*.

28. León Pinelo, *Velos antiguos i modernos en los rostros de las mugeres*, chapter 8; Fernández, *La mujer en la conquista y la evangelización en el Perú*, 451.

29. AAL, LC, leg. II, exp. 14, "Solicitud . . . doña Florencia Barreto."

30. AAL, LC, leg. III, exp. 6, "Solicitud . . . doña Andrea de Salas." In *Los negros y la Iglesia en el Perú*, 1:393, Tardieu cites the *Definiciones . . . Santissima Trinidad*, cap. 18.5.

31. AAL, LC, leg. III, exp. 16, "Causa de nulidad . . . Francisca de Valencia."

32. AAL, Papeles Importantes, 24, 8, "Auto"; Tardieu, *Los negros y la Iglesia en el Perú*, 1:400; Fernández, *La mujer en la conquista y la evangelización en el Perú*, 141.

33. Meléndez, *Tesoros verdaderos de las Indias*, 2:169.

34. The breakdown of the fifty-three petitions to enter La Concepción that supplied age data is as follows: ages thirteen to sixteen: 20; ages seventeen to twenty: 20; ages twenty-one to thirty: 11; over thirty: 2. Of the forty-three petitions with data for Santa Clara: ages thirteen to sixteen: 13; ages seventeen to twenty: 18; ages twenty-one to thirty: 10; and over thirty: 2. For an example of a couple taking vows of celibacy and as *donados*, see LE, leg. XI, exp. 86, "Autos . . . Antonio de Cordova y Juana Maria Hurtado, esposos." Some older women entered the novitiate because the abbess found them "useful"; see AAL, LC, leg. XXV, exp. 7, "Expediente . . . Juana de Añazgo."

35. *Constituciones generales para todas las monjas, y religiosas, sujetas a la obediencia de la Órden de nuestro Padre San Francisco* (hereafter *Constituciones*), 101. The papal bull of Gregory VIII (1583) stated that the convent should have no more than one *criada* for every ten nuns. On the excessive comings and goings, see AAL, LT, leg. III, exp. 10, "Auto arzobispal por Fernando Arias de Ugarte"; AAL, LE, leg. XI, exp. 30, "Auto dado por el arzobispo de Lima, Villagómez." On the expulsion of servants and slaves in 1664, see AAL, LC, leg. XVI, exp. 30, "Relacion dc las criadas." On the concern over children in convents, see AAL, Monasterio de Santa Catalina de Sena (hereafter Santa Catalina), leg. VIII, exp. 87, "Auto seguido"; and AAL, SC, leg. XXI, exp. 10, "Testimonios dados."

36. *Constituciones*, 145; AAL, Santa Catalina, leg. VIII, exp. 4, "Autos . . . María Micaela de Jesús Nazareno."

37. *Constituciones*, 145; Fernández, *La mujer en la conquista y la evangelización en el Perú*, 451.

38. Aguilar, *Sermones varios*, 257r–270v.

39. AAL, LC, leg. XVI, exp. 49, "Solicitud . . . Josefa de la Concepcion y Meneses."

40. Dickey, "Mutual Exclusions," 52–53; Minh-ha, "Not You/Like You," 1.

41. AAL, SC, leg. XVIII, exp. 41, "Solicitud . . . doña Juana de Melendez."

42. AAL, LC, leg. XXV, exp. 33, "Profesión de Ursula de la Concepcion"; AAL, LC, leg. XXV, exp. 35, "Oficios . . . 1688." For a description of tasks in Puebla's convents, see Loreto López, *Los conventos femeninos*, 125–133.

43. Fernández, *La mujer en la conquista y la evangelización en el Perú*, 315; AAL, LC, leg. XXV, exp. 13, "Expediente . . . Mariana de Jesus"; AAL, LC, leg. XXVII, exp. 45, "Oficios . . . 1697."

44. AAL, LC, leg. XX, exp. 3, "Solicitud . . . Maria de Escobar."

45. Teresa de Ávila, *Libro de las fundaciones*, 1:143.

46. Loreto López, "Prácticas alimenticias en los conventos de mujeres en la Puebla del siglo XVIII," 493; AAL, LC, leg. V, exp. 44, "Autos . . . doña Jerónima de Sejas," 3r; Ursula de Jesús, *The Souls of Purgatory*, 30–31.

47. Martín, *Daughters of the Conquistadores*, 191; Fernández, *La mujer en la conquista y la evangelización en el Perú*; van Deusen, *Between the Sacred and the Worldly*; Burns, *Colonial Habits*.

48. AAL, Papeles Importantes, leg. XXIV, exp. 8, "Cuaderno de Autos," doc. 7, "Sobre los oficios . . . La Encarnación"; and AAL, SC, leg. XVII, exp. 47, "Oficio . . . para cubrir los oficios."

49. See AAL, SC, leg. V, exp. 42, "Autos . . . doña Ana de Zarate"; AAL, LE, leg. V, exp. 26, "Autos . . . Juan Gómez, labrador"; AAL, Causas de Negros (hereafter CN), leg. VII, exp. 37, "Autos . . . Juana de Aguilar"; AAL, SC, leg. XX, exp. 66, "Autos . . . Antonia María y Juana de Leiba"; AAL, LC, leg. V, exp. 44, "Autos . . . doña Jerónima de Sejas"; AAL, LE, leg. III, exp. 8A, "Autos . . . doña Melchora de los Reyes."

50. AAL, LC, leg. V, exp. 44, "Autos . . . doña Jerónima de Sejas"; LE, leg. III, exp. 22, "Solicitud de la abadesa"; LE, leg. V, exp. 26, "Autos . . . Juan Gomez, labrador"; AAL, LC, leg. IX, exp. 29, "Carta de libertad de Ursula, negra criolla"; AAL, CN, leg. XII, exp. 4, "Expediente de Ines de Guevara"; AAL, SC, leg. V, exp. 42, "Autos . . . doña Ana de Zarate"; AAL, CN, leg. X, exp. 11, "Autos de la demanda."

51. Archivo General de la Nación, Lima (hereafter AGNP), Protocolos, Joseph de Aguirre Urbina, 2–3v.

52. *Constituciones*, 99v, 144.

53. Fernández, *La mujer en la conquista y la evangelización en el Perú*, 316; Ursula de Jesús, *The Souls of Purgatory*, 25–30.

54. AAL, LC, leg. XXI, exp. 43, "Oficios . . . 1679"; AAL, LC, leg. XXI, exp. 77, "Oficios . . . 1680." See also AAL, SC, leg. XII, exp. 99, "Autos . . . Josefa Maria"; Fernández, *La mujer en la conquista y la evangelización en el Perú*, 214; Real Academia Española, *Diccionario de autoridades*, 5:581; AAL, SC, leg. XX, exp. 73, "Oficios."

55. AAL, LE, leg. XIII, exp. 87, "Autos . . . Lorenza de Mesa, mulata." See also LT, leg. III, exp. 3, "Autos . . . María de San José"; and AAL, SC, leg. XII, exp. 112, "Autos . . . Lorenza de la Madre de Dios de la Soledad."

56. Of the total number of *donadas* known (n = 237), ninety-six stated that they had been raised in the convent, 124 had no data, and eighteen had not been raised there. Based upon the 114 cases where the data is known (ninety-six + eighteen), the calculation reaches 85 percent.

57. AAL, LC, leg. XX, exp. 3, "Solicitud . . . María de Escobar (50 años)."

58. Because the numbers of servants vary, I calculated an overall average of 130 for La Encarnación and 150 for Santa Clara and La Concepción before 1670. After 1670, the numbers of servants increased dramatically. One can assume that after 1690, the percentage of *donadas* selected from the overall number of servants raised in the convent decreased significantly.

59. *Constituciones*, 9; AAL, Monasterio de la Encarnación (hereafter EN), leg. XIII, exp. 6, "Autos . . . María de Mancilla"; AAL, EN, leg. XIII, exp. 10, "Autos . . . Catalina de San Antonio."

60. Van Deusen, *Between the Sacred and the Worldly*, 173–174.

61. AAL, SC, leg. XIX, exp. 81, "Autos . . . Ursula, mulata esclava"; AAL, LC, leg. XXIV, exp. 10, "Expediente . . . Ana de la Santíssima Trinidad"; AAL, LE, leg. II, exp.

5, "Autos . . . doña Antonia Clavijo"; AAL, SC, leg. XIX, exp. 81, "Autos . . . Ursula, mulata esclava"; AAL, SC, leg. XXI, exp. 28, "Autos . . . la esclava de la abadessa."

62. AAL, LC, leg. XX, exp. 4, "Autos . . . Ana de Heredía, mulata de Panama"; AAL, LC, leg. XXV, exp. 17, "Profesión . . . Beatriz del Arco."

63. AAL, LC, leg. XXIII, exp. 23, "Expediente . . . Ana Casilda, de Pisco"; AAL, LC, leg. XXV, exp. 33, "Autos . . . Ursula de la Concepcion"; AAL, LC, leg. XXIV, exp. 14, "Expediente . . . Margarita de Jesus"; AAL, LC, leg. XXVI, exp. 60, "Bernarda de San Joseph"; AAL, LE, leg. XI, exp. 59, "Autos . . . Maria de Cristo"; AAL, LE, leg. XI, exp. 103, "Autos . . . doña Luisa Ordoñes de Pineda"; AAL, LE, leg. XI, exp. 106, "Autos . . . doña Maria Josefa de Jesús."

64. AAL, SC, leg. XXI, exp. 10, "Testimonios dados por algunas religiosas"; AGNP, Protocolos, Gregorio de Urtazo, 1103, 1709, "Testamento, Lorensa de la Encarnación," 67r–69v.

65. AGNP, Protocolos, Joseph de Aguirre Urbina, 69, 1644–1645, 7/10/1645, "Donación," 2–3v.

66. Of the forty nuns listed with cells in La Trinidad, seven lived with *donadas*. AAL, LT, leg. I, exp. 38, s/f.

67. AAL, LC, leg. XXII, exp. 51, "Solicitud de María Marchan"; AAL, LC, leg. XVII, exp. 55, "Solicitud de María Marchan."

68. AAL, EN, leg. III, exp. 17, "Autos . . . doña Ana de Pineda."

69. AAL, LT, leg. I, exp. 38 s/f, "Relación de las sirvientas."

70. AGNP, Protocolos, Francisco de Acuña, 29 (1648), 7/II/1648, "Donation, María de San Cristóbal," 80–80v; AGNP, Protocolos, Francisco de Acuña, 34 (1653), 21/IV/1653, "Will . . . doña Francisca Vásquez"; AAL, SC, leg. XII, exp. 74, "Autos . . . Isabel de Ulloa"; AAL, SC, leg. XII, exp. 58, "Autos . . . Josefa de Herrera."

71. AAL, LE, exp. 88, "Autos . . . Ana Maria de los Santos, mulata esclava"; AAL, SC, leg. XVIII, exp. 38, "Autos . . . Andrea de Solorzano"; AAL, SC, leg. XIX, exp. 37, "Autos . . . Andrea de Solorzano"; AAL, LC, leg. V, exp. 8, "Solicitación . . . don Martín Riquelme."

72. AAL, SC, leg. XII, exp. 42, "Autos . . . Lorenza Agustina del Carmen"; Martín, *Daughters of the Conquistadores*, 186.

73. AAL, LE, leg. XIII, exp. 10, "Autos . . . Catalina de San Antonio."

74. AAL, SC, leg. XVIII, exp. 91, "Autos . . . Ventura de la Fuente."

75. AGNP, Protocolos, Francisco de Acuña, "Testament of Bernalda de la Palma," 33, 1652, folios 294–296.

76. AAL, LC, leg. II, exp. 6, "Causa . . . Luis de Alvarado Bracamonte"; Premo, *Children of the Father King*, 220–221.

77. Premo, *Children of the Father King*, 84, 86–88.

78. I have borrowed this term from Cope, *The Limits of Racial Domination*, 93. See AAL, CN, leg. VI, exp. 25, "Expediente . . . Fernando de Sotomayor."

79. Real Academia Española, *Diccionario de autoridades*, 3:334–335. On "condi-

tional" freedom, see AAL, LC, leg. XXV, exp. 60, "Solicitud . . . doña Juana de Tello"; AGNP, Protocolos, FA, 33, 1652, "Testament of Isabel de Espinoza," 25/VI/1652, 315–316v; AGNP, Protocolos, FA, 35, 1654, "Letter of Freedom by doña Antonia de San Francisco Coello," 21/V/1654, folios 281–282.

80. AAL, SC, leg. XII, exp. 120, "Autos que sigue Ana de Mora, negra libre," 12r–15v.

81. Ibid., 19r, 34r–v.

82. See also AGNP, Protocolos, FA, 29 "Testament of Doña Juana de Contreras," 1648, 27/VI/1648, 400v–401v; and AAL, Monasterio de Las Descalças, leg. IV, exp. 79, "Solicitud . . . Maria Pascuala, mulata."

83. AAL, SC, leg. XII, exp. 120, 34v.

84. AAL, LC, leg. V, exp. 27, "Causa de nulidad . . . Maria de San Francisco."

85. AAL, Monasterio de Las Descalças, leg. II, exp. 50, "Autos . . . Leonor de San Nicolás"; AAL, LC, leg. XIX, exp. 64, "Autos . . . Juana de Santa Rosa."

86. AAL, LT, leg. VI, exp. 70, "Autos . . . María de Carbajal Galindo, Petronila de Oviedo San José, mulata, y Nicolasa de Aguilar, mulata libre."

87. AAL, LC, leg. VII, exp. 22, "Expediente . . . de Lucia Bravo"; AAL, LC, leg. XXIV, exp. 14, "Expediente . . . Margarita de Jesús"; AAL, SC, leg. XVI, exp. 47, "Autos . . . Magdalena de Espinoza, una hija legítima"; Fernández, *La mujer en la conquista y la evangelización en el Perú*, 336; AAL, LC, leg. V, exp. 44, "Autos . . . doña Jerónima de Sejas."

88. AAL, Monasterio de Las Descalças, leg. II, exp. 49, "Autos . . . Isabel de San José"; AAL, LT, leg. V, exp. 69, "Autos . . . Josefa Duarte"; AAL, LE, leg. XI, exp. 59, "Autos . . . Maria de Cristo." On mothers working, see AAL, LC, leg. XXV, exp. 7, "Expediente . . . Juana de Añazgo"; AAL, LC, leg. XXV, exp. 74, "Expediente . . . Petronila de la Visitación"; AAL, SC, leg. XVI, exp. 15, "Autos . . . Francisca de la Concepcion"; AAL, SC, leg. XII, exp. 64, "Autos . . . doña Beatriz de Herrera."

89. AAL, SC, leg. XIV, exp. 72, "Autos . . . de doña Nicolasa del Puerto."

90. AAL, LC, leg. XXVI, exp. 28, "Expediente . . . María Magdalena y Francisca de Jesús de Lima, 15 y 11"; AAL, LC, leg. XXVIII, exp. 11, "Autos . . . Magdalena y Francisca de Lomba"; AAL, LE, leg. XIII, exp. 29, "Autos . . . Francisca Rebollo, india, Bartola y Francisca Rebollo, pardas."

91. AGNP, Protocolos, FA, 38, 1657, "Testament of Isabel de Atocha," 650v–652v; van Deusen, *Between the Sacred and the Worldly*, chapters 4 and 6.

92. Martín, *Daughters of the Conquistadores*, 188; AAL, LE, leg. I, exp. 6, "Solicitud . . . Antonia de los Reyes."

93. AAL, Cofradías, leg. XXXI, exp. 2, "Cuentas presentadas."

94. AGNP, Protocolos, Francisco Acuña, 32, 1651, 4/IV/1651, 253r–v; "Testament of Francisca Terranova," 32, 1651, 23/V/1651, Joana Quispe, hermana of the Cofradía de Nuestra Señora de Loreto; "Testament, Teresa de la Cruz," 14/VI/1651, hermana of the Cofradía of Nuestra Señora de Loreto, 431v–432v; Francisco Acuña, 34, 1653, 13/IX/1653, "Testament of Ana de Tierra Folupa," morena libre, cófrada de los Fo-

lupos (in San Francisco), 510–511; 40, 1660, 29/VIII/1660, 347v–349v, "Testament, Francisca de Vallalba," morena libre de tierra Bran, cófrada de la Cofradía de los Bañones; Gómez Acuña, "Las cofradías de negros en Lima (siglo XVII)," 36.

95. Martín, *Daughters of the Conquistadores*, 184; AAL, LE, leg. I, exp. 7, "Autos . . . María de los Reyes"; Fernández, *La mujer en la conquista y la evangelización en el Perú*, 184; Tardieu, *Los negros y la Iglesia en el Perú*, 1:399.

96. AAL, LC, leg. XXV, exp. 83, "Solicitud de Petrona Roldán."

97. AAL, LC, leg. XXV, exp. 66, "Solicitud . . . Agustina de los Rios"; AAL, SC, leg. XXI, exp. 66, "Autos . . . Maria de Mora."

98. AAL, SC, leg. XII, exp. 157, "Doña Manuela de Billaruela y Mendosa."

99. AAL, LE, leg. XI, exp. 68, "Autos . . . Magdalena de San Jose, mulata"; AAL, LC, leg. XXIII, exp. 18, "Solicitud . . . Lucia Bravo de Laguan y Catalina de la Madre de Dios."

100. AAL, LC, leg. XXI, exp. 24, "Solicitud . . . María de la Cueva"; AAL, LC, leg. XXII, exp. 4, "Solicitud . . . Petrona de Avendaño"; AAL, LC, leg. XVI, exp. 49, "Solicitud . . . Josefa de la Concepcion."

101. AAL, LE, leg. XIII, exp. 28, "Autos . . . Jerónima Clavijo, Luisa Rebata y Beatríz Rodríguez."

102. Aguilar, "De la Presentación," in *Sermones varios*.

103. AAL, LE, leg. III, exp. 8A, "Autos . . . Bartolomé Delgado"; AAL, LE, leg. IX, exp. 39, "Traslado . . . doña Magdalena Carrillo."

104. AGNP, Protocolos, FA, 32, 1651, "Testament, Josefa del Espíritu Santo," 24/VI/1652, 471–472v.

105. Aguilar, "De la Presentación," in *Sermones varios*, 257r–270v.

106. Biblioteca Nacional del Perú, Ms. B 124, "Relación de la fundación," 50r; Morabito, "San Benedetto il Moro," 241–243; Busto Duthurburu, *San Martín de Porras*, 57n20.

107. Echave y Assu, *La estrella de Lima*, 232, 228–229; AAL, Las Descalças, leg. IV, exp. 32 1668, "Autos . . . María Josepha de Todos los Santos y Juana Maria de la Resurrección"; Fernández, *La mujer en la conquista y la evangelización en el Perú*, 243–244; AAL, LE, leg. VI, exp. 21, "Solicitud . . . Maria de la O"; AAL, LC, leg. XII, exp. 14, "Memoria de los oficios . . . 1657."

108. Meléndez, *Tesoros verdaderos de las Indias*, 2:72.

109. Bhabha, *The Location of Culture*, 127; Real Academia Española, *Diccionario de autoridades*, 2:657; AAL, LT, leg. VI, exp. 70, "Autos . . . María de Carbajal Galindo, Petronila de Oviedo San José, mulata, y Nicolasa de Aguilar," 1r.

110. AAL, LC, leg. XX, exp. 3, "Solicitud . . . Maria de Escobar."

111. AAL, Descalças, leg. IV, exp. 86, n.d., "Solicitud . . . abadesa Juana del Niño Jesus."

112. AAL, SC, leg. XII, exp. 96, "Autos . . . Francisca de la Cruz, parda."

113. AAL, LC, leg. XVII, exp. 15.

114. Ursula de Jesús, *The Souls of Purgatory*, 30.

115. Archivo del Convento de Santa Clara de Lima, "Vida de la Hermana Ursula," 1928, 32r; Granada, *Guía de pecadores*, 375.

116. Tardieu, *Los negros y la Iglesia en el Perú*, 1:394–395.

117. Fernández Alvárez, *Casadas, monjas, rameras y brujas*, 197.

118. Martín, *Daughters of the Conquistadores*, 185.

119. Boyer, "Respect and Identity," 492; Adams and Dickey, *Home and Hegemony*.

120. Matthew 24:13; Granada, *Guía de pecadores*, 375.

121. Granada, *Guía de pecadores*, 375.

PART 3

Comparisons and Whitening Revisited: Race and Gender in Colonial Cuba

7

Whitening Revisited

Nineteenth-Century Cuban Counterpoints

KAREN Y. MORRISON

Two unreconciled perspectives on "whitening" have shaped the historiography on Latin America's African descended people for the past forty years. On the one hand, scholars have defined whitening as a reproductive strategy pursued by black and mulatto individuals in the effort to improve their social standings.[1] On the other hand, other writers have viewed whitening as a political and social ideology promoted by members of the Latin American elite to presumably improve the racial qualities of their nations.[2] The connections between the two frequently are left as implicit assumptions, including the notion that people of color tacitly accepted racist, elite principles.[3] In an effort to reconcile these distinct approaches, I empirically investigate the race-making behaviors from late colonial Cuba that once might have suggested complicity with whitening and develop from them an alternate interpretation of race mixture's many realities. I prioritize the historical ambiguity of *blanqueamiento* (the whitening process) and demonstrate that it has been much less linear and predictable than the older literature would suggest, especially as the family replaces the individual as the unit of analysis.

A central issue in Afro–Latin American identity construction has been the extent to which the racial expectations of the white elite have been historically adapted into the behaviors of African-descended masses. In his useful review of the racial ideologies experienced by Latin America's black and mulatto populations, George Reid Andrews describes the shifts from early nineteenth-century independence-era racial inclusiveness to late nineteenth-century visions of national whitening and finally to the emergence of cultural and political "browning" (the glorification of race mixture) and "blackening" (the reclamation of African ancestry) in the twentieth century.[4] This ideological trajectory suggests an inherent instability of whitening behaviors and philosophies that once had been thought so pervasive. If their force had been hegemonically complete, then few African-descended populations would have survived into the twentieth century. After all, an absolute acceptance of whitening would lead nonwhites to restrict their own group-sustaining reproduction. Other Afro-Latin American populations would eventually go the way of the Afro-Argentines, leaving little physical traces in the general public or recognition in the national consciousness.[5] Conversely, if we acknowledge the incomplete nature of whitening, then the survival of Afro-Latin groups demands a thorough investigation of its limits. How have these populations resisted its ideological onslaught? Have they actively sought alternatives to whitening or passively remained in marginal, unrecognized isolation?[6] And, most important for our purposes, if resistance to whitening has coexisted with its fulfillment, how are the historical dimensions of both to be explored? This chapter critiques the visions of a thoroughgoing whitening offered in historical studies of both colonial and modern Latin America. It then uses examples from late colonial Cuba, of the nineteenth century, to propose greater precision in describing the time frame through which "whitening" operated and to expand the comprehension of the human actions that constituted this presumed process.

In contemplating new empirical approaches to study whitening, it is important to begin with the issue of its unit of analysis. Who whitens? As the term is currently used in histories of Afro-Latin populations, individual women of color have whitened their children through procreation with white men in the hope of improving their own material conditions or those of the next generation.[7] By contrast, white men have been left out of explanations of the process. Their input has been presented in minimal terms, and they appear largely unaffected by whitening. They are not acknowledged as involved fathers; instead, they have been considered men for whom the interaction with darker women was little more than sexual dalliance.[8] So while the women of color whitened, white men remained above the experience. They were not socially disadvantaged or darkened by these sexual contacts.

At another, broader level of analysis, Latin American nations also seem to have whitened as policy makers vigorously encouraged European immigration, as the mortality of non-whites increased (with wars, for example), and as nonwhite reproduction decreased. All these occurrences have been measured through demographics that drew upon essentialized notions of race. A priori racial categories abound in the resulting studies. Pure blackness and Indianness, then, are defined as oppositional poles to a pure whiteness. Whereas American scholarly interpretations of Latin American racial dynamics posited mulattos, mestizos, and other mixed-race populations as the intermediate stages of whitening—"the mulatto escape hatch," as it were—in countries with nonwhite majorities, twentieth-century Latin American intellectuals often celebrated racial hybridity or *mestizaje* as a positive end unto itself.[9] In Cuba, the racial proportion of the population did not suggest any clear intellectual direction and nationalists varied in their beliefs about a racial future. While a desire for national whitening remained a subtle political presence, early twentieth-century commentators acknowledging the importance of race mixture, such as Fernando Ortiz, Alejo Carpentier, and Nicolás Guillén, were cautious in their approach. Their complex vision of *mestizaje* accommodated a multiracial national unity, the continuation of European cultural preeminence, and the social survival of Afro-Cuban peoples.[10]

These considerations lead us into an important concern when reconceptualizing whitening—the problems of its boundaries. To ask the question in another way, whether the unit of analysis remains the individual or the nation, are all instances of biological reproduction that involve whites and nonwhites to be interpreted as whitening? Such a position would seem to promote a white hypodescent in which the African-descended contributing elements are minimized. The very existence of a multitude of Latin-American racial categories obviously would call such claims into question. The mulatto and the mestizo are still differentiated from their white countrymen and at times have been viewed with great suspicion. Moreover, their socioeconomic advancement as measured against blacks appears to be negligible in many areas.[11]

Such categorical limitations to any short-term whitening might also prompt one to extend the timeframe through which whitening is studied beyond one instance of interracial mating and instead envision whitening as a multigenerational process. In that case, one must ask at what point was successful whitening achieved. The determination of its endpoint remains unclear. Were the colonial legal designations of *casta* identities discontinued after recognition of less than 1/32 of nonwhite heritage?[12] Or should we only identify whitening with those few individuals who purchased the royal dispensation of legal whiteness with *gracias al sacar*, regardless of our lack of awareness of their subsequent social status?[13] In asking these questions, I reconsider the utility of applying the term "whitening" to the reproductive choices made by people of color in colonial Latin America.

Most important, this chapter suggests a path out of the slippery problems of examining whitening and rejects definitions of race that rely on fixed (biological) or essentializing characteristics. It offers a methodology that emphasizes the social construction of race and is similar to other studies that emphasize the ideological components of race. Moreover, I also highlight race's construction in the sexual domain, where it develops out of intimate experiences and is not defined solely by official mandates or political expediencies.[14] This study moves beyond these perspectives to consider the meaning of race and of whitening in terms of reproductive and family formation practices. In comprehending whitening as a process that required both families and nations to force ideological and behavioral commitments on individuals, this chapter concentrates on the late colonial period in Cuba and reveals the means through which racialized reproductive choices manipulated the standard system of racial classification and fostered whitening in some cases and discouraged it in others.[15] It is within this context that the family (the publicly recognized bonds of biological kinship and social affinity) becomes the unit of analysis, as it defined group self-identity and differentiated the racial "us" from the racial "other."

Although race has been omnipresent in Cuban processes of family formation, late colonial Cubans of the nineteenth century manipulated concepts of race and family in mutually constructive ways. The archival records show that many members of the colonial community—from ordinary individuals to the Spanish monarch himself—used varied notions of family to undermine the racial restrictions around which the society was presumably constructed. Briefly, between racially endogamous marriage and marginalized interracial consensual unions, colonial Cuban families were formed in a variety of recognized social and legal practices.[16] Each form in turn reproduced racial meaning because it was also shaped by race. Shifts in racial classifications for individuals, families, and (at times) the whole society were the outcomes of these practices. Most specifically, those transformative actions included those of white fathers who openly recognized their mixed race children, women of color who bore offspring who received white jural classification, and a colonial church that maintained an ambiguous relationship to the more rigid rules by which it was to assign racial labels. The exploration of these acts allows us into those intimate areas that created the true Cuban counterpoints of race formation and whitening. Their implications also extend to other African diasporan populations, as they participated in this constant renegotiation of race.

Valuing a Sexual Economy of Race

As a counterpoint to the older view that whitening was the predominant force in the reproductive history of colonial Latin America, this study suggests that such essentializing views of race and social reproduction need to be modified in favor of a more process-oriented analysis of the social construction of social categories within the context of family formation. Based on such a feminist insight, I begin from the premise that in addition to their material determinants and political expediencies, races exist because people have historically chosen—or, one could argue, have been forced—to reproduce themselves in racially determined ways. In racially heterogeneous societies, race has value in the selection of mates, the acknowledgment of relationships, and the initial social positioning of offspring. An explicit calculus of racialized reproduction often exists, what Caribbean social theorist Frantz Fanon initially outlined as a "sexual economy of race."[17]

I modify Fanon's approach away from its original emphasis on the desire of people of color to advance socially through sexual contact with whites. I also move beyond the notion that particular racial inputs into the reproductive equation are expected to generate a limited set of fixed outputs, of racial and color categories.[18] My goal is to trace the historical patterns in the Cuban resolution of situations of intimate racial negotiation to comprehend the resultant collective identities that later contributed to collective political action. The notion of a sexual economy of race becomes a means of examining the conjunction between reproductive behavior and the social construction of race. This concept is defined here as a repetitive and iterative process structured by four salient features. First is the designation of social agents (potential contributors to a sexual relationship) according to gender, race, and class. Second is the selection of mates and the classification of the relationship. This step both uses the labels defined in stage one and has the potential to generate new labels based on racial perceptions of the couple. These racial notions assist in its designation as a marriage, a consensual union, a visiting relation, a concubinage, or even a rape, depending on its public perceptions. This stage, like all others, is proscribed by official sanctions, social taboos, and individual preferences.

In the third stage, the procreation and categorization of offspring offers another opportunity for either maintaining or transforming group boundaries. Offspring can assume social categories similar to either of the parents or they may be positioned under radically different social labels. The fourth and final stage of the sexual economy of race is one that should resonate most profoundly with historians. It is created by the enduring memory of the procreative process, or the development of an understanding of ancestry. This is the area where individuals assume racial identities based on the memory—or the forgetting—of the racial identity of their ancestors. The public and private acknowledgement of genealogy may also differ based on a host of social expediencies. Generally, in the Americas, one becomes white as the self and the community loses any sense of a familial connection to the racial other.[19] These steps are repeated in subsequent generations, either in normative forms that adhere to the forefathers' standards or disruptive ones that forge new directions. These practices delineated the boundaries between social groups. At times, these means minimized distinction, and at others, they amplified it. The meanings of whiteness and of otherness were negotiated at these points.

This outline of the sexual economy of race makes apparent some of the limitations of the traditional literature on the formation of class and race in colonial Latin American societies. That literature has emphasized a tripartite division of society—black, white, and racially mixed—that aligned closely with a racial division of reproductive actions. White males controlled the reproductive potential of white women by linking honor to procreation solely in legitimate marriage. This act (re)produced a racially defined ruling class. In the next stratum, white males acquired the reproductive potential of nonwhite women through the projection of images of the former's own social and economic superiority. The women who entered these relationships presumably saw greater personal benefit if they reproduced lighter children with white men. The resulting offspring were to have benefited from the "mulatto [or mestizo] escape hatch," or a degree of upward social mobility gained due to whitening.[20] Reproducing among themselves over several generations, persons in this category were perceived as intermediaries between a white elite and a less racially mixed lower class. A few were to have been so "fortunate" as to have engaged in a generational succession of sexual encounters with whites in order to whiten their heirs into the higher social ranks. In the lowest social level, insufficiently "*adelantado*" (racially advanced) women and men, whose phenotypes do not reflect sufficient race mixture, had limited social and economic possibilities. Men in this station experienced racially restrictive sexual limitations more profoundly than their female counterparts. The reproductive potential of these men was constrained by a lack of opportunity to mate with higher-status women. The women of this sector had some access to higher-status partners, despite the generally low rate of legitimizing these relationships. By contrast with the conscious efforts at racial preservation attributed to endogamous high-status groups, one is left with the impression that endogamy reproduction within the lower-status group resulted from the lack of other opportunities.[21]

What is missing in this picture is a sense of historical change in the meaning of various racial labels. While it is noteworthy that such accounts of colonial Latin American social reproduction acknowledged the coexistence of endogamous, or equal status, marriage alongside hypergamous, consensual unions for women of color and contrasted it with the United States, where the possibility of hypergamous mating for people of color historically was denied,[22] shifts in the meaning of specific racial categories were not recognized in either region. In both, white and black are viewed as essential positions. In terms of reproduction, whiteness was associated with unquestioned European descent and blackness with some degree of African ancestry. For many making regional comparisons in race relations, Latin American exceptionalism has often been defined through a recognition of a valuable, intermediate social role for mestizos and mulattos. These scholars suggest and emphasize that the rules of racial reproduction remained as fixed as did the social meanings of each racial category. Again, white men possessed several options in how they chose to procreate and socially position the next generation. If they did not deviate from social expectation, their children were reproduced as white, through the bodies of pedigreed women who were selected for their *limpieza de sangre* (purity of blood). Otherwise children were publicly constituted as racially mixed, or *pardo*, when the procreative contributions of women of color were recognized.

But what of those moments when whites themselves transcended the norms? Admittedly, endogamous marriage and marginalized interracial consensual unions exemplify the norm within the sexual economy of colonial Latin America. Nineteenth-century Cuba was no different. Yet Cubans of that period also departed from the standard to generate more disruptive means of socially (re)producing race. As we shall see below, these critical strategies included 1) the paternal recognition of interracial children born out of wedlock; 2) familial or clerical falsification of race in baptismal certificates; 3) self-selected racial reclassification; and 4) official classification of racially questionable, "royal" orphans as white. These methods constructed the varied family types through which Cubans mediated social distinctions and preexisting racial concepts. "Whitening" was only one experience that these families could either foster or limit as they sought the best social outcomes for their members.

Restricted Interracial Marriage and Alternate Methods of Family Formation

Cuba's colonial administration perceived the maintenance of a racial hierarchy as central to its political interests. The restriction (and at times outright prohibition) of interracial marriages was one means through which colonial officials reinforced racial differences. Beginning with the military ordinances of 1728, which required that military officers have permission from their superiors to marry, and continuing with the *Real Pragmática de Matrimonio* of 1776, race became a factor in the state's sanction of marriage in colonial Spanish America.[23] Additionally, scholars such as Verena Stolcke (formerly Martínez-Alier) have often interpreted an 1805 Cuban clarification to the *Pragmática* as a broad prohibition on interracial marriages involving persons of African descent. These policies effectively ended subsequent formation of legitimate interracial families. The most intensive application of these restrictions coincided with the height of Cuban slavery, in the period between 1820 and 1860. Thus, in an institutionalized manner, interracial reproduction was relegated to illegitimate forms and the racial hierarchy was presumably preserved.[24]

Stolcke's text remains seminal for its clear demonstration of the racial discrimination practiced in Spanish colonial marriage policies. In developing her outline of the of racial controls on marriage in nineteenth-century Cuba, Stolcke reviewed petitions related to interracial marriage that were brought before Cuban colonial officials and found that a slight majority (56 percent) were not permitted. And of those that were accepted, the whites were of undistinguished, if not marginal, status. Yet the picture may not be as rigid as the one she paints. Slightly less than half of her cases (or 44 percent) allowed for the interracial marriages.[25] Beyond the twenty-five resolved cases that Stolcke highlights, a review of the same archives finds another ten cases in which interracial marriages were permitted, bringing the acceptance rate to 66 percent.[26] Also, although Stolcke was diligent in her effort to find evidence of interracial marriage outside the governmental petitions, she limited her search to the registries of people of color. Just before the 1881 revocation of the marriage restriction, a small number of these marriages were also found in the marriage registries for whites. In those few cases, the choice of the registry appears to follow the husband's racial status. Thus, marriages between white men and *parda* women were recorded in the white registries.[27] More important, however, ecclesiastical registries often allowed for a degree of flexibility in recording race that Stolcke discussed only briefly. In highlighting marriages between low-status whites and people of color, she revealed what she saw as the exceptional moments in the general pattern of strict racial definitions. For this reason, she also read racial classifications as largely fixed and inconsistently addressed the explicit contestations of racial labels seen within the documents. We will see below that although these points of racial contestation demonstrate Cuban methods of "whitening" and the forces that opposed it, they also reveal weak points in Cuba's racial hierarchy.

Examples of Cuban flexibility in racial classification began at the highest levels of the colonial administration. In 1786, the Marqués de Sonora, José de Gálvez, one of the most important officials in Spain's colonial administration, as Minister of the Indies and uncle to the governor of Cuba, petitioned the Spanish monarch to mediate an end to the social embarrassment experienced by a loyal Havana family by declaring the wife white. The unfortunate family had been the brunt of vicious public gossip that suggested that the wife, Doña Mariana, was actually the daughter of a previously enslaved *parda* woman who now worked in the Havana streets selling flowers. In rejecting these rumors, her husband claimed that nothing could have been further from the truth. Instead, the home of Doña Mariana's honorable, yet unwed, grandmother had been frequently visited by a young *parda* slave with the same name and approximate same age as Doña Mariana's mother and people had maliciously assumed that the two young girls were the same. However, now the family presented thirty witnesses, including clerics and the former owner of the slave women, who testified in support of their claims of whiteness. All attested that the family was an honorable one that did not deserve such a perpetual stain on its reputation.[28]

Despite these testimonies, Doña Mariana's racial identity remained open to skepticism. When the petition reached the Spanish court, the king's advisors urged him to dismiss this request. They found it most irregular. Generally, people of quality and significant wealth would have first requested that an illegitimate child receive a royal legitimization through an aspect of *gracias al sacar*. The relatives of the petitioner would testify to the claimant's familial ties and his or her white racial purity extending back at least four generations. Failing the ability of family members to testify, an extensive genealogy based on ecclesiastical records would have been used to support the family's claims. Doña Mariana had neither the public testimony of relatives nor the documents from the Church proving her claim. Where were her parents or the documentary proof of their existence? Without either, court advisors felt that the king should deny the petition. Moreover, they asked why the royal declaration of Doña Mariana's whiteness was more important than the restoration of honor through her legitimization. Despite these objections and questions, King Charles III granted the request. He did so on the stated grounds that it was his desire to bring happiness to one of his subjects by removing this dark mark against the family and allowing it to continue to receive social distinction.[29]

Doña Mariana's story could be interpreted as revealing one individual's success at "passing," hiding any negative aspects of her ancestry. But we could also interpret the story more broadly by shifting the focus from the individual to the community. From that perspective, whitening was not simply attributed to the public conduct or sexual choices of one person. It required a broader range of social behaviors and participants. In this case, a number of good citizens and even the monarch were willing to bend the rules of racial classification for the pleasure of one family. They valued the family more than they valued upholding racially restrictive law. They were willing to confer whiteness on Doña Mariana despite her lack of merit based on traditional measures. In doing so, they engaged in what could be considered a conspiracy in racial identification and whitening. Her supporters engaged in the collective practice of erasing any possible mention of African ancestry for Doña Mariana. Any public memory of its existence was officially denied.

Although this case may initially appear anecdotal, it raises some important questions. Did the social benefit achieved by this one family also threaten the society's entire racial hierarchy? If one woman of questionable background could enter the ranks of the honorable, couldn't others have done so? As will be demonstrated below, when family and social reproduction are placed at the center of race relations studies, the processes through which racial meanings were transformed become more visible. It was possible for children born of illegitimate unions between white men and women of color to simply become baptized as white and enjoy that designation on a legal basis. Within the central archives of the Catholic Church in Havana are several cases in which white men had their racially mixed children baptized as white. They demonstrate the significant fissures that existed in the racial hierarchy established by the colonial state and the dominant class.[30]

In one such case, in 1865, the free *pardo* Federico Mainolo petitioned the Cuban Church for the correction of his fiancée's baptismal record so as to permit them to marry. According to Federico, his fiancée, María del Pilar Genoveva de Rosa y Acosta, had been mistakenly baptized as white when in fact she was a free *parda*. She had lived her twenty-three years under the mistaken white classification, but she would have to be reclassified to the correct *parda* status if the couple was to legally marry. María del Pilar's *parda* status was readily confirmed by her appearance before the local priest. But the Church inquired further. Her mother, the *negra* María del Carmen Acosta, came to testify on her daughter's behalf and to explain the cause of the initial confusion. María del Carmen readily acknowledged that facts of maternal identity listed on her daughter's baptismal certificate had been falsified. Although María del Pilar's father had been correctly listed as the white Havana native Don Manuel de la Rosa, the document incorrectly listed the mother as Doña María del Carmen Acosta, and the maternal grandparents were also given the honorific title of Don and Doña to indicate their fictitious white status. María del Carmen's own baptismal certificate revealed her to be the legitimate daughter of two enslaved Africans. Don Manuel had also falsified the racial identities of the couple's two other children, similarly baptizing them as whites. María del Carmen claimed that these distortions had been created by the now-deceased Don Manuel against her wishes. Faced with such evidence, the Church allowed María del Pilar to marry her *pardo* fiancé by agreeing to her reclassification as *parda*. However, it left the racial status of her siblings unchanged.[31]

María del Pilar's various transformations in racial classification are just one example of the multiple levels of intrigue surrounding social positioning in late colonial Cuba. Her experience reveals some of the methods Cubans used to cross the boundaries of racial identity. Here, beyond just one individual, a host of others—including family members, the Church, and the state—all participated in these actions. First, the state's role had begun well before María del Pilar's birth and continued into the time of her engagement. Again, with the 1776 *Real Pragmática Sanción de Matrimonio* and additional early nineteenth-century controls on marriage, the state imposed racial limits to the selection of marital partners. Next, familial intervention was also involved. Almost three-quarters of a century later, a white father (Don Manuel) circumvented these limitations through the ethically questionable act of baptizing his racially mixed children as white. This allowed him both to openly acknowledge his children and obscure their socially disadvantageous black ancestry. Finally, in contradiction of her father's goals, the daughter made alternate racial choices, adhered to the restrictions of the *Pragmática*, and displayed a certain level of respect for both the state and the Church. María del Pilar reclaimed a *parda* identity and married another *pardo* instead of enjoying the legal whiteness her family had secured for her.

The archival record reveals the existence of similar shifts in racial classification. Another case indicates how two of the mixed-race children of French émigré Don Juan Bautista Susan had been baptized as white, with the mother unknown, while three others were listed as orphans of color. To ensure all a share of his estate, the paternity of each child had to be clarified. The names of both parents were added to the certificates of the orphans. Yet it is interesting that the entries for the children who had been listed as white were not moved to the baptismal registries for people of color, and there is no clear indication that the mother's name was added to their records.[32] In this instance, the Church's awareness that these "white" children had been born of a woman of color did not prompt a correction. High-ranking officials of the local Church did not enforce a rigid racial classification. These children of color had become "white" with tacit Church complicity.

A more deliberate effort to achieve white status also proved successful for the children of another interracial couple. In 1885, Doña Bartolomea Blanco asked the Church to re-certify the missing baptismal certificate of her illegitimate daughter, Celestina. The two were gathering the requisite documents for the daughter's upcoming wedding. In written testimony, Doña Bartolomea and the child's father presented themselves as white. They also had the confirmation of several witnesses. The bishop's office quickly agreed to the petition. A local priest was about to present the restored certificate to the father when he casually asked why the couple had not married. The father answered that the couple could not marry because of the obvious racial difference between them. With indignant reaction, the priest quickly contacted higher Church officials, requesting the denial of the new birth certificate that listed the child as white. However, the Church again did not take action against the child's white classification.[33]

Another example also demonstrates that even when local priests complained of the falsification of white identities for a child of color, higher-level officials often did not engage in the argument. In 1851, a priest initially baptized an infant as white because he could attest to the whiteness of the father and the godparents. He was untroubled by the absence of the mother, who remained listed as "*madre reservada*" (mother reserved) on the baptismal certificate. This situation changed when the priest later discovered that the mother was in fact a slave. He then called upon the Church to change the child's classification from white to *pardo*. The bishop's office responded that without documentation of her mixed-race ancestry, no such change was warranted.[34] In these cases, the Church's lack of interest in the precise maintenance of racial categories aided the corruption of the very meaning of whiteness. The white jural label lost some of its validity.

In spite of the 1778 restriction and the historical value of race in maintaining political and social hierarchy, many people were moved by a variety of motives, such as love or material considerations, to change their jural classifications from white to racially mixed in order to marry someone of color. These were situations in which Cuban flexibility with racial labels continued beyond their initial baptismal assignments. In 1817, 30-year-old José Bonifacio Garcia had lived his entire life as legally white, but to Church officials he then claimed to be a fair-skinned *pardo*. He had been baptized as a white orphan who had not known his parents or grandparents. However, he had been raised by his mother's brother. José Bonifacio now rejected his white status in order to marry his fiancée, who was clearly *parda*. The white uncle strongly objected and pled with colonial authorities to prevent the marriage.[35] Perhaps the uncle's own claims to whiteness and honor would have been threatened by the nephew's racial classification. The racial status of one family member would have had implications for all members of the same lineage. White privilege could be threatened if people of color were acknowledged within the family.

This familial nature of racial status in 1847 prompted another white man, Don Ramón Moya, to attempt to prevent his wife's sister, Doña Encarnación, from marrying her *pardo* fiancé. That marriage would create an unacceptable stain on his family's reputation. The young woman responded with claims that in reality her family was not white but racially mixed. She then made the family's private secret public: her grandmother had been a woman of color. In fact, her fiancé was also her uncle. His mother and Doña Encarnación's grandmother were the same person. The fiancé had been conceived in her relationship with a man of color, while his older sister was conceived in a relationship with a white man. After the deaths of her parents, Doña Encarnación had been raised in the household of her fiancé's father. Residing with a family of color would have been truly exceptional for a young white woman of good social standing. To drive home her point, Doña Encarnación went even further with her revelations of *pardo* racial identity, challenging even her brother-in-law Don Ramón's claims of being white. She suggested instead that he was really the illegitimate son of a priest and a *mulata* slave woman. By the end of the record, colonial officials had allowed Doña Encarnación to marry without further comment.[36] These types of situations reveal the precarious nature of white identity for many Cuban families of the period. If white privilege had been achieved through deceptive circumstances, it could have been easily lost in the subsequent generation if children made racial choices that were distinct from those of their parents.

Beyond the shifts in racial identity associated with marriage, an even more institutional strategy allowed racially mixed children to achieve a designation as white. This often occurred after they were deposited as orphans in Havana's Real Casa de Maternidad, also known as the Casa Cuna. It had been created under the auspices of both the Spanish Crown and the Catholic Church to protect abandoned white children, offering them a chance for adoption to a good family or the right to be raised in the name of the Spanish Crown with legal acknowledgment of a fictive legitimacy. In recognition of the Casa Cuna's founder, Archbishop Jeronimo Valdés, the family name of Valdés was granted to all such children in support of this idea.[37] However, below we will see that in practice, nonwhite children were often also accepted under the same circumstances as whites.

Children of all racial categories were abandoned at various private doorsteps throughout the country and received by the Church. Many were then baptized with the annotation "appears to be white." In this way, anyone could receive a white jural classification. Considerate parents would then return to "adopt" or act as patrons to their own abandoned but newly whitened and legitimated children. One mid-nineteenth-century priest noted that it was not unusual for adults who were obviously mulattoes to receive copies of their baptismal certificates that listed them as white orphans. The most famous case of the value of the Casa Cuna in reproducing and transforming racial categories comes from the tragic heroine at the center of the nineteenth-century Cuban novel *Cecilia Valdés*. Cirilio Villaverde's fictional story presented the title character as the illegitimate daughter of a quadroon woman and an elite white man. Cecilia received her surname as the result of a temporary placement in the Real Casa in an ultimately futile attempt to hide her background. Her removal from the institution to the home of her *mulata* grandmother ended any possibility of hiding African ancestry. In this case, even her fair complexion still did not allow her to enter the world of creole whites. Her racial background was an ever-present force in limiting her social mobility.[38]

The available sources do not indicate how successful this strategy was for real orphans registered under similar circumstances. What they do suggest is that some continued to live as jural whites and others did not. One black mother petitioned the Church to change her son's record to reflect his true parentage. She argued that if he remained listed as white, it would become so obviously false as to make him the object of ridicule. Other orphans requested deletion of their white identities as a result of an unfavorable application of the 1778 impediment against interracial marriage. Take for example the case of Juana Valdés and her desire to marry her *pardo* boyfriend. Initially, colonial officials had denied the couple permission to marry based on racial inequality. As a royally recognized orphan, Juana was presumed to be white.

After the first official rejection of her case, Juana resubmitted the petition and went to greater lengths to prove that she was in fact *mulata* and that she had always associated with other people of color. She presented the required number of witnesses to affirm that point. Only then were the change to her racial designation and the marriage license approved.[39]

Some of the orphans who received their legal whiteness from the Casa Cuna realized the dubiousness of these designations. Late in the nineteenth century, a small number of these orphans insisted on additional medical confirmation of their whiteness. They submitted themselves to physical examination in the process of verifying their anthropometric characteristics as belonging to the Caucasian race. The first record of this type appeared in 1879, in the midst of the gradual abolition of Cuban slavery.[40] It is unclear what motivated these petitions, whether it was a declining prestige for the Real Casa, other local changes in the meaning of race associated with the close of slavery, or, possibly, the spread of scientific racism in the Euro-American world. Of the twenty-four such petitions encountered for the period between 1879 and 1892, five were requested in 1880, when slavery was replaced by the *patronato* apprenticeship system. An additional ten were found for 1886 and 1887, when slavery was completely terminated.[41]

Not all interracial unions actively pursued a surreptitious whiteness or the whitening of their children. The public process of acknowledging paternity for children born outside wedlock also provided another institutional form for reproducing the boundaries of race and class within the context of the family. Between 1860 and 1894, 169 white or Asian men in western Cuba claimed paternity of their mixed-race children. The majority of these children were legally baptized under the *pardo*, or racially mixed, label. These actions created openly recognized families that did not conform to the limits the state had placed on racial reproduction. Despite legal impediments to interracial marriages, these Cuban families transcended attempts to define family in racially exclusive terms in which legitimacy and social recognition were reserved for whites and illegitimacy and marginalization defined the reproductive space of people of color.

The first interracial recognition encountered in the records dates from 1860. It contains the angry lament of a white father about the difficulties he had faced in attempting to legally recognize his *parda* daughter. Don Enrique Urbina noted that by a royal order of December 1, 1837, illegitimate children were no longer to be baptized with their parents labeled as unknown, as long as both parents acknowledged paternity to the officiating priest. Don Enrique could not understand why a local priest had refused to annotate proper paternity for his daughter, Enriqueta Dorotea. The Church's initial response was that since an official impediment to the marriage of the parents existed, neither parent could be recognized on the baptismal document. This impediment sprang from their obvious racial difference and the royal *cédula* (order) of October 15, 1805, which stated "that it has come into practice that marriage cannot be celebrated between people of recognized nobility and cleanliness of blood and someone of the black, mulatto, and other mixed races, unless the presidents of the municipal courts, after reviewing the evidence, grant their permission."[42] Despite the Church's negative reaction, the child's paternity was later annotated to her baptismal certificate without further explanation.[43]

From that time forward, a small trickle of white and Asian men chose to so claim their mixed-race children. In fact, in a subsequent 1861 petition, a church official indicated that because "there did not occur any impediment to contract marriage" between an Asturian (Spanish) man and an enslaved woman, acknowledgment of their child's paternity was accepted without further comment.[44] These types of recognition crossed many social boundaries. They occurred among Spaniards and Cubans and property holders and the penniless. Only the Cuban nobility were not counted within this set. Through such recognition mulattoes, blacks, and whites were united by openly acknowledged family bonds. These acts could be interpreted as whitening only if the black and mulatto elements were ignored.

Despite these examples of the disjuncture between the policies of the state and the actions of the Church related to issues of racial identity, at times the two converged, or at least the Church's position appeared ambivalent. Take for example the handful of cases in which single, presumably white women petitioned the Church to correct their mistaken *parda* identities found in their children's baptismal records. In all cases, both mother and child had been initially listed in the baptismal registries of people of color. With documentation of the mother's white ancestry, the children's records were readily transferred to the registries of whites.[45]

The original listings and subsequent corrections suggest several explanations. One could easily accept that the initial *parda* listings may have been simple errors. However, given the colonial association of whiteness and legitimacy, these petitions may suggest a tendency to record out-of-wedlock baptisms under people of color. Any possible reclassification of white mothers as *parda* would have confused even further the meaning of whiteness in Cuba's late colonial period by forcing "true" whites into the *pardo* jural category. Another interpretation of these cases is that they represent more evidence of women of color successfully "passing." Such a view would only further support the hypothesis that when requested, Church officials preferred to list someone as white and aided the construction of ambiguous racial identities.

With these possibilities in mind, the uncertainty in racial positioning is revealed in one additional case. In one 1840 request, Antonio Soto declared himself to be a free *pardo* and acknowledged that his ability to marry a *parda* woman was compromised by the fact that his 1805 birth certificate falsely listed him as white. Since his mother was white and his father remained unnamed, Antonio had lived with white status for thirty-five years. But the restrictions on interracial marriage led him to seek clerical redefinition of his status. The local parish began to investigate the matter. In a report on the background and conduct of the mother and son, the local priest stated that he did not personally know Antonio's mother, María Paula Soto, but according to other witnesses, "yes, she does belong to the class of poor whites and her son, who opened this investigation, is the result of her union with a man of color as indicated by his phenotype and, for this reason, has been and is reputed to be mulatto."[46] Therefore, the mother's racial category stood without question and was not changed. If her status was true, then this is one of the few cases in which a white woman of the colonial period was registered as the mother of a *pardo* child.

This possibility is further suggested in the oral family histories I collected in Havana.[47] Of my twenty Afro-Cuban informants over the age of seventy-five, three discussed knowledge of white grandmothers. One such case recounted the story of the grandmother's painful banishment from her white family when she chose a black spouse.[48] These prevalent family memories of white grandmothers contrast with the historical documentation. In the approximately 5,800 baptisms of color recorded at the Havana parish of Espíritu Santo between 1876 and 1904, only two white mothers were listed.[49] While there is no direct correlation between these two data sets, the difference between them is suggestive. They may speak either to an exaggeration of white ancestry or a jural denial of the possibility of interracial reproduction between men of color and white women. In the latter situation, few members of either group could reproduce publicly themselves in the bodies of the racial other, a fact that stands in great contrast to the reproductive possibilities of white men and women of color.

The background of the well-remembered nineteenth-century Cuban poet "Plácido" Concepción Valdés also speaks to the existence of this practice of intentionally obscuring reproductive or familial links between whites and people of color. He was born in 1809, the son of a mulatto craftsman and a

Spanish actress. Although he was raised in his father's home, he had been initially placed in the Real Casa de Maternidad and baptized as a white orphan with the surname Valdés.[50] What motivated this action? Did his parents wish to protect his mother's honor, hide his father's race, or both? In either case, the official baptismal record did not recognize Placido's African descent, although it became public knowledge from the moment his mulatto father recovered him from the orphanage. If whitening had been this family's strategy, they also accepted its limits.

A final case highlights the gendered politics of racialized reproduction in late colonial Cuba and the agency of Cuban women in exercising their reproductive options. In defending her *pardo* lover, José de Leon, against charges of kidnapping and rape brought by her parents, the white Doña María Navarro testified that they had intended to marry and that she had threatened him "that if he didn't do it [carry her to his home], he wasn't a man." In this way Doña María declared herself to have been an active participant in challenging the sexual boundaries of race by defending her socially unacceptable relationship. And even more surprisingly, a local official supported the couple's plans. In a letter to the president of the Real Audiencia (regional court), he cited a similar case against the *pardo* Juan Escalona for the alleged rape and kidnapping of the white Doña Eusevia Yzquierdo, where a license to marry had been granted. The official suggested that based on this precedent, José de Leon and Doña María should have been allowed to marry.[51] While such cases admittedly occurred infrequently, they testify to the reality of sexual and familial encounters between men of color and white women. In this way, race continued to impose different limitations for men and women of color, just as it did for white women and men. The various ways that they chose to shape family sometimes had the power to overcome these differences and sometimes only reinforced them.

Conclusions and Implications

This chapter places family-formation practices at the center of an analysis of racial meaning in late colonial Cuba. It develops and uses the concept of the sexual economy of race to argue that in choosing alternate family forms, a number of nineteenth-century Cubans initiated unintended changes in how race was lived and perceived. At various points, familial relationships crossed the traditional boundaries between races. The above examples reveal the existence of these dissident acts. Between the recognition white men gave to their racially mixed children, the norms of reproductive endogamy, and the isolation determined by class and race, several possibilities existed. Those of African ancestry could enter the ranks of the white and the white person could choose to reclassify himself as a person of color. In terms of class, the man of wealth could choose to bear his heirs with an enslaved woman. Also, the white laborer could choose to create family alliances with people of color in an act that also fostered an intra-class unity that transcended race.

The examples I have presented highlight the flexibility of racial categories. In the late colonial Cuban context, all such categories were subject to internal transformations; they were either expanded or contracted to fit a variety of sociopolitical situations. Even the "whiteness" that the dominant elements of Euro-American societies have held as paramount had undergone shifts in meaning.[52] The uncertainty associated with these shifts was not driven only by the actions of people of color. The person of color did not simply "whiten" or "pass" into whiteness by repeated, reproductive lessening of nonwhite physical characteristics accompanied by unproblematic socioeconomic advancement.[53] Instead, the very definition of whiteness was consciously expanded to fit certain people of recognized mixed descent. While the old idiom that "money whitens" remained in play, economic considerations were only one factor in that process. In addition, "whitening" was a process that required the active participation of whites beyond the biological contribution.

Another important implication of this evidence is to question assumptions that all social actors were striving for advancement vis-à-vis the colonial state. It would be incorrect to interpret all public actions, including reproduction, through this lens and thus falsely understand the procreative choices of the majority of people of color as directed toward "whitening." One can be critical of this perspective because of its emphasis on a unidirectional orientation and its dismissal of other possibilities in racialized reproduction.

One of the concerns of this chapter is with scholarly descriptions of whitening that use either the individual or the nation as the unit of analysis. The nation whitens as the demographic presence of nonwhite individuals decreases. The dark individual whitens in the choice of lighter individuals as reproductive partners. As shown here, a great deal more often was at play. What of the choice made by the lighter partner? Since race mixture in colonial Latin America occurred most often in consensual unions between white men and nonwhite women, it has been assumed that these men did not have a social investment in the offspring and did not seek to reproduce themselves in the nonwhite bodies of either mother or child. The literature does not consider these relations as families but defined them as concubinage or promiscuity with diluted social value and positioned the offspring as marginal, depending on if they had passed some threshold in white phenotype. Thus, according to the literature, the partner of color whitens while the white partner remains unaffected by his or her reproductive choice.

While it is likely true that many black and mulatto individuals did hope to whiten subsequent generations, viewing the process of whitening through the lens of the family or the community instead of the individual makes its legal and social limitations more apparent. The "whitening" individual did not live in isolation. He or she was associated with a family and a community. For one to become white, both family and community had to unite in the rejection of an African past. Many did, while others did not. As we have seen, a few people made familial choices to be *pardo* rather than live as white.

In colonial Cuba's interracial environment, the social reproduction of race did not follow a unitary paradigm. The Latin American rejection of the U.S.-type black hypodescent or "one-drop rule" did not just create an alternate mulatto hypodescent or an inevitable whitening. Interracial procreation did not have a fixed result. The offspring of the same couple could have been labeled white or mulatto, depending not only on skin color and economic status but also on the various strategies individuals used to group themselves collectively into families. The public memory is an important factor in distinguishing the act of race mixture from one of *blanqueamiento*. It is not simply the racial inputs into the sexual equation that matters as much as the description and recollection of the process. Recognition of *mestizaje* provides for dual or multiple heritage, while *blanqueamiento* acknowledges only one, white past. Ultimately, colonial Cuban families, created by a variety of recognized social practices and legal procedures, struggled with these choices. And each form in turn reproduced racial meaning, just as race shaped family forms. The colonial reproductive practices provided the foundations for the "whitening," "browning," and "blackening" of subsequent generations within independent Latin American nations.

Notes

1. See the statement that in Latin America "the constant endeavors on the part of the colored populations to advance socially by whitening themselves through marriage, or rather through informal affairs with lighter, if not white people, conflicted with the downgrading principle [the black hypodescent prevalent in U.S. race discourse]"; Martínez-Alier, *Marriage, Class and Colour in Nineteenth-Century Cuba*, 18.

2. Thomas Skidmore notes that "the whitening ideal remained firmly entrenched among the [Brazilian] elite"; *Black into White*, 192.

3. Valuable here are the essays in Richard Graham, ed. *The Idea of Race in Latin America*, especially Skidmore, "Racial Ideas and Social Policy"; and Helg, "Race in Argentina and Cuba."

4. Andrews, *Afro-Latin America.*

5. See Andrews, *Blacks and Whites in São Paulo, Brazil.*

6. In *Blackness and Race Mixture*, Wade speaks of a geographic-based "moral topography" of race. Also see Appelbaum, "Whitening the Region."

7. In a few studies, black and mulatto men are revealed to have pursued whitening for their families. See the brief biographies of early nineteenth-century Nicaraguans Pedro Benito Pineda and his son Laureano Pineda in Wolfe, "'The Cruel Whip.'"

8. Exceptions to this general picture have appeared in the literature on the early colonial Spanish American society in regions with large indigenous populations. There, a number of male Spanish settlers acknowledged and supported their children born to indigenous mothers. See Lockhart, *Spanish Peru*; and Burns, *Colonial Habits*. However, no comparable studies have considered sociologically the results of miscegenation between white men and women of African descent.

9. On the "mulatto escape hatch," see Degler, *Neither Black nor White*, 226–232. The classic example of the promotion of *mestizaje* is seen in Vasconcelos, *Raza cósmica.*

10. De la Fuente, *A Nation for All*, chapter 5; and Bronfman, *Measures of Equality*, chapter 5.

11. See Lowell and Wood, "Skin Color, Racial Identity, and Life Chance in Brazil"; and de la Fuente, "Race, National Discourse, and Politics in Cuba."

12. See Rout, *The African Experience in Spanish America*, 126–131.

13. For a good description of this and other forms of *gracias al sacar*, see Twinam, *Public Lives, Private Secrets*, 43. Interestingly, Twinam notes few cases of official bestowal of whiteness to people of color through that type of *gracias al sacar*. From other sources, only two such cases were documented for Cuba. See Castellanos and Castellanos, *Cultura Afrocubana*, 1:90.

14. This approach is informed by Omi and Winant, *Racial Formation in the United States*. However, I will deemphasize political constructions of race and consider a longer historical process.

15. As will be demonstrated below, the concept of family is not limited to the unit defined by marriage. Other forms can exist and have existed. For additional treatment of this topic for Cuba, see Morrison, "Creating an Alternative Kinship"; and Morrison, "White Fathers and Slave Mothers in Nineteenth-Century Cuba."

16. For discussion of colonial restrictions on the selection of marriage partners, see Martínez-Alier, *Marriage, Class and Colour in Nineteenth-Century Cuba*; for elsewhere, see Ardanaz, *El matrimonio en Indias*, 3–18; Lavrin, "Introduction: The Scenario, the Actors, and the Issues"; Socolow, "Acceptable Partners: Marriage Choice in Colonial Argentina, 1778–1810"; and Gutiérrez, *When Jesus Came, the Corn Mothers Went Away*, 227–297.

17. See Fanon, *Black Skin, White Masks*, 42–47; and Anne McClintock's reading of Fanon's implicit assessment of a "sexual economy of race" in "No Longer in a Future Heaven: Nationalism, Gender, and Race," 264–270.

18. See Lancaster, *Life Is Hard*, 18–20 and 280–282, although Lancaster does not explicitly define the concept of "sexual economy."

19. Compare this fourth point with recent studies of the social construction of whiteness in the United States. See Allen, T*he Invention of the White Race*; Delgado and Stefancic, *Critical White Studies*; Ignatiev, *How the Irish Became White*; and Roediger, *Working toward Whiteness*. While many such works emphasize the value of whiteness in formal politics and labor relations, such insights can also be turned toward the construction of race in the familial domain.

20. Degler, *Neither Black nor White*, 107 and passim.

21. See Harris, *Patterns of Race in the Americas*; Hoetink, *Slavery and Race Relations in the Americas*; and Degler, *Neither Black nor White*.

22. Martínez-Alier, *Marriage, Class and Colour*, 117.

23. Seed, *To Love, Honor, and Obey in Colonial Mexico*; Socolow, "Acceptable Partners"; and Gutiérrez, *When Jesus Came, the Corn Mothers Went Away*, 284–292 and 317. For a valuable interpretation of the minimal importance of race in the original design and implementation of the 1776/1778 *Real Pragmática*, see Saether, "Bourbon Absolutism and Marriage Reform in Late Colonial Spanish America." However, Cuban developments were not treated extensively in this latter work.

24. Martínez-Alier, *Marriage, Class and Colour*.

25. Ibid., 60–62.

26. This study found interracial marriages allowed in the following petitions: Archivo Nacional de Cuba (hereafter ANC), Gobierno Superior Civil: leg. 888, no. 29871, 1813; leg. 888, no. 29913, 1813; leg. 888, no. 29969, 1814; leg. 890, no. 30044, 1815; leg. 891, no. 30091, 1816; leg. 893, no. 30297, 1818; leg. 895, no. 30472, 1820; leg. 895, no. 30487, 1820; leg. 895, no. 3052, 1821; leg. 897, no. 30698, 1822; leg. 897, no. 30724, 1822; leg. 899, no. 30829, 1826; leg. 900, no. 30881, 1827; leg. 912, no. 31671, 1849; leg. 913, no. 31731, 1850; leg. 935A, no. 32840, 1853; leg. 935B, no. 32963, 1858; leg. 921, no. 32129, 1859 (includes three approved petitions); leg. 924, no. 32284, 1862. Also ANC, Gobierno General, leg. 348, no. 15760A, 1868. However, this review admittedly did not cover all the available records.

27. Archive of the Parroquia de Santo Ángel Custodio (Havana), *Libro 9 de matrimonios blancos*, entries 79 and 122; Archive of the Parroquia de Espíritu Santo (Havana), *Libro 55 de bautismos de pardos y morenos*, entry 760 and *Libro 56*, entries 78 and 455; Archivo del Arzobispado de la Habana (hereafter AAH), Fondo de Legitimaciones y Reconocimientos (hereafter "Reconocimientos"), leg. 100, expediente 73, leg. 101, exp. 22, leg. 106, exp. 7, leg. 113, exp. 3, and leg. 114, exp. 100.

28. Konetzke, *Colección de documentos para la historia de la formación social de Hispanoamérica*, vol. 3, tomo 2, num. 291, pp. 594–597.

29. Ibid.

30. See Cope, *The Limits of Racial Domination*, for discussion of popular rejection of dominant forms of racial categorization.

31. AAH, Reconocimientos, leg. 11, exp. 5, 1865.

32. AAH, Reconocimientos, leg. 25, exp. 6, 1868.

33. AAH, Reconocimientos, leg. 81, exp. 68, 1885.

34. AAH, Reconocimientos, leg. 2, exp. 6, 1851.

35. ANC, Fondo Gobierno Superior Civil, leg. 892, no. 30240. Another example is found in leg. 906, no. 31309. Examples from Church records include Reconocimientos, leg. 69, exp. 78 and leg. 7, exp. 97.

36. ANC, Fondo Gobierno Superior Civil, leg. 910, no. 31527, 1847.

37. González, "Abandonment in Havana," 12–14.

38. Villaverde, *Cecilia Váldes*.

39. ANC, Fondo Gobierno Superior Civil, leg. 935A, no. 32823, 1851.

40. AAH, Reconocimientos, leg. 55, exp. 81, 1879.

41. AAH, Reconocimientos, leg. 52, exp. 52, 1878; leg. 55, exp. 81, 1879; leg. 59, exp. 87, 1880; leg. 61, exp. 45, 1880; leg. 61, exp. 65, 1880; leg. 66, exp. 79, 1881; leg. 78, exp. 72, 1884; leg. 78, exp. 100, 1884; leg. 79, exp. 93, 1884; leg. 88, exp. 78, 1886; leg. 88, exp. 93, 1886; leg. 89, exp. 35, 1887; leg. 89, exp. 38, 1887; leg. 89, exp. 41, 1887; leg. 89, exp. 46, 1887; leg. 90, exp. 78, 1887; leg. 91, exp. 101, 1887; leg. 92, exp. 44, 1888; leg. 92, exp. 72, 1887; leg. 95, exp. 33, 1888; leg. 109, exp. 29, 1891; leg. 109, exp. 48, 1891; leg. 109, exp. 86, 1892; and leg. 110, exp. 14, 1892.

42. AAH, Reconocimientos, leg. 4, exp. 57, 1860.

43. AAH, Reconocimientos, leg. 4, exp. 57, 1860.

44. AAH, Reconocimientos, leg. 4, exp. 83, 1861.

45. AAH, Reconocimientos, leg. 19, exp. 80; leg. 46, exp. 2; leg. 68, exp. 61; leg. 79, exp. 54; and leg. 93, exp. 78.

46. ANC, Fondo Gobierno Superior Civil, leg. 906, no. 31309, 1840.

47. Morrison, "'And Your Grandmother, Where Is She?'" chapter 9.

48. Interview with anonymous respondent by author, tape recording, Havana, August 14, 1999.

49. Archive of the Parish of Espíritu Santo, *Libros de bautismos de pardos y morenos*, 56–59.

50. Calcagno, *Poetas de color*, 9–10.

51. ANC, Fondo de Gobierno Superior Civil, leg. 914, no. 31756.

52. In U.S. history, Roediger's *The Wages of Whiteness* takes much of the lead in the deconstruction of white identity. Also important is Allen, *The Invention of the White Race*, vol. 1, *Racial Oppression and Social Control*. For Latin American history, see Kuznesof, "Ethnic and Gender Influences on 'Spanish' Creole Society in Colonial Spanish America."

53. Notions of economic advantages enjoyed by people of notable mixed-race descent have been challenged by several authors. For example, see Wood and Lovell, "Skin Color, Racial Identity, and Life Chances in Brazil."

8

Tensions of Race, Gender, and Midwifery in Colonial Cuba

MICHELE REID-VAZQUEZ

In February 1828, the Cuban newspaper *El Diario de la Habana* reported a "truly painful" discovery: the "honorable" profession of midwifery had become "disgraced." Its demise, the article claimed, centered on shifts in the female population and overall deficiencies in midwife training. Initially, the article suggested that the decline of the profession could be traced, in part, to the "scarcity" of white women on the island. It alleged that the insufficient numbers of Spanish women and *criollas* (women of Spanish descent born in Cuba) had naturally hindered the increase of white *parteras* (midwives). The true reason for the damaged character of the field, however, seemed to stem directly from the fact that it had been "abandoned" to women of African descent, particularly free women of color. The author contended that black women's lack of institutional expertise threatened public health and their designated low socioracial status jeopardized "the art of midwifery."[1] These assertions demand closer scrutiny, particularly in nineteenth-century Cuban society, where few women of any racial background pursued and prospered in a skilled occupation. To what degree did the proportions of African- and European-descended women in Cuba contribute to the shifting racial composition of midwifery? How did Cuba's social hierarchy inform occupational choices for women, specifically for medical practice? If more formal education and a larger number of white female practitioners would restore honor to the field, what did that mean for black *parteras* and, more broadly, the economic opportunities for free women of color in Cuba?

In the early nineteenth century, the intersections of slavery, freedom, gender, empire, and medicine produced fissures in colonial Cuban society. As one of the last strongholds of Spanish colonialism in the Americas, Cuba stood at a political crossroads. On the one hand, imperial authorities and elites embraced the island's economic growth in sugar production. The fact that slavery in Cuba had expanded in such close proximity to the new black republic of Haiti fostered suspicions of Cuba's numerically significant free population of African descent (*libres de color*) as well as slaves. On the other hand, efforts to counteract the demise of its empire in the Americas dictated that Spain imitate the approach of its European and American rivals to bolstering imperial and national progress by modernizing its Caribbean territories. To that end, Spanish colonial authorities in Cuba embraced the surge in the professionalization of medicine, which was aimed primarily at men of European descent in an attempt to expand and whiten all realms of medical practice. Midwives' contributions to reproduction, understood as both the physical act of giving birth to healthy Spanish and creole heirs and new members of the slave labor pool and the symbolic act that perpetuated colonial identity and authority, took on new meanings in an era of geopolitical restructuring. Consequently, supplanting midwives in Cuba, who traditionally were black women, became an ardent goal.

Using the tensions surrounding local and international debates over midwives in the nineteenth century, I explore how Cuba's medical establishment and free women of African descent deciphered conflicting interpretations of midwifery as an occupational avenue. This chapter compares midwife traditions in Europe and Africa and their development in the Americas; addresses representations of honor, gender, race, and labor in a colonial Cuban context; and traces the impact of Atlantic World medical trends in the late eighteenth and nineteenth centuries by examining contestations over midwifery in Cuba. By demonstrating that free black and mulatto women secured a labor niche that challenged established socioracial codes of conduct, I argue that these women understood the value of their labor to Cuban society and used it to bolster their economic and social condition within a framework of honor. In essence, free women of African descent engaged the terms of honor that elites used and appropriated them for themselves. In doing so, some of them deflected efforts by the colonial state to diminish their participation in midwifery.

This chapter suggests ways that free women of color used occupational choice as a marker of identity and honor despite the limits of race and gender within Cuba's slave society. Indeed, as the editors of this volume point out, individuals of African descent influenced local knowledge and cultural systems. Although midwifery had the potential to become a unifying endeavor based on gendered occupational patterns from Africa and Europe, in Cuba the intertwined processes of racialization, medical professionalization, and colonial politics produced cleavages that forced women of African descent to reshape their roles as midwives. Their participation in this diasporic paradigm emphasizes the tensions of freedom, race, and gender from the multiple perspectives that informed colonial Cuba's slave society and the broader issues within the African Diaspora in Latin America.

Midwives in the New World

Contexualizing the broader regional and trans-Atlantic tensions over race, labor, and gender is key to understanding nineteenth-century Cuban debates over midwives. African and European traditions transferred to the New World dictated that women work in this occupation. In these regions, women predominated the field of midwifery in which they shared knowledge of the trade through oral transmission, used medicinal plants, and incorporated religious rituals in their practices. Differences, however, emerged in the social perception of midwives. For instance, the typical midwife in early modern Spain practiced in an urban area and had little education.[2] The European practitioner's low social status, lack of formal training, and perceived superstitious nature often produced representations of her as "drunken, dirty and immoral" and left her vulnerable to persecution.[3] In contrast, midwives in pre-colonial and colonial sub-Saharan Africa were identified as figures of authority and high social status. Their skill and knowledge made them revered throughout their communities.[4] The fact that numerous societies encouraged reproduction as a means of maintaining regional authority and labor needs through natural population increase accentuates this point. Correspondingly, some women used their high fertility, combined with the assistance of a skilled midwife, to establish political and cultural prestige.[5] Despite the ways that midwifery overlapped or diverged in Africa and Europe, practitioners in both regions served a key role in the care of mothers and infants during and after childbirth.

In the New World, racial slavery and colonialism dictated the hierarchy of labor, and midwifery was no exception. African and African-descended midwives in rural and urban areas served populations throughout the Americas, often monopolizing the field in plantation-based societies in the Caribbean, South America, and North America.[6] Similarly, in colonial territories such as New Spain and Guatemala, which had large indigenous populations, Indian or *mestiza* women served as *parteras*.[7] As the primary health care providers, especially on plantations, women of color performed a range of tasks. In addition to their service as midwives, they were frequently called upon by community members to perform related activities as nurses and healers.[8] An enslaved woman could also be hired out as a wet nurse or as a domestic and through this means earn money to eventually purchase her freedom. Once free, women of color typically continued these duties while adding other activities, such as operating a small business, to their limited repertoire of economic options.[9]

The majority of *parteras* in Latin America gained experience through traditional cultural practices.[10] Midwives generally learned their craft through hereditary apprenticeship. For instance, Mexican surgeons noted that most practitioners acquired their skills from a "mother, sister, or relative" and had a working knowledge of local plants and their medicinal properties. Furthermore, it was not uncommon for birthing attendants to be widows. Nineteenth-century census records for Mexico City listed fifteen widows among the city's twenty-four registered midwives.[11] *Partera* training programs instituted in Cuba required widows to provide proof of their former marital status for admission.[12] Whether midwives fostered skills through hereditary practice or more formal methods, they continued to pass them on to female relatives to ensure the perpetuation of knowledge that had been preserved through oral tradition. It also afforded these women, especially widows, a measure of economic stability and social autonomy.

Because they predominated in the field, black women's contributions to midwifery did not go unnoticed in the colonies. Political and medical elites acknowledged midwives in the Americas for their rudimentary knowledge of the body and their reliability in providing testimony regarding cases of rape or incest.[13] Moreover, plantation owners conceded that midwives proved crucial to the expansion of the slave population. Some slave holders offered incentives, such as money or livestock, to secure the healthy development of a newborn slave. As one planter in eighteenth-century Saint-Domingue commented, "It is customary to give the midwife a small gratuity for every successful delivery."[14] An English plantation owner in Virginia specified payments by race, commenting that the typical fee for a slave with birthing skills "was about ten shillings, while a white woman often charged as much as 4 pounds." In Cuba, even as Havana's Royal Protomedicato attempted to regulate healthcare practitioners in 1728, colonists continued to rely on traditional herbalists and *parteras*.[15] Nevertheless, the praise for and reliance on midwives could easily shift to condemnation when infant mortality spiked.[16]

With life literally in their hands, women of color came under intense colonial scrutiny. As Saint-Domingue coffee planter P. J. Laborie noted in his journal in 1789, "During the first nine days [of a child's birth], no one except the midwife, not even the reputed father, must be permitted to enter the [mother's] chamber. Both she and the mother must be acquainted that no excuses will be admitted, nor accidents of neglect overlooked. If accidents should happen, the ordinary gratuity will not be paid, and even severe penalties may be inflicted."[17] If the infant died, punishments, such as whipping, could be exacted on both women.[18] Given the importance of infant survival to the colonies, authorities often regarded birth attendants of African and indigenous background with disdain and characterized them as "ignorant Indians and mulattos."[19] Slave owner Thomas Chaplin of South Carolina expressed his racial preference when his wife went into labor, commenting, "Old Judy, a black midwife, has been summoned . . . to the Chaplin house in the village until Maria Cook, a white midwife, is available."[20] Because of midwives' racial heritage and their social position, as either slaves or free women from the poor classes, authorities persistently questioned their training, accused them of being illiterate and superstitious, and suggested that they "crossed the boundary of science" into sorcery.[21]

As medical professionalization began in the late eighteenth century, midwives in Cuba and throughout Spanish America suffered mounting condemnation for their informal training. The "traditional" realm of midwifery and the "scientific" sphere of medicine clashed, producing scathing criticism.[22] Some officials chastised Peruvian *parteras* for practicing "without principles and rules."[23] Mexican physician Antonio Serrano declared that the colony contained a "plague of *curanderos*, destroyers of humanity" whose "wild prognostics" tainted the work of licensed practitioners.[24] Cuba's medical establishment levied similar accusations and characterized free black and mulatto midwives as "ignorant beings" who threatened public health.[25] The persistent portrayal of midwives as unskilled, despite colonial acknowledgement to the contrary, and the fact that most practitioners were women of color made African and African-descended women prime targets for reform and displacement at the hands of the medical profession.

Constructing Race, Gender, and Honor in Colonial Cuba

In colonial Spanish America, codes of honor permeated the political and social ordering of society. Understood and accepted as a tangible characteristic, honor structured Spanish America by maintaining established hierarchies between the elites and the masses. In effect, it sanctioned discrimination in favor of the privileged based on a variety of qualities, including economic standing, social activities, racial ancestry, and gender. Individuals of African ancestry, particularly women, were subject to constant exclusion from the honor norms of Spanish and creole society. Assertions of dishonor were clear attempts to highlight the inferiority of others. Honor, however, was not static, but malleable and negotiable. It had the power to reflect and validate the shifting public personas and reputations of elites and plebeians.[26]

The flexible nature of honor enabled non-elites to fashion their own interpretations of this social code. Scholars have noted that members of the masses, like those of high social status, had a vested interest in their honor, especially in terms of their public standing and integrity.[27] For instance, when a mainland Spanish American newspaper accused Cuban militia men of color of being dangerous, untrustworthy, and thus dishonorable, black officers responded to the government and the general community, asserting that "commissions of high importance have trusted us and we have fulfilled [our military duty] with precision and pure honor with the appreciation and recommendation of the Leaders and the Magistrates."[28] They staked their political reputations on their proven loyalty to the Spanish Crown. In a more personal and individual case, political tensions in Cuba forced Carlota Molina to establish her honor with the aid of foreign authorities. After Molina obtained her freedom in Cuba in 1818, she decided to reunite with family, first in Curaçao and later in Jamaica. When she had difficulty securing reentry to Cuba a few years later, Molina sought a personal reference from the Jamaican consul. His characterization of her behavior as "always honorable" and his elite political position helped her enter Cuba at a time when authorities had closed its ports to Jamaican freedmen, whom Cuban officials deemed "a dangerous class . . . contagious with the false and fictitious doctrines of revolutionaries."[29] These examples illustrate a few of the ways individuals of African descent interpreted the importance of honor on a public and personal level, particularly in the Cuban context.

Notions of honor also shaped gender ideals. Spanish society, and Spanish colonies constructed definitions of femininity that often included contrasting characterizations based on race in the Americas. Depictions of the ideal proper woman centered on women of European descent who adhered to codes of *limpieza de sangre* (blood purity) and were virginal, chaste, passive, respectable.[30] Elites viewed those who varied from this description as deviant and dishonorable. The dominant social codes for upper-status women, who were considered the "keepers of morality," frequently forced them to conduct their lives in the isolation of the domestic sphere.[31] Travelers to Cuba noted this seclusion, remarking repeatedly that they rarely saw Spanish women and *criollas* in the streets. Instead, as Benjamin Moore Norman, an American visitor to Cuba in the 1840s, noted, it was behind "the iron gratings of the windows . . . that the females enjoy the luxury of the air, and display their charms. . . . Many a bright lustrous eye, and fairy-like foot, have I thus seen through the wires of her cheerful cage, which were scarcely ever seen beyond it."[32] In addition, the social status of elite women, who had access to higher levels of education, excluded them from manual labor. Indeed, after British traveler James Phillippo's visit to Cuba in the 1850s, he described white women as "guiltless of manual labour."[33] In other words, race and gender excluded upper-status white women from the public streets and the work that took place in these spaces. Simultaneously, from an elite standpoint, these factors marked women of color as racial and social inferiors who lacked virtue, morality, and honor.

Efforts to maintain racial purity and social hierarchy fostered corresponding divisions of labor. Colonial traditions in the Americas blocked upper-status *criollas* and Spanish women from pursuing scientific study and training, despite the honor that derived from their gender and racial status.[34] Elite men deemed women in general, particularly those of African descent, as too limited intellectually for formal professions, especially those in the medical field.[35] Poor women, consequently, had few opportunities for educational advancement. For instance, few schools existed for individuals of color in Cuba at the start of the nineteenth century, and the number of educated *pardas* (women of mixed African and European ancestry who had light to brown skin) and *morenas* (women of primarily African descent who had dark skin) persistently lagged behind the number of educated white women. A government report for Havana in 1861 revealed that only 10 percent of free women of color were literate, compared to 52 percent of white women.[36] Similarly, an 1861 assessment of schools in Havana indicated that of the 4,184 students who attended the city's 53 public and 61 private facilities, black females comprised only 3 percent, while white females accounted for 37 percent. Regulations from the 1860s prohibited black women and men and white women from attending the city's colleges.[37] Nevertheless, women of African descent often managed to obtain limited access to a wide array of knowledge, training, and skills through both informal and formal means.[38]

In Cuba, the low-status designation of *pardas* and *morenas* gave such individuals access to arenas traditionally prohibited to Spaniards and *criollas*: the streets.[39] Indeed, as Massachusetts lawyer and abolitionist Richard Henry Dana Jr. remarked during his visit to Havana in the 1850s, "There are no women walking in the streets, except negresses."[40] Every day, black women's activities took them unaccompanied into Cuba's public corridors and squares.[41] For example, planters called on the services of midwives and wet nurses late into the night.[42] An array of foreign visitors commented on the ubiquitous presence of black women, including one who noted that they could "be seen at all hours hanging up washed clothes," haggling with creole men in the market over the price of chickens, or selling fruit or "spruce beer" on a street corner.[43] Others noted black female domestic servants "passing to and fro, carrying mats on which their mistresses were to kneel" during morning church services.[44] Foreign travelers gave vivid descriptions of the attire of free black women they saw in the streets. Several observers commented specifically on the "splendid apparel" worn by nurses, housekeepers and other black women.[45] They described how women of African descent appeared "in shining calico frocks, with silk shoes worn slipshod, red shawls, their hair arranged in fine braids and a bandanna or other handkerchief as a head-dress."[46] Others were adorned in "French wraps and gold jewelry."[47] Thus, free black and mulatto women became a familiar sight as they traversed the city, some in distinctive attire, often selling fruit, shopping for daily meals, or doing laundry—or traveling to attend pregnant women or infants.[48] Bound by race and gender, free women of color, like their male counterparts, filled both an occupational role and a public social space that the absence of higher-status women created.

In the context of the racial and gendered parameters that informed honor and occupation in colonial society, midwifery proved to be a high-profile professional niche for female *libres de color*. The *Diario de la Habana*'s claims about the sparse representation of white women as midwives had little to do with the numerical reality. Censuses taken in 1827 and 1841 indicate that white women comprised approximately 20 percent of the total population, while free women of color constituted only about 8 percent.[49] Thus, cultural and occupational norms of colonial Cuban society, rather than demographics, dictated that free *pardas* and *morenas* take a prominent role in one of the few skilled professions available to women. Those with formal midwife training who were licensed by Spain's Protomedicato publicized their specializations. In 1828, María del Carmen Alfonso promoted herself as a "teacher of the art of midwifery." María Vicente Carmona emphasized the availability of her services "regardless of the hour."[50] A list of reputable midwives appeared in the island's *Guía de Forasteros* (Visitors' Guide) in 1834, 1839, 1840, 1841, and 1845. Each roster showed a majority of women of color, and the names of the same individuals often appeared over the course of several years. For example, Vicente Carmona's name appeared in at least three of the *Guías*.[51]

These activities shed light on the appropriation of honor through occupation. Free women of color used the opportunities afforded them as midwives to validate their public reputation—their public honor. The vital role *parda* and *morena* midwives played in births and legal cases garnered them a level of respectability throughout broader Cuban society. Public announcements highlighted their abilities and their elite position in the free community of color and served as markers of their influence and leadership among *libres de color*; it took money to attend midwifery school and place an advertisement. The language the visitors' guides used to advertise midwives' services emphasized their skill and dedication to the field. These endeavors helped shape the broader social persona of free women of color within the realities of occupation and honor in a slave society. Nevertheless, race, honor, and changes in the medical field at the end of the eighteenth century and political events in nineteenth-century Cuba tempered the ability of free black women to work and prosper.

Midwives and the Medical Revolution

By the late eighteenth and early nineteenth centuries, a medical revolution had emerged in Western Europe that would have major repercussions in Cuba. At the turn of the century, French, British, and Spanish authorities took steps to professionalize medical practice, effectively displacing female practitioners from access to formal training.[52] The Protomedicato, Spain's medical regulatory authority, followed suit. In colonial Cuba, however, pursuing the goals of the "medical revolution" proved difficult. Formally trained doctors often skirted obstetrics because the bulk of male practitioners were not required to prove *limpieza de sangre*.[53] The dearth of licensed physicians in the colony forced the local population to incorporate indigenous and African healing practices performed by individuals with primarily informal training. Despite the colony's regulations and licensing procedures, Cuba's dependence on traditional and extralegal medicine cast it as "backward." With the advent of medical reform, Cuba sought to correct its less-than-modern position.[54]

Patterns of medical professionalization also advocated exclusion based on gender and race. Although physicians recognized that birthing practices had been the almost-exclusive domain of women for centuries, efforts to displace female midwives became prominent during the era of medical reform.[55] French laws focused on the distinction between legal and illegal practitioners. English efforts to homogenize and raise the status of the medical field solidified medicine as a male arena. Male midwives ultimately supplanted female birth attendants in Europe, although some places, such as the Netherlands, managed to retain more women in the field than other locales. A similar phenomenon occurred in the United States, where male physicians began competing with midwives for childbirth cases, particularly for elite women.[56] Essentially, the international rise of modern medicine established itself by negating the legitimacy of competing medical forms.[57] In Cuba, healing practices that were deemed informal or traditional or were practiced predominantly by women, especially women without blood purity, came under attack.

Colonial Cuban elites sought to prove their civilized status within European models, and they embraced the discriminatory changes in medical practice. Moreover, Spain's categorization in the early nineteenth century as a second-rank European power dependent on the economic stability of its colonies dictated that it heed trends in Europe.[58] In accordance with public health advances, Cuba's medical authorities undertook efforts to construct a colonial identity based on European paradigms of medical reform. Because of Cuba's diverse population and racial and gender hierarchies, European approaches to professionalization proved challenging to copy and apply in the Spanish colony. Nevertheless, public discourse and medical programs implemented during the first half of the nineteenth century demonstrate the efforts of Cuban elites to conform to these trends.

Midwifery in Cuba

In the early decades of the nineteenth century, Havana's expanding population and the growing number of informally trained midwives prompted increased discussion and regulation of practitioners and licensing. The medical establishment published the *Manual on Theory and Practice for Midwives* in 1824, which emphasized the need to shift the profession into the hands of Spanish women and *criollas*. Commentaries in the colony's official newspaper brought issues related to race and education into the public arena. Meanwhile, the medical council prohibited unlicensed midwives from practicing in the colony.[59] Cuban elites created an idealized medical field in an effort to restore the honor of midwifery and highlight the colony's efforts to establish a modern identity.

Accordingly, the medical establishment made concerted attempts to recruit *criolla* and Spanish midwives. The newspaper article of February 6, 1828, illuminates this point. In addition to railing against the state of midwifery in the hands of "ignorant" women of color, the article highlighted the positive attributes white women would bring to the field:

> The exercise of the art of midwifery must be viewed as an honorable application and the most useful and beneficial to which a woman dedicates herself. What other profession can have a nobler objective than the public good, the public health? What persons can be the most upheld and regarded in society than those who employ their services in comforting and bringing happiness to a grieving family? What persons receive more gifts, compliments, and attention, acquire more friendships, receive and enjoy more correspondence and earnings?[60]

This exaggerated characterization conflicted with numerous aspects of the dominant gender codes of society. Middle- and upper-status women maintained honor by attending to the private domestic sphere. In addition, customs of decency prohibited these women from traversing public streets unaccompanied. While the article asserted that they would garner "gifts," "attention," "compliments," "friendships," and "income" from their actions, these incentives competed weakly with long-standing associations of race, gender, honor, and occupation.

In this same article, the medical establishment announced plans to train white midwives. Although few cities in Latin America in the early nineteenth century could boast of a sizeable cadre of white *parteras*, Cuban medical elites projected ambitious results. They predicted that within two years Havana would offer the public "several white well-trained . . . and intelligent midwives."[61] The final paragraphs of the article outlined a course of study aimed at achieving this goal. The plan boasted that graduates of the program would not only be well trained, they would also execute their position in a "refined manner." In turn, the combination of formal education and idealized racial and behavioral elements would restore the honor of the profession and repair the island's besmirched reputation. White midwives would propel Cuba back into its rightful place at "the level of civilization enjoyed by the cities of Europe."[62] Cuba's success at institutionalizing midwifery in the public discourse would reinforce the colony's standing on the international stage as a modern imperial territory.

However, conflict emerged about fostering white women's interest in becoming *parteras*. Recruitment lagged. Indeed, how could authorities attract *criollas* and Spanish women to the ranks of midwifery when social norms deemed it distasteful to work in a field predominated by free *pardas* and *morenas*? Furthermore, women of European descent continued to maintain a higher level of basic education than free women of color. In other words, the social parameters of racial purity and a professional occupation marked two key aspects of honor. To maintain this ideal, white women necessarily shunned manual labor—even the skilled labor of midwives. Despite white women's numerical advantage over free women of color in the population, *blancas* of any social level were reluctant to become *parteras*. Who then, other than black women, would provide the vital care and comfort for pregnant women, particularly the wives of elite officials, planters, and merchants? Under these circumstances, being a midwife was honorable for a free woman of African descent, even if elite white colonial women did not deem it so for themselves.

Nevertheless, medical institutionalization continued to encroach upon midwifery. Attempts to regulate *parteras* continued into the 1830s. The Royal Council of Medicine and Surgery increased penalties for unauthorized midwives, stipulating fines of up to 300 pesos for transgressions.[63] Enforcement proved difficult, however, and the Spanish medical establishment expressed a general dissatisfaction with efforts to enforce licensure in its colonies. The explicit criticism of the profession as being "abandoned to women of color" and dishonored underscored the pervasive and informal nature of midwife activities and training.[64] The traditions that made race, occupation, and honor inextricable in the Spanish empire now seemed paradoxical. As elsewhere in Latin America, Cuban authorities lamented the fact that literate white women, who could afford the costs associated with midwife training, eschewed the practice, in part because they would be forced to share the field with "rustic" women of color.[65] The difficulties involved in persuading Spanish and creole women to pursue careers as midwives continued to mar the island's perceived progress.

Decades of recruitment efforts designed to whiten midwifery finally gained headway in the mid-1840s. It was not professionalization trends that solidified this shift, however. Rather, the Conspiracy of La Escalera, a series of slave rebellions in 1843, shook colonial Cuba's social and political structure. Authorities accused free blacks of leading a plot in collaboration with slaves, white dissidents, and British abolitionists to overthrow slavery and colonial rule on the island. The subsequent repression prompted colonial authorities in Cuba to radically alter policies toward free people of color.[66] It limited the influence and demographic growth of *libres de color* by executing and banishing accused free black and slave leaders of the conspiracy, restricting their occupational avenues, curtailing their social activities, and expelling hundreds from the colony. In addition, the revised slave codes of 1844 diminished opportunities in the medical field. Regulations forbade free people of color from becoming apothecaries or making prescriptions. Midwives came under close surveillance from the Military Commission and the medical establishment.[67] The case of María del Pilar Poveda, a prominent *parda* midwife, illustrates the effects of elite fears.

Charged as an accomplice to the conspiracy, primarily because the accused rebellion leader, Gabriel de la Concepción "Plácido" Valdés, was her son-in-law, María del Pilar Poveda was sentenced by the Military Commission to a year of service in Havana's San Francisco de Paula Hospital. Commission officials deemed her capable of abusing her position as a *partera* to harm the white women and children she attended. Consequently, authorities barred Poveda from working as a midwife under penalty of life imprisonment and prohibited her from living with her family in Matanzas.[68] Although the Military Commission commonly sentenced women to hospital labor, their stipulation that Poveda complete her sentence in Havana, far from her family, appeared extreme when compared to the treatment of other women charged as accomplices in the conspiracy. For instance, when the Military Commission sentenced Mercedes Mederos to work in a Havana women's hospital, commission officers agreed to allow Mederos' young daughter to remain with her.[69] By isolating Poveda from her family and banning her from midwifery, authorities succeeded in making an example of her to the free community of color. Forbidding Poveda from attending pregnant women damaged her public reputation as a skilled *partera*. Furthermore, it tarnished her personal character by depriving her and her family of the income she derived from a highly specialized profession. In other words, colonial elites stripped Poveda of her honor.

After completing her sentence, Poveda, like many others affected by the repression, petitioned for the right to return to her occupation. In a letter that asked the Cuban government to lift the occupational ban, she explained how the separation from her family had caused an economic vacuum. Her three sons and "aging and ailing husband . . . had been reduced to the greatest misery" without her earnings as a midwife. Poveda emphasized the support she had from the "elite ladies of her town." She instructed the notary who prepared the letter to highlight that these women "could not criticize her actions in any way" and that "they did not limit themselves to pay[ing] her at the level to which her expertise distinguished her."[70] Officials granted her request. In spite of her success, however, Poveda's conviction in the Conspiracy of La Escalera seemed to aggravate government apprehensions regarding race, gender, and midwifery. In combination with Poveda's case, the continued predominance of free women of color as midwives over the first half of the nineteenth century and the less-than-successful efforts to attract more white women to the field prodded officials to make a more focused effort to change the racial composition of midwives in Cuba.

Immediately following the Military Commission trials in 1845, concern about the state of midwife training and practices prompted colonial authorities to take renewed action. They established a director to oversee the women studying obstetrics at the San Francisco de Paula Hospital and organized new classes. The program required all female candidates, *pardas, morenas*, and *criollas*, to provide a variety of documents to meet the entrance criteria. To demonstrate religious integrity and sound moral character, student applicants submitted baptismal records and a certificate of good conduct from their church or local judge. Literacy regulations stipulated they show an ability to read and write. Each married woman had to provide written permission to participate in the program from her husband, and each widow had to present her husband's death certificate.[71] In 1849, the Council of Development and the Economic Society of Havana recommended that a school be established where midwife trainees could gain practical experience.[72] Similar to the requirements of the hospital program, the council's guidelines specified that "midwives must have the combined qualities of good conduct, religious devotion, and empathy . . . necessary to inspire trust" in their patients and the families of their patients.[73]

Efforts to establish additional midwife schools and regulate the character of candidates continued over the next two decades. Controlling the quality of midwife applicants helped ensure that the profession would be upheld as honorable. Meanwhile, the search for preferred students encouraged middle- and upper-status white women to take positions they had previously perceived as being beneath them because of associations with manual labor and the work of women of color. In essence, by institutionalizing midwifery programs and regulating the participants in those programs, the medical establishment sought to reshape previous notions of white female honor and occupation. Doing so, however, meant stripping free *parda* and *morena* midwives of their reputation and presence in the field.

By the late 1850s, legislation and public debate about the need for more white midwives had produced modest signs of progress. Indications of more *criollas* and Spanish women showing interest in becoming *parteras* began to emerge.[74] But the expense of formal training hindered many free women of color. Midwife programs required all students to make a "contribution to the treasury" ranging from 120 to 200 pesos.[75] However, the financial burden did not completely displace black midwives. Free women of color comprised six of the fourteen *parteras* listed in the 1862 census for Havana. This trend proved even stronger in Matanzas, María del Pilar Poveda's home, where eight of the nine women registered as midwives were free *pardas* and *morenas*.[76]

Nevertheless, it is likely that potential *parda* and *morena* candidates, particularly in Havana, where the debates over medical practice and Cuba's imperial status remained particularly sensitive, could not afford to enroll in the midwife programs. Indeed, some may have sought training as nurses, since medical reform did not appear to displace free women of color from this arena. At least one hospital in Havana requested and received permission to regularly employ black nurses.[77] Interestingly, Englishman Henry Latham, who traveled to Havana in the late 1860s, wrote of being spellbound by the "material comforts" displayed by the "splendid apparel of some of the nurses,"[78] suggesting that nursing had become another source of employment that women of color could take pride in. The official participation of black midwives, however, appeared to decline in the late 1860s. Industry records from 1869 indicate a significant drop in the number of registered birthing attendants of African descent. Commerce records enumerated fifteen women who had matriculated as midwives, but none of these were women of color.[79] Given that the free and slave populations continued to increase, *pardas* and *morenas* most likely persisted in practicing without a license or explored other avenues, such as nursing, to engage their understanding of honor within the bounds of race and gender in colonial Cuba.

Conclusion

The convergence of medical professionalization, feminine ideals, honor, occupational whitening, and racial denigration defined the social and economic parameters for free women of African descent in colonial Cuba. Bound by their gender and race, they negotiated notions of female behavior to create an occupational niche for themselves. As midwives who were often cast simultaneously as skilled practitioners and negligent caregivers, free *pardas* and *morenas* used their skills throughout Cuba's population, serving both elites and plebeians. Operating within Hispanic social codes, free women of color understood the terms of honor, particularly regarding their public reputation and personal character. In the process, they demonstrated their adaptability to the changes in medical practice emanating from within and beyond the Spanish colony. In Cuba, Atlantic World medical reforms displaced black female birth attendants in favor of a more "scientific" approach and a whiter cadre of midwives. As Karen Morrison's chapter in this volume suggests, the whitening process involved both an ideological presumption of racial superiority and behavioral modifications at the individual level to implement this inherently political agenda. Whether in terms of reproductive choice or occupational endeavors, whitening as a means of asserting colonial control produced incomplete and often unintended results.

This certainly proved true for midwives in Cuba. Analysis of imperial discourses, colonial data, local advertisements, travelers' and planters' accounts, sociopolitical events, and, where possible, individual voices of free women of color reveal the fragmented nature of colonial efforts to assert Spanish authority by whitening the field of midwifery. Reformers' attempts ran counter to established interpretations of both white and black female behavior. New midwife training programs and recruitment activities designed to dislodge women of color in favor of Spaniards and *criollas* had mixed results. White women reluctantly embraced the new occupational prospects, and free *pardas* and *morenas* refused to abandon the field. Instead, free women of color embraced the professional opportunities offered by the colonial state. In a locale where the concept of honor permeated the social order and women of African descent were classified as disgraceful, these women sought to modify elite notions of respectability and credibility to suit their particular context. The uneven effects of medical reform underscore the tensions of race and gender in nineteenth-century colonial Cuba. Moreover, they suggest avenues for further investigation regarding the continuities in and adaptations to female identities that Africans and their descendants forged through the dynamics of honor, freedom, and slavery in colonial Spanish America.

Notes

My thanks to the participants of the Workshop on Race and Blackness in Latin America held at the Center for Africana Studies at Johns Hopkins University for their comments and criticisms on an earlier version of this work. Summer support from the Newberry Library contributed significantly to the completion of this chapter. I especially thank Ben Vinson III, Jane Landers, Sherwin Bryant, Rachel Sarah O'Toole, Bianca Premo, and the anonymous readers for their suggestions.

1. *El Diario de la Habana*, February 6, 1828.

2. McGregor, *From Midwives to Medicine*, 30; Ortiz, "From Hegemony to Subordination," 100, 102.

3. McGregor, *From Midwives to Medicine*, 38; Lanning, *The Royal Protomedicato*, 298; Deacon, "Midwives and Medical Men in the Cape Colony before 1860," 273.

4. McGregor, *From Midwives to Medicine*, 38.

5. Bleek, "Did the Akan Resort to Abortion in Pre-Colonial Ghana?" 124; Hanretta, "Women, Marginality and the Zulu State," 393.

6. McGregor, *From Midwives to Medicine*, 38.

7. Hernández Sáenz and Foster, "Curers and Their Cures in Colonial New Spain and Guatemala," 38.

8. Moitt, *Women and Slavery in the French Antilles*, 62; Geggus, "Slave and Free Colored Women in Saint Domingue," 261; McGregor, *From Midwives to Medicine*, 38; Bush, *Slave Women in Caribbean Society*, 141n36; Ortiz, "From Hegemony to Subordination," 100, 102.

9. Casteñeda, "The Female Slave in Cuba," 144; Landers, *Black Society in Spanish Florida*, 149.

10. Hernández Sáenz and Foster, "Curers and Their Cures in Colonial New Spain and Guatemala," 38.

11. Palmer, *From Popular Medicine to Medical Populism*, 140; McGregor, *From Midwives to Medicine*, 41.

12. Archivo Nacional de Cuba (hereafter ANC), Instrucción Pública, leg. 40, no. 2115, 1845.

13. Palmer, *From Popular Medicine to Medical Populism*, 140.

14. Moitt, *Women and Slavery in the French Antilles*, 62; Laborie, *The Coffee Planter of Saint Domingo*, 172.

15. Sheridan, *Doctors and Slaves*, 53.

16. Moitt, *Women and Slavery in the French Antilles*, 62.

17. Laborie, *The Coffee Planter of Saint Domingo*, 173.

18. Moitt, *Women and Slavery in the French Antilles*, 95.

19. Lanning, *The Royal Protomedicato*, 298.

20. Chaplin, *The Journal of Thomas B. Chaplin*, 366n267.

21. Lanning, *The Royal Protomedicato*, 298, 320; Hernández Sáenz and Foster, "Curers and Their Cures in Colonial New Spain and Guatemala," 38.

22. Peard, *Race, Place, and Medicine*, 123; see also Lanning, *The Royal Protomedicato*, 298, 303.

23. Lanning, *The Royal Protomedicato*, 304.

24. Ibid., 303.

25. *El Diario de la Habana*, February 6, 1828.

26. Twinam, *Public Lives, Private Secrets*, 32–33; Johnson and Lipsett-Rivera, "Introduction," 3; Lauderdale-Graham, "Honor among Slaves," 203.

27. Lauderdale-Graham, "Honor among Slaves," 204, 206; Boyer, "Honor among Plebeians," 156.

28. ANC, Comisión Militar, leg. 60, no. 2.

29. ANC, Asuntos Políticos, Leg. 140, Exp. 36, 1844; ANC, Reales Órdenes y Cédulas, leg. 133, exp. 220, 1832.

30. Martínez-Alier, *Marriage, Class and Colour in Nineteenth-Century Cuba*, 120–121, 75; Kuzinski, *Sugar's Secrets*, 22; Landers, *Black Society in Spanish Florida*, 137; Beckles, "Sex and Gender in the Historiography of Caribbean Slavery," 133; Chambers, *From Subjects to Citizens*, 164–169.

31. McGregor, *From Midwives to Medicine*, 11; Martínez Fernández, "The 'Male City' of Havana," 105.

32. Norman, *Rambles by Land and Water*, 29; Dana, *Two Years before the Mast and Other Voyages*, 416, 422.

33. Ortiz, "From Hegemony to Subordination," 102; Phillippo, *The United States and Cuba*, 419.

34. Nye "Medicine and Science as Masculine 'Fields of Honor,'" 68.

35. Ibid., 68, 71.

36. Archivo General de Indias, Seville (hereafter AGI), Indiferente, leg. 1533, no. 7, Cuba, 1774–1861, folio 332. The report listed the following data: among 20,058 free women of color: literate = 2,072 (10.3 percent), illiterate = 17,986 (89.7 percent); among 47,240 white women: literate = 21,975 (52 percent), illiterate = 25,295 (48 percent).

37. Pezuela, *Diccionario geografico, estadístico, historico de la isla de Cuba*, 14–17. Of 220 students of color, 130 were girls and 90 were boys. Of 3,964 white students, 1,549 were girls and 2,415 were boys.

38. Ortiz, "From Hegemony to Subordination," 102.

39. Dimock, *Impressions of Cuba in the Nineteenth Century*, 67; Martínez-Fernández, *Fighting Slavery in the Caribbean*, 68.

40. Dana, *Two Years before the Mast*, 416.

41. Reid, "Negotiating a Slave Regime," 41.

42. Chaplin, *The Journal of Thomas B. Chaplin*, 366.

43. Murray, *Lands of the Slave and the Free*, 285, 291; see also Abbot, *Letters Written in the Interior of Cuba*, 97; and Latham, *Black and White*, 200.

44. Bryant, *Letters of a Traveller*, 360–361.

45. Latham, *Black and White*, 200.

46. Phillippo, *The United States and Cuba*, 432.

47. Martínez-Fernández, *Fighting Slavery in the Caribbean*, 68–69; Pérez, *Slaves, Sugar, and Colonial Society*, 225.

48. Kimball, "Letters from Cuba," 545; Pérez, *Slaves, Sugar, and Colonial Society*, 226.

49. Kiple, *Blacks in Colonial Cuba*, 88–90; Superintendencia General Delegada de Real Hacienda, *Informe fiscal sobre fomento de la población blanca en la isla de cuba*, 6. The 1827 census reported a total population of 704,487, of which 142,398 were white women (20 percent of the total population), 54,532 were free women of color (27.7 percent), and 103,652 were slave women (14 percent). The 1841 census reported a total population of 1,007,624, of which 191,147 were white women (10 percent of the total population), 77,135 were free women of color (7.6 percent), and 155,245 were slave women (15 percent).

50. *El Diario de la Habana*, August 11, 1828; *El Diario de la Habana*, December 1, 1833, quoted in Deschamps Chapeaux, *El negro en la economía habanera del siglo XIX*, 173.

51. Deschamps Chapeaux, *El negro en la economía habanera del siglo XIX*, 172–173.

52. Ramsey, *Professional and Popular Medicine in France*, 279–280; Marland, *Medicine and Society in Wakefield and Huddersfield*, 302; Palmer, *From Popular Medicine to Medical Populism*, 53; Risse, "Medicine in New Spain," 29–30; Sheridan, *Doctors and Slaves*, 53; Danielson, *Cuban Medicine*, 5–21.

53. Lanning, *The Royal Protomedicato*, 298.

54. Sheridan, *Doctors and Slaves*, 3, 52–53; Danielson, *Cuban Medicine*, 5–21.

55. Lebsock, *The Free Women of Petersburg*, 169.

56. Ramsey, *Professional and Popular Medicine in France*, 79; Marland, *Medicine and Society in Wakefield and Huddersfield*, 302; Deacon, "Midwives and Medical Men in the Cape Colony before 1860," 273; Lebsock, *The Free Women of Petersburg*, 169.

57. Marland, *Medicine and Society in Wakefield and Huddersfield*, 303.

58. Brading, *The First America*, 468.

59. *El Diario de la Habana*, February 6, 1828; AGI, Cuba, leg. 2350A, folios 25–26, 1835.

60. *El Diario de la Habana*, February 6, 1828.

61. Mexico City appears as the main exception, listing twenty-four midwives in its 1811–1812 census. Palmer, *From Popular Medicine to Medical Populism*, 140; Hernández Sáenz and Foster, "Curers and Their Cures in Colonial New Spain and Guatemala," 38; Lanning, *The Royal Protomedicato*, 298.

62. *El Diario de la Habana*, February 6, 1828.

63. AGI, Cuba, Leg. 2350A, Miguel Tacón to the Spanish Ministry of Interior, October 29, 1835, "Reglamento de la Real Junta Superior de Medicina y Cirugía, establecida en la Siempre Fiel Isla de Cuba, Conformó la real cédula espedida en nueve de enero de mil ochocientos treinta," Oficina de Don José Doloña, Impresor de la Real Marina por S.M., Habana, 1834, 25–26.

64. *El Diario de la Habana*, February 6, 1828.

65. Lanning, *The Royal Protomedicato*, 305–306.

66. For the most recent account of the Conspiracy of La Escalera, see Paquette, *Sugar Is Made with Blood*. For a discussion of the impact of the repression, see Reid-Vazquez, *The Year of the Lash*.

67. Zamora y Coronada, *Biblioteca de legislación ultramarina en forma de diccionario alfabético*, 3:139–141; Paquette, *Sugar Is Made with Blood*, 273–274.

68. Deschamps Chapeaux, *El negro en la economía habanera*, 180–182.

69. *El Diario de la Habana*, December 26, 1844.

70. ANC, Instrucción Pública, leg. 40, exp. 2114, 1845.

71. ANC, Instrucción Pública, leg. 40, exp. 2115, 1845.

72. Sociedad Económica de Amigos del País, *Anales de las Reales Juntas de Fomento y Sociedad Económica de La Habana*, 1:38.

73. Gonzáles del Valle, *Manuel de obstetricia*, 110.

74. ANC, Reales Órdenes y Cédulas, leg. 196, exp. 10, 1857.

75. ANC, Gobierno General, leg. 478, exp. 23542, 1869–1870.

76. Pezuela, *Diccionario geografico, estadístico, historico de la isla de Cuba*, 3:357, 360, 363, 371; 4:30.

77. ANC, Gobierno Superior Civil, leg. 406, no. 15929, 1857.

78. Latham, *Black and White*, 200.

79. ANC, Gobierno General, leg. 478, exp. 23542, 1869–1870.

9

The African American Experience in Comparative Perspective

The Current Question of the Debate

HERBERT S. KLEIN

I would like to return to a theme that has been much neglected in the recent discussions on the African Diaspora in the Americas, and that is the question of the comparative differences and similarities between slave regimes in the Americas and the influence of those differences on the post-manumission integration of Africans. This is a theme that goes back to the first modern studies of Africans in the Americas. From Fernando Ortiz in Cuba to Nina Rodrigues in Brazil, there was a general awareness among Latin American scholars that there were differences in the way Africans were integrated into the various societies in the Americas.[1] North American scholars such as Donald Pierson, Frank Tannenbaum, and Stanley Elkins picked up on these themes and tried to place the U.S. experience in this comparative framework.[2] For a time, from the 1940s to the 1970s, it appeared that this comparative analysis was leading to some interesting questions and debates about institutions, cultures, and social organizations.[3] But this discussion has died with the rejection of the comparative differences school in North American historiography and in turn the concentration on detailed local studies within Latin American historiography, both movements that have failed to return to this question in any detail.

For the earlier Latin American authors, the harsh racism of the United States, as they examined it in the postslavery period, was a result of what they all saw as a more restrictive slave regime in the United States compared to all other systems. The two-color racial model that evolved in the United States, the extraordinarily harsh nineteenth-century legal system that Ortiz referred to as the "iron law of slavery,"[4] the long hostility to freed blacks, and their marginalization among free people in the Jim Crow post-emancipation South were all taken to mean that the United States was different from most Latin American societies. This is not to say that these authors did not recognize the inherent racism in all the post-slave systems in the Americas, but they conceived the United States as a case apart.[5]

The post-1970s attack on the comparative school came from U.S. scholars who denied the exceptionalism of U.S history in the context of slavery studies, even as they celebrated it in other areas. The work of Eugene Genovese was crucial in this respect. He argued that the harsh legal system did not express the true nature of the slave system, which in fact was mitigated by paternalism into a regime that differed little from other slave societies in the Americas.[6] Others scholars such as C. Vann Woodward argued that the positive natural demographic growth of the U.S. slave population compared to the more normal negative population growth of the slave societies in the rest of the Americas was clear evidence that the treatment of slaves was better in the United States and that therefore, if anything, the Latin American societies had a harsher slave system.[7]

But the existence of laws in the southern states must be explained and they do in fact signify something about the reality of ideas, beliefs and actions. They did have a profound impact in defining both the North American slave and free colored societies that emerged as a result. The demographic variation in fertility and mortality of slaves among various American societies has more to do with the intensity of the Atlantic slave trade and its impact on the age and sex of arriving Africans, with differing health conditions between Latin America and North America, and with varying lactation practices that influenced fertility than it has to do with the "better" or "worse" treatment of the slave population.[8] Slavery was nasty and brutish in all societies, and the labor extracted from all slaves everywhere was harsh and far more demanding than the labor ever requested of free wage workers. It was also extracted everywhere by the use of corporal punishment.

This concentration on the "better" or "worse" treatment of slaves shifted the ground away from institutions and social and economic practices and led to a total rejection of the comparative school as a viable model, at least in North American historiography. Except for the recent attempts to deal with the "slave community" theme in comparative perspective,[9] there is little new discussion on this theme, and most scholars in North America assume that all slave systems were equal and that if anything, the Latin American slave regimes were "worse."

I would argue that in fact important differences did exist among slave regimes in the Americas and that these differences had important social, economic, and political consequences for the Afro-American populations. Let us start this comparative analysis by examining what is similar in all slave regimes. To begin with, almost all the major slave systems created in the Americas had the same economic ends. In a world where land was cheap and labor was costly and where alternative European labor could not be attracted by prevailing American free wages, Africans were employed as the cheapest alternative labor force.[10] But given their high costs, they were associated in most cases with the most advanced export sectors in the given societies, producing for a world market.[11] The only major variation from this model was the more domestic and urban slavery practiced by the Spaniards in the heavily Amerindian societies, where Africans were concentrated in domestic service and crafts and the primary producers of domestic and exportable products were the Indian peasants.

Except for the French and English West Indies, roughly one-third of the population of almost all the major slave societies consisted of slaves and roughly one-third of the free persons owned slaves. Moreover, the majority of slave owners held just one slave, while the average slave holding was on the order of 5–10 slaves per owner and owners of average-sized plantations owned roughly 50–100 slaves. It was the non-Hispanic sugar islands that stand out as different with a majority of the population being slaves and average plantations holding several hundred slaves.[12]

But there was little difference in the organization of this plantation slave labor in export agriculture. All plantations, whatever their product or size, organized labor in a similar fashion. Workers were grouped into unisex gangs based on their age and physical abilities. These field labor gangs were supervised by slave drivers who routinized the work tasks and administered them with the use of whips, creating "factories in the field" types of labor organization. In these gangs women and men equally performed the basic field work tasks of planting, maintaining, and harvesting the crops. Beyond the field hands, there was work for everyone to do, no matter what their age or sex. These slave labor systems were unusual in that the economically active population was the highest of any laboring populations at the time—on the order of 80 percent of all slaves performed some economic task—compared to around 50–60 percent among most peasant groups.[13]

There were of course differences in the plantation regimes based on the technology of production. Sugar was a harsher labor regime for slaves than coffee, plantations that had three growing seasons required more labor than those that might have two or fewer harvests, and so on. Some crops required a great deal of technical work to produce, such as sugar, and others required few skilled tasks to create a final product, such as coffee, and these differences influenced relative skill levels in the slave population. All plantation regimes tended to reserve skilled labor for male slaves, though in non-plantation labor women slaves performed a wide variety of skilled occupations. These rural servile labor regimes thus shared common features across all societies, and a nineteenth-century traveler would have noticed little difference in work routines in plantations anywhere in the Americas.

Although gang labor and slave discipline were the same everywhere, there were some important economic differences among these regimes. The skill level of the slaves often depended on the relative scarcity or availability of competitive white labor. When blacks and mulattoes, free and slave, formed the majority of laborers in a given society, slaves were often better trained for skills than they were in societies where competitive white artisans existed. Equally, in societies that lacked large groups of competitive white, Indian, or mestizo laborers and could import large numbers of Africans, it was more common to find slaves in many more occupations than in societies where there was more competitive non-Afro-American labor. Brazil of course stands out as a prime case where slaves could be found in virtually every occupation and at every level of skill. Afro-Brazilian slave sailors were even used as crews on slavers going to Africa to purchase slaves.[14] But in all urban centers of Latin America from the sixteenth to the early nineteenth centuries, Afro-Latin Americans were well represented in most of the major crafts, and although they were more likely to be apprentices and journeymen than their white co-workers, some of them were masters of their crafts.[15]

This openness of the labor market for slaves and free colored workers makes for some crucial differences in slave regimes, since in a country such as Brazil, for example, only about a third of the slaves were working on plantations in the first national census of 1872 and the majority worked at every occupational level and in every occupation, from unskilled urban work to rural produce farming, from mule transportation to whaling.[16] Many worked in family units alongside the slave owner families themselves or with free landless workers at their side. This same pattern can also be found in Cuba and Puerto Rico.[17] All this made for a more complex labor market for Afro-Americans than was to be found in North America. Although plantation slaves remained relatively isolated, slave laborers everywhere else mingled with colored, white, Indian, and mestizo free workers. Thus, the relative importance of rural and urban slave labor is as significant as the relative importance of plantation labor within the rural context. In this, for example, the United States was more like the non-Hispanic West Indies than like the other continental and Hispanic island slave regimes.

Slaves were used in every conceivable task these societies needed to function. They were rented out, apprenticed, and even allowed to live on their own in large numbers. Although renting slaves and urban slavery existed in the United States, they occurred on a smaller scale than in most Latin American countries and declined over time. Moreover, just as state and owner control over urban slaves became ever more strict in the United States in the nineteenth century, these controls seemed to become more loose in Latin America as time went on. Municipal governments in Latin America were forever complaining about the failure of urban slave owners to discipline, house, and feed their slaves, but little was done to control them.[18] In contrast, in nineteenth-century North America, the state asserted effective and increasing control over the lives of urban slaves and restricted them to the homes of their owners.[19] These changes were not related to economic efficiency. In fact, economically, it was more effective to allow slave labor the greatest mobility possible for it to be profitable. Allowing slaves to make contracts and arrange for their own housing, clothing, and food reduced maintenance costs for owners. Restraining owners and increasing their maintenance expenses, all in the name of security, was in fact an uneconomic policy. Reversing Elkins's model of the "dynamics of unopposed capitalism," we could say that Brazil and Cuba were the true capitalist societies and that the United States was willing to sacrifice economic rationality for other preferred ends.

How did the state and its laws respond to these emerging American realities? All slave legal systems shared much in common. As Orlando Patterson has shown, all slave systems have to legally destroy the rights of slaves if they are to be economically mobile. Owners everywhere could discipline their slaves, use them in any occupations they wanted, and sell them to anyone. In all cases their rights as owners were backed by the state.[20] By the nineteenth century, however, some differences were emerging within the American slave regimes. Most of these differences grew out of local customary practices that modified the rights of owners. If slaves were living on their own and providing their owners with rent, they had to make contracts and handle their own finances. Although legally no slaves could own property or make contracts, urban slaves in fact tended to own property and make contracts independent of their owners. On all plantations slaves produced much of their own foods, and they often sold this food to itinerant peddlers who went around the farms—an issue much commented upon in Cuba. Thus, slaves sold food and other goods that they produced on their own plots, though they had no legal rights to do so. In fact, if not in law, these garden plots were often considered the property of the slaves who worked them. With their own property, slaves soon were allowed by the state to purchase their own freedom, a system that evolved in customary law and soon became fully elaborated in the local slave codes. In Brazil and Cuba, self-purchase by slaves was a customary act that eventually received legal support. This was the primary way for African-born slaves to obtain their freedom and was of course far more common in urban than in rural areas. Nevertheless, it was part of a complex set of rules that supported a normal process of manumission.[21]

It would seem that in the eighteenth century all slave systems in the Americas produced roughly the same proportion of manumitted slaves. In all societies fathers freed their slave children and their mistresses, owners freed their slaves for religious or moral reasons, and loyal support was sometimes rewarded with freedom. There are even cases of self-purchase to be found in all slave regimes. All this began at a slow pace and produced a free colored class that grew at a modest rate. But in the nineteenth century some slave societies began to close these avenues of manumission, while others progressively expanded the right of self-purchase and encouraged other processes of manumission. In Brazil, for example, not only could slaves be freed with formal contracts (*cartas de alforria*) before notaries, but large numbers were simply declared free at their baptism, a process that occurred in most Latin American countries.[22] State laws and courts accepted all these manumission procedures and protected them. In turn, these legal encouragements for manumission led to a free colored population that expanded ever more rapidly and soon exceeded the slave population in the nineteenth century. By the first national census of Brazil in 1872, some sixteen years before emancipation, for example, there were 4.2 million free colored and only 1.5 million slaves. For the United States in 1860 the figures were reversed with almost 4 million slaves and less than half a million free colored. In no other major slave society were the free colored so numerous and so important a part of the population as in Brazil. But by the early part of the nineteenth century, free colored either equaled the number of slaves or were quickly passing them in importance everywhere in the Iberian world. Nothing like this occurred in either the French or English colonies and nations.[23]

In North America, nineteenth-century state legislation progressively restricted the manumission process and tried to isolate and even expel the free colored from their territories. Owners were progressively restricted in their right to manumit slaves within their borders, no support was given to self-purchase arrangements, and there were ever increasing restrictions for the African Americans who were free, and even their physical mobility was curtailed. This legislation was successful and the free colored population was kept to a low ratio of the total Afro-American population before 1860. Moreover over half of these free colored lived outside the southern slave states. It has been estimated that in 1860, only 3 percent of the free population in the southern states were colored freedpeople.[24] It is worth exploring why this increasing fear of manumission was dominant in the United States by the nineteenth century; this topic has until now received little attention. It has been suggested that this hostility toward freedpeople emerged from a defense of the slave system began by English planters who saw slavery as the only proper condition for African Americans. Why did other slave societies not view this in the same way? Why did an emerging and large free colored class in Latin America not threaten traditional owner-slave relations?

A great deal of this difference in attitude toward the freedpeople can be seen as well in the differing political, economic, and social roles of the free colored population within each of the slave societies. Once free, Afro-Americans played a much more important role in their respective Latin American societies than in the English colonies and nations. Both Spain and Brazil organized the free colored into military units and used them to deal with international wars and internal rebellions. In Spanish America, Indians were prohibited from serving in the militia, but the free colored, organized into units of mulattoes and blacks, were required to serve the state. Everywhere they were a very important element in the military. In many cases these troops were even used outside their home territories by the imperial governments. In the case of Brazil, *pardo* and *preto* units were the norm until the 1830s, and even after the creation of a unified National Guard under the empire, free colored were vital within the military establishment. Thus, everywhere in Latin America the free colored were granted the right to bear arms, and they used this right to extend their own private rights. In all Latin American countries the militiamen obtained access to privileged military courts, and in Mexico they succeeded in escaping the tribute tax free colored and Indians were required to pay. Also, elite free colored gained power as officers of these units. This is not to say that these colored militias were not discriminated against in terms of occupations within the army or in being assigned the worst duties. But it is clear that they were an important part of the state apparatus from early in the slave periods.[25] In fact, many of the revolutionary leaders in the independence movements of the early and late nineteenth century in such countries as Mexico and Cuba came from this free colored class.

The free colored in Latin America had few impediments to their geographic mobility, which were the same as all free persons within their societies. In Brazil they moved about freely between urban and rural areas and from province to province, as the judicial records of the time demonstrate. The restrictions to geographic mobility that developed within nineteenth-century North America did not occur in Latin America. Free colored resided everywhere they could afford to live. Studies of residence by color for such cities as Mexico or San Juan have also shown that free colored lived next to and often intermingled with white and mestizo families and that it was as common for free colored to rent spaces in their apartments to whites as it was for whites to rent spaces to free colored.[26] Though the urban ghettos of the United States are usually assumed to have originated in the post-emancipation era, it is nevertheless telling that no such systematic intermingling of the races by individual residence has been shown for the United States.[27]

Although all but the elite occupations were open to the free colored, even royal restrictions on this economic mobility progressively declined over the colonial period and were eliminated altogether in the Latin American republics during the nineteenth century. From Lima to Mexico City, there are numerous cases of free colored who obtained royal permission to engage in elite occupations that were officially denied to them. This included everything from government and church positions to occupations in restricted crafts.

A minority of free colored even owned slaves, a phenomenon that occurred in all the slave societies, including the United States. In Brazil, where colored slave owners have been well studied, they were a significant minority of slave owners in most regions and were mostly artisans running small workshops. In this context, free colored women were a significant part of the slave-owning free colored class. In the United States colored owners represented a far smaller proportion of the slave-owning class, were far more male, and were more restricted to farming occupations than was the case in Brazil.[28]

The slaves and free colored in both the rural and urban areas of Latin America mingled rather freely with whites. Although most African manifestations of religious practices were severely repressed and religions such as Candomblé and Santería were underground in the slave period and were often violently suppressed, blacks and whites mingled at numerous fiestas and other public events and gathering places, and we even find slaves appearing at these places. The Latin American judicial records are filled with slaves who socialized with whites and free colored in the local taverns that were major social gathering places. There are also numerous cases of slaves escaping to cities and living as free colored.

There were even large numbers of free colored communities that emerged by illegal means in these societies. Although it has been suggested that slave rebellions were more numerous and more violent in Latin America than in North America, these events were few and far between in most slave societies. Runaway slaves were common to all slave regimes, but where the Latin American and even West Indian societies differ from North America is in the size and extraordinary number of runaway slave communities in the former regions and their scarcity in the latter. Brazil is filled with hundreds of towns named Quilombo, which was the designation for runaway communities, and the Cimarron communities all over Latin America and the Caribbean islands were quite important and numerous. The reasons for the relative importance of these slave communities outside North America were primarily due to ecological conditions such as mountainous semi-tropical and tropical terrain where isolated communities could be successfully maintained. Also, the permanent loss of escaping slaves into the free colored population was far more common in Latin America than in North America because of the existence of larger free colored communities and of more urban centers, both of which gave significant cover to escaped slaves. Moreover, once they had been established over several generations, most of these runaway communities in fact converted into free colored agricultural communities and became a part of the free rural landscape.

Possibly because of their economic importance or their inability to seriously influence elite politics, the free colored were offered a wide range of rights that were denied to them in North America. They could vote if they had the property qualifications, they could bear arms, they could live wherever they could find work and housing, and, by the nineteenth century, they had few restrictions on their occupations or educational opportunities. Though the state sometimes treated the free colored more harshly than their white peers, free colored nevertheless were treated quite differently from their slave counterparts.[29] They could appear in court cases as witnesses and complainants, and they could make legal contracts. As Tannenbaum was wont to say, they were "citizens" within all the republics and empires they lived in.

This is not to say that the free colored were equal to whites or that discrimination did not occur. In Brazil there was even some measure of discrimination between those who were born free and those who were freed during the course of their lifetimes. All ex-slaves emerged from slavery with no savings and only the human capital they carried with them in terms of skills, languages, and abilities. They thus formed the base of the poor in all Latin American societies, a position they shared with an important minority of downwardly mobile whites. It has been suggested in studies of Mexico City, for example, that discrimination among the poor was quite limited and that color was a very fluid marker that could change during the course of a lifetime. For those who moved up the economic and social scale, discrimination clearly increased the higher they rose.[30] The cases of children suing parents for the right to marry in late eighteenth-century Spanish America show that middle-ranking whites were highly discriminatory toward blacks and mulattoes.[31] Among the very elite, should a free colored make it that far—and very few outside of the French West Indies reached these exalted ranks—discrimination was probably less pronounced since class was a far more rigid barrier. But even this status did not guarantee equality, and the free colored planter class of Saint-Domingue faced bitter hostility from the white planter elite, which was one of the key factors that prepared the way for the slave rebellion of 1791.[32] Nor was a frightened white elite above attacking the free colored as a dangerous element in their societies, as occurred in the supposed Escalera affair in Cuba in the early 1840s.[33] Color was clearly a marker of status in Latin American society, but the definition of status, class, and identity involved more markers than just skin color. This was in sharp contrast to the United States and the English colonies, where skin color was the only marker used to discriminate among peoples, thus making it easier for prejudice to function.

What of the religious and social life of the slaves and free colored? Clearly although the Catholic countries baptized their African slaves from the earliest days of their residence in the Americas, the Church had only a moderate impact on their daily lives. Religious holidays and Sunday rest days were usually enforced, and most slaves were taught the basics of Christianity. The Roman Catholic Church did not hesitate to incorporate Africans as members, in contrast to the Protestant churches, which substantially delayed their acceptance. There is also no question that slaves took the sacraments and participated in Catholic rituals if a priest was available to them.[34] But there were relatively few priests, especially in rural areas. The Church, however, enforced the holidays, and most Catholics respected these days without labor.[35] The church was also a place for manumissions, and there is ample evidence to show various levels of church support for slaves who were married. Also, slaves observed godparenthood rituals, mostly using their fellow slaves as godparents for their children. Finally, in Brazil, there is abundant evidence in the south central zones of significant legal slave marriages and of systematic efforts of the Church to guarantee that married couples remained together, even if teenage children were not always protected in the process. Although slave marriages could be found in Mexico and other Latin American societies, they were relatively more important in Brazil.[36]

Where the Church had a greater impact was among the free colored. It was the free colored who organized many of the famous religious brotherhoods and even succeeded in constructing their own churches, as can be seen in numerous Brazilian towns and cities. The brotherhoods of free colored probably involved a large proportion of the free colored community and became an important part of the social life and festive activities of members of this community. They also served as effective mutual aid and burial societies. This is not to say that religious activity was not important in Protestant societies, but the autonomy of the brotherhoods was formally recognized by the priesthood and they were a fundamental part of both white and free colored society. Like the militia, the religious brotherhoods were also important outlets where upwardly mobile free colored could find expression and recognition.[37]

The longer history of the slave trade to the major slave states of Latin America was a fundamental factor in the transfer and survival of African cults and religious ideas in Latin America.[38] But the survival of African religious practices, so important to Afro-Americans in Latin America, was also due in part to their ability to syncretize these practices with folk Catholic practices, something that was less viable within Protestant practice.[39]

So what can we then say about the comparative similarities and differences among all of these societies? It would seem to me that most of the major continental slave societies up to 1800 were more or less moved in the same direction in terms of labor organization, the rates of manumission, the relative importance of slaves and slave owners, and the size of slave holdings in the various societies. Cuba and Puerto Rico shared most of the features of these continental regimes, and the West Indies, because of their unusual demographic structures, represented quite alternative models. But after 1800 the United States began to move in a different direction and essentially began to oppose the normal tendencies toward opening the system through increasing manumission and incorporating the free colored as welcomed members of free society.

How this occurred is easy to see, but understanding why is much more complicated. Instead of permitting the normal economic and social evolution of the slave regime, as was occurring in all the Latin American countries in the nineteenth century, the slave-owning elite of the United States decided that the system had to be closed down. Thus, they denied slaves access to literacy and freedom on an ever-increasing scale of harshness. It is no accident that the United States was the only society to produce a positive defense of slavery.[40] It might be that in democratic societies white elites and free white workers feel more frightened by the potential social and economic mobility of free colored. This fear of the emancipated slave probably also existed in Latin America, but it was never powerful enough to create rigid barriers against the normal economic functioning of the market economies. Elites felt secure in highly stratified and nonrepresentative systems, and the working class was so infiltrated with free colored that systematic discrimination was virtually impossible and would have led to economic chaos. Intermarriage, craft identity, military participation, and other cross-boundary institutions weakened the fear that blacks would displace upper-level white artisans or threaten their status, even if blacks entered the ranks of master craftsmen in a few of the trades. What is most strange about this is that the North Americans were dealing with a far less African-influenced population than, say, Brazil or Cuba. Few Africans lived in North America in the mid-nineteenth century, compared to the large numbers of Africans who could be found in the societies that did not end their slave trades until this period. Nor would a far more active emancipation rate on the level of that of Latin American societies have threatened the U.S. slave population with extinction. The North American slave population was increasing at a rate of over 2 percent per annum; the slave force easily could have lost 1 percent of that growth to manumission and still survived.

It is also clear that when emancipated, the North American free colored played a far less decisive market role than their counterparts in Latin America.[41] Small white farmers and artisans blocked their integration in numerous ways in the U.S. South. It has been suggested that even after the Civil War, the land market in the South was closed to most blacks.[42] Whether in Latin America it was the more established guild system which guaranteed effective education in skills and crafts or the lack of a competitive white artisan class which challenged their skills, there is little question that ex-slaves had the ability to carry their skills successfully into the free labor market, something that was far more difficult to achieve in the United States. With restricted physical mobility, active market competition from whites, and probably handicapped with rudimentary plantation skills, emancipated slaves found it extremely difficult to transfer their skills across the barrier of freedom in North America.

This closing of opportunities for ex-slaves was even more apparent when final emancipation occurred in the United States. Until 1900, in fact, well over 90 percent of African Americans still resided in the South, and discrimination against them was pervasive.[43] In contrast, in Brazil, few ex-slaves were to be found in the core plantation areas of the West Paulista plains or the advanced sugar and coffee municipalities of Rio de Janeiro after abolition occurred in 1888. Though some regions had higher ratios of black and mulatto residents, in general ex-slaves could be found everywhere after final emancipation. In contrast, the geographic immobility of ex-slaves in the U.S. South lasted into the early twentieth century. By contrast, black geographic mobility was the norm, not just in Brazil but in all Latin American societies both before and after emancipation.

While it is true that freedpeople everywhere formed the poorest element in all slave and ex-slave societies, it is nevertheless evident that the laws and attitudes that promoted or rejected manumission and accepted or opposed the economic and geographic mobility of freedpeople and ex-slaves were crucial in defining the nature of these African American populations long after the end of slavery. If this argument of essential differences on these key variables makes sense, then it is evident that we can explain the differences and their causal factors only with more detailed comparative work on the attitudes of the white slave-owning elite in each society and the nature of the local labor markets. Why one slave-owning class fears changes in the status of slaves while another accepts change without fear of loss of control may be due to a host of different political and demographic factors. Are democratic regimes more racist than nondemocratic ones? Are societies with less European immigration more willing to rely on the skilled and unskilled labor of Afro-Americans than societies with a steady immigration of free white workers? Do Catholic cultural values make slave owners more accepting of manumission than do Protestant societies? How do the French West Indies fit into this schema?

Much of the new social and cultural research of recent years, which is well reflected in the essays in this volume, has shown the importance of African survivals in the Diaspora and has suggested their effective utility for individuals facing integration in New World white-dominated societies. But as yet, much of this scholarship has been based on single case studies or the experiences of a very few individuals without explaining their uniqueness or commonality with larger groups. In addition, the necessary linkages have not been established in many of these studies to the basic social and economic structures of the slave societies in which these individual slaves and free colored functioned. Without this context, it will be difficult to see how these individual experiences functioned within differing societies or how these societies differed, if at all, from each other.

Clearly I believe that if we are to answer these questions of comparative differences among slave regimes, several areas are worth investigating in detail. To begin with are the economic role of slaves, the human capital they accumulated under slavery, and the availability of alternative roles within slavery that could provide access to skills, to space away from the owner's daily control, and other forms of social and economic autonomy, be they individual or collective, religious or civil. Next to be considered is the rate and importance of manumission and the legal and effective support given to it by the slave-owning elite. Finally, we need to consider the role of the free colored class well before final slave emancipation. How did this class emerge, how many free colored people were there relative to whites and slaves, where did they live, what were their institutions and communities like, and how much of the skills they learned in slavery were available to them as freedpeople? What was the nature of racism and how did it function by class and color? This requires studying the nature of white-black competition within the free labor market and the attitude of the white working classes toward their Afro-American peers. These questions also require us to study the elite and their attitude toward slavery, slaves and the free colored within their midst. As I have argued for many years, we need to examine free colored people under slavery to fully understand the slave regimes. These are just a few of the areas worth exploring if we are to explain the obvious differences that did exist among these slave societies in the Americas. Moreover, explaining both the common and different features of slave and free colored societies throughout the Americas will go a long way toward explaining the different patterns of integration of all Afro-Americans in the period after slavery.

Notes

1. Nina Rodrigues, *Os Africanos no Brasil*, 2nd ed.; and Ortiz y Fernández, *Hampa afro-cubana*.

2. Pierson, *Negroes in Brazil*; Tannenbaum, *Slave and Citizen*; and Elkins, *Slavery: A Problem in American Institutional and Intellectual Life*.

3. The works of the Brazilian sociologist Gilberto Freyre were extremely important in this debate, see especially his *Casa-grande & senzala*, which was published in English as *The Masters and the Slaves*.

4. "A legislation of iron, is what the North American colonists had given to themselves, independently of the Britannic Metropolis." Ortiz y Fernández, *Hampa afro-cubana*, 362.

5. The standard reference for these state laws is Hurd, *The Law of Freedom and Bondage in the United States*, 2:2–150. After examining these laws, which became ever more draconian after 1800, one scholar concluded that "whites had pushed free Negros into a place of permanent legal inferiority. Like slaves, free Negros were

generally without political rights, were unable to move freely, were prohibited from testifying against whites, and were often punished with the lash." Berlin, *Slaves without Masters*, 97. For the post-emancipation laws, see Johnson, *The Development of State Legislation Concerning the Free Negro*.

6. See Genovese, *Roll, Jordan, Roll*, part 1.

7. Woodward, *American Counterpart*.

8. See Klein and Engerman, "Fertility Differentials between Slaves in the United States and the British West Indies," 357–374.

9. See, for example, Kolchin, *Unfree Labor*.

10. The classic article which provides the model for explaining land/labor ratios and their influence on the turn to slavery is Domar, "The Causes of Slavery or Serfdom: A Hypothesis."

11. See Klein, *African Slavery in Latin America and the Caribbean*. Although this statement is generally true in all slave societies, there is a lively discussion as to whether the state of Minas Gerais in Brazil in the 19th century was a possible exception. There a very large slave population seemed to maintain itself via local craft and food production for the domestic market. For the debate on this theme see Filho and Martins, "Slavery in a Nonexport Economy: Minas Gerais Revisited," with comments by Robert Slenes, Warren Dean, Eugene Genovese, and Stanley Engerman; and Martins and Filho, "'Slavery in a Nonexport Economy': A Reply." The arguments of the Martins brothers is most fully critiqued in Bergad, *Slavery and the Demographic and Economic History of Minas Gerais*. For a temporary use of slaves in food production in São Paulo in the early coffee period, see Klein and Luna, "African Slavery in the Production of Subsistence Crops."

12. See the suggestive essay of Schwartz, "Patterns of Slaveholding in the Americas: New Evidence from Brazil."

13. See for example, Fogel and Engerman, *Time on the Cross*; Debien, *Les esclaves aux Antilles françaises*; Craton, *Sinews of Empire*; Higman, *Slave Population and Economy in Jamaica, 1807–1834*; Higman, *Slave Population of the British Caribbean, 1807–1834*; Moreno Fraginals, *El ingenio*; Luna and Klein, *Slavery and the Economy of São Paulo, 1750–1850*; and Bergad, *Slavery and the Demographic and Economic History of Minas Gerais*.

14. See Klein, *The Middle Passage*, chapter 3.

15. On urban craft activities, for example, one of the best surveys is found in Bowser, *The African Slave in Colonial Peru, 1524–1650*. For some of these urban activities for free colored in Cuba, see Klein, *Slavery in the Americas*, chapter 9.

16. Klein, *African Slavery*, chapter 6.

17. Knight, *Slave Society in Cuba during the Nineteenth Century*; Bergad, *Cuban Rural Society in the Nineteenth Century*; Scarano, *Sugar and Slavery in Puerto Rico*.

18. See Bowser, *The African Slave in Colonial Peru*; and Karasch, *Slave Life in Rio de Janeiro, 1808–1850*.

19. Wade, *Slavery in the Cities*; Golden, *Urban Slavery in the American South*.

20. Patterson, *Slavery and Social Death.*

21. Pedrigao Maiheiro, *A escravidão no Brasil*; Schwartz, "The Manumission of Slaves in Colonial Brazil: Bahia, 1684–1745"; Nishida, "Manumission and Ethnicity in Urban Slavery: Salvador, Brazil, 1808–1888"; Ortiz y Fernández, *Hampa afro-cubana*, 285–290; Meiklejohn, "The Implementation of Slave Legislation in Eighteenth-Century New Granada." On the difficulties in carrying out self-purchase in the United States, see Matison, "Manumission by Purchase."

22. Kiernan, "The Manumission of Slaves in Colonial Brazil: Paraty, 1789–1822"; Kiernan, "Baptism and Manumission in Brazil: Paraty, 1789–1822."

23. See Klein, *African Slavery in Latin America and the Caribbean*, appendix tables.

24. Gray, *History of Agriculture in the Southern United States to 1860*, 1:481–482.

25. Among other studies, see Klein "The Colored Militia of Cuba, 1568–1868"; Vinson, *Bearing Arms for His Majesty*; Kraay, *Race, State, and Armed Forces in Independence-Era Brazil*; Sanchez, "African Freedmen and the Fuero Militar: A Historical Overview of Pardo and Moreno Militiamen in the Late Spanish Empire"; Kuethe, "The Status of the Free-Pardo in the Disciplined Militia of New Granada"; and the special issue on this subject edited by Ben Vinson III and Stewart King for the *Journal of Colonialism and Colonial History* 5, no 2 (2004). On the French experience, see King, *Blue Coat or Powdered Wig?*

26. See, e.g., Cope, *The Limits of Racial Domination, 1660–1720*; and Kinsbruner, *Not of Pure Blood.*

27. See Cutler, Glaeser, and Vigdor, "The Rise and Decline of the American Ghetto."

28. For recent studies showing the relative importance of free colored persons as slave owners in various *municípios* of Brazil, see Luna, *Minas Gerais*; Luna, "São Paulo: população, atividades e posse de escravos em vinte e cinco localidades—(1777–1829)"; Klein and Paiva, "Free Persons in a Slave Economy: Minas Gerais in 1831"; and Paiva and Klein, "Slave & Free in 19th Century Minas Gerais: Campanha in 1831." For two *municípios* in Bahia, see Barickman, "As cores do escravismo: escravistas 'pretos,' 'pardos' e 'cabras' no Recôncavo Baiano, 1835." Also see Nero da Costa, *Arraia-miúda*; and Luna and Klein, *Slavery and the Economy of São Paulo, 1750–1850*, chapter 7. On the few hundred free colored who owned slaves, see the classic study by Woodson, *Free Negro Owners of the Slaves in the United States in 1830*. For an updating of Woodson's study for one particular state, see Koger, *Black Slave Owners*. For a pessimistic assessment over the situation of the free colored under slavery in the United States, see Berlin, *Slaves without Masters.*

29. See, e.g., Algranti, *O feitor ausente.*

30. See Cope, *The Limits of Racial Domination.*

31. Socolow, "Acceptable Partners: Marriage Choice in Colonial Argentina, 1778–1810."

32. On the free colored in the French West Indies, see Debbasch, *Couleur et liberte.*

33. Paquette, *Sugar Is Made with Blood.* On the free colored in general, see the recent work of Howard, *Changing History.*

34. While slaves had limited access to the civil courts, there are innumerable recordings of slaves appearing as legal witnesses in ecclesiastical proceedings, especially in marriage contracts. See Bennett, *Africans in Colonial Mexico*.

35. See Schwartz, *Sugar Plantations in the Formation of Brazilian Society*, 102–103.

36. On slave marriages among rural slaves in the province of São Paulo, see Luna and Klein, *Slavery and the Economy of São Paulo, 1750–1850*, chapter 6. For Rio de Janeiro, see Góes, *O cativeiro imperfeito*; and Florentino and Góes, *A paz das senzalas*. In his recent study of slave marriages, Slenes found that São Paulo had a much higher rate of slave marriages than the norm, and far higher than in Rio de Janeiro. See Slenes, *Na senzala, uma flor*, 82–86.

37. The literature on the colored *cofradías* (brotherhoods) is quite extensive; see Russell-Wood, "Black and Mulatto Brotherhoods in Colonial Brazil: A Study in Collective Behavior"; Bastide, *Les religions africaines au Brésil*; Scarano, *Devoção e escravidão*. On the relationship of the Rosario devotion to Bantu religion, see Souza, "Viagens do Rosário entre a Velha Cristandade e o Além-Mar." For the Mexican experience, see von Germeten, "Corporate Salvation in a Colonial Society: Confraternities and Social Mobility for Africans and Their Descendants in New Spain."

38. For a survey of the relevant literature on this subject, see Klein, *The Atlantic Slave Trade*.

39. This is most evident when we compare the findings of Bastide, with those of Raboteau, *Slave Religion*; and Sobel, *Trabelin' On*.

40. See Weinstein, "The Destruction of Slavery and the Construction of National Identity: Brazil and the United States South Compared." For a survey of the positive defense school, see Faust, *The Ideology of Slavery*.

41. On the relative deprivation of the free colored in the United States, see Berlin, *Slaves without Masters*. Although some free colored were able to own property in various southern states, the law was bitterly opposed to their mobility. For the economic holdings of the wealthiest few hundred free colored in the southern slave states, see Schweininger, *Black Property Owners in the South, 1790–1915*; and Schweininger, "Prosperous Blacks in the South, 1790–1880." Although a few succeeded, the norm was for a great deal of active legal discrimination and blocked mobility. In Virginia, for example, they were legally denied access to mobility and property in the slave period. See Jackson, *Free Negro Labor & Property Holding in Virginia, 1830–1860*. All this is in sharp contrast to the relative prosperity and mobility in Brazil. On the wealth of the free colored in Brazil, see Klein and Paiva, "Free Persons in a Slave Economy"; and Klein and Luna, "Free Colored in a Slave Society: São Paulo and Minas Gerais in the Early Nineteenth Century." The wealth of a sample of first-generation ex-slaves has been analyzed in Oliveira, *O liberto*.

42. This is the argument sustained by Ransom and Sutch, *One Kind of Freedom*.

43. See Klein, *A Population History of the United States*, chapter 4.

Glossary

N.B.: Except where otherwise noted, all foreign-language terms listed below are Spanish.

adelantado, -da (adjective; masculine and feminine) advanced, developed, precocious; in the multiethnic societies of the Spanish Americas, occasionally used to mean "racially advanced"

apostolado (noun; masculine) instruction in Christian doctrine, or propagation of the faith; apostleship

atezado, -da (adjective; masculine and feminine) bronzed or dark-skinned; used in the context of a *negra atezada*

audiencia (noun; feminine) a royal court often charged with executive and legislative powers and judicial authority

auto de ingreso (noun; masculine) a formal petition requesting admission to a convent

avería (noun; feminine) a tax levied on the transoceanic transport of goods; in this context, a fee for taking a slave across the Atlantic from Spain

bachiller, -ra (noun; masculine and feminine) someone who is educated, learned; formerly a person who had attained a university degree

baxon (also spelled ***bajón***) (noun; masculine) a flute

beata (noun; feminine) a woman affiliated with a third order of the regular clergy; a woman who lived according to a religious rule; someone very devout

beaterio (noun; masculine) a lay pious house for women

blanca (noun; feminine) a white woman; a woman of European descent

blanqueamiento (noun; masculine) literally, "whitening"; a process whereby a person of mixed ancestry would acknowledge only his or her white heritage or past

bozal (adjective) term used to describe someone who is African born but is removed from the land of his or her birth

cajón (noun; masculine) a kiosk; a wooden shack or stand from which goods are sold

calidad (noun; feminine) personal quality or status that differentiated individuals by cultural, social, and economic status; often summarized in documents by racial or ethnic terms

canario, -a (noun; masculine and feminine) a native of the Canary Islands or someone descended from the indigenous inhabitants of the Canary Islands

Candomblé (Portuguese) a religion of African origins practiced in Brazil

capitanes (noun; masculine plural) appointed subordinates to the leaders of expeditions

carta de alforria (Portuguese) (noun; feminine) in Brazil, a formal legal contract executed before a notary whereby a slave was manumitted

carta de libertad (noun; feminine) in Spanish America, a formal legal contract executed before a notary whereby a slave was manumitted

casta (noun; feminine) caste, descent, lineage, marker of status or a colonial resident of mixed descent

cédula (noun; feminine) a royal order or privilege; an official document

celador, -ora (noun; masculine and feminine) an attendant; a guard appointed to the dormitories and individuals' cells in a convent

celdita (noun; feminine) (diminutive) a "little cell," referring here to a cell in a monastic or conventual community; a small space that serves as living quarters

chirimía (noun; feminine) hornpipes; a wooden wind instrument

cirial (plural *ciriales*) (noun; masculine) tall candlesticks of the type carried by acolytes in religious processions

cofrada (noun; feminine) a woman belonging to a religious association or guild

cofradía (sometimes ***confradía***) (noun; feminine) a religious brotherhood or association

color membrillo, de (adjective) *membrillo* is the quince tree or its fruit; *de color membrillo* refers to a yellowish complexion

contratación (noun; feminine) hiring, contracting; can refer to *contratación* records, meaning records from the Casa de la Contratación, or the bureaucratic entity in Seville (founded 1503) that controlled and documented trade between Spain and its overseas possessions

criado, -da (noun; masculine and feminine) a servant

criollo, -lla (adjective and noun; masculine and feminine) an individual of non-Amerindian descent (i.e., European, African, or mixed) who was born in the Spanish colonies of the Americas; initially the term was primarily applied to individuals of European descent born in the Americas

curandero (noun; masculine) a faith healer; someone who practiced medicine without an official license

desventurado, -da (adjective and noun; masculine and feminine) unlucky, unfortunate; a person who has suffered hardship

doctrina (noun; feminine) a settlement of Indians recently converted to Christianity that was governed by members of the religious orders, who emphasized instruction in religious doctrine

don, -ña (noun; masculine and feminine) a sign of respect in addressing an individual; similar to "Sir" or "Lady" in English; formerly used only with people of an elevated social rank

donado, -da (noun; masculine and feminine) in monastic life, a category of religious servants reserved for men and women of African and indigenous heritage who were, by virtue of canon law, unable to become nuns or priests; an intermediate category between full monastic status and servitude

embusteiro, -a (Portuguese) (noun; masculine and feminine) a false visionary; disparagingly used to describe someone as a cheat or a liar

encomienda (noun; feminine) an institution used in the Spanish colonization of the Americas whereby a colonizer was "given" land and a group of indigenous people to work the land, in exchange for which the colonizer was expected to offer protection and Catholic evangelization

entonador, -ra (noun; masculine and feminine) in a religious house or cathedral, someone who kept the organ in tune; one who modulated the wind for the organ pipes

epístola (adjective) the quality of being ordained with permission to chant the epistles and prepare the Eucharist but not to say Mass or perform the sacraments

esclavo, -a (adjective and noun; masculine and feminine) a slave

español, -a (adjective and noun; masculine and feminine) a Spaniard, generally understood in this context to mean a white European; the Spanish language

estrecho, -a (adjective; masculine and feminine) close, tight, intimate; can be used to describe a relationship

examen de profesión (noun; masculine) an exam taken by a novice at the end of her year as a novitiate

expediente de profesión (noun; masculine) document related to the formal profession of vows in a monastic order; a dossier or file related to the profession of vows

facistol (noun; masculine) a lectern used in churches

fraile (noun, masculine) friar, monk

freila (noun; feminine) a female religious servant; synonymous with *donada* or *hermana*

frontal (noun; masculine) the frontal covering of an altar

fuellera (noun; feminine) in a religious house, church, or cathedral, an individual who stoked and fanned the fires

gobernador (noun; masculine) literally a governor, one charged with governing a particular territory; a conquistador (or his successor) with full authority over a specified region

gracias al sacar (noun; feminine plural) a set of legal procedures or dispensations through which an individual's social status received enhancement from the Spanish Crown; these included the shift from mulatto to white status and from illegitimate to legitimate birth; a 1795 royal decree established the prices for these procedures

grumete (noun; masculine) a page, cabin boy, or ship boy; a person of low rank on a sailing vessel

hermana (noun; feminine) a nun; sister (in the context of a religious house)

incensorio (noun; masculine) a censer, or jar used to burn incense in religious ceremonies (particularly one swung on a chain during these ceremonies)

indio, -a (adjective and noun; masculine and feminine) Amerindian; Native American; the indigenous peoples of the Americas

informaciones (noun; feminine plural) literally, "information"; the data sheets collected as part of passengers' petitions for a license (*licencia*) to embark for the Indies from Spain

lego, -a (adjective and noun; masculine and feminine) a religious servant, or lay brother or sister in a religious house

libres de color (noun; masculine plural) free people of color; free population of African descent

licencia (noun, feminine) permission, license; a legal document allowing travel from Spain to the Americas

limeño, -ña (adjective and noun; masculine and feminine) a resident of the city of Lima, Peru; of or pertaining to this city

limpieza de sangre (noun; feminine) literally "cleanliness of blood"; an early modern Iberian conception of racial purity dependent on the quality of not having non-Christian and nonwhite ancestors

loro, -ra (adjective; masculine and feminine) olive-colored, referring here to a person's complexion

"***madre reservada***" (noun; feminine) literally, "mother reserved" or "mother's identity withheld"; this was sometimes listed on a child's baptismal certificate in circumstances when the mother's status could be socially disadvantageous to the child; for instance, if the mother was a slave and the father was free

marinero, -a (noun; masculine and feminine) a sailor

mayorala (noun; feminine) a woman occupying a position of authority in a religious house; a mother superior

mestizaje (noun; masculine) miscegenation; racial and cultural mixing between Spaniards and Indians

mestizo, -za (adjective and noun; masculine and feminine) person of mixed race, especially of combined Spanish and Indian heritage

moreno, -na (adjective and noun; masculine and feminine) a person of primarily African descent; a person with dark skin and hair; *morenas conventuales* were women of African heritage who lived a conventual life

morisco, -ca (adjective and noun; masculine and feminine) in the context of Spain and North Africa, a Muslim living under Christian rule; in the Americas the term was sometimes applied to the offspring of a *mulato/a* and a European

moro, -a (adjective and noun; masculine and feminine) a Moor; a Muslim from North Africa or Spain, whether Arab or Berber; when used in the phrase "*indios moros*," the term likely referred to Indians who had not accepted baptism, suggesting something along the lines of "infidel"

mosa (often spelled ***moza***) (noun; feminine) a young girl, a lass

mulato, -ta (adjective and noun; masculine and feminine) (diminutive = ***mulatilla***) typically used to describe the offspring of African and European unions; in the early colonial period, it was often applied to African intermarriage with a person of any other "race"

nefando, -a (adjective; masculine and feminine) unspeakable; nefarious

negro, -a (adjective and noun; masculine and feminine) used to refer to individuals of sub-Saharan African ancestry, generally those born in the Americas (as opposed to ***bozales***, born in Africa)

obediencia (noun; feminine) obedience; the vow of obedience taken upon entering a religious order

obrero, -a (noun; masculine and feminine) worker; laborer

oficial (adjective and noun; masculine and feminine) an official or officer, typically of the court or other government office

oidor (noun; masculine) a judge or magistrate in an *audiencia* who heard cases and pronounced sentences

palenque (noun; masculine) an isolated, or well-hidden, hamlet or settlement; frequently used to describe settlements of escaped slaves

palia (noun; feminine) a cloth placed over the chalice during the Eucharist

panadero, -a (noun; masculine and feminine) a baker

pardo, -da (adjective and noun; masculine and feminine) a person with any combined degree of African and European heritage; not necessarily limited to someone with one black and one white parent

partera (noun; feminine) a midwife; a woman with or without formal training who assists in the delivery of children

pasajero, -ra a Indias (noun; masculine and feminine) a passenger traveling to the Indies, departing from Spain

patronato (noun; masculine) a system of apprenticeship that replaced slavery when the institution was outlawed in Cuba

peninsular (adjective and noun; masculine and feminine) a native of the Iberian Peninsula; in the Spanish Americas generally used to refer to a Spaniard

piloto mayor (noun; masculine) the office of chief pilot, or harbor captain, in Seville

poste (noun; masculine) a pole, or post

preto, -a (Portuguese) (adjective and noun; masculine and feminine) an individual of African descent

promotor, -ora fiscal (noun; masculine and feminine) a public prosecutor
pulpero, -a (noun; masculine) owner of a small dry-goods store
puntal (noun; masculine) a structural support; a prop or brace
quarterona de mestiza (noun; feminine) a woman who is one-quarter *mestiza*
quarteronas de mulata (noun; feminine) women who are one-quarter *mulata*
Real Casa de Maternidad (noun; feminine) a name given to any one of the public maternity hospitals and orphanages established by the Spanish imperial government
reales (noun; masculine) a unit of currency
recogimiento (noun; masculine) a secluded living arrangement designed to avoid distractions; an institution for lay and religious women and girls
religión (noun; feminine) a religious order
religioso, -sa (noun) a cleric or a nun
sacristana mayor (noun; feminine) a nun of the white veil; a nun in charge of the sacristy
sambo, -a (often spelled ***zambo, -a***) (noun; masculine and feminine) in Latin America, a person who is descended from Amerindians and Africans
Santería a syncretic religion practiced in the Caribbean and other parts of Latin America that conjoins Catholic saints with gods of African origin
señora (noun; feminine) a woman, a lady; a formal form of address
siglo (el siglo) (noun; masculine) literally, "century" or "age"; a term derived from the Latin word *seculum* to refer to the secular world; the world "in time," in opposition to the world of the religious life, which stood outside of time
sillero, -a (noun; masculine and feminine) a person in charge of the pantry and the distribution and storage of foodstuffs
tablas de oficios (noun; feminine) annually designated task lists in convents
testigo (noun; masculine and feminine) a witness, for instance of a marriage
traza (noun; feminine) literally, "outline"; name for the non-indigenous city center
vecindad (noun; feminine) a building composed of small apartments
vecino, -na (noun; masculine and feminine) resident, citizen
velo simple (noun; masculine) literally, a "simple veil"; shoulder-length white veil given to *donadas* to distinguish them from the nuns
vidas (noun; feminine) literally, "lives," used here to refer to the lives of the saints; a relation, or history, of the notable deeds performed during a person's life
votos simples (noun; masculine) the simple religious vows: poverty, obedience, chastity, enclosure
votos solemnes (noun; masculine) formal vows in the canonical or juridical sense that were made publically
zambo, -a (sometimes spelled ***sambo, -a***) (noun; masculine and feminine) in Latin America, a person who is descended from Amerindians and Africans

Bibliography

Archival Sources

CUBA

Archivo del Arzobispado de la Habana (AAH): Fondo de Legitimaciones y Reconocimientos.
Archivo Nacional de Cuba, Havana (ANC): Asuntos Políticos; Comisión Militar; Gobierno General; Gobierno Superior Civil; Instrucción Pública; Reales Órdenes y Cédulas.
Archive of the parish of Espíritu Santo, Havana: *Libro 55 de bautismos de pardos y morenos.*
Archive of the parish of Santo Ángel Custodio, Havana: *Libro 9 de matrimonios blancos.*

ECUADOR

Archivo Nacional Historico, Quito: Cédulas.

MEXICO

Archivo General de la Nación de México (AGN), Ciudad de México: Inquisición; Ramo de Matrimonios.

PERU

Archivo Arzobispal de Lima (AAL): Apelaciones de Trujillo; Causas de Negros (CN); Cofradías; Monasterio de La Concepción (LC); Monasterio de La Encarnación (LE); Monasterio de La Trinidad (LT); Monasterio de Las Descalças; Monasterio de Santa Catalina de Sena; Monasterio de Santa Clara (SC); Papeles Importantes.
Archivo Arzobispal de Trujillo: Testamentos.

Archivo del Convento de Santa Clara de Lima: "Vida de la Hermana Ursula," Libro 5, 1928.
Archivo Departamental de La Libertad (ADL), Trujillo: Cabildo Ordinarias; Protocolos.
Archivo Franciscano del Perú (AFP), Lima: Registro 17, no. 45. "Vida de la Venerable Ursula de Jesús," 585r–607v.
Archivo General de la Nación (AGNP), Lima: Protocolos; Testamentos de Indígenas.
Archivo Parroquia El Sagrario, Iglesia San Francisco, Trujillo: Libro de bautismos de mistis, 1717–1729.
Biblioteca Nacional del Perú, Lima: Ms. B 124, Diego Córdova y Salinas, "Relación de la fundación de la Santa Provincia de los Doce Apóstoles."

SPAIN

Archivo General de Indias (AGI), Seville: Audiencia de Quito; Contratación; Escribania; Indiferente; Inquisición; Justicia; Pasajeros; Patronato.
Archivo Histórico Nacional (AHN), Madrid: Inquisición, Canarias; Inquisición, Sevilla.

UNITED STATES OF AMERICA

DeGolyer Library, Southern Methodist University, Dallas, Texas: Archivo del Duque del Infantado, Madrid, Sección Montesclaros.
Huntington Library, San Marino, California: Huntington Manuscript Collection.

Newspapers

El Diario de la Habana, 1828–1844

Printed Primary Sources

Abbot, Abiel. *Letters Written in the Interior of Cuba, between the Mountains of Arcana, to the East, and of Cuscu, to the West, in the Months of February, March, April, and May 1828*. Boston: Bowles and Dearborn, 1829.
Aguilar, José de. *Sermones varios*. Brussels: Mercador de Libros, 1684.
Baquaqua, Mahommah Gardo. *The Biography of Mahommah Gardo Baquaqua: His Passage from Slavery to Freedom in Africa and America*. Ed. Robin Law and Paul E. Lovejoy. Princeton, N.J.: Markus Wiener Publishers, 2001.
Barbot, Jean. *Barbot on Guinea: The Writings of Jean Barbot on West Africa, 1678–1712*. Vols. 1–2. Ed. P. E. H. Hair, Adam Jones, and Robin Law. London: The Hakluyt Society, 1992.
Bryant, William Cullen. *Letters of a Traveller: or, Notes of Things Seen in Europe and America*. London: Richard Bentley, 1850.
Cabello Balboa, Miguel. "Verdadera descripción y relación larga de la provincia y tierra de Las Esmeraldas, de las Esmeraldas, contenida desde el cabo comúnmente

llamado Pasao, hasta la bahía de la Buena Ventura, que es en la costa del Mar del Sur del Reino del Piru; dirigida al muy Illustre Señor Licenciado Jhoan López de Cepeda de el Concejo de su Majestad y su Presidente en la provincia de los Charcas, Reinos del Piru; hecha por Miguel Cabello Balboa, clérigo; donde se contiene una breve suma del alzamiento y rebelión de los indios de la provincia de los Quixios y de la entrada del inglés en el Mar del Sur." In Miguel Cabello Balboa, *Obras*, vol. 1, ed. Jacinto Jijón y Caamaño, 7–76. Quito: Editorial Ecuatoriana, 1945.

Calancha, Antonio de, Bernardo de Torres, and Manuel Merino. *Crónicas agustinianas del Perú*. Madrid: C.S.I.C., 1972.

Calcagno, Francisco. *Poetas de color*. Havana: Militar de la V. de Soler, 1878.

Cavazzi, Giovanni Antonio. "Istorica Descrizione de' Tre Regni Congo, Matamba, et Angola. (Milan, 1690)." In *Un Cappuccino nell'Africa nera del seicento: I disegni dei Manoscritti Araldi del Padre Giovanni Antonio Cavazzi da Montecuccolo*, ed. Ezio Bassani. [Milan?]: Quaderni Poro, 1987.

Chaplin, Thomas B. *The Journal of Thomas B. Chaplin (1822–1890), Tombee: Portrait of a Cotton Planter*. Ed. Theodore Rosengarten. New York: William Morrow and Company, Inc., 1986.

Chimalpahín, Domingo. *Diario*. Trans. Rafael Tena. Mexico: Conaculta, 2001.

Constituciones generales para todas las monjas, y religiosas, sujetas a la obediencia de la Órden de nuestro Padre San Francisco, en toda la Familia Cismontana. Madrid: Imprenta Real, 1748.

Cooke, Edward. *A Voyage to the South Sea, and Round the World, Performed in the Years 1708, 1709, 1710, and 1711*. London: Printed by H.M. for B. Lintot and R. Gosling, 1712.

Córdova y Salinas, Diego de. *Crónica franciscana de las provincias del Perú*. Ed. Lino G. Canedo. 1651; facsimile ed., Washington, D.C.: Academy of American Franciscan History, 1957.

Covarrubias Orozco, Sebastián de. *Tesoro de la lengua castellana o española*. Ed. Felipe C. R. Maldonado. Rev. Manuel Camarero. Madrid: Editorial Castalia, 1995.

Dana, Richard Henry, Jr. *Two Years before the Mast and Other Voyages*. New York: Literary Classics of the United States, 2005.

Definiciones, y constituciones, que han de guardar la Abadesa, y Monjas de el Monasterio de la Sanctissima Trinidad, de esta Ciudad de los Reyes. Lima: Antonio Ricard, 1604; facsimile ed., Lima: Casa de los Niños Expósitos, 1759.

Dimock, Joseph J. *Impressions of Cuba in the Nineteenth Century: The Travel Diary of Joseph J. Dimock*. Ed. Louis A. Pérez. Wilmington, Del.: Scholarly Resources, 1998.

Echave y Assu, Francisco de. *La estrella de Lima convertida en sol sobre svs tres coronas el B. Toribio Alfonso Mogrobexo, sv segvndo arzobispo: celebrado con epitalamios sacros, y solemnes cultos*. Amberes: J. B. Verdussen, 1688.

Equiano, Olaudah. *The Interesting Narrative of the Life of Olaudah Equiano*. Ed. Robert J. Allison. Boston: Bedford Books of St. Martin's Press, 1995.

Fernández, Josef. *Apostólica y Penitente Vida de el V.P. Pedro Claver de la Compañía de Jesus sacada principalmente de informaciones juridicas hechas antes el Ordinario de la Ciudad de Cartagena de Indias. A su religiosisima provincial de el Nuevo Reyno de Granada*. Zaragoza: Diego Dormer, 1666.

Gonzáles del Valle, Ambrosio. *Manuel de obstetricia*. Havana: Imprenta y Liberia de A. Graupera, 1854.

Granada, Luis de. *Guía de pecadores*. Ed. José María Balcells. Barcelona: Editorial Planeta, 1986.

Hurd, John Codman. *The Law of Freedom and Bondage in the United States*. 2 vols. Boston: Little Brown & Co, 1858–1862.

Johnson, Franklin. *The Development of State Legislation Concerning the Free Negro*. New York: Arbor Press, 1916.

Kimball, Richard. "Letters from Cuba." *Knickerbocker* 26 (October 1845): 544–554.

Konetzke, Richard, ed. *Colección de documentos para la historia de la formación social de Hispanoamérica, 1493–1810*. 4 vols. Madrid: Consejo Superior de Investigaciones Científicas, 1953–1962.

Laborie, P. J. *The Coffee Planter of Saint Domingo; with an Appendix, Containing a View of the Constitution, Government, Laws, and State of That Colony, Previous to the Year 1789*. London: T. Cadell and W. Davies, 1798.

Latham, Henry. *Black and White: A Journal of a Three Months' Tour in the United States*. London: Macmillan, 1867.

Manzano, Juan Manzano. *Recopilación de leyes de los Reinos de las Indias*, 4 vols. 1681; rep., Madrid: Ediciones Cultura Hispánica, 1973.

Meléndez, Juan. *Tesoros verdaderos de las Indias: historia de la Provincia de S. Juan Baptista del Perú, del Órden de Predicadores*. Vols. 1–3. Rome: Nicolás Tinassio, 1681.

Montalvo, Francisco Antonio. *El sol del Nuevo Mundo, ideado y compuesto en las esclarecidas operaciones del bienaventurado Toribio Arçobispo de Lima*. Rome: Imp. Angel Bernavò, 1683.

Morton, Louis. *Robert Carter of Nomini Hall: A Virginia Tobacco Planter of the Eighteenth Century*. Charlottesville: Dominion Books, 1945.

Murray, Henry A. *Lands of the Slave and the Free: or, Cuba, the United States, and Canada*. London: John W. Parker and Son, 1855.

Norman, Benjamin Moore. *Rambles by Land and Water, or, Notes of Travel in Cuba and Mexico; Including a Canoe Voyage up the River Panuco, and Researches among the Ruins of Tamaulipas*. New York: Paine & Burgess, 1845.

"Ordenanzas acerca de la orden que se ha de tener en el tratamiento con los negros para la conservación de la política que han de tener (ca. 1545)." In *Colección de documentos para la historia de la formación social de Hispanoamérica, 1493–1810*, ed. Richard Konetzke, 237–240. Madrid: Consejo Superior de Investigaciones Científicas, 1955.

Pedrigao Maiheiro, Agostinho. *A escravidão no Brasil*. 2 vols. Rio de Janeiro: Typographia Nacional, 1866.

Pezuela, Jacobo de la. *Diccionario geografico, estadístico, historico de la isla de Cuba.* 4 vols. Madrid: Imprenta del establecimiento de Mellado, 1863.

Pérez, Louis A., Jr., ed. *Slaves, Sugar, and Colonial Society: Travel Accounts of Cuba, 1801–1899.* Wilmington, Del.: Scholarly Resources, 1992.

Phillippo, James M. *The United States and Cuba.* London: Pewtress & Co., 1857.

Real Academia Española. *Diccionario de autoridades.* Vols. 1–6. Facsimile edition. Madrid: Editorial Gredos, 1963.

———. *Diccionario de la lengua española.* Vols. 1–2. Decimanovena edición. Madrid: Espasa Calpe, 1970.

Rogers, Woodes. *A Cruising Voyage Round the World: First to the South-Sea, Thence to the East-Indies, and Homewards by the Cape of Good Hope. Begun in 1708, and Finish'd in 1711.* 2nd ed. 1712; London: Bell & Lintot, 1718.

Rojas Villandrando, Agustín de. *El viaje entretenido.* Vol. 1. Madrid: Espasa-Calpe, 1977.

Rumazo, José González, ed. *Documentos para la historia de la audiencia de Quito.* 8 vols. Madrid: Afrodisio Aguado, S.A., 1948–1950.

Sandoval, Alonso de. *De instauranda aethiopum salute: El mundo de la esclavitud negra en América.* Bogotá: Empresa Nacional de Publicationes, 1956.

———. *Un Tratado sobre la esclavitud.* Madrid: Alianza, 1987.

Sociedad Económica de Amigos del País. *Anales de las Reales Juntas de Fomento y Sociedad Económica de La Habana.* Vol. 1. Havana: Imprenta del Gobierno y Capitanía General, 1849.

Superintendencia General Delegada de Real Hacienda. *Informe fiscal sobre fomento de la población blanca en la isla de cuba y emancipación progresiva de la esclava con una breve resena de las reformas y modificaciones que para conseguirlo convendría establecer en la legislación y constitución coloniales.* Madrid: Imprenta de J. M. Alegria, 1845.

Teresa de Ávila. *Libro de las fundaciones de Santa Teresa de Jesús.* 2 vols. Madrid: Espasa-Calpe, 1957.

Ursula dc Jcsús. *The Souls of Purgatory: The Spiritual Diary of a Seventeenth-Century Afro-Peruvian Mystic, Ursula de Jesús.* Ed. and trans. Nancy E. van Deusen. Albuquerque: University of New Mexico Press, 2004.

Villaverde, Cirilo. *Cecilia Váldes: o, La loma del angel. Novela de costumbres cubanas.* Havana: Editorial excelsior, 1879.

Voyages: The Trans-Atlantic Slave Trade Database. Available at http://www.slavevoyages.org/tast/index.faces.

Zamora y Coronada, José María. *Biblioteca de legislación ultramarina en forma de diccionario alfabético.* 7 vols. Madrid: Imprenta de Alegría y Charlain, 1844–1849.

Secondary Sources

Acosta Saignes, Miguel. *Vida de los esclavos negros en Venezuela.* Caracas: Hespérides, 1967.

Adams, Kathleen M., and Sara Dickey, eds. *Home and Hegemony: Domestic Service and Identity Politics in South and Southeast Asia*. Ann Arbor: University of Michigan Press, 2000.

Aguirre, Carlos. *Agentes de su propia libertad: Los esclavos de Lima y la desintegración de la esclavitud: 1821–1854*. Lima: Pontificia Universidad Católica del Perú, Fondo Editorial, 1993.

Aguirre Beltrán, Gonzalo. *La población negra de México. Estudio etnohistórico*. 3rd ed. México, D.F.: Fondo de Cultura Económica, 1989.

———. *Medicina y magia: el proceso de aculturación en la estructura colonial*. 1963; repr., México, D.F.: Fondo de Cultura Económica, 1992.

Alberro, Solange. *Inquisición y sociedad en México, 1571–1700*. México, D.F.: Fondo de Cultura Económica, 1988.

Alcina Franch, José. "Penetración Española en Esmeraldas tipología del descubrimiento." *Revista de Indias* 36, nos. 143–144 (1976): 65–121.

———. "Textos para la etnohistoria de Esmeraldas." Madrid: Departamento de antropologia y etnologia de America Universidad Complutense de Madrid, 1974.

Algranti, Leila Mezan. *O feitor ausente: Estudos sobre a escravidão urbana no Rio de Janeiro, 1808–1822*. Petrópolis:Vozes, 1988.

———. *Honradas e devotas: Mulheres da colônia: condição feminina nos conventos e recolhimentos do sudeste do Brasil, 1750–1822*. Rio de Janeiro: José Olympio, 1993.

Allen, Theodore. *The Invention of the White Race*. 2 vols. London and New York: Verso, 1994 and 1997.

Altman, Ida. *Emigrants and Society: Extremadura and America in the Sixteenth Century*. Berkeley: University of California Press, 1989.

Anderson, Rodney D. "Race and Social Stratification: A Comparison of Working-Class Spaniards, Indians, and Castas in Guadalajara, Mexico in 1821." *Hispanic American Historical Review* 68, no. 2 (1988): 209–241.

Andrews, George Reid. *Afro-Latin America, 1800–2000*. Oxford: Oxford University Press, 2004.

———. *Blacks and Whites in São Paulo, Brazil, 1888–1988*. Madison: University of Wisconsin Press, 1991.

Appelbaum, Nancy. "Whitening the Region: Caucano Mediation and 'Antioqueno Colonization' in Nineteenth-Century Colombia." *Hispanic American Historical Review* 79, no. 4 (1999): 631–667.

Ardanaz, Daisy Rípodas. *El matrimonio en Indias: realidad social y regulación juridical*. Buenos Aires: Fundación para la Educación, la Ciencia y la Cultura, 1977.

Ares Queija, Berta. "Mestizos, mulatos y zambaigos (Virreinato del Perú, siglo XVI)." In *Negros, mulatos, zambaigos: Derroteros africanos en los mundo ibéricos*, ed. Berta Ares Queija and Alessandro Stella, 45–88. Seville: Consejo Superior de Investigaciones Científicas, Escuela de Estudios Hispano-Americanos, 2000.

Ares Queija, Berta, and Alessandro Stella, eds. *Negros, mulatos, zambaigos: Derroteros africanos en los mundo ibéricos*. Seville: Consejo Superior de Investigaciones Científicas, Escuela de Estudios Hispano-Americanos, 2000.

———. "Presentación." In *Negros, mulattos, zambaigos: Derroteros africanos en los mundos ibéricos*, ed. Berta Ares Queija and Alessandro Stella, 11–16. Seville: Escuela de Estudios Hispano-americanos, 2000.

Arrazola, Roberto. *Palenque: Primer pueblo libre de América*. Cartagena: Ediciones Hernández, 1970.

Arrelucea Barrantes, Maribel. "Conducta y control social colonial. Estudio de las panaderías limeñas en el siglo XVIII." *Revista del Archivo General de la Nación* [Lima] 13 (1996): 133–150.

———. "Slavery, Writing, and Female Resistance: Black Women Litigants in Lima's Late Colonial Tribunals of the 1780s." In *Afro-Latino Voices: Narratives from the Early Modern Ibero-Atlantic World, 1550–1812*, ed. Kathryn Joy McKnight and Leo J. Garofalo, 285–301. Indianapolis/Cambridge: Hackett Publishing Company, 2009.

Arrom, Sylvia. *The Women of Mexico City, 1790–1857*. Stanford, Calif.: Stanford University Press, 1985.

Banerjee, Swapna M. "Down Memory Lane: Representations of Domestic Workers in Middle Class Personal Narratives of Colonial Bengal." *Journal of Social History* 37, no. 3 (2004): 681–708.

Baralt, Guillermo. *Esclavos rebeldes: Conspiraciones y sublevaciones de esclavos en Puerto Rico (1795–1873)*. Río Piedras, P.R.: Ediciones Huracán, 1981.

Barickman, B. J. "As cores do escravismo: escravistas 'pretos', 'pardos' e 'cabras' no Recôncavo Baiano, 1835." *População e Família* 2, no. 2 (Jul–dez. 1999): 7–62.

Barnet, Miguel. *The Autobiography of a Runaway Slave: Esteban Montejo*. London: Bodley Head, 1968.

Bassani, Ezio, ed. *Un cappuccino nell'Africa nera del seicento: I disegni dei Manoscritti Araldi del Padre Giovanni Antonio Cavazzi da Montecuccolo*. Milan: Quaderni Poro, 1987.

Bastide, Roger. *African Civilisations in the New World*. New York: Harper & Row, 1971.

———. *Les religions africaines au Brésil. Contribution à une sociologie des interpénétrations de civilisation*. 2ème édn. Paris: PUF, 1995.

Beatty, Charles Edward. "Rebels and Conquerors: African Slaves, Spanish Authority, and the Domination of Esmeraldas, 1563–1621." Ph.D. diss., Brown University, 2002.

Beatty-Medina, Charles. "Fray Alonso de Espinosa's Report on Pacifying the Fugitive Slaves of the Pacific Coast." In *Documenting Latin America: Gender, Race, and Empire*, vol. 1, ed. Erin E. O'Connor and Leo J. Garofalo, 69–74. New York: Prentice Hall, 2010.

Beckles, Hilary. "Sex and Gender in the Historiography of Caribbean Slavery." In *Engendering History: Caribbean Women in Historical Perspective*, ed. Verene Sheperd, Bridget Brereton, and Barbara Bush, 125–140. New York: St. Martin's Press, 1995.

Behar, Ruth. "Sex and Sin, Witchcraft and the Devil in Late-Colonial Mexico." *American Ethnologist* 14, no. 1 (1987): 34–53.

Bennett, Herman L. *Africans in Colonial Mexico: Absolutism, Christianity, and Afro-Creole Consciousness, 1570–1640*. Bloomington: Indiana University Press, 2003.

———. *Colonial Blackness: A History of Afro-Mexico*. Bloomington: Indiana University Press, 2009.

———. "Lovers, Family and Friends: The Formation of Afro-Mexico, 1580–1810." Ph.D. diss., Duke University, 1993.

———. "Sons of Adam": Text, Context, and the Early Modern African Subject." *Representations* 92 (Fall 2005): 16–41.

———. "The Subject in the Plot: National Boundaries in the History of the Black Atlantic." *African Studies Review* 43:1 (2000): 101–124.

Bergad, Laird W. *Cuban Rural Society in the Nineteenth Century: The Social and Economic History of Monoculture in Matanzas*. Princeton, N.J.: Princeton University Press, 1990.

———. *Slavery and the Demographic and Economic History of Minas Gerais, Brazil, 1720–1888*. New York: Cambridge University Press, 1999.

Berlin, Ira. "From Creole to African: Atlantic Creoles and the Origins of African-American Society in Mainland North America." *William and Mary Quarterly*, 3rd ser., 53, no. 2 (1996): 251–288.

———. *Many Thousands Gone: The First Two Generations of Slavery in North America*. Cambridge: Belknap Press of Harvard University Press, 2004.

———. *Slaves without Masters: The Free Negro in the Antebellum South*. New York: Pantheon Books, 1974.

Bernard, Alexis. "Les esclaves à Séville au XVIIe siècle." Thesis Université de Paris X-Nanterre, 2000.

Bhabha, Homi K. *The Location of Culture*. New York: Routledge 1994.

Blanchard, Peter. *Slavery & Abolition in Early Republican Peru*. Wilmington, Del.: SR Books, 1992.

Bleek, Wolf. "Did the Akan Resort to Abortion in Pre-Colonial Ghana? Some Conjectures." *Africa: Journal of the International African Institute* 6, no. 1 (1990): 121–131.

Borah, Woodrow, and Sherburne F. Cook. "Marriage and Legitimacy in Mexican Culture: Mexico and California." *California Law Review* 54, no. 2 (1966): 946–997.

———. "Sobre las posibilidades de hacer el estudio histórico del mestizaje sobre una base demografica." *Revista de Historia de América* 53–54 (1962): 181–190.

Bourdieu, Pierre. *An Outline of a Theory of Practice*. Chicago: University of Chicago Press, 1991.

Bowser, Frederick P. "The African Experience in Colonial Spanish America: Reflections on Research Achievements and Priorities." *Latin American Historical Review* 7, no. 1 (1972): 77–94.

———. *The African Slave in Colonial Peru, 1524–1650*. Stanford, Calif.: Stanford University Press, 1974.

Boxer, C. R. *The Golden Age of Brazil, 1695–1750*. Berkeley: University of California Press, 1962.

Boyer, Richard. "Caste and Identity in Colonial Mexico: A Proposal and an Example." Occasional Paper No. 7. Latin American Studies Consortium of New England, 1997.

———. "Honor among Plebeians." In *The Faces of Honor: Sex, Shame, and Violence in Colonial Latin America*, ed. Lyman L. Johnson and Sonya Lipsett-Rivera, 152–178. Albuquerque: University of New Mexico Press, 1998.

———. "Respect and Identity: Horizontal and Vertical Reference Points in Speech Acts." *Americas: A Quarterly Review of Inter-American Cultural History* 54, no. 4 (1998): 491–509.

Brading, David A. *The First America: The Spanish Monarchy, Creole Patriots, and the Liberal State, 1492–1867*. Cambridge: Cambridge University Press, 1991.

Bristol, Joan C. "'Although I am black, I am beautiful': Juana Esperanza de San Alberto, Black Carmelite of Puebla." In *Gender, Race and Religion in the Colonization of the Americas*, ed. Nora E. Jaffary, 67–80. Burlington, Vt.: Ashgate Publishing, 2007.

———. *Christians, Blasphemers, and Witches: Afro-Mexican Ritual Practice in the Seventeenth Century*. Albuquerque: University of New Mexico Press, 2007.

———. "Negotiating Authority in New Spain: Blacks, Mulattos, and Religious Practice in the Seventeenth Century." Ph.D. diss., University of Pennsylvania, 2001.

Brockington, Lolita G. *The Leverage of Labor: Managing the Cortés Haciendas in Tehuantepec, 1588–1688*. Durham, N.C.: Duke University Press, 1989.

Bronfman, Alejandra. *Measures of Equality: Social Sciences, Citizenship, and Race in Cuba, 1902–1940*. Chapel Hill: University of North Carolina Press, 2004.

Brooks, George E. *Eurafricans in Western Africa: Commerce, Social Status, Gender, and Religious Observance from the Sixteenth to the Eighteenth Century*. Athens: Ohio University Press, 2003.

Brown, Kathleen M. *Good Wives, Nasty Wenches, and Anxious Patriarchs: Gender, Race, and Power in Colonial Virginia*. Chapel Hill: Published for the Institute of Early American History and Culture by the University of North Carolina Press, 1996.

Bryant, Sherwin K. "Enslaved Rebels, Fugitives, and Litigants: The Resistance Continuum in Colonial Quito." *Colonial Latin American Review* 13. no. 1 (2004): 7–46.

———. "Finding Gold, Forming Slavery: The Creation of a Classic Slave Society, Popayán, 1600–1700." *The Americas* 63 (2006): 81–112.

———. "Slavery and the Context of Ethnogenesis: Africans, Afro-Creoles and the Realities of Slavery in the Kingdom of Quito, 1600–1800." Ph.D. diss., Ohio State University, 2005.

Burgos Guevara, Hugo. *Primeras doctrinas en la real audiencia de Quito, 1570–1640: Estudio preliminar y transcripción de las relaciones eclesiales y misionales de los siglos XVI y XVII*. 1st ed. Quito, Ecuador: Ediciones ABYA-YALA, 1995.

Burns, Kathryn. *Colonial Habits: Convents and the Spiritual Economy of Cuzco, Peru*. Durham, N.C.: Duke University Press, 1999.

———. *Into the Archive: Writing and Power in Colonial Peru*. Durham, N.C.: Duke University Press, 2010.

———. "Notaries, Truth, and Consequences." *American Historical Review* 110, no. 2 (2005): 350–379.

Burton, Antoinette M. *Dwelling in the Archive: Women Writing House, Home, and History in Late Colonial India*. New York: Oxford University Press, 2003.

Bush, Barbara. *Slave Women in Caribbean Society, 1650–1838*. Bloomington: Indiana University Press, 1990.

Busto Duthurburu, José Antonio del. *San Martín de Porras (Martín de Porras Velásquez)*. Lima: Pontificia Universidad Católica del Perú, Fondo Editorial, 2001.

Butler, Kim D. "Defining Diaspora, Refining a Discourse." *Diaspora* 10, no. 2 (2001): 189–219.

———. *Freedoms Given, Freedoms Won: Afro-Brazilians in Post-Abolition São Paulo and Salvador*. New Brunswick, N.J.: Rutgers University Press, 1998.

Byrd, Alexander X. *Captives and Voyagers: Black Migrants across the Eighteenth-Century British Atlantic World*. Baton Rouge: Louisiana State University Press, 2008.

———. "Eboe, Country, and Nation in Gustavus Vassa's *Interesting Narrative*." *William and Mary Quarterly*, 3rd ser., 63, no. 1 (2006): 123–148.

———. "The Slave Trade from the Biafran Interior to Jamaica: Commerce, Culture Change, and Comparative Perspective." Paper presented at The International Seminar on the History of the Atlantic World, 1500–1800, Harvard University, 1998.

Cabrera, Manuel Lobo. *La esclavitud en las Canarias orientales en el siglo XVI (negros, moros y moriscos)*. Las Palmas: Ediciones del Cabildo Insular de Gran Canaria, 1982.

———. *Los libertos en la sociedad canaria del siglo XVI*. Madrid: Instituto de Estudios Canarios, 1983.

Cáceres Gómez, Rina. *Del olvido a la memoria: Los afromestizos en la historia colonial de Centroamérica*. San José: Oficina Regional de la UNESCO, 2008.

———. *Negros, mulatos, esclavos y libertos en la Costa Rica del siglo XVII*. Mexico City: Instituto Panamericano de Geografía e Historia, 2000.

———. *Rutas de la esclavitud en África y América Latina*. San José: Editorial de la Universidad de Costa Rica, 2001.

Calvo, Thomas. *Guadalajara y su región en el siglo XVII: Población y economía*. Guadalajara: Ayuntamiento de Guadalajara, 1992.

Cândido, Mariana. "Merchants and the Business of the Slave Trade in Benguela, c. 1750–1850." *African Economic History* 35 (2008): 1–30.

Carmagnani, Marcelo. "Demografía y sociedad: La estructura social de los centros mineros del norte de México, 1600–1720." In *Historia y población en México (Siglos XVI–XIX)*, ed. Thomas Calvo, 122–162. México, D.F.: El Colegio de México, 1994.

Caron, Peter. "'Of a nation which others do not Understand': Bambara Slaves and African Ethnicity in Colonial Louisiana, 1718–60." *Slavery & Abolition* 18, no. 1 (April 1997): 98–121.

Carrera, Magali M. *Imagining Identity in New Spain: Race, Lineage, and the Colonial Body in Portraiture and Casta Painting*. Austin: University of Texas Press, 2003.

Carroll, Patrick J. *Blacks in Colonial Veracruz: Race, Ethnicity, and Regional Development*. Austin: University of Texas Press, 2001.

———. "Los Mexicanos negros, el mestizaje y los fundamentos olvidados de la 'raza cósmica': una perspectiva regional." *Historia Mexicana* 44, no. 3 (1995): 403–438.

Carter, Donald. "Preface." In *New African Diasporas*, ed. Khalid Koser, ix–xix. London: Routledge, 2003.

Castellanos, Jorge, and Isabel Castellanos. *Cultura Afrocubana*. Vol. 2, *El negro en Cuba 1845–1959*. Miami: Universal, 1990.

Casteñeda, Digna. "The Female Slave in Cuba during the First Half of the Nineteenth Century." In *Engendering History: Caribbean Women in Historical Perspective*, ed. Verene Sheperd, Bridget Brereton, and Barbara Bush, 141–154. New York: St. Martin's Press, 1995.

Castillero Calvo, Alfredo. *Los negros y mulatos libres en la historia social panameña*. Panama: Comisión de Estudios Interdisciplinarios para el Desarrollo de la Nacionalidad, 1969.

Castillo Mathieu, Nicolás del. *Esclavos negros en Cartagena y sus aportes léxicos*. Bogotá: Instituto Cara y Cuervo, 1982.

Chambers, Douglas B. "Ethnicity in the Diaspora: The Slave-Trade and the Creation of African 'Nations' in the Americas." *Slavery and Abolition* 22, no. 3 (2001): 25–39.

———. "'My own nation': Igbo Exiles in the Diaspora." *Slavery and Abolition* 18, no. 1 (1997): 72–97.

———"Tracing Igbo into the African Diaspora." In *Identity in the Shadow of Slavery*, ed. Paul E. Lovejoy, 55–71. London: Continuum, 2000.

Chambers, Sarah C. *From Subjects to Citizens: Honor, Gender, and Politics in Arequipa, Peru, 1780–1854*. University Park: Pennsylvania State University Press, 1999.

Chance, John K. *Race and Class in Colonial Oaxaca*. Stanford: Stanford University Press, 1978.

———, and William B. Taylor. "The Ecology of Race and Class in Late Colonial Oaxaca." In *Studies in Spanish American Population History*, ed. David J. Robinson, 93–117. Boulder, Colo.: Westview Press, 1981.

———. "Estate and Class: A Reply." *Comparative Studies in Society and History* 21, no. 3 (1979): 443–442.

———. "Estate and Class in a Colonial City: Oaxaca in 1792." *Comparative Studies in Society and History* 19 (1977): 454–487.

Chandler, David L. "Health and Slavery in Colonial Colombia." Ph.D. diss., Tulane University, 1972.

———. "Slave over Master in Colonial Colombia and Ecuador." *The Americas* 38, no. 3 (1982): 315–326.

Chavés, María Eugenía. *Honor y libertad: Discursos y recursos en la estrategia de libertad de una mujer esclava (Guayaquil a fines del período colonial)*. Departamento de Historia e Instituto Iberoamericano de la Universidad de Gotemburgo, 2001.

———. *María Chiquinquirá Díaz, un esclava del siglo VIII: Acerca de las identidades de amo y esclavo en el Puerto colonial de Guayaquil*. Guayaquil: Archivo Histórico del Guayas, 1998.

———. "Slave Women's Strategies for Freedom and the Late Spanish Colonial State." In *Hidden Histories of Gender and the State in Latin America*, ed. Elizabeth Dore and Maxine Molyneux, 108–126. Durham, N.C.: Duke University Press, 2000.

Chávez-Hita, Adriana Naveda. *Pardos, mulatos y libertos: Sexto encuentro de afromexicanistas*. Mexico D.F.: Universidad Veracruzan, 2001.

Collo, Paola, and Silvia Benso, eds. *Sogno: Bamba, Pemba, Ovando e altre contrade dei regni di Congo, Angola e adjacenti*. Milan: Franco Maria Ricci, 1986.

Colmenares, Germán. *Historia económica y social de Colombia*. Tomo 1, *1537–1719*. Bogota Columbia: Universidad del Valle, Division de Humanidades, 1972.

———. *Historia económica y social de Colombia*. Tomo 2, *Popayán: una sociedad esclavista 1680–1800*. Santafé de Bogotá: TM Editores 1997.

Cope, R. Douglas. *The Limits of Racial Domination: Plebeian Society in Colonial Mexico City, 1660–1720*. Madison: University of Wisconsin Press, 1994.

Cortés Jácome, María Elena. "La memoria familiar de los negros y mulatos. Siglos XVI–XVIII." In *La memoria y el olvido*, ed. Segundo Simposio de Historia de las Mentalidades, 125–133. México, D.F.: Instituto Nacional de Antropología e Historia, 1985.

———. "Negros amancebados con indias, siglo XVI." In *Familia y Sexualidad en Nuevo España: Memoria del Primer Simposio de Historia de la Mentalidades—Familia, Matrimonio y Sexualidad en Nueva España*, 285–293. México, D.F.: SEP, 1982.

Cortés López, José Luis. *La esclavitud negra en la España peninsular del siglo XVI*. Salamanca: Universidad de Salamanca, 1989.

Craemer, Willy de, Jan Vansina, and Renée C. Fox. "Religious Movements in Central West Africa: A Theoretical Study." *Comparative Studies in Society and History* 18, no. 4 (1976): 458–475.

Craton, Michael. *Sinews of Empire: A Short History of British Slavery*. New York: Doubleday, 1974.

Crespo, Alberto. *Esclavos negros en Bolivia*. La Paz: Academia Nacional de Ciencias de Bolivia, 1977.

Crosby, Alfred W. *Ecological Imperialism: The Biological Expansion of Europe, 900–1900*. New York: Cambridge University Press, 1986.

Cuetos, María Luisa Laviana. *Guayaquil en el siglo XVIII: recursos naturales y desarrollo económico*. Seville: Escuela de Estudios Hispano-Americanos, 1987.

Curtin, Philip D. *The Atlantic Slave Trade: A Census*. Madison: University of Wisconsin Press, 1969.

———. *Economic Change in Precolonial Africa: Senegambia in the Era of the Slave Trade*. Madison: University of Wisconsin Press, 1975.

Cussen, Celia. "Fray Martín de Porres and the Religious Imagination of Creole Lima." Ph.D. diss., University of Pennsylvania, 1996.

———. "The Search for Idols and Saints in Colonial Peru: Linking Extirpation and Beatification." *Hispanic American Historical Review* 85, no. 3 (2005): 417–448.

Cutler, David M., Edward L. Glaeser, and Jacob L. Vigdor. "The Rise and Decline of the American Ghetto." *Journal of Political Economy* 107, no. 3 (1999): 455–506.

Danielson, Roswell S. *Cuban Medicine*. New Brunswick, N.J.: Transaction Books, 1978.

Dantas, Mariana M.L. *Black Townsmen: Urban Freedom and Slavery in the Eighteenth Century Americas*. New York: Palgrave-Macmillan, 2008.

Davis, Darién J. "Introduction: The African Experience in Latin America—Resistance and Accommodation." In *Slavery and Beyond: The African Impact on Latin America and the Caribbean*, ed. Darién J. Davis, xi–xxv. Wilmington, Del.: Scholarly Resources, 1995.

Deacon, Harriet. "Midwives and Medical Men in the Cape Colony before 1860." *The Journal of African History* 39, no. 2 (1998): 271–292.

Dean, Warren. "Comments on 'Slavery on a Nonexport Economy.' II." *Hispanic American Historical Review* 63, no. 3 (1983): 582–584.

Debbasch, Yvan. *Couleur et liberte. Le jeu du critère ethnique dans un order juridique esclavagiste*. Paris: Dalloz, 1967.

Debien, Gabriel. *Les esclaves aux Antilles françaises*. Basse-Terre & Fort-de-France: Societies d'historie de la Guadeloupe and Martinique, 1974.

Degler, Carl. *Neither Black nor White: Slavery and Race Relations in Brazil and the United States*. New York: Macmillan, 1971.

Delgado, Richard, and Jean Stefancic, eds. *Critical White Studies: Looking Beyond the Mirror*. Philadelphia: Temple University Press, 1997.

Deschamps Chapeaux, Pedro. *El Negro en la economía habanera del siglo XIX*. Havana: Unión de Escritores y Artístas de Cuba, 1971.

Díaz, María Elena. *The Virgin, the King, and the Royal Slaves of El Cobre: Negotiating Freedom in Colonial Cuba, 1670–1780*. Stanford, Calif.: Stanford University Press, 2000.

Dickey, Sara. "Mutual Exclusions: Domestic Workers and Employers on Labor, Class, and Character in South India." In *Home and Hegemony: Domestic Service and Identity Politics in South and Southeast Asia*, ed. Kathleen A. Adams and Sara Dickey, 31–62. Ann Arbor: University of Michigan Press, 2000.

Dodds, Jerrilynn D., María Rosa Menocal, and Abigail Krasner Balbale. *The Arts of Intimacy: Christians, Jews, and Muslims in the Making of Castilian Culture*. New Haven, Yale University Press, 2008.

Domar, Evsey D. "The Causes of Slavery or Serfdom: A Hypothesis." *Journal of Economic History* 30, no. 1 (1970): 18–32.

Dubois, Laurent, and Julius S. Scott. *Origins of the Black Atlantic*. New York: Routledge, 2010.

Duncan, Quince, and Carlos Meléndez. *El Negro en Costa Rica*. San Jose: Editorial Costa Rica, 1972.

Edwards, Brent Hayes. "The Uses of Diaspora." *Social Text* 19, no. 1 (2001): 45–73.

Elkins, Stanley M. *Slavery: A Problem in American Institutional and Intellectual Life*. Chicago: University of Chicago Press, 1959.

Elliott, John H. *Empires of the Atlantic World: Britain and Spain in America, 1492–1830*. New Haven, Conn.: Yale University Press, 2006.

Eltis, David, Paul E. Lovejoy, and David Richardson. "Slave-Trading Ports: Towards an Atlantic-Wide Perspective, 1676–1832." In *Ports of the Slave Trade (Bights of Benin and Biafra): Papers from a Conference of the Centre of Commonwealth Studies, University of Stirling June 1998*, ed. Robin Law and Silke Strickrodt, 12–34. Stirling: Centre of Commonwealth Studies, University of Stirling, 1999.

Engerman, Stanley L., and Eugene D. Genovese. "Comments on 'Slavery on a Nonexport Economy.' III." *Hispanic American Historical Review* 63, no. 3 (1983): 585–590.

Epstein, Steven A. *Speaking of Slavery: Color, Ethnicity, and Human Bondage in Italy*. Ithaca: Cornell University Press, 2001.

Estenssoro, Juan Carlos. *Del paganismo a la santidad: la incorporación de los indios del Perú al catolicismo, 1532–1750*. Trans. Gabriela Ramos. Lima: IFEA, Instituto Francés de Estudios Andinos, Pontificia Universidad Católica del Perú, Instituto Riva-Agüero, 2003.

Fairchilds, Cissie. *Domestic Enemies: Servants & Their Masters in Old Regime France*. Baltimore and London: Johns Hopkins University Press, 1984.

Fanon, Frantz. *Black Skin, White Masks*. Trans. Charles Lam Markmann. New York: Grove Press, 1967.

Faust, Drew Gilpin, ed. *The Ideology of Slavery: Proslavery Thought in the Antebellum South, 1830–1860*. Baton Rouge: Louisiana State University Press, 1981.

Feliú Cruz, Guillermo. *La abolición de la esclavitud en Chile*. Santiago: Universidad de Chile, 1942.

Fernandes, Florestan. *A Integraço do Negro na Sociedade de Classes*. 3rd ed. São Paulo: Ática, 1978.

Fernández Álvarez, Manuel. *Casadas, monjas, rameras y brujas: La olvidada historia de la mujer española en el renacimiento*. Madrid: Espasa Calpe, 2002.

Fernández Fernández, Amaya, et al., eds. *La mujer en la conquista y la evangelización en el Perú (Lima 1550–1650)*. Lima: Pontificia Universidad Católica del Perú, 1997.

Filho, Amilcar Martins, and Roberto B. Martins. "Slavery in a Nonexport Economy: Minas Gerais Revisited." *Hispanic American Historical Review* 63, no. 3 (1983): 537–568.

Fischer, Kirsten. *Suspect Relations: Sex, Race, and Resistance in Colonial North Carolina*. Ithaca: Cornell University Press, 2002.

Fisher, Andrew B., and Matthew O'Hara, eds. *Imperial Subjects: Race and Identity in Colonial Latin America*. Durham, N.C.: Duke University Press, 2009.

Florentino, Manolo, and José Roberto Góes. *A paz das senzalas. Famílias escravas e tráfico Atlântico, Rio de Janeiro, c. 1790–c. 1850*. Rio de Janeiro: Civilização Brasileira, 1998.

Fogel, Robert William, and Stanley L. Engerman. *Time on the Cross: The Economics of American Negro Slavery*. Boston, Little, Brown, 1974.

Fournié-Martinez, Ch. "Contribution à l'étude de l'esclavage en Espagne au Siècle d'or: les esclaves devant l'Inquisition." Thesis École Nationale des Chartes, Paris, 1987–1988.

Fra Molinero, Baltasar. "Ser mulato en España y América: discursos legales y otros discursos literarios." In *Negros, mulatos, zambaigos: Derroteros africanos en los mundo ibéricos*, ed. Berta Ares Queija and Alessandro Stella, 123–147. Seville: Consejo Superior de Investigaciones Científicas, Escuela de Estudios Hispano-Americanos, 2000.

Franco Silva, Alfonso. *La esclavitud en Sevilla y su tierra a fines de la Edad Media.* Seville: Diputación Provincial de Sevilla, 1979.

Frey, Sylvia R., and Betty Wood. *Come Shouting to Zion: African American Protestantism in the American South and the British Caribbean to 1830.* Chapel Hill: University of North Carolina Press, 1998.

Freyre, Gilberto. *Casa-grande & senzala; formação da familia brasileira sob o regime de economia patriarcal.* Rio de Janeiro: J. Olympio, 1943.

———. *The Masters and the Slaves: A Study in the Development of Brazilian Civilization.* New York: Knopf, 1946.

Friedemann, Nina de. "Estudios de negros en la antropología colombiana." In *Un siglo de investigacion social: antropología en Colombia*, ed. Jaime Arocha and Nina S. de Friedemann, 507–572. Bogotá: Etno, 1984.

———. *Presencia Africana en Colombia. La saga del negro.* Bogotá: Pontificia Universidad Javeriana, 1993.

Fuente, Alejandro de la. "Esclavos africanos en La Habana: Zonas de procedencia y denominaciones étnicas, 1570–1699." *Revista Española de Antropología Americana* 20 (1990): 135–160.

———. *Havana and the Atlantic in the Sixteenth Century.* Chapel Hill, University of North Carolina Press, 2008.

———. *A Nation for All: Race, Inequality, and Politics in Twentieth-Century Cuba.* Chapel Hill: University of North Carolina Press, 2001.

———. "Race, National Discourse, and Politics in Cuba." *Latin American Perspectives* 23, no. 3 (May 1998): 43–69.

Ganster, Paul. "Churchmen." In *Cities and Society in Colonial Latin America*, ed. Louisa Schell Hoberman and Susan Migden Socolow, 137–163. Albuquerque: University of New Mexico Press, 1986.

Garay Arellano, Ezio. "La Elite económica de los negros en Guayaquil de 1742 a 1765." In *Actas del primer congreso de historia del negro en el Ecuador y sur de Colombia. Esmeraldas 14–16 de octubre, 1988*, ed. Rafael Savoia, 113–121. Quito: Centro Cultural Afro-Ecuatoriano, 1988.

Garofalo, Leo J. "Afro-Iberian Sailors, Soldiers, Traders, and Thieves on the Spanish Main." In *Documenting Latin America: Gender, Race, and Empire*, vol. 1, ed. Erin E. O'Connor and Leo J. Garofalo, 25–34. New York: Prentice Hall, 2010.

———. "Conjuring with Coca and the Inca: The Andeanization of Lima's Afro-Peruvian Ritual Specialists, 1580–1690." *The Americas* 63, no. 1 (July 2006): 53–80.

———. "The Ethno-Economy of Food, Drink, and Stimulants: The Making of Race in Colonial Lima and Cuzco." Ph.D. diss., University of Wisconsin-Madison, 2001.

Geggus, David P. "Slave and Free Colored Women in Saint Domingue." In *More than Chattel: Black Women and Slavery in the Americas*, ed. David Barry Gaspar and Darlene Clark Hine, 257–278. Bloomington: Indiana University Press, 1996.

Genovese, Eugene. *Roll, Jordan, Roll: The World the Slaves Made*. New York: Pantheon Books, 1972.

Gerhard, Peter. "A Black Conquistador in Mexico." *Hispanic American Historical Review* 58, no. 3 (1968): 451–459.

Gilroy, Paul. *The Black Atlantic: Modernity and Double-Consciousness*. Cambridge, Mass.: Harvard University Press, 1993.

Góes, Roberto. *O cativeiro imperfeito. Um estudo sobre a escravidão no Rio de Janeiro da primeria metade do século XIX*. Vitória, ES: Lineart, 1993.

Golden, Claudia. *Urban Slavery in the American South, 1820–1860*. Chicago: University of Chicago Press, 1976.

Gomez, Michael A. *Exchanging Our Country Marks: The Transformations of African Identities in the Colonial and Antebellum South*. Chapel Hill: University of North Carolina Press, 1998.

Gómez Acuña, Luis. "Las cofradías de negros en Lima (siglo XVII). Estado de la cuestión y análisis de caso." *Páginas* 129 (1994): 28–39.

Gonzalbo Aizpuru, Pilar. "Familias y viviendas en la capital del virreinato." In *Casas, vivienda sy hogares en la historia de México,* ed. Rosalva Loreto López, 75–107. México: El Colegio de México, Centro de Estudios Históricos, 2001.

González, Ondina E. "Abandonment in Havana: The Response of the State and the Church, 1700–1750." Paper presented at the Latin American Studies Association Meeting, 2000.

González Díaz, Antonio Manuel. *La esclavitud en Ayamonte durante el antiguo régimen (siglos XVI, XVII y XVIII)*. Huelva: Diputación provincial, 1996.

Gosner, Kevin. *Soldiers of the Virgin: The Moral Economy of a Colonial Maya Rebellion*. Tucson: University of Arizona Press, 1992.

Gould, Jeffrey. "Gender, Politics, and the Triumph of Mestizaje in Early 20th-Century Nicaragua." *Journal of Latin American Anthropology* 2, no. 1 (1996): 4–33.

Graham, Richard, ed. *The Idea of Race in Latin America, 1870–1940*. Austin: University of Texas Press, 1990.

Gray, Lewis Cecil. *History of Agriculture in the Southern United States to 1860*. 2 vols. Washington, D.C.: Carnegie Institute, 1932.

Greene, Sandra E. "Cultural Zones in the Era of the Slave Trade: Exploring the Yoruba Connection with the Anlo-Ewe." In *Identity in the Shadow of Slavery*, ed. Paul E. Lovejoy, 86–101. London: Continuum, 2000.

Greer, Margaret R., Walter D. Mignolo and Maureen Quilligan, eds. *Rereading the Black Legend: The Discourses of Religious and Racial Difference in the Renaissance Empires*. Chicago: University of Chicago Press, 2007.

Guardia, Roberto de la. *Los Negros del istmo de Panamá*. Panamá: Instituto Nacional de Cultura. 1977.

Guridy, Frank. *Forging Diaspora: Afro-Cubans and African Americans in a World of Empire and Jim Crow*. Chapel Hill: University of North Carolina Press, 2010.

Gutiérrez, Ramón. *When Jesus Came, the Corn Mothers Went Away*. Stanford, Calif.: Stanford University Press, 1991.

Hall, Gwendolyn Midlo. "African Ethnicities and the Meanings of 'Mina.'" In *Trans-Atlantic Dimensions of Ethnicity in the African Diaspora*, ed. Paul E. Lovejoy and David V. Trotman, 43–65. London: Continuum, 2003.

Hammerly, Michael. *El comercio de cacao de Guayaquil durante el período colonial: un estudio cuantitativo*. Quito, Ecuador: Comandancia General de Marina, 1976.

———. *Historia social y económica de la Antigua provincia de Guayaquil, 1763–1842*. Guayaquil, Ecuador: Archivo Historico del Guayas, 1973.

Hanger, Kimberly S. "Patronage, Property and Persistence: The Emergence of a Free Black Elite in Spanish New Orleans." In *Against the Odds: Free Blacks in the Slave Societies of the Americas*, ed. Jane G. Landers, 44–64. London: Frank Cass, 1996.

Hanretta, Sean. "Women, Marginality and the Zulu State: Women's Institutions and Power in the Early Nineteenth Century." *Journal of African History* 39, no. 3 (1998): 389–415.

Harris, Leslie M. *In the Shadow of Slavery: African Americans in New York City, 1626–1863*. Chicago: University of Chicago Press, 2003.

Harris, Marvin. *Patterns of Race in the Americas*. New York: Walker and Co., 1964.

Harth-Terré, Emilio. *Negros e indios: Un estamento social ignorado en el Perú colonial*. Lima: Editorial Juan Mejía Baca, 1974.

Hartman, Saidiya. "Venus in Two Acts." *Small Axe* 12, no. 2 (June 2008): 1–14.

Helg, Aline. *Liberty and Equality in Caribbean Colombia, 1770–1835*. Chapel Hill: University of North Carolina Press, 2004.

———. *Our Rightful Share, The Afro-Cuban Struggle for Equality, 1886–1912*. Chapel Hill: University of North Carolina Press, 1995.

———. "Race in Argentina and Cuba, 1880–1930: Theory, Policies, and Popular Reaction." In *The Idea of Race in Latin America, 1870–1940*, ed. Richard Graham, 37–70. Austin: University of Texas Press, 1990.

Hernández Sáenz, Luz María, and George M. Foster. "Curers and Their Cures in Colonial New Spain and Guatemala." In *Mesoamerican Healers*, ed. Brad R. Huber and Alan R. Sandstrom, 19–46. Austin: University of Texas Press, 2001.

Hernando i Delgado, Josep. *Els esclaus islàmics a Barcelona: blancs, negres, llors i turcs de l'esclavitud a la llibertat (s. XIV)*. Barcelona: Consell Superior d'Investigacions Científiques, Institució Milà i Fontanals, Departament d'Estudis Medievals, 2003.

Herrera, Robinson A. *Natives, Europeans, and Africans in Sixteenth-Century Santiago de Guatemala*. Austin: University of Texas Press, 2003.

Herskovits, Melville J. *The Myth of the Negro Past*. Boston: Beacon Press, 1970.

Hesse, Barnor. "Racialized Modernity: An Analytics of White Mythologies." *Ethnic and Racial Studies* 30, no. 4 (2007): 643–663.

Heywood, Linda. "Queen Njinga Mbandi Ana de Sousa of Ndongo/Matamba: African Leadership, Diplomacy, and Ideology, 1620s–1650s." In *Afro-Latino Voices: Narratives from the Early Modern Ibero-Atlantic World, 1550–1812*, ed. Kathryn Joy McKnight and Leo J. Garofalo, 38–51. Indianapolis/Cambridge: Hackett Publishing Company, 2009.

———, and John K. Thornton, ed. *Central Africans, Atlantic Creoles, and the Foundation of the Americas, 1585–1660*. New York: Cambridge University Press, 2007.

Higman, Barry W. *Slave Population and Economy in Jamaica, 1807–1834*. Cambridge: Cambridge University Press, 1976.

———. *Slave Population of the British Caribbean, 1807–1834*. Baltimore, Md.: Johns Hopkins University Press, 1984.

Hilton, Anne. *The Kingdom of Kongo*. Oxford: Clarendon Press, 1985.

Hine, Darlene Clark, Trica Danielle Keaton, and Stephen Smallwood, eds. *Black Europe and the African Diaspora*. Urbana: University of Illinois Press, 2009.

Hine, Darlene Clark, and Jacqueline McLeod, eds. *Crossing Boundaries: Comparative History of Black People in Diaspora*. Bloomington: Indiana University Press, 1999.

Hoerder, Dirk. "How the Intimate Lives of Subaltern Men, Women, and Children Confound the Nation's Master Narratives." *Journal of American History* 88, no. 3 (2001): 874–881.

Hoetink, H. *Slavery and Race Relations in the Americas: Comparative Notes on Their Nature and Nexus*. New York: Harper & Row, 1973.

Holt, Thomas C. "Slavery and Freedom in the Atlantic World: Reflections on the Diasporan Framework." In *Crossing Boundaries: Comparative History of Black People in Diaspora*, ed. Darlene Clark Hine and Jacqueline McLeod, 33–44. Bloomington: Indiana University Press, 1999.

Howard, Philip A. *Changing History: Afro-Cuban Cabildos and Societies of Color in the Nineteenth Century*. Baton Rouge: Louisiana State University Press, 1998.

Hünefeldt, Christine. *Paying the Price of Freedom: Family and Labor among Lima's Slaves, 1800–1854*. Berkeley: University of California Press, 1994.

Ibsen, Kristine. *Women's Spiritual Autobiography in Colonial Spanish America*. Gainesville: University Press of Florida, 1999.

Ignatiev, Noel. *How the Irish Became White*. London: Routledge, 1995.

Instituto Colombiano de Cultura Hispánica. *Geografía humana de Colombia*. Tomo 6, *Los Afrocolombianos*. Santafé de Bogotá: Instituto Colombiano de Cultura Hispánica, 1998.

Jackson, Luther Porter. *Free Negro Labor & Property Holding in Virginia, 1830–1860*. 2nd ed. New York: Atheneum, 1968.

Jackson, Robert H. *Race, Caste, and Status: Indians in Colonial Spanish America*. Albuquerque: University of New Mexico Press, 1999.

Jamieson, Ross. "Bolts of Cloth and Sherds of Pottery: Impressions of Caste in the Material Culture of the Seventeenth Century Audiencia of Quito." *The Americas* 60, no. 3 (January 2004): 431–446.

Janzen, John M. *Lemba, 1650–1930: A Drum of Affliction in Africa and the New World.* New York: Garland Publishing, 1982.

Jaramillo Urbe, Jaime. *Ensayos de historia social colombiana.* Bogotá: Universidad Nacional de Colombia, Dirección de Divulgación Cultural 1968.

Johnson, Lyman L. and Sonya Lipsett-Rivera. "Introduction." In *The Faces of Honor: Sex, Shame, and Violence in Colonial Latin America*, ed. Lyman L. Johnson and Sonya Lipsett-Rivera, 1–19. Albuquerque: University of New Mexico Press, 1998.

Jouve Martín, José Ramón. *Esclavos de la ciudad letrada: Esclavitud, escritura y colonialismo en Lima (1650–1700).* Lima: IEP, 2005.

Kabo, R. "Les esclaves africains face à l'Inquisition espagnole: les procès de sorcellerie et de magie." Thesis Université de Montpellier, 1984.

Kamen, Henry. *Empire: How Spain Became a World Power, 1492–1763.* New York: Harper Collins, 2003.

Karasch, Mary C. "Free Women of Color in Central Brazil, 1779–1832." In *Beyond Bondage: Free Women of Color in the Americas*, ed. David Barry Gaspar and Darlene Clark Hine, 237–270. Urbana: University of Illinois Press, 2004.

———. *Slave Life in Rio de Janeiro, 1808–1850.* Princeton, N.J.: Princeton University Press, 1987.

Katzew, Ilona. *Casta Painting: Images of Race in Eighteenth-Century Mexico.* New Haven, Conn.: Yale University Press, 2004.

———, and Susan Deans-Smith, eds. *Race and Classification: The Case of Mexican America.* Stanford, Calif.: Stanford University Press, 2009.

Kicza, John E. *Colonial Entrepreneurs: Families and Business in Bourbon Mexico City.* Albuquerque: University of New Mexico Press, 1983.

Kiddy, Elizabeth W. *Blacks of the Rosary: Memory and History in Minas Gerais, Brazil.* University Park: Pennsylvania State University Press, 2005.

Kiernan, James Patrick. "Baptism and Manumission in Brazil: Paraty, 1789–1822." *Social Science History* 3, no. 1 (1978): 56–71.

———. "The Manumission of Slaves in Colonial Brazil: Paraty, 1789–1822." Ph.D. diss., New York University, 1976.

King, Stewart R. *Blue Coat or Powdered Wig? Free People of Color in Pre-Revolutionary Saint-Domingue.* Athens: University of Georgia Press, 2001.

———. "Introducing the 'New' African Diasporic Military History in Latin America." *Journal of Colonialism and Colonial History* 5, no. 2 (2004): 1–24.

Kinsbruner, Jay. *Not of Pure Blood: The Free People of Color and Racial Prejudice in Nineteenth-Century Puerto Rico.* Durham, N.C.: Duke University Press, 1996.

Kiple, Kenneth F. *Blacks in Colonial Cuba, 1774–1899.* Gainesville: University Presses of Florida, 1976.

Klein, Herbert S. *African Slavery in Latin America and the Caribbean.* New York: Oxford University Press, 1986.

———. *The Atlantic Slave Trade.* New York: Cambridge University Press, 1999.

———. "The Colored Militia of Cuba, 1568–1868." *Caribbean Studies* 6, no. 2 (1966): 17–27.

———. *The Middle Passage: Comparative Studies in the Atlantic Slave Trade*. Princeton, N.J.: Princeton University Press, 1978.

———. *A Population History of the United States*. Cambridge: Cambridge University Press, 2004.

———. *Slavery in the Americas: A Comparative History of Cuba and Virginia*. Chicago: University of Chicago Press, 1967.

———, and Stanley Engerman. "Fertility Differentials between Slaves in the United States and the British West Indies: A Note on Lactation Practices and Their Implications." *William and Mary Quarterly* 35, no. 2 (1978): 357–374.

Klein, Herbert S., and Francisco Vidal Luna. "African Slavery in the Production of Subsistence Crops: The Case of São Paulo in the 19th Century." In *Slavery in the Development of the Americas*, ed. David Eltis, Frank Lewis, and Kenneth L. Sokoloff, 120–149. Cambridge: Cambridge University Press, 2004.

———. "Free Colored in a Slave Society: São Paulo and Minas Gerais in the Early Nineteenth Century." *Hispanic American Historical Review* 80, no.4 (2000): 913–942.

Klein, Herbert S., and Clotilde Paiva. "Free Persons in a Slave Economy: Minas Gerais in 1831." *Journal of Social History* 29, no. 4 (1996): 933–962.

Knight, Franklin. *Slave Society in Cuba during the Nineteenth Century*. Madison: University of Wisconsin Press, 1970.

Koger, Leonard. *Black Slave Owners: Free Black Slave Masters in South Carolina, 1790–1860*. Jefferson, N.C.: McFarland, 1985.

Kolchin, Peter. *Unfree Labor: American Slavery and Russian Serfdom*. Cambridge, Mass: Harvard University Press, 1987.

Kopytoff, Barbara K. "Religious Change among the Jamaican Maroons: The Ascendance of the Christian God within a Traditional Cosmology." *Journal of Social History* 20 (1987): 463–484.

Koser, Khalid. "New African Diasporas: An Introduction." In *New African Diasporas*, ed. Khalid Koser, 1–16. London: Routledge, 2003.

Kraay, Hendrik. *Race, State, and Armed Forces in Independence-Era Brazil: Bahia, 1790s–1840s*. Stanford: Stanford University Press, 2001.

Kristjanson, Lowell Gudmundson. *Estratificación socio-racial y económica de Costa Rica: 1700–1850*. San José, Costa Rica: Ed. Univ. Estatal a Distanci, 1978.

Kuethe, Alan. "The Status of the Free-Pardo in the Disciplined Militia of New Granada." *Journal of Negro History* 56, no. 2 (1971): 105–117.

Kuzinski, Vera M. *Sugar's Secrets: Race and the Erotics of Cuban Nationalism*. Charlottesville: University Press of Virginia, 1993.

Kuznesof, Elizabeth A. "Ethnic and Gender Influences on 'Spanish' Creole Society in Colonial Spanish America." *Colonial Latin American Review* 4, no. 1 (1995): 153–176.

Lancaster, Roger. *Life Is Hard: Machismo, Danger, and Intimacy of Power in Nicaragua*. Berkeley: University of California Press, 1992.

Landers, Jane. *Atlantic Creoles in the Age of Revolutions*. Cambridge, Mass.: Harvard University Press, 2010.

———. *Black Society in Spanish Florida*. Urbana: University of Illinois Press, 1999.

Lane, Kris E. "Captivity and Redemption: Aspects of Slave Life in Early Colonial Quito and Popayán." *The Americas* 57 (2000): 225–246.

———. *Quito 1599: City and Colony in Transition*. Albuquerque: University of New Mexico Press, 2002.

Lanning, John Tate. *The Royal Protomedicato: The Regulation of the Medical Professions in the Spanish Empire*. Ed. John Jay TePaske. Durham, N.C.: Duke University Press, 1985.

Lasso, Marixa. *Myths of Harmony: Race and Republicanism during the Age of Revolution, Colombia 1795–1831*. Pittsburgh, Pa.: University of Pittsburgh Press, 2007.

Lauderdale-Graham, Sandra. "Honor among Slaves." In *The Faces of Honor: Sex, Shame, and Violence in Colonial Latin America*, ed. Lyman L. Johnson and Sonya Lipsett-Rivera, 201–228. Albuquerque: University of New Mexico Press, 1998.

Lavallé, Bernard. "Lógica esclavista y resistencia negra en los Andes ecuatorianos a finales del siglo XVIII." *Revista de Indias* 53, no. 199 (1993), 699–722.

———. *Recherches sur l'apparition de la conscience Creole dans la Vice-Royaute du Perou: L'antagonisme hispano-creole dans les orders religieux (XVIè–XVIIème siecles)*. Vols. 1–2. Lille: Atelier National de Reproduction des Theses, Universite de Lille III, 1982.

Lavrín, Asunción. "Indian Brides of Christ: Creating New Spaces for Indigenous Women in New Spain." *Mexican Studies/Estudios Mexicanos* 15, no. 2 (1999): 225–260.

———. "Introduction: The Scenario, the Actors, and the Issues." In Lavrín, *Sexuality and Marriage in Colonial Latin America*, 1–43. Lincoln: University of Nebraska Press, 1989.

Law, Robin. "Ethnicity and the Slave Trade: 'Lucumi' and 'Nago' as Ethnonyms in West Africa." *History in Africa* 24 (1997): 205–219.

———. *The Kingdom of Allada*. Leiden: Research School CNWS. School of Asian, African, and Amerindian Studies, 1997.

———. *Ouidah: The Social History of a West African Slaving "Port," 1727–1892*. Athens: Ohio University Press. 2004.

———. *The Oyo Empire, c. 1600–c. 1836: A West African Imperialism in the Era of the Atlantic Slave Trade*. Oxford: Clarendon Press, 1977.

———. *The Slave Coast of West Africa, 1550–1750: The Impact of the Atlantic Slave Trade on an African Society*. Oxford: Clarendon Press, 1991.

Lebsock, Suzanne. *The Free Women of Petersburg: Status and Culture in a Southern Town, 1784–1860*. New York: Norton, 1985.

Leiva Vivas, Rafael. *Tráfico de esclavos negros a Honduras*. Tegucigalpa, Honduras: Editorial Guaymuras, 1982.

León Pinelo, Antonio de. *Velos antiguos i modernos en los rostros de las mugeres*. Santiago de Chile: Centro de Investigación de la Historia de América, 1966.

Lewis, Laura. *Hall of Mirrors: Power, Witchcraft, and Caste in Colonial Mexico*. Durham, N.C.: Duke University Press, 2003.

Lockhart, James. "The Social History of Colonial Spanish America: Evolution and Potential." *Latin American Research Review* 7, no. 1 (1972): 6–45.

———. *Spanish Peru, 1532–1560: A Colonial Society*. Madison: University of Wisconsin Press, 1968.

Lohse, Russell. "Slave-Trade Nomenclature and African Ethnicities in the Americas: Evidence from Early Eighteenth-Century Costa Rica." *Slavery and Abolition* 23, no. 3 (2002): 73–92.

Lohse, K. Russell. "Africans and Their Descendants in Colonial Costa Rica." Ph.D. diss., University of Texas, Austin, 2006.

Lokken, Paul. "Marriage as Slave Emancipation in Seventeenth-Century Rural Guatemala." *The Americas* 58, no. 2 (2001): 175–200.

Lombardi, John V. *The Decline and Abolition of Negro Slavery in Venezuela, 1820–1854*. Westport, Conn.: Greenwood Publishing Co., 1973.

Lombardo de Ruiz, Sonia, and Yolanda Terán Trillo. *Atlas histórico de la Ciudad de México*. Vol. 1. México: Smurfit Cartón y Papel de México, Instituto Nacional de Antropología y Historia, 1996.

López Molina, Manuel. *Una década de esclavitud en Jaén: 1675–1685*. Jaén: Ayuntamiento de Jaén, 1995.

Loreto López, Rosalva. "Familial Religiosity and Images in the Home: Eighteenth-Century Puebla de Los Angeles, Mexico." *Journal of Family History* 22, no. 1 (January 1997): 26–49.

———. *Los conventos femeninos y el mundo urbano de la Puebla de los Ángeles del siglo XVIII*. México: El Colegio de México, Centro de Estudios Históricos, 2000.

———. "Prácticas alimenticias en los conventos de mujeres en la Puebla del siglo XVIII." In *Conquista y comida: consecuencias del encuentro de dos mundos*, ed. Janet Long. 481–503. México: Universidad Nacional Autónoma de México, 1996.

Lovejoy, Paul E. "Ethnic Designations of the Slave Trade and the Reconstruction of the History of Trans-Atlantic Slavery." In *Trans-Atlantic Dimensions of Ethnicity in the African Diaspora*, ed. Paul E. Lovejoy and David V. Trotman, 9–42. London: Continuum, 2003.

———. "Identifying Enslaved Africans in the African Diaspora." In *Identity in the Shadow of Slavery*, ed. Paul E. Lovejoy, 1–29. London: Continuum, 2001.

———. *Transformations in Slavery: A History of Slavery in Africa*. New York: Cambridge University Press, 2000.

———, and David Vincent Trotman. "Introduction: Ethnicity and the African Diaspora." In *Trans-Atlantic Dimensions of Ethnicity in the African Diaspora*, ed. Paul E. Lovejoy and David Vincent Trotman, 1–8. London: Continuum, 2003.

Lowell, Peggy A., and Charles H. Wood. "Skin Color, Racial Identity, and Life Chance in Brazil." *Latin American Perspectives* 25, no. 3 (1998): 90–109.

Luna, Francisco Vidal. *Minas Gerais: Escravos e senhores*. São Paulo: IPE/USP, 1981.

———. "São Paulo: população, atividades e posse de escravos em vinte e cinco localidades—(1777–1829)." *Estudos Econômicos* 28, no. 1(jan–mar. 1998): 99–169.

———, and Herbert S. Klein. *Slavery and the Economy of São Paulo, 1750–1850*. Stanford, Calif.: Stanford University Press, 2003.

Lutz, Christopher H. *Santiago de Guatemala, 1541–1773: City, Caste and the Colonial Experience*. Norman: University of Oklahoma Press, 1994.

MacLachlan, Colin M., and Jaime E. Rodríguez O. *The Forging of the Cosmic Race: A Reinterpretation of Colonial Mexico*. Berkeley: University of California Press, 1990.

Mann, Kristin. "Shifting Paradigms in the Study of the African Diaspora and of Atlantic History and Culture." *Slavery & Abolition* 22, no. 1 (2001): 3–21.

———. *Slavery and the Birth of an African City: Lagos, 1760–1900*. Bloomington: Indiana University Press, 2008.

———, ed. *Rethinking the African Diaspora: The Making of a Black Atlantic World in the Bight of Benin and Brazil*. Studies in Slave and Post-Slave Societies and Cultures. Portland: Frank Cass, 2001.

Manning, Patrick. "Africa and the African Diaspora: New Directions of Study." *Journal of African History* 44, no. 3 (2003): 487–506.

———. *The African Diaspora: A History through Culture*. New York: Columbia University Press, 2009.

Mark, Peter. "Constructing Identity: Sixteenth- and Seventeenth-Century Architecture in the Gambia-Geba Region and the Articulation of Luso-African Ethnicity." *History in Africa* 22 (1995): 307–327.

Marland, Hilary. *Medicine and Society in Wakefield and Huddersfield, 1780–1879*. Cambridge: Cambridge University Press, 1987.

Martín, Luis. *Daughters of the Conquistadores: Women of the Viceroyalty of Peru*. Dallas, Tex.: Southern Methodist University, 1989.

Martín Casares, Aurelia. *La esclavitud en la Granada del siglo XVI*. Granada: Universidad de Granada, 2000.

Martínez, José Luis. *Pasajeros de Indias. Viajes trasatlánticas en el siglo XVI*. Mexico: Fondo de Cultura Económica, 1999.

Martínez, María Elena. "The Black Blood of New Spain: *Limpieza de Sangre*, Racial Violence, and Gendered Power in Early Colonial Mexico." *William and Mary Quarterly* 61, no. 3 (2004): 479–520.

———. *Genealogical Fictions: Limpieza de Sangre, Religion, and Gender in Colonial Mexico*. Stanford, Calif.: Stanford University Press, 2008.

Martínez-Alier, Verena. *Marriage, Class and Colour in Nineteenth-Century Cuba: A Study of Racial Attitudes and Sexual Values in a Slave Society*. 2nd ed. Ann Arbor: University of Michigan Press, 1989.

Martínez Fernández, Luis. *Fighting Slavery in the Caribbean: The Life and Times of a British Family in Nineteenth-Century Havana*. Armonk, N.Y.: M. E. Sharpe, 1998.

———. "The 'Male City' of Havana: The Coexisting Logics of Colonialism, Slavery, and Patriarchy in Nineteenth-Century Cuba." In *Women and the Colonial Gaze*, ed. Tamara L. Hunt and Micheline R. Lessard, 104–116. New York: New York University Press, 2002.

Martínez i Alvarez, Patricia. *La libertad femenina de dar lugar a Dios: Discursos religiosos de poder y formas de libertad religiosa desde la Baja Edad Media hasta el Perú colonial.* Lima: Universidad Nacional Mayor de San Marcos, Facultad de Ciencias Sociales, 2004.

Martínez Montiel, Luz María. *Negros en América.* Madrid: Editorial MAPFRE, 1992.

———, ed. *La presencia africana en México.* México, D.F.: Consejo Nacional para la Cultura y las Artes, 1995.

Martins, Roberto B., and Amilcar Martins Filho. "'Slavery in a Nonexport Economy': A Reply." *Hispanic American Historical Review* 64, no. 1 (1984): 135–146.

Matison, Sumner Eliot. "Manumission by Purchase." *Journal of Negro History* 33, no. 2 (1948): 146–167.

McAlister, Lyle N. "Social Structure and Social Change in New Spain." *Hispanic American Historical Review* 63, no. 2 (1963): 349–370.

McCaa, Robert. "*Calidad, Clase,* and Marriage in Colonial Mexico: The Case of Parral, 1788–90." *Hispanic American Historical Review* 64, no. 3 (1984): 477–501.

———, Stuart B. Schwartz, and Arturo Grubessich. "Race and Class in Colonial Latin America: A Critique." *Comparative Studies in Society and History* 21, no. 3 (1979): 421–433.

McClintock, Anne. "No Longer in a Future Heaven: Nationalism, Gender, and Race." In *Becoming National: A Reader,* ed. Geoff Eley and Ronald Grigor Suny, 89–112. Oxford: Oxford University Press, 1996.

McGregor, Deborah Kuhn. *From Midwives to Medicine: The Birth of American Gynecology.* New Brunswick, N.J.: Rutgers University Press, 1998.

Meiklejohn, Norman. "The Implementation of Slave Legislation in Eighteenth-Century New Granada." In *Slavery and Race Relations in Latin America,* ed. Robert Brent Toplin, 176–203. Westport, Conn.: Greenwood Press, 1974.

Meillassoux, Claude. *The Anthropology of Slavery: The Womb of Iron and Gold.* Trans. Alide Dasnois. Chicago: University of Chicago Press, 1991.

Mellafe, Rolando. *La introducción de la esclavitud en Chile. Tráfico y rutas.* Santiago de Chile: Universidad de Chile, 1959.

Mena García, Maria del Carmen. *La sociedad de Panamá en el siglo XVI.* Sevilla: Diputación de Sevilla, 1984.

Metcalf, Alida C. *Go-Betweens and the Colonization of Brazil, 1500–1600.* Austin: University of Texas Press, 2005.

Miller, Joseph C. "Central Africa during the Era of the Slave Trade, c. 1490s–1850s." In *Central Africans and Cultural Transformations in the American Diaspora,* ed. Linda M. Heywood, 21–70. Cambridge: Cambridge University Press, 2002.

———. *The Way of Death: Merchant Capitalism and the Angolan Slave Trade.* Madison: University of Wisconsin Press, 1988.

Mills, Kenneth, and Anthony Grafton, eds. *Conversion: Old Worlds and New.* Rochester: University of Rochester Press, 2003.

Minh-ha, Trinh T. "Not You/Like You: Post-Colonial Women and the Interlocking Questions of Identity and Difference." *Inscriptions* 3–4 (1988): 71–77.

Mintz, Sidney W. *Maroon Societies: Rebel Slave Communities in the Americas*. Garden City, N.Y.: Anchor Press, 1973.

———, and Richard Price. *An Anthropological Approach to the Afro-American Past: A Caribbean Perspective*. ISHI Occasional Papers in Social Change. Philadelphia: Institute for the Study of Human Issues, 1976.

———. *The Birth of African-American Culture: An Anthropological Perspective*. Boston: Beacon Press, 1992.

Moitt, Bernard. *Women and Slavery in the French Antilles, 1635–1848*. Bloomington: Indiana University Press, 2001.

Monroy, Joel L. *Los Religiosos de la Merced en la Costa del Antiguo Reino de Quito*. Quito: Editorial Labor, 1935.

Morabito, Vittorio. "San Benedetto il Moro, da Palermo, prottetore degli africani di Siviglia, della penisola iberica e d'America latina." In *Negros, mulatos, zambaigos: Derroteros africanos en los mundo ibéricos*, ed. Berta Ares Queija and Alessandro Stella, 223–273. Seville: Consejo Superior de Investigaciones Científicas, Escuela de Estudios Hispano-Americanos, 2000.

Morales, Ricardo. "Arquitectura virreynal: Don Evaristo, un alarife negro en Trujillo." *Arkinka: Revista arquitectura, diseño y construcción* [Lima] 11 (Octubre 1996): 74–80.

Morales Padrón, Francisco. *Historia de Sevilla: la ciudad del quinientos*. Seville: Editorial Universidad de Sevilla, 1989.

Moreno Fraginals, Manuel. *El ingenio: complejo económico social cubano del azúcar*. 3 vols. Habana: Editorial de Ciencias Sociales, 1978.

Morgan, Philip D. "The Cultural Implications of the Atlantic Slave Trade: African Regional Origins, American Destination and New World Developments." *Slavery and Abolition* 18, no. 1 (1997): 122–145.

Mörner, Magnus. *Race Mixture in the History of Latin America*. Boston: Little, Brown, 1967.

Morrison, Karen Y. "Creating an Alternative Kinship: Slavery, Freedom, and Nineteenth-Century Afro-Cuban Hijos Naturales." *Journal of Social History* 41, no. 1 (2007): 55–80.

———. "White Fathers and Slave Mothers in Nineteenth-Century Cuba: Defining Family and Social Status." *Slavery & Abolition* 31, no. 1 (2010): 29–55.

———. "'And Your Grandmother, Where Is She?': Reproducing Family, Race, and Nation in Cuba." Ph.D. diss., University of Florida, 2003.

Mott, Luiz. *Rosa Epigpcíaca: Uma santa africana no Brasil*. Rio de Janeiro: Editora Bertrand Brasil, 1993.

Mullin, Michael. *Africa in America: Slave Acculturation and Resistance in the American South and the British Caribbean, 1736–1831*. Urbana: University of Illinois Press, 1994.

Muriel, Josefina. "La habitación plurifamiliar en la ciudad de México." In *La ciudad y el campo en la historia de México: Memoria de la VII Reunión de Historiadores Mexicanos y Norteamericanos*, tomo 1, ed. Comite Organizador Conjunto, 267–282. México: Universidad Nacional Autónoma de México, 1992.

Nero da Costa, Iraci. *Arraia-miúda: um estudo sobre os não-proprietários de escravos no Brasil*. São Paulo: MGSP Ed., 1992.

Ngou-Mve, Nicolás. *El África Bantú en la colonización de México (1595–1640)*. Madrid: Consejo Superior de Investigaciones Científicas, 1994.

Nina Rodrigues, Raimundo. *Os Africanos no Brasil*. São Paulo: Companhia editora nacional, 1932. 2nd ed. São Paulo: Companhia Editora Nacional, 1935.

Nishida, Mieko. "Manumission and Ethnicity in Urban Slavery: Salvador, Brazil, 1808–1888." *Hispanic American Historical Review* 73, no. 3 (1993): 361–391.

Northrup, David. *Africa's Discovery of Europe: 1450–1850*. Oxford: Oxford University Press, 2002.

Nye, Robert A. "Medicine and Science as Masculine 'Fields of Honor.'" *Osiris*, 2nd ser., 12 (1997): 60–79.

O'Hara, Matthew D. *A Flock Divided: Race, Religion, and Politics in Mexico, 1749–1857*. Durham, N.C.: Duke University Press, 2010.

Okpewho, Isidore. "Introduction." In *African Diaspora: African Origins and New World Identities*, ed. Isidore Okpewho, Carole Boyce Davies, and Ali A. Mazrui, xi–xxviii. Bloomington and Indianapolis: Indiana University Press, 1999.

Olaechea, Labayen, and Juan Bautista. *El mestizaje como gesta*. Madrid: Editorial Mapfre, 1992.

Oliveira, Maria Inês Côrtes de. *O liberto: O seu mundo e os outros, Salvador, 1790–1890*. São Paulo: Corrupio, 1988.

Omi, Michael, and Howard Winant. *Racial Formation in the United States: From the 1960s to the 1980s*. New York: Routledge, 1986.

Ortiz, Teresa. "From Hegemony to Subordination: Midwives in Early Modern Spain." In *The Art of Midwifery: Early Modern Midwives in Europe*, ed. Hilary Marland, 95–114. London: Routledge, 1993.

Ortiz y Fernández, Fernando. *Hampa afro-cubana: Los negros esclavos, estudio sociologico y de derecho publico*. Havana: Revista Bimestre Cubana, 1916.

O'Toole, Rachel Sarah. "Castas y representación en Trujillo colonial." In *Más allá de la dominación y la resistencia: Ensayos de historia peruana*, ed. Paulo Drinot and Leo J. Garofalo, 48–76. Lima: Instituto de Estudios Peruanos, 2005.

———. "From the Rivers of Guinea to the Valleys of Peru: Becoming a Bran Diaspora within Spanish Slavery." *Social Text* 25, no. 3 (2007): 19–36.

———. "Inventing Difference: Africans, Indians, and the Antecedents of 'Race' in Colonial Peru (1580s–1720s)." Ph.D. diss., University of North Carolina at Chapel Hill, 2001.

———. "The Making of a Free *Lucumí* Household: Ana de la Calle's Will and Goods, Northern Peruvian Coast, 1719." In *Afro-Latino Voices: Narratives from the Early

Modern Ibero-Atlantic World, 1550–1812, ed. Kathryn Joy McKnight and Leo J. Garofalo, 142–153. Indianapolis/Cambridge: Hackett Publishing Company, 2009.

Owensby, Brian P. "How Juan and Leonor Won Their Freedom: Litigation and Liberty in Seventeenth-Century Mexico." *Hispanic American Historical Review* 85, no. 1 (February, 2005): 39–79.

Paiva, Clotilde, and Herbert S. Klein. "Slave & Free in 19th Century Minas Gerais: Campanha in 1831." *Slavery & Abolition* 15, no.1 (1994): 1–21.

Palmer, Colin A. "The African Diaspora." *The Black Scholar* 30, nos. 3–4 (2000): 56–60.

———. "Defining and Studying the Modern African Diaspora." *American Historical Association Perspectives* 36, no. 6 (1998): 1, 22–25.

———. "From Africa to the Americas: Ethnicity in Early Black Communities of the Americas." *Journal of World History* 6, no. 2 (1995): 223–235.

———. *Slaves of the White God: Blacks in Mexico, 1570–1650*. Cambridge, Mass.: Harvard University Press, 1976.

Palmer, Steven. *From Popular Medicine to Medical Populism: Doctors, Healers, and Public Power in Costa Rica, 1800–1940*. Durham, N.C.: Duke University Press, 2003.

Paquette, Robert L. *Sugar Is Made with Blood: The Conspiracy of La Escalera and the Conflict between Empires over Slavery in Cuba*. Middletown, Conn.: Wesleyan University Press, 1988.

Patterson, Orlando. *Slavery and Social Death: A Comparative Study*. Cambridge, Mass.: Harvard University Press, 1982.

Patterson, Tiffany Ruby, and Robin D. G. Kelley. "Unfinished Migrations: Reflections on the African Diaspora and the Making of the Modern World." *African Studies Review* 43, no. 1 (2000): 11–45.

Peard, Julyan G. *Race, Place, and Medicine: The Idea of the Tropics in Nineteenth-Century Brazilian Medicine*. Durham, N.C.: Duke University Press, 1999.

Pérez-Mallaína, Pablo E. *Spain's Men of the Sea: Daily Life on the Indies Fleets in the Sixteenth Century*. Trans. Carla Rahn Phillips. Baltimore, Md.: John Hopkins University Press, 2005.

Pérez y Valdivia, Diego. *Aviso de gente recogida*. Madrid: Universidad Pontificia de Salamanca, Fundación Universitaria Española, 1977.

Phelan, John Leddy. *The Kingdom of Quito in the Seventeenth Century*. Madison: University of Wisconsin Press, 1967.

Pierson, Donald. *Negroes in Brazil: A Study of Race Contact at Bahia*. Chicago: University of Chicago Press, 1942.

Pike, Ruth. "Sevillian Society in the Sixteenth Century: Slaves and Freedmen." *Hispanic American Historical Review* 47 (1967): 344–359.

Premo, Bianca. *Children of the Father King: Youth, Authority, and Legal Minority in Colonial Lima*. Chapel Hill: University of North Carolina Press, 2005.

Proctor, Frank "Trey," III. "Afro-Mexican Slave Labor in the Obrajes de Paños of New Spain, Seventeenth and Eighteenth Centuries." *The Americas* 60, no. 1 (2003): 33–58.

———. *"Damned Notions of Liberty": Slavery, Culture, and Power in Colonial Mexico, 1640–1769*. Albuquerque: University of New Mexico Press, 2010.

———. "Slavery, Identity, and Culture: An Afro-Mexican Counterpoint, 1640–1763." Ph.D. diss., Emory University, 2003.

Raboteau, Albert J. *Slave Religion: The "Invisible Institution" in the Antebellum South* New York: Oxford University Press, 1978.

Ramos, Arthur, and Richard Patee. *The Negro in Brazil.* Washington, D.C.: Associated Publishers, 1939.

Ramsey, Matthew. *Professional and Popular Medicine in France, 1770–1830: The Social World of Medical Practice.* Cambridge: Cambridge University Press, 1988.

Ransom, Roger L., and Richard Sutch. *One Kind of Freedom: The Economic Consequences of Emancipation.* 2nd ed. New York: Cambridge University Press, 2001.

Reid, Michele B. "Negotiating a Slave Regime: Free People of Color in Cuba, 1844–1868." Ph.D. diss., University of Texas at Austin, 2004.

Reid-Vazquez, Michele. *The Year of the Lash: Free People of Color in Cuba and the Nineteenth-Century Atlantic World.* Athens: University of Georgia Press, 2011.

Reis, João José. *Slave Rebellion in Brazil: The Muslim Uprising of 1835 in Bahia.* Trans. Arthur Brakel. Baltimore, Md.: Johns Hopkins University Press, 1993.

Restall, Matthew. "Black Conquistadors: Armed Africans in Early Spanish America." *The Americas* 57, no. 2 (2000): 171–205.

———. *The Black Middle: Africans, Mayas, and Spaniards in Colonial Yucatan.* Stanford, Calif.: Stanford University Press, 2009.

———, ed. *Beyond Black and Red: African-Native Relations in Colonial Latin America.* Albuquerque: University of New Mexico Press, 2005.

Restrepo, Luz Adriana Maya. *Brujería y reconstruccción de identidades entre los Africanos y sus descendientes en la Nueva Granada, Siglo XVII.* Bogota: Ministerio de Cultura, 2003.

Rey, Terry. "Kongolese Catholic Influences on Haitian Popular Catholicism: A Sociohistorical Exploration." In *Central Africans and Cultural Transformations in the American Diaspora*, ed. Linda M. Heywood, 265–285. Cambridge: Cambridge University Press, 2002.

Risse, Guenter B. "Medicine in New Spain." In *Medicine in the New World: New Spain, New France, and New England*, ed. Ronald L. Numbers, 29–30. Knoxville: University of Tennessee Press, 1987.

Roediger, David. *The Wages of Whiteness: Race and the Making of the American Working Class.* The Haymarket Series in North American Politics and Culture. New York: Verso, 1991.

———. *Working toward Whiteness: How America's Immigrants become White. The Strange Journey from Ellis Island to the Suburbs.* New York: Basic Books, 2005.

Rollins, Judith. *Between Women: Domestics and Their Employers.* Philadelphia, Pa.: Temple University Press, 1985.

Romero, Mario Diego. "Sociedades negras: esclavos y libres en la Costa Pacífica de Colombia." *América Negra* 2 (Diciembre 1991): 137–152.

Rout, Leslie B., Jr. *The African Experience in Spanish America, 1502 to the Present Day.* Princeton, N.J.: Markus Wiener Publishers, 2003.

Rueda Novoa, Rocio. *Zambaje y autonomía: Historia de la gente negra de la provincia de Esmeraldas, siglos XVI–XVIII.* Quito: Abya-Yala, 2001.

Russell-Wood, A. J. R. "Black and Mulatto Brotherhoods in Colonial Brazil: A Study in Collective Behavior." *Hispanic American Historical Review* 54, no. 4 (1974): 567–602.

Saco, José Antonio, and Ortiz, Fernando. *Historia de la esclavitud de la raza Africana en el Nuevo Mundo y en especial en los paises Americo-Hispanos.* Havana: Habana Cultural, 1938.

Saether, Steinar A. "Bourbon Absolutism and Marriage Reform in Late Colonial Spanish America." *The Americas* 59, no. 4 (April 2003): 475–509.

Sanchez, Joseph P. "African Freedmen and the Fuero Militar: A Historical Overview of Pardo and Moreno Militiamen in the Late Spanish Empire." *Colonial Latin American Historical Review* 3, no. 2 (1994): 165–184.

Saunders, A. C. de C. M. *A Social History of Black Slaves and Freedmen in Portugal, 1441–1555.* Cambridge: Cambridge University Press, 1982.

Savoia, Rafael, ed. *Actas del primer congreso de historia del negro en el Ecuador y sur de Colombia.* Quito: Centro Cultural Afro-Ecuatoriano, 1988.

Scarano, Francisco A. *Sugar and Slavery in Puerto Rico: The Plantation Economy of Ponce, 1800–1850.* Madison: University of Wisconsin Press, 1984.

Scarano, Julita. *Devoção e escravidão: a irmandade de Nossa Senhora do Rosário dos Pretos do Distrito Diamantino do século XVIII.* São Paulo: Cia. Editora Nacional, 1976.

Scheuss de Studer, Elena Fanny. *La trata de Negros en Rio de la Plata durante el siglo XVIII.* Buenos Aires: Universidad de Buenos Aires, Departamento Editorial, 1958.

Schwartz, Stuart B. "The Manumission of Slaves in Colonial Brazil: Bahia, 1684–1745." *Hispanic American Historical Review* 54, no. 4 (1974): 603–635.

———. "Patterns of Slaveholding in the Americas: New Evidence from Brazil." *American Historical Review* 87, no. 1 (1982): 55–86.

———. *Sugar Plantations in the Formation of Brazilian Society: Bahia, 1550–1835.* Cambridge: Cambridge University Press, 1985.

Schweininger, Loren. *Black Property Owners in the South, 1790–1915.* Urbana: Univ. of Illinois Press, 1990.

———. "Prosperous Blacks in the South, 1790–1880." *American Historical Review* 95, no. 1 (1990): 31–56.

Scott, Rebecca J. *Slave Emancipation in Cuba: The Transition to Free Labor.* Princeton, N.J.: Princeton University Press, 1985.

Seed, Patricia. *To Love, Honor, and Obey in Colonial Mexico: Conflicts over Marriage Choice, 1514–1821.* Stanford, Calif.: Stanford University Press, 1988.

———. "The Social Dimensions of Race: Mexico City 1753." *Hispanic American Historical Review* 62, no. 4 (1982): 569–606.

Sharp, William F. *Slavery on the Spanish Frontier: The Colombian Chocó, 1680–1810*. Norman: University of Oklahoma Press, 1976.

Sheridan, Richard B. *Doctors and Slaves: A Medical and Demographic History of Slavery in the British West Indies, 1680–1834*. Cambridge: Cambridge University Press, 1985.

Silverblatt, Irene. *Modern Inquisitions: Peru and the Colonial Origins of the Civilized World*. Durham: Duke University Press, 2004.

Skidmore, Thomas. *Black into White: Race and Nationality in Brazilian Thought*. 2nd ed. Durham, N.C.: Duke University Press, 1993.

———. "Racial Ideas and Social Policy in Brazil, 1870–1940." In *The Idea of Race in Latin America, 1870–1940*, ed. Richard Graham. Austin: University of Texas Press, 1990.

Slamoral, Manuel Lucena. *Sangre sobre piel negra: La esclavitud quiteña en el contexto del refomismo borbónico*. Quito: Abya-Yala, 1991.

Slenes, Robert. "Comments on 'Slavery on a Nonexport Economy.' I." *Hispanic American Historical Review* 63, no. 3 (1983): 569–581.

———. "*Malungu, ngoma vem*: Africa coberta e descoberta do Brazil." *Revista Universidão de São Paulo* 12 (1991–1992): 48–67.

———. *Na senzala, uma flor. Esperanças e recordações na formação da família escrava: Brasil Sudeste, século XIX*. Rio de Janeiro: Nova Fronteira, 1999.

Smith, Carol D. "Myths, Intellectuals, and Race/Class/Gender Distinctions in the Formation of Latin American Nations." "Mestizaje." Special issue, *Journal of Latin American Anthropology* 2, no. 1 (1996): 148–169.

Sobel, Mechal. *Trabelin' On: The Slave Journey to an Afro-Baptist Faith*. 2nd ed. Princeton, N.J.: Princeton University Press, 1988.

Socolow, Susan M. "Acceptable Partners: Marriage Choice in Colonial Argentina, 1778–1810." In *Sexuality and Marriage in Colonial Latin America*, ed. A. Lavrin, 209–251. Lincoln: University of Nebraska Press, 1989.

Souza, Juliana Beatriz de Almeida. "Viagens do Rosário entre a Velha Cristandade e o Além-Mar." *Estudos afro-asiáticos* 23, no.2 (2001): 1–17.

Souza, Laura de Mello e. *O Diabo e a Terra de Santa Cruz*. São Paulo: Companhia das letras, 1985.

Steedman, Carolyn. "Servants and Their Relationship to the Unconscious." *Journal of British Studies* 42, no. 3 (2003): 316–350.

Stella, Alessandro. *Histoires d'esclaves dans la péninsule ibérique*. Paris: Editions de l'Ecole des Hautes Etudes en Sciences Sociales, 2000.

———. "'Mezclandose carnalmente.' Relaciones sociales, relaciones sexuales y mestizaje en Andalucía Occidental." In *Negros, mulatos, zambaigos. Derroteros africanos en los mundos ibéricos*, ed. Berta Ares Queija and Alessandro Stella, 175–188. Seville: Escuela de Estudios Hispano-americanos, 2000.

Stoler, Ann Laura. *Carnal Knowledge and Imperial Power: Race and the Intimate in Colonial Rule*. Berkeley: University of California Press, 2002.

———. "Tense and Tender Ties: The Politics of Comparison in North American History and (Post)colonial Studies." *Journal of American History* 88, no. 3 (2001): 829–865.

Stuckey, Sterling. *Slave Culture: Nationalist Theory and the Foundations of Black America*. New York: Oxford University Press, 1987.

Sweet, James. *Domingos Álvares, African Healing, and the Intellectual History of the Atlantic World*. Chapel Hill: University of North Carolina Press, 2011.

———. *Recreating Africa: Culture, Kinship, and Religion in the African-Portuguese World, 1441–1770*. Chapel Hill: University of North Carolina Press, 2003.

———. "Mistaken Identities? Olaudah Equiano, Domingos Álvares, and the Methodological Challenges of Studying the African Diaspora." *American Historical Review* 114, no. 2 (2009): 279–306.

———. *Domingos Álvares, African Healing, and the Intellectual History of the Atlantic World*. Chapel Hill: University of North Carolina Press, 2011.

Szaszdi, Adam. "El transfondo de un cuadro: 'Los mulatos de Esmeraldas' de Andrés Sánchez Galque." *Cuadernos Prehispánicos* 12 (1986–1987): 93–142.

Tannenbaum, Frank. *Slave and Citizen, the Negro in the Americas*. New York: Alfred A. Knopf, 1947.

Tardieu, Jean-Pierre. "Jesuitas y la 'lengua de Angola' en Peru (siglo XVII)." *Revista de Indias* 53, no. 198 (1993): 627–637.

———. *El Negro en el Cuzco: Los caminos de la alienación en la segunda mitad del siglo XVII*. Lima: PUCP/Banco Central de Reserva del Perú, 1998.

———. *El negro en la Real Audiencia de Quito, siglos XVI–XVIII*. Quito: Ediciones Abya-Yala, 2006.

———. *Los negros y la Iglesia en el Perú. Siglos XVI–XVII*. 2 vols. Quito: Centro Cultural Afroecuatoriano, 1997.

Taussig, Michael. *Mimesis and Alterity: A Particular History of the Senses*. New York: Routledge, 1993.

Taylor, William B. *Magistrates of the Sacred: Priests and Parishioners in Eighteenth-Century Mexico*. Stanford, Calif.: Stanford University Press, 1996.

———. "Mexico's Virgin of Guadalupe in the Seventeenth Century." In *Colonial Saints: Discovering the Holy in the Americas*, ed. Allan Greer and Jody Bilinkoff, 277–298. New York: Routledge, 2003.

Tellis-Nayak, V. "Power and Solidarity: Clientage in Domestic Service." *Current Anthropology* 23, no. 1 (1982): 67–79.

Thornton, John K. *Africa and Africans in the Making of the Atlantic World, 1400–1800*. 2nd ed. Cambridge: Cambridge University Press, 1992.

———. "The Development of an African Catholic Church in the Kingdom of the Kongo, 1491–1750." *Journal of African History* 25 (1984): 147–167.

———. *The Kingdom of Kongo: Civil War and Transition, 1641–1718*. Madison: University of Wisconsin Press, 1983.

———. "Religious and Ceremonial Life in Kongo and Mbundu Areas, 1500–1700." In *Central Africans and Cultural Transformations in the African Diaspora*, ed. Linda M. Heywood, 71–90. Cambridge: Cambridge University Press, 2002.

Tibesar, Antonine. "The Franciscan Doctrinero Versus the Franciscan Misionero in Seventeenth-Century Peru." *The Americas* 14 (1957): 115–124.

Turner, Victor. *The Drums of Affliction: A Study of Religious Processes among the Ndembu of Zambia*. Oxford: Clarendon Press, 1968.

Twinam, Ann. *Public Lives, Private Secrets: Gender, Honor, Sexuality, and Illegitimacy in Colonial Spanish America*. Stanford, Calif.: Stanford University Press, 1999.

Twine, France W. *Racism in a Racial Democracy: The Maintenance of White Supremacy in Brazil*. New Brunswick, N.J.: Rutgers University Press, 1998.

Valencia Villa, Carlos Eduardo. *Alma en boca y huesos en costal: Una aproximación a los contrastes socio-económicos de la esclavitud Santafé, Mariquita y Mompox 1610–1660*. Bogotá: Instituto Colombiano de Antropología e Historia, 2003.

Valtierra, Ángel. "El Padre Alonso de Sandoval, S.J." In Alonso de Sandoval, *De instauranda Aethiopum salute: El mundo de la esclavitud negra en America*, v–xxxvii. Bogotá: Empresa Nacional de Publicaciones, 1956.

van Deusen, Nancy E. *Between the Sacred and the Worldly: The Institutional and Cultural Practice of Recogimiento in Colonial Lima*. Stanford, Calif.: Stanford University Press, 2001.

———. "Circuits of Knowledge among Women in Early Seventeenth-Century Lima." In *Gender, Race and Religion in the Colonization of the Americas*, ed. Nora E. Jaffary, 137–151. Burlington, Vt.: Ashgate Press, 2007.

———. "Úrsula de Jesús." In *Encyclopedia of African American Culture and History: The Black Experience in the Americas*, vol. 3, ed. Colin Palmer, 1175–1176. Detroit: MacMillan Reference USA, 2006.

———. "Ursula de Jesús, a Seventeenth-Century Afro-Peruvian Mystic." In *The Human Tradition in Colonial Latin America*, ed. Kenneth J. Andrien, 88–103. Wilmington, Del.: Scholarly Resources, Inc., 2002.

Vanhee, Hein. "Central African Popular Christianity and the Making of Haitian Vodou Religion." In *Central Africans and Cultural Transformations in the American Diaspora*, ed. Linda M. Heywood, 243–264. Cambridge: Cambridge University Press, 2002.

Vansina, Jan. "Equatorial Africa and Angola: Migrations and the Emergence of the First States." In *General History of Africa*, vol. 4, *Africa from the Twelfth to the Sixteenth Century*, ed. J. Ki-Zerbo and D. T. Niade, 551–577. Berkeley: UNESCO, 1984.

———. "Foreword." In *Central Africans and Cultural Transformations in the American Diaspora*, ed. Linda M. Heywood, xi–xiii. Cambridge: Cambridge University Press, 2002.

———. "The Kongo Kingdom and Its Neighbors." In *General History of Africa*, vol. 5, *Africa from the Sixteenth to the Eighteenth Centuries*, ed. B. A. Ogot, 546–587. Berkeley: UNESCO, 1992.

———. *Paths in the Rainforests: Toward a History of Political Tradition in Equatorial Africa*. Madison: University of Wisconsin Press, 1990.

———. "Western Bantu Expansion." *Journal of African History* 25 (1984): 129–145.

Vasconcelos, José. *La Raza cósmica: Misión de la raza iberoamericana*. Paris: Agencia Mundial de Librería, 1920.

Vergara Ormeño, Teresa. "Migración y trabajo femenino a principios del siglo XVII: el caso de las indias en Lima." *Histórica* 21, no. 1 (1997): 135–157.

Vial Correa, Gonzalo. *El africano en el Reino de Chile. Ensayo histórico-juridico*. Santiago, Chile: Universidad Católica de Chile, Facultad de Ciencias Jurídicas y Sociales, Instituto de Investigaciones Históricas, 1957.

Vila Vilar, Enriqueta. "La evangelización del esclavo negro y su integración en el mundo americano." In *Negros, mulatos, zambaigos: Derroteros africanos en los mundo ibéricos*, ed. Berta Ares Queija and Alessandro Stella, 189–206. Seville: Consejo Superior de Investigaciones Científicas, Escuela de Estudios Hispano-Americanos, 2000.

Villa-Flores, Javier. "To Lose One's Soul: Blasphemy and Slavery in New Spain, 1596–1669." *Hispanic American Historical Review* 82, no. 3 (2002): 435–468.

Villaseñor Black, Charlene Marianna. "Saints and Social Welfare in Golden Age Spain: The Imagery of the Cult of Saint Joseph." Ph.D. diss., University of Michigan, 1995.

Vinson, Ben, III. "African (Black) Diaspora History, Latin American History—A Comment." *The Americas* 63, no. 1 (July 2006): 1–18.

———. *Bearing Arms for His Majesty: The Free-Colored Militia in Colonial Mexico*. Stanford, Calif.: Stanford University Press, 2001.

Viotti da Costa, Emília. *Crowns of Glory, Tears of Blood: The Demerara Slave Rebellion of 1823*. New York: Oxford University Press, 1994.

Viquiera Albán, Juan Pedro. *Propriety and Permissiveness in Bourbon Mexico*. Trans. Sonya Lipsett-Rivera and Sergio Rivera Ayala. Wilmington, Del.: Scholarly Resources, 1999.

Von Germeten, Nicole. *Black Blood Brothers: Confraternities and Social Mobility for Afro-Mexicans*. Gainesville: University Press of Florida, 2006.

———. "Corporate Salvation in a Colonial Society: Confraternities and Social Mobility for Africans and Their Descendants in New Spain." Ph.D. diss., University of California, Berkeley, 2003.

Wade, Peter. *Blackness and Race Mixture: The Dynamics of Racial Identity in Colombia*. Baltimore, Md.: Johns Hopkins University Press, 1993.

———. *Race and Ethnicity in Latin America*. Chicago: Pluto Press, 1997.

Wade, Richard C. *Slavery in the Cities: The South, 1820–1860*. New York: Oxford University Press, 1964.

Walker, Tamara J. "'He outfitted his family in notable decency': Slavery, Honour and Dress in Eighteenth-Century Lima, Peru." *Slavery and Abolition* 30, no. 3 (2009): 383–402.

Weinstein, Barbara. "Slavery, Citizenship, and National Identity in Brazil and the South." In *Nationalism in the New World*, ed. Don H. Doyle and Marco Antonio Pamplona, 248–271. Athens: University of Georgia Press, 2006.

West, Robert. *Colonial Placer Mining in Colombia*. Baton Rouge: Louisiana State University Press, 1952.

Whitten, Norman E. *Black Frontiersmen: Afro-Hispanic Culture of Ecuador and Colombia*. 2nd ed. Prospect Heights, Ill.: Waveland Press, 1986.

Williams, Eric. *Capitalism and Slavery*. Chapel Hill: University of North Carolina Press, 1944.

Wolfe, Justin. "'The Cruel Whip': Race and Place in Nineteenth-Century Nicaragua." In *Blacks & Blackness in Central America: Between Race and Place*, ed. Lowell Gudmundson and Justin Wolfe, 177–208. Durham, N.C.: Duke University Press, 2010.

Wood, Alice. "Religious Women of Color in Seventeenth-Century Lima: Estefania de San Joseph and Ursula de Jesu Christo." In *Beyond Bondage: Free Women of Color in the Americas*, ed. David Barry Gaspar and Darlene Clark Hine, 286–316. Urbana: University of Illinois Press, 2004.

Wood, Charles H., and Peggy Lovell. "Skin Color, Racial Identity, and Life Chances in Brazil." *Latin American Perspectives* 25, no. 3 (1998): 90–109.

Woodson, Carter G. *Free Negro Owners of the Slaves in the United States in 1830*. New York: Negro Universities Press, 1924.

Woodward, C. Vann. *American Counterpart: Slavery and Racism in the North-South Dialogue*. Boston: Little, Brown, 1971.

Wu, Celia. "The Population of the City of Queréetaro in 1791." *Journal of Latin American Studies* 16, no. 2 (1984): 277–295.

Young, Jason R. *Rituals of Resistance: African Atlantic Religion in Kongo and the Lowcountry South in the Era of Slavery*. Baton Rouge: Louisiana State University Press, 2007.

Zeleza, Paul Tiyambe. "Rewriting the African Diaspora: Beyond the Black Atlantic." *African Affairs* 104, no. 414 (2005): 35–68.

Contributors

SHERWIN K. BRYANT Northwestern University, Department of History
Colonial Latin America and Comparative Slavery

Sherwin K. Bryant is an Associate Professor of African American Studies and History at Northwestern University, specializing in colonial Latin American History, slavery, race, and the early modern African Diaspora. His publications include "Enslaved Rebels, Fugitives, and Litigants: The Resistance Continuum in Colonial Quito," *Colonial Latin American Review* 13, no. 1 (2004): 7–46; "Finding Gold, Forming Slavery: The Creation of a Classic Slave Society, Popayán, 1600–1700," *The Americas* 63 (2006): 81–112; and "Finding Freedom: Slavery in Colonial Ecuador," in *The Ecuador Reader*, ed. Carlos de la Torre and Steve Striffler, 52–67 (Durham, N.C.: Duke University Press: 2008). Currently, he is revising his book manuscript, *Rivers of Gold, Sweet Valleys and Cities of Squalor: Slavery and the Struggle for Autonomy and Rights in Colonial Quito.*

RACHEL SARAH O'TOOLE University of California, Irvine, Department of History
Colonial Latin America, the Andes, the African Diaspora, the Atlantic World, the History of Race, Gender

Rachel Sarah O'Toole is an Associate Professor of History at the University of California, Irvine, specializing in indigenous colonial Peru and the African Diaspora. Her publications include "From the Rivers of Guinea to the

Valleys of Peru: Becoming a Bran Diaspora within Spanish Slavery," *Social Text* 25 (Fall 2007); "Danger in the Convent: Colonial Demons, Idolatrous *Indias*, and Bewitching *Negras* in Santa Clara (Trujillo del Perú)," *Journal of Colonialism and Colonial History* 7 (Spring 2006); "In a War against the Spanish": Andean Protection & African Resistance on the Northern Peruvian Coast," *The Americas* 63 (July 2006); and manuscript entitled *Bound Lives: Africans, Indians, and the Making of Race in Colonial Peru* (University of Pittsburgh Press, 2012).

BEN VINSON III George Washington University, Columbian College of Arts and Sciences

Ben Vinson is Dean of the Columbian College of Arts and Sciences at The George Washington University. Prior to his time at GW, Vinson was a Latin American historian in the Department of History at Johns Hopkins University with particular interests in race relations and the African Diaspora and served as director of the Center for Africana Studies until 2010. Before going to Hopkins, Vinson was an associate professor at Penn State University and taught at Barnard College. He has held fellowships from the Fulbright Commission, the National Humanities Center, the Social Science Research Council, the University of North Carolina at Chapel Hill, and the Ford, Rockefeller, and Mellon foundations. An expert on colonial Mexico, Vinson is interested broadly in the nineteenth and twentieth centuries and transnational networks, including the interactions between African Americans and Latinos.

LEO J. GAROFALO Connecticut College, Department of History

Latin American and Caribbean History, the History of Race and Ethnicity, the African Diaspora and Afro–Latin America, Peru and the Andes

Leo J. Garofalo is an Associate Professor of the History Department at Connecticut College. Garofalo's research in Peru draws attention to the central roles of Native Andeans and Afro-Peruvians in shaping daily life in colonial cities. His current work focuses on the Afro-Iberian roots of Andean witchcraft and the Atlantic and European routes of the West African Diaspora to the Andes in the sixteenth and seventeenth centuries. He was recently awarded a Social Science Research Council Grant and a Fulbright-Hays Research Grant. He is the author of "Conjuring with Coca and the Inca: The Andeanization of Lima's Afro-Peruvian Ritual Specialists, 1580–1690," *The Americas* 63, no. 1 (July 2006): 53–80; and he is the editor (with Kathryn Joy

McKnight) of *Afro-Latino Voices: Narratives from the Early Modern Ibero-Atlantic World, 1550–1812* (Indianapolis: Hackett, 2009) and (with Erin O'Connor) *Documenting Latin America*, vols. 1 and 2 (Upper Saddle River, N.J.: Pearson Education, 2010).

CHARLES BEATTY-MEDINA University of Toledo, Department of History

Latin America, the African Diaspora, and the Southern Atlantic and Circum-Caribbean Region

Charles Beatty-Medina is an Associate Professor of Latin America. He has done research at numerous U.S. archives and collections and has undertaken archival research in Ecuador, Spain, Colombia, and Mexico. Beatty-Medina's article "Caught between Rivals: The Spanish-African Maroon Competition for Captive Indian Labor in the Region of Esmeraldas during the Late Sixteenth and Early Seventeenth Centuries" is part of the special issue of *The Americas* entitled "The African Diaspora in the Colonial Andes" (edited by Ben Vinson III).

NANCY E. VAN DEUSEN Queen's University—Kingston, Ontario, Department of History

Colonial Latin America, Iberian Atlantic World

Nancy E. van Deusen teaches at Queen's University in Kingston, Ontario, and specializes in the histories of bondage, gender relations, and female Catholic spirituality in colonial Peru. She is currently completing a book project about indigenous slaves who pressed for their freedom in the Spanish courts between 1530 and 1585.

FRANK "TREY" PROCTOR III Denison University, Department of History

Mexico, Colonial Latin America, Comparative Slavery

Frank "Trey" Proctor III is an Associate Professor of History at Denison University. He is the author of *"Damned Notions of Liberty": Slavery, Culture, and Power in Colonial Mexico, 1640–1769* (University of New Mexico Press, 2010). His work on African slavery in New Spain has appeared in the *Hispanic American Historical Review* and *The Americas*.

JOAN C. BRISTOL George Mason University, Department of History and Art History

World History: Latin America, Social and Cultural History

Joan C. Bristol is an Associate Professor of History at George Mason University. She is the author of *Christians, Blasphemers, and Witches: Afro-Mexican Ritual Practice in the Seventeenth Century* (University of New Mexico Press, 2007). Her articles have appeared in the *Boletín del Archivo General de la Nación* (Mexico) and the *Journal of Colonialism and Colonial History* and in several edited volumes.

KAREN Y. MORRISON, University of Massachusetts Amherst, Department of Afro-American Studies

African Diasporan Studies

Karen Y. Morrison specializes in the social and cultural histories of Latin America, the Caribbean, the African Diaspora, and Cuba of the nineteenth and twentieth centuries, approaching these through an emphasis on family history and race theory. Her articles have appeared in *Cuban Studies/Estudios Cubanos*, the *Journal of Social History*, and *Slavery & Abolition*. She is currently completing a book-length manuscript that analyzes the intersection of family formation and the social construction of race in Cuba.

MICHELE REID-VAZQUEZ Georgia State University, Department of History

Atlantic World History, Nineteenth-Century Cuba, the Comparative Caribbean and Latin America, the African Diaspora in Latin America

Michele Reid-Vazquez is an affiliated faculty member of the Program in World History and Cultures and the Center for Latin American and Latino/a Studies at Georgia State University. Her publications include *The Year of the Lash: Free People of Color in Cuba and the Nineteenth-Century Atlantic World* (Athens: University of Georgia Press, 2011), which explores issues of race relations, slavery, exile, and empire. She is also a contributor to *Documenting Latin America: Gender and Race, Empire and Nation* and has forthcoming essays in *The Encyclopedia of Free Blacks and Free People of Color in the Americas*. Her ongoing projects include an exploration of comparative free black emigration to the Caribbean during the American, Haitian, and Latin American revolutions.

HERBERT S. KLEIN Stanford University, Department of History

Latin American History

Herbert S. Klein is Gouverneur Morris Emeritus Professor at Columbia University, Research Fellow Hoover Institution, and former director of the Center of Latin American Studies at Stanford University. Klein received his B.A. from the University of Chicago in 1957 and his Ph.D. from Chicago in 1963. He is the author of some 20 books and 165 articles in several languages on Latin America and on comparative themes in social and economic history. His long-term interests are in comparative economic and social history, and he is currently working on international migration in contemporary Spain and the United States and on the history of Brazil. Klein has been a Guggenheim fellow, a Woodrow Wilson Fellow, and a Fulbright Lecturer and was a postdoctoral fellow at Yale and Oxford.

Acknowledgments

This volume is an outgrowth of a 2005 international conference, "The African Diaspora to Latin America: New Directions," sponsored by the Center for African American History at Northwestern University. The symposium communicated an effort to complicate our understanding of what is meant by "African American history" and a desire to signal the center's commitment to a more expansive vision of the early modern African Diaspora. The center's inaugural director, Darlene Clark Hine, provided the vision and resources for the symposium. We owe a debt of gratitude to Darlene, her staff, the various units at Northwestern that cosponsored the event, and the conference participants and attendees.

We would like to thank each of the contributors for making us stewards of their work, for prodding our thinking, and for offering suggestions along the way. Each of them engaged our queries, comments, and critiques with good humor, rigor, and patience. We thank the anonymous readers of the University of Illinois Press for their advice. A special thanks goes to Andre Devereux for his work on the glossary, bibliography, and administrative assistance. Kate Babbitt's copyediting helped improve the book significantly. We also thank Joan Catapano for believing in the importance of this work.

Portions of chapter 2 appeared as "'To Marry in the Holy Mother Church': Marriage and Community Formation," in Frank T. Proctor III's *"Damned Notions of Liberty": Slavery, Culture, and Power in Colonial Mexico, 1640–1769* (Albuquerque: University of New Mexico Press, 2010): 37–67. We are grateful for permission to reuse the material.

Finally, we would be remiss if we did not acknowledge the personal, intellectual, and institutional debts owed to friends, colleagues, and funding units at Northwestern University, the Center for Africana Studies at Johns Hopkins University, and the Humanities Center at the University of California, Irvine.

Index

THE NEW BLACK STUDIES SERIES

Beyond Bondage: Free Women of Color in the Americas *Edited by David Barry Gaspar and Darlene Clark Hine*

The Early Black History Movement, Carter G. Woodson, and Lorenzo Johnston Greene *Pero Gaglo Dagbovie*

"Baad Bitches" and Sassy Supermamas: Black Power Action Films *Stephane Dunn*

Black Maverick: T. R. M. Howard's Fight for Civil Rights and Economic Power *David T. Beito and Linda Royster Beito*

Beyond the Black Lady: Sexuality and the New African American Middle Class *Lisa B. Thompson*

Extending the Diaspora: New Histories of Black People *Dawne Y. Curry, Eric D. Duke, and Marshanda A. Smith*

Activist Sentiments: Reading Black Women in the Nineteenth Century *P. Gabrielle Foreman*

Black Europe and the African Diaspora *Edited by Darlene Clark Hine, Trica Danielle Keaton, and Stephen Small*

Freeing Charles: The Struggle to Free a Slave on the Eve of the Civil War *Scott Christianson*

African American History Reconsidered *Pero Gaglo Dagbovie*

Freud Upside Down: African American Literature and Psychoanalytic Culture *Badia Sahar Ahad*

A. Philip Randolph and the Struggle for Civil Rights *Cornelius L. Bynum*

Queer Pollen: White Seduction, Black Male Homosexuality, and the Cinematic *David A. Gerstner*

The Rise of Chicago's Black Metropolis, 1920–1929 *Christopher Robert Reed*

Living with Lynching: African American Lynching Plays, Performance, and Citizenship, 1890–1930 *Koritha Mitchell*

Africans to Spanish America: Expanding the Diaspora *Edited by Sherwin K. Bryant, Rachel Sarah O'Toole, & Ben Vinson III*

Rebels and Runaways: Slave Resistance in Nineteenth-Century Florida *Larry Eugene Rivers*

The Black Chicago Renaissance *Edited by Darlene Clark Hine and John McCluskey Jr.*

The University of Illinois Press
is a founding member of the
Association of American University Presses.

University of Illinois Press
1325 South Oak Street
Champaign, IL 61820-6903
www.press.uillinois.edu